Cheap. Fast. Good!

CHEAP. FAST. GOOD!

A Cookbook by Beverly Mills *&* Alicia Ross

Illustrations by Steven Guarnaccia

Workman Publishing • New York

Library of Congress Cataloging-in-Publication Data
Mills, Beverly.
    Cheap, fast, good! / by Beverly Mills and Alicia Ross.
       p. cm.
    ISBN 0-7611-3176-0 (alk. paper)—ISBN 0-7611-3818-8
    1. Cookery. 2. Consumer education. I. Ross, Alicia. II. Title.
    TX714.M5547 2005
    641.5—dc22   2004066444

Cover design by Paul Hanson
Book design by Barbara Balch
Cover photographs by Zeva Oelbaum
Cover food styled by Sara Neumeier
Book illustrations by Steven Guarnaccia

Workman books are available at special discount when purchased in
bulk for premiums and sales promotions as well as for fund-raising or
educational use. Special editions or book excerpts can be created to
specification. For details, contact the Special Sales Director at the
address below.

Workman Publishing Company, Inc.
708 Broadway
New York, NY 10003-9555
www.workman.com
www.desperationdinners.com

Manufactured in the U.S.A.
First printing December 2005

10 9 8 7 6 5 4 3 2 1

For my mother
Dorothy Mills

Standing between the rows of your vegetable garden,
I learned the importance of hard work and its ultimate rewards.
At your kitchen counter, I witnessed a passion
for wholesome meals perfectly prepared.
It was at your table that I first tasted love.

—Beverly

For the most important women in my life,
my "moms"—Gayle Brady and Betty Ross
And my daughters—Hannah and Rachel Ross

May our times together in the kitchen continue to be blessed
by wisdom, laughter, and lots of wonderful food.

—Alicia

A Hearty Plateful of Thanks

Writing a book when we are thousands of miles apart has been an incredible journey, and we could have never completed it if it hadn't been for Monday morning two-hour phone conversations and countless emails. Thank goodness for technology and overnight package delivery.

We have to say how wonderful it has been working once again with our editor, Suzanne Rafer. Thank you for believing we had something worthwhile to say about budget cooking. To Carla Glasser, our number one cheerleader and agent extraordinaire, we thank you once again for steering us through the maze that is book publishing.

There's nothing like a good friend (and a few family members) with good recipes to share, and we're grateful to Fred and Louanne Bisel, Janice McDaniel, Liz Cilem, Herschel Freeman, Gayle Brady, Dot Mills, Betty Ross, Pauline Byron, Myra Fisher, Susan Umstead, Sheri Castle, Ada Winters, Cheryl Andrassy, Christy Veeder, Avis June Thompson, and the readers of our weekly Desperation Dinners newspaper column who keep sharing family favorites. Thank you for opening your hearts and your recipe boxes to us.

Thanks go to our recipe testers for your careful attention to detail and hard work: Julie Realon, Tony and Elizabeth Voiers, Dot Mills, Denise Deen, Debi Williams, Rhett Holladay, Jeff Strickland, Flo Strickland, Marietta Wynands, Ann Mendenhall, and Carmel Dunlop.

A special note of thanks goes to Karen Chan in consumer and family economics at the University of Illinois for getting us off to a good start with our research for this book. And to Chris Loudon of Nutrition Resources, who ran cost analyses for us.

Our parents, Dot and Jay and Gayle and Jim, are, as always, a big part of our continued success. We so cherish your love, your example, and your unfailing support. We know your friends will be glad to hear we finally have another book for you to talk about.

All of the terrific people at Workman are to be applauded. Kudos go to Peter and Carolan Workman for their leadership, Kathie Ness for her excellent copy editing, Paul Hanson for the creative cover design, Barbara Balch for her fun and inviting interior design, Steven Guarnaccia for his imaginative illustrations, Helen Rosner for help on the editorial front, and Joelle Herr and Barbara Peragine for shepherding it all through.

To Sarah O'Leary Burningham, Jennifer Pare, and all of the great folks in the publicity department and to Katie Workman and Jenny Mandel—thank you so much for your continued support of all of our projects and willingness to go the extra mile for us.

The readers of our Desperation Dinners column are simply wonderful. Your letters of support and reports of successes with desperation cooking are such an encouragement. We hope that this book, too, makes for great satisfaction in the kitchen (and adds to the bottom line in your checkbook). To Lisa Wilson, Marianne Goldstein, and all of the terrific people at United Media who keep the column alive and well, thank you for your continued support.

And finally to our husbands, Anders and Ron, and our children, Sam and Grey, Hannah and Rachel—you are awesome! We know that having wives and moms who do weird things like test recipes all day and feed you strange conglomerations of the leftovers and call it dinner must be foreign to others, but you always come to the dinner table with appetites and enthusiasm. May you always have happy memories of our times together in the kitchen and at the dinner table.

—*Beverly and Alicia*

CONTENTS

CHAPTER THREE
SUMPTUOUS SKILLET MEALS 116

When you're short on time, skillet meals come to the rescue.
Fast and fabulous (not to mention cost-conscious, as well) recipes
include Salsa-Cheese Beef and Rice, Mu-shu Pork at Home, Fiery
Chicken with Vegetables, Chicken and Apples with Dijon Cream,
and Fisherman's Seafood Creole.

CHAPTER FOUR
EMPOWERING PASTAS 178

You can't go wrong with pasta—the price is right, and it couldn't
be faster to prepare. Quickie Cacciatore, Thai
Spaghetti Toss, Corkscrews with Chicken and
Zucchini, Hungry Man's Macaroni, Tex-Mex
Noodles—the shapes, the sauces, the toppings
are so appealing and varied, there's something
for everyone.

Eating Like a Big Spender for Just a Few Dollars

We're the Desperation Dinners Duo, and for the past decade, we have concentrated our energy on finding every trick and technique imaginable for saving time in the kitchen. The results have been published in two Desperation Dinners cookbooks, on our Web site, and in our syndicated newspaper column. A few years ago, we both encountered desperation of a different sort. Like many people, we watched our household expenses spin out of control while our retirement accounts took a dive and college savings accounts dwindled. Since then, we've weathered corporate downsizing and job changes, and, at times, we've worried whether the checkbook would balance.

While we realized that we were fortunate to still have investments to fret over and jobs to go to, the economic downturn jabbing at us—and at our friends and relatives—presented significant challenges. And then it hit us: What would happen if we shifted our energies a bit and started concentrating on saving *money* in the kitchen, in addition to time?

We went in looking for pennies, but what we found were dollars. After spending months researching every avenue we could find, developing thrifty recipes, and rethinking our eating habits, we hold these four truths to be self-evident:

First, saving money in the kitchen is as simple as one four-letter word: *Cook.* Yes, our Desperation Dinners cookbooks strongly advocate cooking, but good times allowed for plenty of dinners out, too. When we started to examine just a couple of months' worth of restaurant bills (including fast-food drive-through and pizza delivery), we were shocked. And we weren't alone. The average U.S. family of four spends nearly $240 a month eating out. In a typical year, Americans eat 70 billion meals at 870,000 restaurants. The good news was that, since we were spending so much eating out, we knew we could save all the more by eating more often at home. What we quickly figured out was that cooking amazing meals at home—even on a budget—is as basic as getting a plan, picking a recipe, and heating up the stove.

Saving money in the kitchen isn't really about pinching pennies, and, truthfully, we just weren't motivated to reuse tea bags and wash out used plastic storage bags. For us, saving money in the kitchen is about good stewardship—making wise buying decisions and then making the most of the ingredients once we get them home. We were startled to discover that the average American household throws away 470 pounds of food every year and that as much as 12 percent of purchased grocery items are never used. Guilty? You bet, and we vowed to change our wasteful ways. Fortunately, it's easy to do, and we've detailed exactly how, step by step, in the following pages.

The second truth is probably the most important: *It's essential to cook meals that you're going to enjoy.* Otherwise, that's money and time right down the garbage disposal. When we started telling family and friends that our next project would be a budget cookbook, we were a little surprised by their reaction. There seemed to be a definite bias against the idea of thrifty food: "You eat a lot of beans and rice, right?" The answer is, yes, we do eat some beans, but we also feast on the likes of Chicken and Apples with Dijon Cream, Moroccan Meatballs over Couscous, Marmalade-Glazed Ham, Stuffed Peppers with Kielbasa Rice, Beef Stew à la Guatemala, and Catfish with a Pecan Crust. And when we do eat beans, we turn them into a gourmet delight. Check out our Sassy Chickpea Burgers with Lemon Aïoli, Very Veggie Lentil Chili, and "Barbecued" Chicken and Black Bean Burritos.

Just in case you're dubious, too, we'd like to make one guarantee: Food doesn't have to cost a fortune to be wonderful! When it comes to cooking, spending a lot of money does not ensure that your soup, pasta sauce, or skillet meal will be delicious. And the opposite is also true: It doesn't take a lot of money to produce amazing meals that you'll be proud to serve to your family, friends, and guests. If you're like us, eating well—really well—is a priority, but it just doesn't need to cost so much.

As for the third essential truth: *Time is a key ingredient.* We will always be the Desperation Dinners Duo, and, probably much like yours, our hectic lives haven't slowed down for a minute. Our recipes must be realistic, easy, and relatively quick to prepare so that, when we're tired or rushed, we won't be forced to eat an expensive meal out or buy costly prepared foods.

The minute you walk through the kitchen door to start dinner, you're automatically saving money. You just need to decide how much money you want to save. After spending months slashing our own food expenses, we landed on our fourth and final essential truth: *The amount of money saved depends on a willingness to take the necessary steps.* For example, the fewer prepped foods we buy, the more money we pocket. The more cooking steps we do ourselves, the more we enhance the budget's bottom line. The more carefully we shop and the more carefully we go out of our way to bag a bargain or clip a coupon, the fatter the wallet is likely to get.

In the following pages, we'll cover each detail of these steps toward creating a smarter, more economical kitchen. Then you can experiment to find what works for you. When all is said and done, this book is simply about making choices. We'll give you the information and the recipes; you need to make smart and realistic ones that fit whatever time you have and whatever efforts you're willing to make. But remember that you don't need to spend half a day in the kitchen to eat well yet save money.

So enough said. Let's get started.

Cheap. Fast. Good! Recipes

CHAPTER ONE

SUPER-SAVER SOUPS AND STEWS

"What other food besides soup is so forgiving, so patient, so comforting?"

From Beverly:

At the first sign of crisis—major or minor, real or imagined—I start a pot of soup or a hearty stew. If there's a snowstorm brewing, I make Hearty Homemade Beef and Vegetable Soup. If somebody's sick, it'll be Cure-All Chicken Soup. If my checkbook hits the skids, I'll rummage around in the refrigerator, gather up all of the leftovers, and surprise myself.

It almost doesn't matter what you put into a pot of soup: Chances are good that the result will be sublime. What other food besides soup is so forgiving, so patient, so comforting? If you're feeling even the slightest bit surly, a tad down in the dumps, a little out of sorts, make soup. Or start a stew. With a steaming cauldron on the stove—a nourishing concoction at your command—any crisis is easier to handle.

The soups and stews on the following pages come with a few guarantees: They are easy. They are versatile. They are inexpensive. And they taste great. When you're in the mood for something old-fashioned, try Grandmother Rose's Mulligan or Almost Ebbie's Corn and Tomato Soup. If it's kid-friendly you need, head straight for Hot Dog and Baked Bean Soup, Mini Ravioli Soup, or Simple Chicken

Stew. Do you have a vegetarian at your dinner table? Pasta e Fagioli, Mixed Bean Meatless Cassoulet, Very Veggie Lentil Chili, or Refried Bean Soup makes a meal so filling, meat-eaters will never miss a beat. Feeling just a little exotic? A pot of Chunky Southwestern Gazpacho, Bayou Stew, or Creamy Wild Rice Soup can take you way beyond the ordinary without straining your imagination or your budget. And if it's speed you need, several of our soups start with some already-cooked building blocks such as meatballs, left-over roast, and peanut sauce. With some of the work already done, Mindless Meatball Minestrone, My Beef and Barley Soup, and Pumpkin Peanut Soup go together in a jiffy for those nights when dinner needs to be *now*. Whatever your need, soup provides perfect sustenance.

You will not believe how easy it is to make this hearty soup.

Adding tomato paste makes for a thicker and richer foundation for the beef, but if you don't have any, you can leave it out. Do add the water, though, so the balance will be correct.

Other frozen vegetables can be substituted for the peas and corn. We like a blend specifically meant for soups when we have it on hand. Just use a total of 2 cups of your favorite vegetables or a vegetable mix.

If you use your Basic Beef from the refrigerator or freezer, this soup is only 10 minutes away!

HEARTY HOMEMADE BEEF AND VEGETABLE SOUP

SERVES: 6 START TO FINISH: UNDER 25 MINUTES

1 pound ground beef, fresh or frozen (see Note)
2 teaspoons olive oil
1 large onion (for about 1 cup chopped)
1 clove fresh garlic, minced, or 1 teaspoon bottled minced garlic
1 can (15 ounces) light red kidney beans or pinto beans, or 1 cup homemade (see page 360), defrosted if frozen
2 cans (about 14 ounces each) fat-free chicken broth, or 4 cups homemade chicken stock (see page 10)
1 can (14½ ounces) chopped tomatoes flavored with onion and herbs
1 can (6 ounces) tomato paste
1 cup frozen yellow or white corn kernels
1 cup frozen green peas
½ teaspoon dried Italian seasoning

1. If the meat is frozen, run it under hot water so you can remove the packaging. Place the meat on a microwave-safe plate and microwave, uncovered, on high power for 3 minutes to partially defrost.

2. Meanwhile, heat the oil in a 4½-quart Dutch oven or soup pot over medium heat. Peel and coarsely chop the onion, adding it to the pot as you chop. Add the partially defrosted meat, raise the heat to medium-high, and cook, breaking up the meat, until it has completely browned, 7 to 8 minutes. Drain away any accumulated fat, if necessary.

3. Add the garlic to the beef. Drain the beans and add them, along with the broth, tomatoes with their juices, tomato paste, and 2 cups water. Raise the heat to high and stir well.

4. Add the corn, peas, and seasoning. Cover and continue to cook until the soup starts to boil. Reduce the heat to low and simmer, stirring occasionally, to blend the flavors, 5 to 7 minutes. Ladle into soup bowls and serve.

NOTE: You can use 3 cups Basic Beef (page 347), defrosted if frozen. Omit the oil, onion, and garlic. Add the defrosted beef to the pot in Step 3 with the beans and broth.

About:
USING CANNED BROTH

When it comes to amounts, all cans of broth are not created equal. On the low end, there's the Campbell's brand at 10½ ounces (1⅓ cups of broth). Most brands hover in the middle at about 14 ounces (1¾ cups), and a few larger cans hold 16 ounces (2 cups).

The good news is that, for our soups, slight variations in broth amounts won't matter. If you're making homemade stock, we suggest freezing it in 2-cup portions because we find it's easy to work with.

There is one caveat: If you're making soup with the smaller, 10½-ounce cans of broth and the recipe calls for two cans, you could be missing 1⅓ cups of liquid. If you're concerned about not having enough soup, just add another third of a can of broth.

Name brands are the most reliable but can be more expensive. We suggest trying the house brand in your grocery store. If you find a rich, not-so-salty broth for significantly less than the national brand, go for it.

After countless hours spent straining our brain cells to be creative in the kitchen, only to have our kids clamor for peanut butter and jelly, we've come to accept the fact that they often prefer simple, even bland, food. Sometimes, even as adults, the simple recipes from childhood are the ones we continue to crave. That's the way one of our readers, Ella Maxwell, feels about her grandmother's tomato-beef-noodle soup.

"This recipe is called Mulligan, and I don't know why," Ella says. "It's not related to what others would call mulligan stew. I loved this as a child and would always request it when we went to Indiana to visit my grandmother Rose."

Ella's grandmother prepared this fast, easy soup using home-canned tomato juice. Because that's not an ingredient most cooks have on hand, we've substituted a tomato-vegetable juice blend. Plain tomato juice will work as well. The original recipe also calls for spaghetti, but in testing, we found that macaroni is easier for kids to eat. This

GRANDMOTHER ROSE'S MULLIGAN

SERVES: 6 START TO FINISH: UNDER 30 MINUTES

Salt for cooking the macaroni
8 ounces elbow macaroni or other small pasta
1 pound ground beef, fresh or frozen (see Note)
2 teaspoons olive oil
1 large onion (for about 1 cup chopped)
1 large bottle (64 ounces) tomato-vegetable juice,
    such as V8
1 tablespoon chili powder
1 tablespoon sugar
Black pepper to taste

1. Bring 2½ quarts lightly salted water to a boil in a covered 4½-quart or larger Dutch oven or soup pot. When the water reaches a rapid boil, add the pasta and cook, uncovered, until firm-tender, following the package directions.

2. Meanwhile, if the meat is frozen, run it under hot water so you can remove the packaging. Place the meat on a microwave-safe plate and microwave, uncovered, on high power for 3 minutes to partially defrost.

3. While the meat is defrosting, heat the oil in a 4½-quart or larger soup pot over medium heat. Peel and coarsely chop the onion, adding it to the pot as you chop. Add the partially defrosted meat to the pot, raise the heat to medium-high, and cook, breaking up the meat, until it has completely browned, 7 to 8 minutes. Drain away any accumulated fat, if necessary.

4. Add the tomato-vegetable juice, chili powder, sugar, and black pepper. Stir well and bring the soup to a boil. Reduce the heat to medium-low and cook at a slow boil to blend the flavors, 5 to 7 minutes.

5. When the macaroni is done, drain it. To serve, spoon some macaroni into each bowl and ladle the soup over it.

NOTE: You can use 3 cups Basic Beef (page 347), defrosted if frozen. Omit the oil and onion. Add the cooked beef in Step 4 with the tomato-vegetable juice.

MY BEEF AND BARLEY SOUP

SERVES: 4 START TO FINISH: UNDER 1 HOUR

SUPER-CHEAP!

1 can (about 14 ounces) fat-free
   chicken broth, or 2 cups homemade
   chicken stock (see page 10)
1 can (about 14 ounces)
   fat-free beef broth
2 medium-size carrots
   (for about 1 cup sliced)
1 large onion (for about 1 cup chopped)
1 cup shredded already-cooked beef roast (see page 348),
   defrosted if frozen
½ cup medium-size pearl barley

1. Pour the two broths into a 4½-quart Dutch oven or soup pot. Add 3 cups water and bring to a boil over high heat.

2. While the liquid is heating, slice the carrots, adding them to the pot as you slice. Peel and chop the onion, adding it to the pot as you chop. Add the beef and barley.

3. When the soup begins to boil, reduce the heat to medium-low. Simmer, covered, stirring occasionally to prevent sticking, until the vegetables and the barley are tender, about 45 minutes.

recipe is indeed a true kid-pleaser, but it also packs enough flavor to satisfy adults, thanks to the just-right sprinkling of chili powder. It's a simple, inexpensive meal.

From Alicia:

Talk about stretching your ingredients! This soup is the definition of s-t-r-e-t-c-h-i-n-g! A cup of cooked beef, half a cup of barley, a couple of carrots, and an onion, and you've got dinner. You simply throw everything in the pot and simmer until it is savory and tender. If you'd like, add a can of diced tomatoes as well. Everyone in my family loves this soup, and no one knows they're eating leftovers.

Thanks to already-cooked meatballs (either your own stash of homemade or a super buy-one-get-one-free special at the store), this recipe is as fast as it is inexpensive. Throw in some frozen vegetables, and it's good for you, too. (Any frozen vegetable mixture that contains carrots, corn, green beans, peas, and such will work just fine.) This is also a great way to use up those odd bits of vegetables languishing in your freezer. We do, however, advise avoiding broccoli, as it tends to taste too srong in this soup.

We use angel hair pasta because it's one of the fastest-cooking, crossing the finish line at about 4 minutes. The soup will be much easier to eat if you break the pasta strands into smaller lengths before adding them to the pot. If you don't mind cooking the soup a little longer, you can substitute any type of pasta you have on hand.

MINDLESS MEATBALL MINESTRONE

SERVES: 4 START TO FINISH: UNDER 25 MINUTES

1 can (about 14 ounces) fat-free chicken broth, or 2 cups homemade chicken stock (see page 10)

1 can (14 ounces) fat-free beef broth

2 cups frozen mixed vegetables, such as corn, carrots, and peas (see headnote)

1 can (14½ ounces) stewed or diced tomatoes

20 already-cooked meatballs (see Note), defrosted if frozen

⅓ cup broken angel hair pasta (1- to 2-inch lengths)

1 can (15 ounces) light red kidney beans, or 2 cups homemade (see page 368), defrosted if frozen

1 teaspoon dried Italian seasoning

½ teaspoon garlic powder

¼ cup shredded or grated Parmesan cheese

1. Pour the two broths into a 4½-quart Dutch oven or soup pot and place it over high heat. While the liquid is heating, add the frozen vegetables, tomatoes, meatballs, and pasta. Cover the pot and bring it to a boil. This will take about 10 minutes.

2. While the soup is heating, rinse and drain the beans.

3. When the soup comes to a boil, uncover it and stir well. (The pasta might stick to the bottom. If so, scrape the bottom of the pot with a wooden spoon to loosen it.) Add the beans, Italian seasoning, and garlic powder and reduce the heat to medium or medium-high (to maintain a vigorous boil). Stir frequently until the pasta is tender, about 3 minutes. Serve at once, garnishing each bowl with 1 tablespoon Parmesan cheese.

NOTE: You can use Marvelous Meatballs (page 353) or purchased frozen meatballs (plain, traditional, or Italian-style).

HOT DOG AND BAKED BEAN SOUP

SERVES: 4 START TO FINISH: UNDER 30 MINUTES

2 teaspoons vegetable oil

3 regular or reduced-fat beef
frankfurters

1 large can (28 ounces)
baked beans seasoned
with onions, bacon,
and brown sugar

2 cans (about 14 ounces each) vegetable broth or fat-free
chicken broth, or 4 cups homemade vegetable stock or
chicken stock (see pages 38 and 10)

½ teaspoon chili powder

1 teaspoon spicy brown mustard

½ large green bell pepper (for ¾ cup chopped; optional)

1. Heat the oil in a 4½-quart Dutch oven or soup pot over medium
heat. Cut the franks into ¼-inch-thick slices and add them to the
pot. Cook until the franks start to brown, 2 to 3 minutes.

2. Add the baked beans with their juice, and the broth, chili
powder, and mustard. Stir well. Raise the heat to high and bring
the soup to a boil. Then reduce the heat to medium to maintain
a moderate boil.

3. Stem, seed, and coarsely chop the green pepper (if using) and
set it aside. Continue to boil the soup to blend the flavors, about
10 minutes. Add the green pepper (if using) to the pot in the last
5 minutes of cooking. Serve at once.

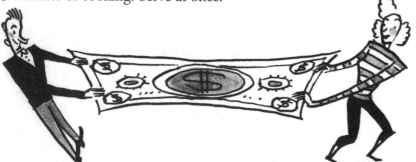

From Beverly:

The first time I served
this to my kids, they
didn't miss a beat.
Recognizing a kinship with
one of their favorite skillet
dinners (see page 172),
they exclaimed: "Oh cool!
Beanie-Weanie Soup!" And
from that day forward,
"Beanie-Weanie Soup"
became a regular request.
I stock up on big cans of
seasoned baked beans when
they go on sale. If there
isn't a special, I often substitute the house brand of
plain baked beans and stir
in my own brown sugar
and onion powder to taste.
(A teaspoon of onion pow-
der usually does the trick.
Add the brown sugar a
tablespoon at a time, tasting until the beans are as
sweet as you like.)

If kids are the main
audience at your house,
you can omit the green
pepper. Or serve the kids
before the adults, then add
the green pepper and sim-
mer the soup for 5 more
minutes before serving the
adults. As we found during
the first winter we lived in
Minnesota, this is a particularly good soup for a
snowstorm.

Making Your Own Chicken Stock

"Making stock truly is a mindless task."

Whenever chicken is on sale—think thighs, drumsticks, and wings—it's time to make some homemade stock. Nothing could be easier. It's less expensive than the cheapest house brand of chicken broth, and you end up with a huge bonus: a stash of tender chicken that's perfect to add to casseroles, soups, salads, or stews.

Contrary to what you might think, making stock truly is a mindless task, and it takes only about 5 minutes to assemble. Here's how:

To make 12 cups of stock (our typical batch), you'll need about 2½ pounds of chicken—12 to 15 wings, or 8 thighs, or 8 drumsticks. The stock will taste better if you include the chicken skin. (You can also use the leftover skin and bones from breasts that you've boned yourself.) If you buy whole chickens that have the neck included, freeze the necks and collect them to add to the stockpot.

Place the chicken in the pot of a 5-quart slow cooker, or use a 4½-quart soup pot. Pour enough cold tap water over the chicken to cover it (about 10½ cups). (The exact amount of water doesn't matter so long as the chicken is covered, but 10½ cups will make enough stock to equal seven cans of purchased broth. The chicken and vegetables will release the additional 1½ cups of liquid.)

Next, add 1 peeled onion cut in half, 2 medium-size carrots cut in half (no need to peel them), and a rib or two of celery cut in half. Cover the pot. If you are using a slow cooker, cook the stock for 5 hours on high or 10 hours on low. If you are using a soup pot, first bring the water to a boil over high heat, then lower the heat and simmer, covered, for 5 hours. Check the stock from time to time, adding more water, if necessary, and spooning off any foam that collects on top.

When the stock has cooked, transfer the chicken pieces to a bowl to cool. (The meat can be removed from the bones for later use.) Discard the vegetables. Ladle the stock through a strainer. (You can cool the stock at room temperature for up to 30 minutes before straining, but it isn't necessary.)

The next step is a secret that comes courtesy of Molly O'Neill's *New York Cookbook.* For a really rich chicken taste, stir a little commercial chicken bouillon into the strained warm stock. (O'Neill actually recommends this step for adding a rich taste to finished chicken soup, but we think this is a great idea for homemade stock as well.) We like to use a tablespoon of reduced-sodium chicken bouillon crystals. If you'd rather use 4 regular chicken bouillon cubes, add them with the vegetables so they'll dissolve.

After the stock has been refrigerated for several hours, scoop off any fat from the surface. The stock can now be used in place of canned broth in all of our recipes.

Although the amount in cans of chicken broth varies (see page 5), we package most of our stock in 2-cup amounts. We also usually package some in 1-cup portions, because that's another common recipe amount. You can put it in containers that hold the amount you think you're most likely to use. For storage, use Tupperware or any airtight, hard plastic containers you have. (Recent studies have cast doubt over whether it's safe to store leftovers in reused, "soft" plastic containers such as margarine tubs and sour cream containers.)

The stock will keep, covered and refrigerated, for up to 2 days; covered and frozen, for up to 2 months. Thaw frozen stock overnight in the refrigerator, or defrost it in the microwave.

CURE-ALL CHICKEN SOUP

Whether you've got an after-work headache or a child with the flu, this soup is good medicine. And when somebody's under the weather (be it the cook or anybody else), we can all use a soup that goes together quickly so as not to add stress to an already stressful situation. This soup will have you feeling better in no time.

Salt for cooking the rice
⅔ **pound skinless, boneless chicken breast halves, fresh or frozen (see Note)**
1 **cup long-grain rice**
2 **teaspoons vegetable oil**
1 **large onion (for about 1 cup chopped)**
2 **medium-size carrots (for about 1 cup chopped)**
3 **medium-size ribs celery (for about 1½ cups diced)**
1 **clove fresh garlic, minced, or 1 teaspoon bottled minced garlic**
1 **teaspoon finely minced fresh ginger or bottled minced ginger**
2 **cans (about 14 ounces each) fat-free chicken broth, or 4 cups homemade chicken stock (see page 10)**
¼ **teaspoon black pepper, or to taste**

1. Bring 2 cups lightly salted water to a boil in a 2-quart saucepan.

2. While the water is heating, if the chicken is frozen, run it under hot water so you can remove the packaging. Place the chicken on a microwave-safe plate and microwave, uncovered, on high power for 2 minutes to partially defrost it.

3. When the water comes to a boil, add the rice, stir, and reduce the heat to low. Cover the pan and simmer until the rice is tender, about 20 minutes.

4. Meanwhile, heat the oil in a 4½-quart or larger Dutch oven or soup pot over medium heat. Peel the onion and finely chop it, adding it to the pot as you chop. Cut the partially defrosted or fresh chicken into bite-size pieces, adding them to the pot as you cut. When all of the chicken is in the pot, raise the heat to medium-high. Cook, stirring, until the chicken is almost cooked through, about 4 minutes.

5. Peel and coarsely chop the carrots, adding them to the pot as you chop. Coarsely dice the celery, adding it to the pot as you dice. Add the garlic and ginger to the pot. Continue to cook, stirring occasionally, until the celery is crisp-tender, about 2 minutes.

6. Add the broth to the pot, raise the heat to high, and bring the soup to a boil. Then reduce the heat to medium and cook at a moderate boil to combine the flavors, 5 minutes. Season with black pepper. To serve, spoon some rice into each bowl and top it with the soup.

NOTE: You can use 2 cups Perfect Poached Chicken (page 362) or Poached Chicken Thighs (page 364), defrosted if frozen. Skip Step 2 and just cook the onions in Step 4. Add the already-cooked chicken in Step 5 after the carrots and celery have cooked for 2 to 3 minutes. Or use 2 cups Chunky Seasoned Chicken (page 358), defrosted if frozen. Omit the onion and garlic. Skip Step 2; in Step 4, just heat the oil, then add the carrots to the pot and continue with Step 5. Add the Chunky Seasoned Chicken with the broth in Step 6.

Chew on This

Every year, the average U.S. household throws away 470 pounds of food, according to research from the University of Arizona's Garbage Project. That equals 14 percent of all the food that's brought into the house.

About:
BOTTLED GINGER

Bottled fresh ginger is a relatively new ingredient that is a perfect replacement for time-consuming minced fresh ginger. Called crushed, ground, minced, or chopped, depending on the brand, bottled fresh ginger is available in the produce section of larger supermarkets. A teaspoon of bottled fresh ginger is the equivalent of 1 teaspoon finely minced fresh ginger.

From Beverly:

Throwing away left-
overs really gets on
my nerves. It's not
just that it's a waste of
money. I guess my mom's
speeches about children
starving in far-off countries
really took root. So I make
it a sport to see if I can use
the last bits and pieces of
everything, and soup is the
perfect vehicle for such
endeavors. Here's a great
way to use up the last bits
of turkey. The nutty flavor
and chewy texture of
brown rice make for a soup
that's hearty enough to be
dinner with just a salad or
a crusty slab of bread.

TURKEY VEGETABLE SOUP WITH BROWN RICE

SERVES: 6 START TO FINISH: UNDER 1 HOUR

1 cup brown rice
2 teaspoons vegetable oil
1 large onion (for about 1 cup chopped)
2 cloves fresh garlic, minced, or 2 teaspoons
    bottled minced garlic
3 cups shredded green cabbage, or 1 bag (8 ounces)
    coleslaw mix
2 cans (about 14 ounces each) fat-free chicken broth,
    or 4 cups homemade chicken stock (see page 10)
1 can (14½ ounces) diced tomatoes (see Notes)
1 bay leaf
¼ teaspoon dried thyme or dried basil
⅛ teaspoon black pepper
1 tablespoon regular or reduced-sodium soy sauce
1 tablespoon Worcestershire sauce
3 cups frozen mixed vegetables
2 cups cooked turkey chunks (see Notes), defrosted
    if frozen

1. Bring 2¼ cups lightly salted water to a boil in a covered 2-quart saucepan. Add the rice, stir, and reduce the heat to low. Cover the pan and simmer until all the water is absorbed, about 30 minutes.

2. While the rice is cooking, heat the oil in a 4½-quart or larger Dutch oven or soup pot over medium heat. Peel and coarsely chop the onion, adding it to the pot as you chop. Cook, stirring occasionally, until the onion starts to soften, about 2 minutes.

3. Add the garlic to the pot, along with the cabbage, broth, tomatoes with their juice, bay leaf, thyme, black pepper, soy sauce, and Worcestershire sauce. Bring the soup to a boil. Reduce the heat to medium-low to maintain a slow boil. If the frozen vegetables have ice crystals, pour them into a colander and rinse with warm tap water. Add the vegetables and turkey chunks to the pot and simmer until ready to serve.

4. When the rice is done, place about ½ cup in each soup bowl, spoon the soup over the rice, and serve.

NOTES: Diced tomatoes seasoned with onions and garlic can be used.

■ Instead of turkey, you can use 2 cups cut-up Perfect Poached Chicken (page 362) or Poached Chicken Thighs (page 364), defrosted if frozen. Add either in Step 3 in place of the turkey. Or use 2 cups Chunky Seasoned Chicken (page 358), defrosted if frozen. Omit the oil, onion, and garlic, and add in Step 3 in place of the turkey.

MoneySaver

For a cheap alternative to canned chicken and beef broths, dissolve 2 bouillon cubes in 2 cups warm water. Most cans of broth measure 1¾ cups, but the ¼ cup extra bouillon won't affect most soups and stews. Since bouillon can be saltier than canned broth, taste before adding any salt called for in the recipe.

Why throw out perfectly good broth when you can use it as the basis of a quick-and-easy dinner? This is the quintessential leftovers soup, but the flavor cries "gourmet restaurant," thanks to the bold, rich broth left over from the Savory Pork Pot Roast. Beverly's daughter liked it so much, she begged for more the following night.

Soup is always a good landing pad for bits of leftovers, and if you have any extra corn kernels or sliced black olives, they make dynamite color and flavor enhancers here as well. A dab of guacamole? Dollop it on top. If you want to make the soup using a cup of pork chunks from the pork roast instead of the chicken, go right ahead. And, by the way, if you have any leftover vegetables from the pot roast, these can be diced and added to the soup as well.

SUPER-SAVER TORTILLA SOUP

SERVES: 4 START TO FINISH: UNDER 25 MINUTES

SUPER-CHEAP!

⅔ **pound boneless, skinless chicken breast halves, fresh or frozen (see Notes)**
2 **teaspoons olive oil**
1 **small onion (for about ½ cup chopped)**
½ **teaspoon ground cumin (optional)**
½ **teaspoon chili powder (optional)**
3 **cups broth from Savory Pork Pot Roast (page 356)**
1 **cup canned fat-free chicken broth or homemade chicken stock (see page 10)**
1 **cup bottled salsa**
4 **ounces (for 2½ cups crushed) tortilla chips (see Notes)**
¼ **cup sour cream (see Notes)**
¼ **cup shredded Monterey Jack, Mexican blend, or Cheddar cheese**

1. If the chicken is frozen, run it under hot water so you can remove the packaging. Place the chicken on a microwave-safe plate and microwave, uncovered, on high power for 2 minutes to partially defrost.

2. While the chicken defrosts, heat the oil in a 4½-quart soup pot over medium heat. Peel the onion and finely chop it, adding it to the pot as you chop. Cut the partially defrosted or fresh chicken into bite-size pieces, adding them to the pot as you cut. When all of the chicken has been added, raise the heat to medium-high and cook, stirring, until the chicken is almost cooked through, about 4 minutes. Add the cumin and chili powder (if desired).

3. Add the Savory Pork Pot Roast broth and the chicken stock, and raise the heat to high. Add the salsa. Cover the pot and cook until the soup is steaming hot, about 6 minutes.

4. To serve, ladle the soup into four bowls and garnish each one with crushed tortilla chips, 1 tablespoon sour cream, and 1 tablespoon cheese.

NOTES: You can use 1 cup cut-up Perfect Poached Chicken (page 362) or Poached Chicken Thighs (page 364), defrosted if frozen, in place of the chicken breasts. Add it in Step 3 after the salsa. Or use 1 cup Chunky Seasoned Chicken (page 358), defrosted if frozen. Omit the onion and oil and add the chicken with the salsa in Step 3.

■ Reduced-fat tortilla chips and sour cream can be used.

CHERYL'S TORTELLINI AND SPINACH SOUP

SERVES: 4 GENEROUSLY   START TO FINISH: UNDER 25 MINUTES

1 package (10 ounces) frozen chopped spinach
2 teaspoons olive oil
1 medium-size onion (for about ¾ cup chopped)
1 clove fresh garlic, minced, or 1 teaspoon bottled minced garlic
2 cans (about 14 ounces each) fat-free chicken broth, or 4 cups homemade chicken stock (see page 10)
1 can (14 ounces) diced tomatoes
1 teaspoon sugar
2 cups frozen cheese tortellini, or 8 ounces other pasta (see Note)
3 tablespoons shredded or grated Parmesan cheese
¼ teaspoon salt
¼ teaspoon black pepper
1 large egg

From Alicia:

I'm not sure whether it was the unselfish kindness my neighbor showed me or the soup she fed me that I couldn't stop thinking about. It was my first migraine headache, and I found myself stranded at the doctor's office, unable to drive home. My husband was out of town. After several calls to friends and family, only to get answering machines, I phoned my neighbor Cheryl Andrassy.

She answered with that nasal sound that always indicates a bad head cold. I immediately wondered who was more pitiful, stranded me or my poor

(continued)

(continued)

neighbor with the stuffy head. I told her my dilemma, and no sooner than the words could pass my lips, Cheryl was on her way.

Several hours later, as I was coming out of a foggy sleep, I heard a light tapping on the front door. There stood Cheryl, soup in hand.

"I know you probably don't want anything to eat, but just in case you do, I brought you some soup," she said.

Later I zapped the soup in the microwave and sat down to sip on it. I am always amazed at the healing powers of food. Feeling pretty miserable and alone, that soup comforted me like a fuzzy blanket on a rainy day. I'll always be grateful to Cheryl for sharing her compassion and her delicious soup. This quick and easy adaptation makes a wonderful meal anytime you need some comfort.

1. Remove the spinach from its packaging and place it in a microwave-safe dish. Microwave, uncovered, on high power until defrosted, about 5 minutes.

2. Meanwhile, heat the oil in a 4½-quart Dutch oven or soup pot over medium heat. Peel and finely chop the onion, adding it to the pot as you chop. Add the garlic. Cook, stirring, until the onion is tender, 2 to 3 minutes. Add 2 cups water and the broth; raise the heat to high and bring the soup to a boil.

3. Remove the spinach from the microwave and drain it well, squeezing out the excess water. Add it to the pot. Add the tomatoes with their juice and the sugar. Stir to mix well.

4. Add the tortellini and bring the soup back to a boil. Reduce the heat to medium, maintaining a slow boil, and cook until the pasta is just tender, 4 to 5 minutes.

5. Meanwhile, combine the Parmesan cheese, salt, black pepper, and egg in a small bowl and stir vigorously with a fork or a small whisk. Set aside.

6. When the pasta is tender, slowly drizzle the egg mixture over the soup, stirring constantly. Cook, stirring, for 2 minutes. Then remove the pot from the heat, spoon the soup into shallow bowls, and serve.

NOTE: Any variety of filled tortellini is wonderful here. For an even more economical soup, substitute a plain short pasta, such as elbow macaroni or rotini, for the tortellini.

MINI RAVIOLI SOUP

SERVES: 4 START TO FINISH: UNDER 20 MINUTES

2 teaspoons olive oil

1 large onion (for about 1 cup chopped)

8 ounces fresh button mushrooms

1 clove fresh garlic, minced, or 1 teaspoon bottled
  minced garlic

2 cans (about 14 ounces each) fat-free chicken broth, or
  4 cups homemade chicken stock (see page 10)

1 can (14½ ounces) diced tomatoes seasoned with garlic
  and onions

1 teaspoon Worcestershire sauce

½ teaspoon dried basil

2 cups mini cheese ravioli

Shredded or grated Parmesan cheese, for serving

1. Heat the oil in a 4½-quart Dutch oven or soup pot over medium heat. While the oil is heating, peel and coarsely chop the onion, adding it to the pot as you chop. Cook, stirring occasionally, until tender, about 3 minutes.

2. Rinse, pat dry, and slice the mushrooms, discarding any tough stems. Add the mushrooms to the pot and cook until they begin to release their liquid, about 2 minutes.

3. Add the garlic, broth, tomatoes with their juice, Worcestershire sauce, and basil. Raise the heat to high, cover the pot, and bring the soup to a boil.

4. When the soup is at a rolling boil, add the ravioli. When it returns to a boil, cook until the ravioli are just tender, 3 to 4 minutes. Serve at once, passing Parmesan cheese around the table to sprinkle on top.

The smiles stretched all around the table when we served this soup to our families, and the most prevalent comment was "This soup is fun!" The kudos go to miniature ravioli, which in proper Italian would be called *ravioletti*. Buitoni makes mini cheese and mini beef ravioli in its line of refrigerated pastas; the 7-ounce packages contain 2 cups. If you can't find mini ravioli, substitute any flavor of refrigerated or frozen tortellini—but because the pasta is larger and takes up more room in the measuring cup, use 3 cups to make sure everyone gets a fair share. If you don't have any mushrooms, substitute 1 cup frozen yellow corn kernels or green peas, or a combination of the two. There are lots of different kinds of seasoned diced tomatoes, and any combination of seasonings that are compatible with Italian food—such as basil, garlic, oregano, and onions—can be used.

The Conventional Wisdom of Food Cost Savings

Saving money on food can go only so far, given the fact that eating and good nutrition are basic human requirements. Do a survey of all the money-saving literature you can find, and what you'll eventually figure out is this: While there are some rules you'll need to follow if you want to save, it's not rocket science. Here's our quick overview of the basic, time-tested, money-saving techniques we've culled from the prevailing conventional wisdom.

To save money and still eat terrific meals, you need to:

- *Avoid restaurants* . . . but we've said that already.

- *Buy items only at their rock-bottom sale price.* Use advertisements to figure out the lowest possible grocery prices. To take full advantage of the lowest possible prices, you must be willing to change your menus and eating habits to use food that happens to be cheap at any given time. This means you can't be a die-hard brand loyalist. (Peter Pan might be cheaper than Jif the week you run out of peanut butter.) And if pork chops are the "featured sale" meat of the week, you need to eat pork rather than the chicken that's not on sale. (Unless, of course, you froze some chicken that you bought when it was cheapest.) As for fresh fruit and vegetables, stick with what's in season.

- *Make a price chart* so you can track the regular prices and sale prices for the grocery items you typically buy. All of the money-saving experts insist that, until you memorize the prices, using a price chart is the only way to know if you're getting the rock-bottom sale price. (See the box on page 158 for complete instructions on how to do this.)

- *Be willing to travel to the store with the lowest prices.* Most of the money-saving gurus shop more than one supermarket each week. Depending on where you live, this may or may not be feasible. (Don't drive so far, however, that you spend your savings on gas!)

- *Make a grocery list* (the easy part), and stick to it (the part that requires self-discipline). The grocery list should be based on a menu plan (see page 74 for menu-planning tips).

- *Don't shop when you're hungry.* Duh! (For information on "The When, Where, and How of Grocery Shopping," see page 54.)

- *Set a realistic grocery budget* (the easy part), and stick to it (the really hard part). (For our experiences while eating on $100 a week, see page 460.)

- If self-discipline is a challenge, *pay with cash.* For most people, it's tougher to part with the real thing.

- *Eat more food that's economical but still nutritionally sound* (think beans, grains, and tougher cuts of meat that tenderize after slow cooking). Eat less food that's expensive (think seafood and steak). Eliminate costly foods that have little or no nutritional value (think junk food and dessert).

- *Use coupons.* This is time consuming, but the savings can be significant. The good news is that most supermarkets run sales on many items in conjunction with manufacturer's coupon drives. Yes indeed, the manufacturer and the super-market are in cahoots! This is a marketing tool that's most often used when a new product is being introduced: The idea is to make the item so cheap that you're willing to give it a try. (For more details on couponing and our individual experiences using them, see page 46.)

- *Look beyond the supermarket.* Most money-saving experts buy produce from farmers' markets and at pick-your-own farms. They also shop at price-club warehouse stores (see details on page 282). Other types of stores that didn't used to sell food items now do, including pharmacies, "mart" stores such as Wal-Mart and Target, and even discount clothing outlets such

"Most money-saving gurus shop more than one supermarket each week."

as Marshall's and TJ Maxx. Bakery outlets are another source for savings (see page 240 for the particulars). Depending on where you live, there may be other unconventional sources for cheaper food. Ask your thrifty friends and watch for advertisements.

- *Make foods from scratch,* particularly convenience items. This area is a bit tricky because some foods are cheaper the more work you do yourself, and some are not. Examples: It's cheaper to slice your own mushrooms and make your own hash browns, but cake mixes (particularly on sale) are cheaper than making cakes from scratch—unless you buy huge quantities of the basic ingredients at a warehouse store and then make a lot of cakes (50 pounds of flour, anyone?). You'll need a calculator to figure out which items are cheaper to make yourself.

- *Grow your own vegetables and herbs.* One penny-pinching expert grew pumpkins, and when the crop came in, she spent entire days carving, seeding, peeling, baking, and pureeing them. When all this was done, she had made fifty-two pumpkin pies. The resulting pies cost just pennies each, but the time involved was substantial. Other gardening endeavors, such as one or two prolific tomato plants, can pay big dividends without such gargantuan efforts. Growing a few favorite herbs in a pot can save on paying a big price for a too-big bunch.

- *Finally, how much you can save depends on how much you already spend.* (Or put another way, it depends on how thrifty you already are.) If your weekly grocery cart is normally brimming with fully cooked entrées, filet mignon, fresh avocados, and peaches out of season, your cost savings can be immediate and huge. But if you're already buying store brands and economy sizes, and eating beans twice a week, trimming a lot more, while possible, may be a challenge.

As you can see, there's one factor that comes into play with every money-saving technique: time. The more time and effort you're willing to spend, the more money you're likely to save. (For more thoughts on this equation, see Time vs. Cost Savings on page 355.)

"To take full advantage of the lowest possible prices, you can't be a die-hard brand loyalist."

LENTIL AND CHICKPEA SOUP WITH CILANTRO

SERVES: 6 START TO FINISH: UNDER 30 MINUTES

2 teaspoons olive oil

1 large onion (for about 1 cup chopped)

2 cans (about 14 ounces each) vegetable broth, or
4 cups homemade vegetable stock (see page 38)

2 cans (14½ ounces each) diced tomatoes seasoned
with onions and garlic

2 cloves fresh garlic, minced, or 2 teaspoons bottled
minced garlic

1 teaspoon finely minced fresh ginger or bottled
minced ginger

1 teaspoon ground turmeric (optional)

½ teaspoon ground cinnamon

¼ teaspoon black pepper

3 ounces (½ bag) fine egg noodles

½ cup loosely packed fresh cilantro leaves

1 can (15 ounces) chickpeas, or 1 cup homemade
(see page 368), defrosted if frozen

3 cups already-cooked brown lentils (see page 369),
defrosted if frozen

1. Heat the oil in a 4½-quart Dutch oven or soup pot over medium heat. Peel and coarsely chop the onion, adding it to the pot as you chop. Cook, stirring frequently, until the onion begins to soften, about 2 minutes.

2. Add the broth and 1 cup water and raise the heat to high. Add the tomatoes with their juice, garlic, ginger, turmeric (if using), cinnamon, and black pepper. Cover the pot until the soup comes to a boil.

3. Uncover the pot and stir in the noodles. Cook, uncovered, until the noodles are tender, about 6 minutes. Meanwhile, rinse the cilantro and dry it with paper towels. Coarsely chop the leaves. Rinse and drain the chickpeas and the lentils.

Like vegetable soup in this country, in Morocco there's no one right way to make lentil soup. Though the recipes vary, the constant is the wonderful abundance of herbs and spices, including cinnamon, turmeric, and cilantro. Turmeric adds a lovely yellow hue, but if you don't have any, just leave it out. The authentic name for this soup is *harira,* and Moroccan families typically eat it to break their fast each night of Ramadan, the ninth and most holy month of the Muslim year. It's also a favorite breakfast of Moroccan farmers. With its hearty mix of chickpeas, lentils, and egg noodles—and the speedy cooking time—we think it makes the perfect midweek dinner. An added bonus is that it is also low in fat, with just 5 grams per serving.

23

4. When the noodles are tender, add the chickpeas, lentils, and chopped cilantro and cook until heated through, about 2 minutes. Serve at once.

From Beverly:

Minestrone is one of my favorite soups, and I'm always experimenting with different ways to make it. This hodgepodge soup is a wonderful way to use the last bits of leftover vegetables, so if you happen to have some extras on hand to throw in, we encourage you to branch out. The extra-special something that sets this minestrone apart is a dollop of our homemade Spinach Parsley Pesto, which adds a bright green flourish and lots of flavor.

Macaroni cooks the quickest in this soup, but feel free to substitute any other short pasta if you have another variety on hand; cook until the pasta is tender.

WINTER MINESTRONE WITH PESTO

SERVES: 4 START TO FINISH: UNDER 30 MINUTES

Salt for cooking the macaroni
½ cup elbow macaroni
2 teaspoons olive oil
1 large carrot (for about ½ cup sliced)
1 large onion (for about 1 cup chopped)
2 cloves fresh garlic, minced, or 2 teaspoons
    bottled minced garlic
1 can (about 14 ounces) fat-free beef broth
1 can (about 14 ounces) fat-free chicken broth,
    or 2 cups homemade chicken stock (see page 10)
1 can (14½ ounces) stewed or diced tomatoes
1½ teaspoons dried Italian seasoning
½ teaspoon sugar
1 cup frozen green beans (see Note)
1 can (15 ounces) white beans, such as Great Northern,
    or 1 cup homemade (see page 368), defrosted if frozen
Black pepper to taste
¼ cup Spinach Parsley Pesto (page 372)

1. Bring 5 cups lightly salted water to a boil in a covered 2-quart pot over high heat. When the water reaches a rapid boil, add the macaroni and cook, uncovered, until just tender, following the package directions.

2. Meanwhile, heat the oil in a 4½-quart Dutch oven or soup pot over low heat. Peel the carrot and thinly slice it, adding the pieces to the pot as you slice. Raise the heat to medium-high and cook, stirring occasionally, while you peel and coarsely chop the onion. Add it to the pot as you chop. Add the garlic to the pot. Cook, stirring frequently, until the carrots are crisp-tender, about 2 minutes more.

3. Add the two broths, the tomatoes with their juice, the Italian seasoning, sugar, and green beans. Raise the heat to high, cover the pot, and bring the soup to a boil. Meanwhile, drain and rinse the white beans. When the soup is boiling, reduce the heat to medium and add the white beans. Let the soup cook at a moderate boil, covered, to blend the flavors, about 5 minutes more.

4. When the macaroni is just tender, drain it. Reduce the heat under the soup pot to low and add the macaroni to the soup. Season with black pepper. Stir the pesto to mix in any oil that may have separated. Ladle the soup into four bowls and top each serving with 1 tablespoon Spinach Parsley Pesto. Serve at once.

NOTE: You can use ½ cup frozen green peas in place of the green beans.

Chew on This

According to figures from a coupon clearinghouse for manufacturers and retailers in Deerfield, Illinois, although some 4 billion coupons were redeemed nationwide in one year, it was only 1.5 percent of all the coupons issued by the manufacturers and retailers.

This Italian pasta and bean soup makes for a hearty—and extremely economical—vegetarian meal. It is so well rounded and so filling that you can serve it alone or simply with bread sticks or crackers.

If staying strictly vegetarian is not a concern, you can add small amounts of leftover cooked turkey or chicken. Just add them in Step 3 and cook until heated through. Chicken broth or homemade chicken stock can also be used in place of the vegetable broth or stock.

PASTA E FAGIOLI

SERVES: 6 START TO FINISH: UNDER 30 MINUTES

SUPER-CHEAP!

2 teaspoons olive oil

1 large onion
  (for about 1 cup chopped)

2 medium-size carrots
  (for about 1 cup sliced)

1 clove fresh garlic, minced,
  or 1 teaspoon bottled minced garlic

3 cans (about 14 ounces each) vegetable broth,
  or 6 cups homemade vegetable stock (see page 38)

2 cans (14½ ounces each) Italian-style stewed tomatoes
  (see Note)

1 teaspoon dried Italian seasoning

1 cup elbow macaroni

1 can (15 ounces) red kidney beans, or 1 cup homemade
  (see page 368), defrosted if frozen

1 can (15 ounces) white beans, such as navy beans, or
  1 cup homemade (see page 368), defrosted if frozen

¼ teaspoon black pepper, or to taste

⅓ cup shredded or grated Parmesan cheese, or to taste

1. Heat the oil in a 4½-quart Dutch oven or soup pot over medium heat. Peel and coarsely chop the onion, adding it to the pot as you chop. Cook, stirring from time to time, while peeling and slicing the carrots into ¼-inch-thick rounds. Add the carrots to the pot and cook, stirring frequently, until they begin to soften, about 3 minutes.

2. Add the garlic, broth, tomatoes with their juice, and Italian seasoning to the pot. Cover, raise the heat to high, and bring the soup to a boil.

3. When the broth comes to a boil, add the macaroni and cook, uncovered, at a rolling boil for 7 minutes. Meanwhile, rinse and drain the beans.

4. Add the beans and bring the soup back to a boil. Continue to cook until the macaroni is tender, about 3 minutes more. Season the soup with black pepper and serve, sprinkling the Parmesan cheese on top.

NOTE: Diced tomatoes flavored with Italian-style seasonings such as garlic, basil, and onions can be substituted.

About:
THE HEALTHY BENEFITS OF BEANS

Everybody knows that beans are cheap —but do you know how healthy they are? They're practically a miracle food.

For starters, beans are a good source of soluble fiber, which lowers cholesterol, keeps your arteries flexible, and helps protect against heart disease and high blood pressure.

That ought to be enough, but no! Beans have almost as much protein as meat but almost none of the fat and cholesterol. They contain folic acid, which is the stuff that helps prevent birth defects and also heart disease. They're a good source of iron, potassium, and other minerals.

When researchers from Tulane University followed 9,500 people over 19 years in a diet and health survey, they found that participants who ate at least four servings of beans a week were 20 percent less likely to suffer from heart disease when compared to those who ate beans less than once a week.

Now pardon us while we go take our medicine—uh, beans.

Now that canned refried beans come in a fat-free version, they're one of our favorite inexpensive pantry staples. Spread some on a flour tortilla, sprinkle with cheese, zap it in the microwave, and you've got an instant snack or emergency dinner. (This is especially helpful if your teenager decides to become the family's only vegetarian.) Refried beans also do a stellar job of thickening soup. Stir in a can, and suddenly you've got the velvety texture it would take hours to achieve otherwise. This soup is a budget-minded, quick-and-hearty, protein-packed, vegetarian meal with only 3 grams of fat per serving.

REFRIED BEAN SOUP

SERVES: 4 START TO FINISH: UNDER 20 MINUTES

SUPER-CHEAP!

2 teaspoons olive oil

1 large onion
   (for about 1 cup chopped)

1 medium-size green bell pepper
   (for about 1 cup chopped)

2 cloves fresh garlic, minced,
   or 2 teaspoons bottled minced garlic

1 can (about 14 ounces) vegetable broth or fat-free
   chicken broth, or 2 cups homemade vegetable stock
   or chicken stock (see pages 38 and 10)

1 can (14½ ounces) Mexican-style stewed tomatoes
   or diced tomatoes seasoned with jalapeño

1 can (15 ounces) black beans, or 1 cup homemade
   (see page 368), defrosted if frozen

1 can (15 ounces) red kidney beans, or 1 cup homemade
   (see page 368), defrosted if frozen

1 can (16 ounces) fat-free refried beans

¼ teaspoon ground cumin

Black pepper to taste

1. Heat the oil in a 4½-quart Dutch oven or soup pot over medium heat. Peel and coarsely chop the onion, adding it to the pot as you chop. Seed and coarsely chop the bell pepper, adding it to the pot as you chop. Raise the heat to medium-high and cook until the vegetables are tender, 2 to 3 minutes.

2. Add the garlic to the pot. Stir in the broth and the tomatoes with their juice. Raise the heat to high. Rinse and drain the black beans and kidney beans and add them to the soup pot. Add the refried beans and the cumin and stir well. Cover the pot and let the soup come to a boil. Reduce the heat to low and simmer, stirring occasionally, until the soup is heated through and the flavors have blended, 5 to 7 minutes. Season with black pepper and serve.

GOOD LUCK SOUP

SERVES: 4 START TO FINISH: UNDER 30 MINUTES

SUPER-CHEAP!

Salt for cooking the rice
1 cup long-grain rice
2 teaspoons olive oil
1 large onion
   (for about 1 cup chopped)
1 clove fresh garlic, minced, or
   1 teaspoon bottled minced garlic
1 can (about 14 ounces) fat-free chicken broth,
   or 2 cups homemade chicken stock (see page 10)
2 cans (15 ounces each) black-eyed peas, packed without pork,
   or 4 cups homemade (see page 368), defrosted if frozen
1 can (14½ ounces) chili-style diced tomatoes or
   diced tomatoes seasoned with jalapeño
1 cup frozen yellow corn kernels
1 teaspoon Worcestershire sauce
1 chicken bouillon cube
½ teaspoon sugar
¼ teaspoon dried thyme

1. Bring 2 cups lightly salted water to a boil in a medium-size saucepan. Add the rice, stir, and reduce the heat to low. Cover the pan and simmer until tender, about 20 minutes.

2. Meanwhile, heat the oil in a 4½-quart Dutch oven or soup pot over medium heat. Peel and coarsely chop the onion, adding it to the pot as you chop. Add the garlic and cook, stirring, for 1 minute.

3. Add the broth and raise the heat to high. Drain and rinse 1 can of the black-eyed peas and add it to the pot. Add the second can with its juices. (If using home-cooked peas, add them with some juice.) Add the tomatoes with their juice, the corn, Worcestershire sauce, bouillon cube, sugar, and thyme. Cover the pot and bring the soup to a boil. Reduce the heat to medium and cook, covered, at a moderate boil, stirring from time to time to blend the flavors, about 10 minutes. At this point, the rice will be done. Spoon some rice into each bowl, pour the soup over the rice, and serve.

From Beverly:

On New Year's Day, the War Between the States still rages at my dinner table. My Southern roots tell me that I simply must have a menu of pork, greens, and, above all, black-eyed peas. The good luck and prosperity of the entire year ahead depends on it.

My northern-born husband, however, has one serious shortcoming: He does not like to eat these particular foods. Since the good fortunes of me and my children are so closely tied to those of my husband, I see it as nothing short of an absolute duty to make sure that he eats an ample supply of the traditional good-luck foods.

Over the years, collard greens have given way to spinach, and I have managed to hide black-eyed peas in everything from dip to meat loaf. This recipe is my latest solution. With the assertive flavors of the chili-style tomatoes mingled with corn and rice, I suspect my husband will hardly notice the peas at all.

LOADED BAKED POTATO SOUP

SERVES: 4 START TO FINISH: UNDER 15 MINUTES

1 tablespoon butter
1 large onion
    (for about 1 cup chopped)
6 already-baked Russet baking
    potatoes (see page 366),
    or 2 packages (1 pound, 4 ounces each)
    refrigerated hash-brown potatoes, such as Simply Potatoes
2 cans (about 14 ounces each) fat-free chicken broth,
    or 4 cups homemade chicken stock (see page 10)
1 cup milk
½ cup sour cream
¼ teaspoon salt, or to taste
⅛ teaspoon black pepper
Real bacon bits (not imitation) to taste (optional; see page 167)
Shredded Cheddar cheese to taste (optional)

SUPER-CHEAP!

1. Melt the butter in a 4½-quart Dutch oven or soup pot over medium heat. Meanwhile, peel and coarsely chop the onion, adding it to the pot as you chop. Raise the heat to medium-high and cook until the onion begins to soften, about 2 minutes. Meanwhile, cut the baked potatoes in half.

2. Add the broth to the soup pot, raise the heat to high, and bring it to a boil. When the broth boils, reduce the heat to medium. Meanwhile, scoop the insides of the baked potatoes into a 2-quart or larger bowl, leaving a ¼-inch-thick shell. (You will have about 3 cups potato.) Reserve the skins for another use. (See page 68 for a recipe.) Cut the potato into bite-size pieces and add them to the pot.

3. Add the milk and sour cream and stir well. Add the salt and black pepper and taste to correct the seasonings. Cook until heated through, 3 to 5 minutes. Serve at once, garnished with bacon bits and cheese, if desired.

AUGUST VICHYSSOISE

SERVES: 6 START TO FINISH: UNDER 20 MINUTES

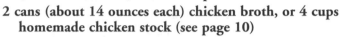

1 medium-size onion
(for about ¾ cup sliced)

1 tablespoon butter

2 to 3 cups sliced cooked
potatoes (see Notes), or 2 cans
(14½ ounces each) sliced new potatoes

2 cans (about 14 ounces each) chicken broth, or 4 cups
homemade chicken stock (see page 10)

1 cup milk or half-and-half

½ teaspoon Worcestershire sauce

¼ teaspoon salt (optional)

Black pepper to taste

Chopped scallions, for garnish (optional)

1. Peel and thinly slice the onion. Melt the butter in a small non-stick skillet over medium heat, add the sliced onion, and cook, stirring occasionally, until tender, 2 to 3 minutes. Do not allow the onion to brown (reduce the heat to low, if necessary).

2. Meanwhile, drain the potatoes if using canned, and put them in a blender or food processor. Add half of the broth and puree until smooth. (If using a food processor, add only half a can of broth to prevent overflow.) Add the cooked onions and process until smooth, about 45 seconds.

3. Pour the potato mixture into a large serving or storage bowl. Add the remaining broth and the milk, Worcestershire sauce, salt (if using), and black pepper. Stir well. Serve immediately if chilled, or refrigerate for up to 4 hours before serving. (See Notes for a quick-chilling technique.) Before serving, garnish the soup with scallions, if desired.

NOTES: See page 366 for our Amazing Baked Potatoes recipe.
■ If the potatoes and broth are not already cold, quick-chill the finished soup by placing it in the freezer for 20 minutes, stirring it once after 10 minutes.

When it's hot outside, we still rely on soup for dinner—we just make it cold. To round out a dinner of chilled soup, all you have to do is add some hearty bread, a chunk of cheese, and a fruit salad.

In some ways, cold soups are even easier than hot. Regardless of what most cookbooks would have you believe, only minimal cooking is necessary. A classic cold soup, traditional vichyssoise (pronounced vishy-swahz) requires peeling potatoes, prying the sand from layers of leeks, and hours of simmering. Our cheap-and-easy version, however, is ready to serve in minutes.

All you have to do is chop and cook a few onions, and then whir the ingredients in a blender or food processor. It does make the process quicker if you think of your refrigerator as part pantry—just keep chicken broth in the back of the fridge for a hot night when you feel like eating liquid velvet.

Many children (and some adults we know) would never agree to sample a soup made from sweet potatoes and pumpkin, even though its slightly sweet, peanut-y taste is perfect for children (or anybody else). If you call it "Jack-O'Lantern Soup," however, you're likely to get a different reaction altogether. What self-respecting child (of any age) could resist?

This recipe makes a lot of soup. Here's an idea: Make the soup for Halloween, then freeze the leftovers and serve them a few weeks later as "Pilgrim Soup" on a night when you're too busy to cook because you're getting ready for the Thanksgiving feast. It's all in the name!

PUMPKIN PEANUT SOUP

SERVES: 6 START TO FINISH: UNDER 20 MINUTES

1 tablespoon butter
1 small onion (for about ½ cup chopped)
3 cups cooked, peeled sweet potatoes (about 2 large),
    or 1 can (29 ounces) sweet potatoes
2 cans (about 14 ounces each) fat-free chicken broth,
    or 4 cups homemade chicken stock (see page 10)
1 can (16 ounces) pure pumpkin (see Notes)
1 cup Thai-Style Peanut Sauce (page 374), defrosted if frozen
¾ cup half-and-half or milk (see Notes)

1. Melt the butter in a 4½-quart Dutch oven or soup pot over low heat. Peel and coarsely chop the onion, adding it to the pot as you chop. Raise the heat to medium and cook until the onion begins to soften slightly, about 3 minutes. Meanwhile, if the sweet potatoes are canned, drain them; if they are packed in syrup, rinse them gently under cold water to remove excess sugar.

2. Put the sweet potatoes and 1 cup of the broth in a blender or food processor and puree until smooth.

3. Add the remaining broth to the soup pot. Add the sweet potato mixture, pumpkin, and peanut sauce. Stir well, cover the pot, and bring the soup to a boil. Reduce the heat to low and simmer, stirring occasionally to prevent sticking, for 5 to 10 minutes, or until ready to serve.

4. Just before serving, remove the pot from the heat and stir in the half-and-half. Serve at once.

NOTES: Be sure to use pure pumpkin (pureed pumpkin), *not* pumpkin pie filling.
■ Skim, low-fat, or whole milk can be used; just be sure the soup is not allowed to boil after adding the milk.

CREAMY WILD RICE SOUP

SERVES: 4 START TO FINISH: UNDER 20 MINUTES

8 ounces fresh button mushrooms

2 teaspoons vegetable oil

1 large onion (for about
1 cup chopped)

2 tablespoons dry sherry
(optional)

1 can (about 14 ounces) fat-free
chicken broth, or 2 cups homemade chicken stock
(see page 10)

1 can (10¾ ounces) regular or reduced-fat condensed
cream of mushroom soup

1 box (6.2 ounces) fast-cooking long-grain and
wild rice blend (see headnote)

Black pepper to taste

SUPER-CHEAP!

1. Rinse, pat dry, and slice the mushrooms, removing and discarding any tough stems. Set them aside.

2. Heat the oil in a 4½-quart Dutch oven or soup pot over medium heat. Peel and coarsely chop the onion, adding it to the pot as you chop. Raise the heat to medium-high. Cook for 1 minute, stirring from time to time. Add the mushrooms and the sherry (if using). Cook, stirring occasionally, until the mushrooms release their liquid, about 3 minutes.

3. Add the broth, cream of mushroom soup, and 2 cups water. Add the rice and 1 tablespoon of the seasoning from the rice's seasoning packet. (Reserve the remaining seasoning for another use or discard it.) Stir well, cover the pot, and raise the heat to high. Bring the soup to a boil. Reduce the heat to low and stir well. Cover and cook at a simmer until the rice is tender, about 5 minutes. Season with black pepper and serve.

The secret ingredient in this soup is a fast-cooking rice blend containing wild rice. Normally wild rice takes about 50 minutes to cook, and it's much more expensive than white rice. The wild rice used here is pre-cooked, and it's blended with white rice—a good way to get the luxury of wild rice without the expense or the long cooking time. We tested this recipe with Uncle Ben's Long Grain & Wild Rice Fast Cook Recipe. There are several brands of wild rice blends on the market, and because they often go on sale, we use whatever is cheapest. Just be sure to choose one that cooks in 5 minutes, and check the package directions to see how much water is required for cooking the rice. If it's not 2 cups, adjust the water you add to this recipe to match whatever is called for on your package.

If you work all day, the way Lorene Cook Lambert does, you don't often have time to head to the farm to pick fresh corn, then cut and scrape the ears. Lorene, one of the readers of our Desperation Dinners column, doesn't have her Grandmother Ebbie's prolific tomato vines, either, but that didn't stop her from craving the corn and tomato soup she remembered from her childhood. Lorene decided to do a little experimenting, and she came up with a version that tastes remarkably similar to her grandmother's. Canned and frozen vegetables replace the fresh, and a few dashes of dried seasonings add dimension. She throws it all in a pot, then serves the soup over corn muffins made from a mix, just the way her grandmother served it over from-scratch cornbread.

"This soup is just as perfect for a summer evening as it is for a cold, snowy night," Lorene says. "When I curl up with a cup of Corn and Tomato Soup, I think of Grandmother Ebbie and her cast-iron stove, warming the kitchen and our hearts."

ALMOST EBBIE'S CORN AND TOMATO SOUP

SERVES: 4 START TO FINISH: UNDER 20 MINUTES

SUPER-CHEAP!

1 package (10 ounces) frozen
   cream-style corn (see Notes)
1 tablespoon butter or margarine
1 medium-size onion
   (for about ¾ cup chopped)
1 clove fresh garlic, minced,
   or 1 teaspoon bottled minced garlic
1 can (about 14 ounces) fat-free chicken broth,
   or 2 cups homemade chicken stock (see page 10)
1 can (14½ ounces) diced tomatoes seasoned with garlic
   and onion
2 cups frozen yellow or white corn kernels
Black pepper to taste
4 corn muffins, for serving (optional; see Notes)

1. Make a small slit to vent the plastic pouch containing the cream-style corn and microwave it for 3 minutes on high power.

2. Meanwhile, melt the butter in a 4½-quart Dutch oven or soup pot over medium heat. Peel and coarsely chop the onion, adding it to the pot as you chop. Cook the onion, stirring occasionally, until slightly softened, about 3 minutes. Add the garlic to the pot, stir, and cook for 30 seconds. Add the broth, tomatoes with their juice, frozen corn kernels, and the defrosted cream-style corn. Season with black pepper. (It's okay if the creamed corn is not completely defrosted.)

3. Raise the heat to high and bring the soup just to a boil, stirring from time to time. Then reduce the heat to medium and cook at a moderate boil, stirring frequently, for 5 minutes. If you are using corn muffins, cut them in half and place 2 halves in each soup bowl. Ladle the soup into the bowls and serve.

NOTES: We did not like the way this soup tasted when we tested it with cream-style corn from a can. (There was a distinct unpleasant aftertaste from the canned corn.) Frozen cream-style corn is available nationally, perhaps most widely under the Green Giant label.
■ This recipe is so quick that there's plenty of time to stir up a box of cornbread mix if you can't find prepared muffins in your local bakery for a good price. The muffins act as a giant crouton when the soup is ladled over them, but the soup is also wonderful without them.

SWEET ONION CHOWDER

SERVES: 4 GENEROUSLY   START TO FINISH: UNDER 25 MINUTES

4 slices bacon

2 tablespoons olive oil

2 pounds (about 4 medium) Vidalia or other sweet onions

3 cloves fresh garlic, minced, or 1 tablespoon bottled minced garlic

2 cans (about 14 ounces each) fat-free chicken broth, or 4 cups homemade chicken stock (see page 10)

2½ cups leftover mashed potatoes or reconstituted instant mashed potatoes, or 1 package (1 pound, 4 ounces) refrigerated mashed potatoes, such as Simply Potatoes

2 cups frozen yellow corn kernels

2 bay leaves

¼ teaspoon dried thyme

⅛ teaspoon black pepper, or more to taste

½ cup sour cream (see Note)

1. Place the bacon on a microwave-safe plate and microwave until crisp, 3 to 4 minutes. Blot with a paper towel to remove any excess grease. Set aside.

2. Meanwhile, heat the oil in a 4½-quart Dutch oven or soup pot over medium heat. Peel the onions and coarsely chop them, adding them to the pot as you chop. When all of the onions have

From Alicia:

I wait all year, gathering recipes, for the beginning of sweet onion season. This used to mean late spring, when the Vidalias appeared in the market. For about two months, sweet onions would show up in nearly everything I cooked: breads, pizzas, sauces, soups, salads, and sides.

Now I can stretch my sweet onion consumption through the summer with Texas 1015 Super Sweets (available June through August), Maui Sweets (available year-round but with limited mainland distribution), and Washington State's Walla Walla Sweets (June through August). Even Arizona, Colorado, and California are getting

(continued)

(continued)

in on the sweet onion production. Depending on where you live, you may be able to enjoy the mild, fresh taste of sweet onions all the way into September.

The attractive qualities of the spring and summer onions are also their biggest limitation. That sweet, mild taste is due in large part to the onions' high water content. But this also means they don't store particularly well, so it's always best to use sweet onions within a few days of purchase. (Or you can try stuffing them into the legs of old panty hose, tying a knot between each onion, and hanging them in a cool, dark place, as some onion growers recommend.)

This chowder can be made with any sweet onion you find available. It's a creamy concoction packed full of delicate onion flavor, accented with sweet corn kernels and thickened with mashed potatoes. (This is a good place to use up leftover mashed potatoes, but it works fine with instant mashed potatoes or even frozen or commercial refrigerated mashed potatoes.)

been added, raise the heat to medium-high and cook, stirring frequently, until they are tender, about 6 minutes.

3. Add the garlic to the soup pot. Cook, stirring, for 1 minute. Add the stock and stir well, scraping the bottom of the pot to remove any brown bits. Add the mashed potatoes, corn, bay leaves, thyme, and black pepper.

4. Cover the pot, raise the heat to high, and bring the soup to a boil. Meanwhile, coarsely crumble the bacon and set it aside. When the soup comes to a boil, remove the pot from the heat. Remove the bay leaves and stir in the sour cream until it is well combined. Serve at once, sprinkling the crumbled bacon on top.

NOTE: Reduced-fat sour cream can be used; just make sure the soup is not allowed to boil once it has been added.

VEG OUT! CHOWDER

SERVES: 4 START TO FINISH: UNDER 25 MINUTES

2 teaspoons olive oil

1 large onion (for about 1 cup chopped)

8 ounces fresh button mushrooms

2 cups Southern-style (cubed) frozen hash-brown potatoes or diced leftover cooked potatoes

2 cans (about 14 ounces each) fat-free chicken broth, or 4 cups homemade chicken stock (see page 10)

1 chicken bouillon cube

1 teaspoon Worcestershire sauce

½ teaspoon dried thyme

1 cup frozen green peas

1 cup frozen yellow or white corn kernels

2 tablespoons real (not imitation) bacon bits (optional)

Black pepper to taste

½ cup sour cream

SUPER-CHEAP!

1. Heat the oil in a 4½-quart Dutch oven or soup pot over medium heat. Peel and coarsely chop the onion, adding it to the pot as you chop. Rinse, pat dry, and slice the mushrooms, removing any tough stems, and add them to the pot. Cook, stirring, for 1 minute.

2. Add the hash browns and raise the heat to high. Cook, stirring frequently, until the hash browns are defrosted, about 3 minutes. (If you are using leftover cooked potatoes, skip this step and add them along with the broth in Step 3.)

3. Add the broth, bouillon cube, Worcestershire sauce, and thyme. Bring the soup to a boil over high heat. Add the peas, corn, and bacon bits (if using) and cover the pot. When the soup boils, reduce the heat to medium-low and cook at a moderate boil, uncovered, to develop the flavors, about 4 minutes. Season with black pepper.

4. Just before serving, remove the pot from the heat and stir in the sour cream. (Reduced-fat sour cream can be used; just make sure the soup doesn't boil once it has been added.)

This recipe doesn't contain any meat to speak of, but your family may never notice, thanks to the filling array of vegetables. The bacon is optional, but it supplies a lot of flavor. (Don't forget to turn any leftover bacon strips into bacon bits and store them in your freezer. See page 167 for tips.) This soup is also a good way to use the odds and ends of vegetables in your freezer. Suddenly leftovers are a cause for celebration!

Instead of the peas and corn, you can use 2 cups of frozen mixed vegetables or any other frozen vegetables you may have on hand. (We do not suggest broccoli or brussels sprouts, however, as the flavor is too strong for the soup.)

Making Your Own Vegetable Stock

D on't you just love getting something for free? If you make your own vegetable stock, that's what you'll get: a lovely broth to add to soups and stews that doesn't cost anything at all. It's not even much trouble to make.

Here's how:

Whenever you're peeling vegetables, collect the trimmings in a 1-gallon-size, zipper-top plastic bag. Anything goes, really, but examples include tough asparagus stalks, mushroom stems, stems from herbs, leafy celery tops, potato and carrot peels, the tops of bell peppers (but not the seeds), tomato cores, tough green parts of scallions, and any parts of an onion that you'd generally discard when peeling (bits of skin are okay, too). Store the bag in the refrigerator.

Just keep adding your trimmings to the bag on a daily basis. The only thing you need to do is to make sure the trimmings are washed and then relatively dry before putting them into the bag. (A lettuce spinner is good for the drying step.) You can keep adding trimmings to the bag for up to about 4 days, but check the bag periodically to make sure the contents are still fresh.

To make the stock, you'll need approximately three-fourths of a gallon bag of trimmings. If you reach the 4-day limit and your bag isn't quite full enough, look in your vegetable bin. You'll be surprised what's lurking there. One limp carrot? Throw it in. But pass on the broccoli, cabbage, cauliflower, and brussels sprouts, which don't make good stock.

Making the stock is especially easy if you use a 5-quart slow cooker. Just place the vegetable trimmings in the pot of the slow cooker and cover them with water. The exact amount of water doesn't matter. Some of the vegetables will float, so just press them down to make sure there's enough water to cover. Cover the crock and cook for 4 to 6 hours on high, or 8 to 12 hours on low.

"Use vegetable stock for making rice pilafs and for cooking dried beans."

If you don't have a slow cooker, place the trimmings in a 4½-quart Dutch oven or soup pot and cover them with water as described. Bring the water to a boil, reduce the heat to low, and simmer, covered, for 4 to 5 hours. Check the stock periodically, and add more water if necessary.

When the stock has cooked, ladle it through a strainer and discard the solids; or if you prefer, let the stock cool overnight in the refrigerator, then strain it. The stock can be used in place of canned vegetable broth in all of our recipes.

One of the fun things about this type of vegetable stock is that it never turns out exactly the same, because you'll have a different assortment of trimmings each time. This won't matter for most soups and stews. We also like to use vegetable stock instead of water for making rice pilafs and for cooking dried beans and lentils. It's the broth of choice for our Very Veggie Lentil Chili (page 58).

As with our chicken stock, we package most of our vegetable stock in 2-cup amounts. We also usually freeze some in 1-cup portions, since that's another common recipe amount. You can put it in containers holding the amount you think you're most likely to use. For storage, use Tupperware or any airtight hard plastic containers you have. (Recent studies have cast doubt on whether it's safe to store leftovers in reused "soft" plastic containers such as margarine tubs and sour cream containers.)

The stock will keep, covered and refrigerated, for up to 3 days; covered and frozen, for up to 2 months. Thaw the stock overnight in the refrigerator, or defrost it in the microwave.

We always loved making Spanish gazpacho in the summertime, when garden tomatoes are at their peak, but the soup never tasted the same when made with less-than-perfect tomatoes. While sitting around in Alicia's kitchen one day, we decided to see what would happen if we put a Tex-Mex spin on the soup, using canned chili-style tomatoes and adding black beans for heft. The result was a wonderful, economical, meatless soup that got raves all around.

Several national brands make diced tomatoes seasoned with cumin, chili powder, and other chili-friendly spices. If you can't find any, just substitute plain diced tomatoes and add roughly ½ teaspoon each of ground cumin and chili powder. Then taste the soup and add more of the seasoning, in ¼-teaspoon increments, if you like it spicy.

CHUNKY SOUTHWESTERN GAZPACHO

SERVES: 4 GENEROUSLY PREP TIME: UNDER 20 MINUTES

SUPER-CHEAP!

1 medium-size cucumber
   (for about ¾ cup pieces)
1 large green bell pepper
   (for about 1½ cups chopped)
1 small onion
   (for about ½ cup chopped)
1 can (14½ ounces) chili-style diced tomatoes
   or diced tomatoes seasoned with jalapeños
1 quart low-sodium tomato-vegetable juice, such as V8
1 can (15 ounces) black beans, or 1 cup homemade
   (see page 368), defrosted if frozen
1 clove fresh garlic, minced, or 1 teaspoon bottled
   minced garlic
2 tablespoons red wine vinegar
1 teaspoon Worcestershire sauce
¼ teaspoon hot pepper sauce, or more to taste

1. Peel the cucumber and cut it in half lengthwise. Scoop the seeds out with a small spoon and discard the seeds. Cut the cucumber into bite-size pieces and put them in a 3-quart or larger bowl.

2. Stem, seed, and cut the bell pepper into bite-size pieces. Add the pieces to the bowl. Peel and finely chop the onion and add it to the bowl.

3. Add the tomatoes and their juice, and the tomato-vegetable juice. Rinse and drain the black beans and add them to the bowl. Add the garlic to the bowl. Stir in the vinegar, Worcestershire sauce, and hot pepper sauce. Refrigerate for 2 hours or until chilled through, then serve.

By Any Name, This Beef Is Still Cheap

From Beverly:

I think of my mother as the queen of many things—good manners, gracious entertaining, and fluffy homemade yeast rolls among them. But perhaps her crowning title should be "Queen of the Sirloin Tip."

A sirloin tip is a large cut of lean beef roast, ranging from 7 to 10 pounds, that goes on sale pretty frequently at per-pound prices that beat ground beef. When I was growing up, Mom would regularly scan the grocery ads looking for the best possible price on a sirloin tip roast. Every few months, when she found a price she liked, Mom would return from the store with pounds upon pounds of beef that she'd freeze for the coming weeks' meals.

When I became a mother myself and moved around to various parts of the country, following in Mom's sirloin-tip footsteps became a challenge. I couldn't always easily identify this versatile, cheap cut of beef. Let's face it—one giant hunk of beef looks pretty much like the next when it's sitting raw and packaged in the supermarket. As it turns out, the name of this cut varies by region and even by store. Its official name is "beef round tip roast." Other names include ball tip roast, cap off roast, and peeled knuckle.

Regardless of what you call it, this cut of meat is lean, with only 5 grams of fat per 3-ounce serving. The low-fat status means that it's most tender when cooked slowly in moisture. It also makes great lean ground beef, and if you ask, the store butcher will grind the roast into hamburger while you wait (usually at no charge). I also like to cut the roast into cubes for use in soups and stews, and while this takes a bit of time and a sharp knife, it's not difficult. I package the cubes in 1-pound portions in freezer-weight zipper-top bags and store them in the freezer for up to 3 months.

With a treasure trove of really cheap beef at the ready, anyone can feel like the Queen of the Sirloin Tip.

From Beverly:

Every year as school starts up, my checkbook balance starts down. First come the notebooks, lunch boxes, and fashionable shelves my teenagers need for their lockers. Next come payments for after-school lessons and sports. Thank goodness beans are cheap.

While the lowly legume can help trim the grocery bill, this homey staple doesn't have to leave the family feeling deprived. In fact, we believe that the low-fat benefits of bean consumption should elevate them to star status—as long as you start with an intriguing recipe. Enter this satisfying and delicious bean soup. All you need to finish this meal off is sliced in-season fruit or canned pineapple.

SOUTH-OF-THE-BORDER BEAN AND TORTILLA SOUP

SERVES: 4 START TO FINISH: UNDER 25 MINUTES

SUPER-CHEAP!

2 teaspoons vegetable oil

1 medium-size onion
(for about ¾ cup chopped)

1 can (15 ounces) red beans or
white beans, or 1 cup homemade
(see page 368), defrosted if frozen

1 can (15 ounces) black beans, or 1 cup homemade
(see page 368), defrosted if frozen

1 can (14½ ounces) diced tomatoes seasoned with
garlic and onion

1 clove fresh garlic, minced, or 1 teaspoon bottled
minced garlic

¾ cup frozen yellow corn kernels

1 teaspoon chili powder

½ teaspoon ground cumin

1 can (about 14 ounces) vegetable broth, or 2 cups
homemade vegetable stock (see page 38; see Note)

½ teaspoon sugar

Juice of ½ lime

4 ounces baked or regular tortilla chips (for 2½ cups
crushed), or to taste

⅓ cup shredded Mexican-blend cheese (optional)

1. Heat the oil in a 4½-quart soup pot over medium heat. Peel and coarsely chop the onion, adding it to the pot as you chop. Raise the heat to medium-high and cook, stirring from time to time.

2. While the onion cooks, rinse and drain the red beans and add them to the skillet. Add the black beans with their juice and the tomatoes with their juice. Add the garlic, corn, chili powder, and cumin to the pot. Stir to blend well. Add the broth, sugar, and lime juice. Bring the mixture to a boil over medium-high heat. Reduce the heat to low and simmer, 7 to 10 minutes to blend the flavors, then serve.

3. When you are ready to serve, crush the chips slightly and divide them among four soup bowls. To serve, ladle the soup over the chips and sprinkle with the cheese, if desired.

NOTE: Fat-free chicken broth or homemade chicken stock can be substituted for the vegetable broth.

BUDGET BEEF STEW

SERVES: 6 PREP TIME: UNDER 20 MINUTES

1½ pounds small beef cubes for stew, defrosted if frozen
¼ teaspoon salt
¼ teaspoon black pepper
1 teaspoon dried basil
1 tablespoon Worcestershire sauce
1 clove fresh garlic, minced, or 1 teaspoon bottled
    minced garlic
2 large onions
4 medium-size carrots
5 medium-size (about 1½ pounds) red or white potatoes
1 can (14½ ounces) diced tomatoes
3 tablespoons cornstarch
¼ cup cold water

1. Place a rack in the middle of the oven and preheat the oven to 300°F.

2. If any of the beef cubes are larger than about 1 inch, cut them into smaller pieces. Place the beef in a 4½-quart Dutch oven or flameproof casserole that has a tight-fitting lid. Sprinkle the salt, black pepper, basil, and Worcestershire sauce evenly over the beef. Sprinkle the garlic over the beef.

There's a trick to stretching a modest amount of beef into a hearty stew. For starters, if the beef cubes are small —about an inch or so—an optical illusion of sorts will make it seem that there's beef for every bite. Next, use a lot of onions, carrots, and potatoes. (And if there's a stray stalk of celery in the bin, throw that in, too!) Finally, the real secret is a wonderfully rich and savory gravy. We accomplish that feat with a few herbs and some canned tomatoes, and by thickening the gravy with cornstarch at the end. You'll want to eat this stew with a spoon so you won't miss a drop!

3. Peel and quarter the onions and scatter the pieces evenly over the mixture. (If the onion quarters are larger than bite-size, cut them into eighths.) Peel the carrots and cut them into 1-inch pieces. Add them to the pot. Peel and quarter the potatoes and scatter the pieces evenly over the mixture. (If you are using thin-skinned red potatoes, leave the skin on if you prefer.) Add the tomatoes with their juice, scattering the tomatoes evenly over the mixture. Add ½ cup water.

4. Bake the stew, covered, for 2 hours. Remove the pot from the oven and stir the stew gently so as not to break up the vegetables. Continue to bake, covered, until the vegetables and meat are very tender, about 1 hour.

5. Remove the pot from the oven and place it on the stovetop over low heat. Mix the cornstarch with the cold water in a jar that has a lid. Cover the jar and shake it well to remove any lumps. Pour the mixture, a little at a time, evenly over the stew. Stir gently, adding the cornstarch mixture as necessary until the liquid reaches the desired thickness, about 3 to 5 minutes. Ladle the stew into large shallow bowls to serve.

BEEF STEW À LA GUATEMALA

SERVES: 4 GENEROUSLY **START TO FINISH:** UNDER 25 MINUTES

Salt for cooking the rice
1⅓ cups long-grain rice
2 teaspoons vegetable oil
1 large onion (for about 1 cup chopped)
1 large green bell pepper (for about 1½ cups chopped)
1 clove fresh garlic, minced, or 1 teaspoon bottled
    minced garlic
1 can (14½ ounces) Mexican-style stewed tomatoes
¼ cup salsa verde, or more to taste (see Note)
1 cup frozen mixed vegetables
2 bay leaves
½ teaspoon dried oregano
⅛ teaspoon ground cloves
2 cups shredded cooked beef (see page 348),
    defrosted if frozen

1. Bring 2⅔ cups lightly salted water to a boil in a covered medium-size saucepan. Add the rice, stir, and reduce the heat to low. Cover the pan and simmer until the rice is tender, about 20 minutes.

2. Meanwhile, heat the oil in an extra-deep 12-inch skillet over medium-high heat. Peel and coarsely chop the onion, adding it to the skillet as you chop. Stem, seed, and coarsely chop the bell pepper, adding it to the skillet as you chop. Add the garlic to the skillet. Continue to cook, stirring, until the onion is tender, about 3 minutes.

3. Add the tomatoes with their juice, the salsa verde, frozen vegetables, bay leaves, oregano, cloves, and beef. Stir well and let the mixture boil until it is thick, about 6 minutes. Remove the bay leaves and serve the stew over a bed of hot rice.

From Alicia:

A few years ago, when my youngest daughter, Rachel, did a report on Guatemala for Spanish class, we were inundated with Guatemalan facts, maps, and—you guessed it—recipes. The Internet, surprisingly, was bursting with traditional Guatemalan recipes printed in English and with American measurements.

Rachel chose a Guatemalan-style banana bread for her final project, but I couldn't stop thinking about the beef stew recipes we had found. Time and again I contemplated the interesting blend of spices and flavors. Finally I launched into a trial recipe using Guatemalan spice blends and ingredients. This recipe is the result of those experiments.

Venturing into the world of exotic recipes can be fun and challenging. While this recipe isn't completely authentic, you can definitely taste the Guatemalan influence. Use leftover beef from the Big Beef Roast, and this is one journey into the exotic your budget can afford.

NOTE: Salsa verde is found in the supermarket alongside the other Mexican foods. It may also be called green taco sauce or tomatillo salsa. Any green sauce that contains tomatillos can be used. Be aware that, while this condiment gives the dish a distinctive flavor, it is fiery hot, and you may want to add it by the tablespoon to taste.

SPEEDY MEATBALL STEW

SERVES: 6 GENEROUSLY START TO FINISH: UNDER 30 MINUTES

Salt for cooking the rice
1 cup long-grain rice
16 ounces frozen mixed vegetables
24 already-cooked meatballs, fresh or frozen (see Notes)
2 teaspoons olive oil
1 large onion (for about 1 cup chopped)
1 clove fresh garlic, minced, or 1 teaspoon bottled minced garlic
8 ounces fresh button mushrooms
1 can (about 14 ounces) fat-free beef broth
¼ cup Madeira or Marsala wine (optional)
1 envelope (about 1 ounce) brown gravy mix (see Notes)

1. Bring 2 cups lightly salted water to a boil in a covered medium-size saucepan. Add the rice, stir, and reduce the heat to low. Cover the pan and simmer until the rice is tender, about 20 minutes.

2. Meanwhile, put the frozen vegetables in a colander and, if there are any ice crystals, run warm tap water over them. Set aside.

3. If the meatballs are frozen, place them on a microwave-safe plate and microwave, uncovered, on high power for 2 to 3 minutes to partially defrost.

This quick-and-easy stew makes good use of our homemade Marvelous Meatballs, but sometimes we do buy a bag of frozen meatballs when they're on sale. The packaged gravy mix adds richness and depth of flavor, as does the Madeira. (You don't have to buy a bottle of the wine just to make the stew, but if you have some, by all means add it.) You can also use the last bits of assorted frozen vegetables or leftover cooked vegetables, so long as you have a total of about 3⅓ cups. If you're feeding a gang of teenage boys or especially hearty eaters, you might want to use a few extra meatballs.

Homemade beef stock is indeed a treasure to have on hand. But these days we find that the gelatin-rich beef bones and quantities of aromatic vegetables

4. Heat the oil in a 4½-quart Dutch oven or soup pot over medium heat. Peel and coarsely chop the onion, adding it to the pot as you chop. Add the garlic to the pot. Rinse, pat dry, and slice the mushrooms and remove any tough stems. Add the mushrooms to the pot. Cook, stirring from time to time, until the mushrooms begin to release their liquid, 2 to 3 minutes.

5. Pour ½ cup water into the pot and raise the heat to high. Add the broth, Madeira (if using), meatballs, and vegetables. Cover the pot and bring the mixture to a boil. Reduce the heat to medium-high and cook, partially covered, at a moderate boil until the mixture is heated through, about 8 minutes.

6. Meanwhile, make the brown gravy mix in the microwave, following the package directions. When the stew is heated through, stir in the gravy. Cook, stirring, until the stew thickens slightly, about 1 minute. Reduce the heat to low and simmer the stew until the rice is done or you're ready to serve, 5 to 10 minutes. To serve, place ½ cup of the steamed rice in each bowl and spoon the stew on top.

NOTES: You can use Marvelous Meatballs (page 353) or purchased frozen meatballs (plain or traditional style).

■ The exact weight of brown gravy mixes varies slightly from brand to brand, but that won't affect the dish. Just be sure to choose a brand that makes at least 1 cup finished gravy. (Some mixes make up to 1½ cups gravy, which is fine, too.)

necessary for making a deep, rich stock are cost-prohibitive. A simple soup bone can cost over $2. Multiply that times several bones, add in all of the veggies, and before you know it you've spent almost $15. And you haven't even walked into the kitchen to start work.

Canned beef broth is simply the best deal. We prefer fat-free beef broth and buy it whenever it is on sale. But if you find a good deal on regular (not fat-free) beef broth, simply skim as much of the fat as possible from the surface of the broth before adding it to your recipe. (Some national brands also now offer reduced-sodium beef broth.)

From Alicia:

This is my family's favorite midweek chili. When I asked my good friend Myra Fisher to try it out, she said she would be glad to but that her kids probably wouldn't like it. Boy, was she ever wrong. They loved it! This is indeed a kid-pleasing, simple chili that you can doctor up if you like. If you are a green pepper fan, start by sautéing half a green bell pepper, finely chopped, in the 2 teaspoons of oil before adding the onion. When the pepper is tender, finish the recipe and enjoy. For those who like it hot, add hot pepper sauce to taste just before serving.

Mild and meaty, this chili is bound to become a favorite at your house, too.

CHOW-DOWN CHILI

SERVES: 4 GENEROUSLY START TO FINISH: UNDER 25 MINUTES

   1 pound ground beef, fresh or frozen (see Note)
   2 teaspoons vegetable oil
   1 large onion (for about 1 cup chopped)
   2 cloves fresh garlic, minced, or 2 teaspoons bottled minced garlic
   2 cans (15 ounces each) light red kidney beans, or 2 cups homemade (see page 368), defrosted if frozen
   1 can (14½ ounces) chopped tomatoes flavored with chili-style seasonings or chopped tomatoes seasoned with jalapeños
   1 can (6 ounces) tomato paste
   1 tablespoon chili powder
   Shredded Cheddar cheese, for serving (optional)
   Sour cream, for serving (optional)

1. If the beef is frozen, run it under hot water so you can remove the packaging. Place the beef on a microwave-safe plate and microwave, uncovered, on high power for 3 minutes to partially defrost.

2. Heat the oil in an extra-deep 12-inch skillet or in a 4½-quart Dutch oven or soup pot over medium heat. Peel and coarsely chop the onion, adding it to the skillet as you chop. Add the garlic and meat (fresh or partially defrosted) to the skillet. Cook, turning and breaking up the meat, until it begins to crumble and brown, 7 to 8 minutes. Drain off any accumulated fat, if necessary.

3. Rinse and drain the beans and add them to the beef. Add the tomatoes with their juice. Add the tomato paste and 6 ounces water (just fill the tomato paste can with tap water). Sprinkle in the chili powder and stir to mix well. Bring the mixture to a boil. Simmer for at least 5 minutes to blend the flavors, stirring occasionally to prevent sticking. Ladle the chili into soup bowls and serve with your toppings of choice.

NOTE: You can use 3 cups Basic Beef (page 317), defrosted if frozen. Omit the oil, onion, and garlic, and begin the recipe at Step 3.

SIMPLE CHICKEN STEW

SERVES: 4 START TO FINISH: UNDER 25 MINUTES

⅔ pound boneless, skinless chicken
    breast halves, fresh or frozen
    (see Note)

2 teaspoons vegetable oil

1 medium-size onion
    (for about ¾ cup chopped)

1 medium-size carrot (for about ½ cup sliced)

1 rib celery (for about ½ cup chopped)

2 cans (about 14 ounces each) fat-free chicken broth,
    or 4 cups homemade chicken stock (see page 10)

4 large (10- to 12-inch) flour tortillas (not fat-free)

SUPER-CHEAP!

1. If the chicken is frozen, run it under hot water so you can remove the packaging. Place the chicken on a microwave-safe plate and microwave, uncovered, on high power for 2 minutes to partially defrost.

2. While the chicken defrosts, heat the oil in a 4½-quart Dutch oven or soup pot over medium heat. Peel the onion and finely chop it, adding it to the pot as you chop. Cut the partially defrosted or fresh chicken into bite-size chunks, adding them to the pot as you cut. When all of the chicken has been added, raise the heat to medium-high and cook, stirring, until the chicken is almost cooked through, about 3 minutes.

3. Peel the carrot and cut it into ¼-inch-thick slices, adding them to the pot as you slice. Finely chop the celery and add it to the pot. Cook, stirring, until the vegetables are tender, about 3 minutes.

4. Add the broth and 4 cups water and raise the heat to high.

5. While the liquid is heating, slice the flour tortillas into thin (about ½-inch-wide) strips. When the liquid is at a boil, add the strips and cook until plumped up, 4 to 5 minutes. (If the liquid begins to boil over, reduce the heat to medium to maintain a slow

True simplicity may just be an illusion in the hustle and bustle of today's world. However, sitting down with your family to enjoy a stress-free, home-cooked, flavorful meal doesn't have to be an illusion, and this stew makes it happen. It's unbelievably quick and satisfying, full of flavors from times gone by, and made with economical ingredients that are easy to keep on hand. But best of all, it's flexible. You can use fresh chicken, leftover chicken or turkey, grilled or rotisserie chicken, or even canned chicken—all with delicious results.

Tortillas fill in for the traditional dumplings here. Some brands of plain flour tortillas are slightly sweet. For this stew, as long as the tortillas are not flavored in any other way and are not fat-free, they will work fine. Kids, especially, enjoy the bit of sweetness.

boil.) When the tortillas are plump, remove the pot from the heat and let the stew stand for about 5 minutes to cool slightly. To serve, divide the stew among four soup bowls.

NOTE: You can use 1 cup Perfect Poached Chicken (page 362) or Poached Chicken Thighs (page 364), defrosted if frozen; add in Step 4 after the broth and water. Or use 1 cup Chunky Seasoned Chicken (page 358), defrosted if frozen. Omit the onion. Add the Chunky Seasoned Chicken in Step 4 after the broth and water. Cooked turkey can also be used.

In many parts of the world, peanuts are called groundnuts, because the nut pods grow underground. Groundnut stew is humble food and typical of West African cuisine. Our Thai-Style Peanut Sauce provides the backbone of flavor for this exotic, slightly sweet stew. It would also be lovely with the nutty taste of brown rice.

CURRIED GROUNDNUT STEW

SERVES: 4 START TO FINISH: UNDER 25 MINUTES

Salt for cooking the rice

1⅓ cups long-grain rice

1 pound skinless, boneless chicken breast halves, fresh or frozen (see Note)

2 teaspoons vegetable oil

1 large onion (for about 1 cup chopped)

3 medium-size carrots (for about 1½ cups sliced)

1 clove fresh garlic, minced, or 1 teaspoon bottled minced garlic

1 cup fat-free canned chicken broth or homemade chicken stock (see page 10)

1 can (6 ounces) tomato paste

1 cup Thai-Style Peanut Sauce (page 374), defrosted if frozen

2 teaspoons curry powder

1 cup frozen green peas

¼ cup chopped unsalted or lightly salted roasted peanuts, for serving (optional)

1. Bring 2⅔ cups lightly salted water to a boil in a covered medium-size saucepan. Add the rice, stir, and reduce the heat to low. Cover the pan and simmer until the rice is tender, about 20 minutes.

2. Meanwhile, if the chicken is frozen, run it under hot water so you can remove the packaging. Place the chicken on a microwave-safe plate and microwave, uncovered, on high power for 2 minutes to partially defrost.

3. While the chicken defrosts, heat the oil in a 12-inch skillet over medium heat. Peel and coarsely chop the onion, adding it to the skillet as you chop. Cook, stirring occasionally. Meanwhile, peel the carrots and cut them into slices about ¼ inch thick, adding them to the skillet as you slice. Continue to stir frequently while you cut the partially defrosted or fresh chicken into bite-size pieces, adding them to the skillet as you cut. Add the garlic to the skillet. Cook, stirring frequently, until the chicken is no longer pink in the center, 5 to 6 minutes.

4. When the chicken is done, add the broth and tomato paste. Stir until the tomato paste is well blended with the broth. Add the peanut sauce and curry powder and stir to blend well. Stir in the frozen peas and cook just until they are heated through, about 2 minutes. Remove the stew from the heat, cover, and set aside until the rice is done.

5. To serve, divide the rice among four bowls and top with chicken, vegetables, and sauce. Garnish each serving with 1 tablespoon chopped peanuts, if desired.

NOTE: You can use 2 cups Perfect Poached Chicken (page 362) or Poached Chicken Thighs (page 364), defrosted if frozen; add it with the garlic in Step 3. Or use 2 cups Chunky Seasoned Chicken (page 358), defrosted if frozen. Omit the onion and garlic, and begin the recipe by cooking the carrots. Add the Chunky Seasoned Chicken with the broth and tomato paste and cook until heated through.

Those Cajuns really know how to cook, and their stews are typically meaty and satisfying. We've limited the overall quantity of meat a bit to make our stew a little less expensive, but with two kinds of meat, plus rice, this stew is more than sufficient for even the very hungry. And the kielbasa and the Cajun seasoning blend make it pop with flavor.

BAYOU STEW

SERVES: 4 START TO FINISH: UNDER 25 MINUTES

Salt for cooking the rice
1 cup long-grain rice
⅔ pound skinless, boneless chicken breast halves, fresh or frozen (see Notes)
2 tablespoons butter
2 large onions (for about 2 cups chopped)
8 ounces kielbasa sausage (see Notes)
1 medium-size green bell pepper (for about 1 cup chopped)
2 cans (about 14 ounces each) fat-free beef broth
2 teaspoons Cajun seasoning blend, or to taste
2 tablespoons all-purpose flour

1. Bring 2 cups lightly salted water to a boil in a covered 2-quart saucepan. Add the rice, stir, and reduce the heat to low. Cover the pan and simmer until the rice is tender, about 20 minutes.

2. Meanwhile, if the chicken is frozen, run it under hot water so you can remove the packaging. Place the chicken on a microwave-safe plate and microwave, uncovered, on high power for 2 minutes to partially defrost.

3. While the chicken defrosts, melt the butter in a 4½-quart Dutch oven or soup pot over medium heat. Peel the onions and finely chop them, adding them to the pot as you chop. Cut the partially defrosted or fresh chicken into bite-size chunks, adding them to the pot as you cut. When all of the chicken has been added, raise the heat to medium-high. Cook, stirring, until the chicken is almost cooked through, about 4 minutes. Meanwhile, cut the sausage link in half lengthwise. Slice both halves into roughly ¼-inch pieces.

4. Add the sausage to the pot and continue to cook, stirring from time to time, while you stem, seed, and cut the bell pepper into bite-size pieces.

5. Add the broth to the pot, raise the heat to high, and add the bell pepper. Cover the pot and bring the soup to a boil.

6. Add the Cajun seasoning. Re-cover the pot, reduce the heat to medium, and cook at a moderate boil until the green pepper is tender, about 3 minutes. (Uncover the pot partially if the soup begins to boil over.)

7. In a small jar that has a lid, mix the flour with 3 tablespoons cold tap water. Cover the jar and shake it until the mixture is well combined and the lumps have disappeared. Gradually add the flour mixture to the soup, stirring constantly, until the soup has thickened slightly. Remove the pot from the heat. Divide the hot cooked rice among four large soup bowls. Ladle the soup over the rice and serve at once.

NOTES: You can use 1 cup Perfect Poached Chicken (page 362), or Poached Chicken Thighs (page 364), defrosted if frozen. Or use Chunky Seasoned Chicken (page 358), defrosted if frozen, and omit the onion. Add the cooked chicken in Step 6 before the Cajun seasoning.

■ Reduced-fat kielbasa sausage (a blend containing turkey) can be used. You can also substitute smoked sausage or Cajun andouille sausage.

The When, Where, and How of Shopping

From Alicia:

G rocery shopping can make me crazy. Knowing this, I've tried to devise the best possible scenario for an optimal grocery-gathering experience. Here's a list of what I try never to do. If I avoid these pitfalls, I'm fine. Your "never-ever" list may be completely different from mine, but it's a good thing to know what your limits are before you head out.

While exact days, times, and execution may vary slightly from week to week, there are some hard and fast "nevers" that, for me, make it all so much more pleasurable.

When to Shop:

- *Never when I'm tired.* There's nothing like trudging through the store when you can barely put one foot in front of the other.

- *Never when I'm hungry.* We've said it before, but it's worth saying again. I know that if I shop when I'm hungry, I will always buy something that's not on the list, simply because it looks good.

- *Never during rush hour.* Tons of folks make a run through the grocery store on their way home from work. This means crowded aisles, too many carts turning corners, and long lines at the checkout.

  If your job makes shopping off-hours impossible, have a snack before you go, and take your time. If you're not in a rush and you're not starving, you're less likely to let temptation get the best of you.

Where to Shop:

- *Never at a store all the way across town.* I have a hard time being excited about savings if I have to endure hideous traffic getting there. Forget real numbers—this is about my perception.

"All the time I spent clipping is out the window if I forget the coupons."

- *Never at more than two stores on the same day.* If the deals at my area grocery stores are so good that I must make two trips each week, I go on different days. This keeps the shopping trips manageable, at least in my mind.

- *Never at a store that is not clean*—no matter what kind of deal they have. I want my grocery stores clean, bright, and with wide aisles. Not to mention that if the store is not clean, you have to wonder about the quality of sanitation in the meat and produce departments.

How to Shop:

- *Never without a list.* I used to be able to remember what that fifteenth item on the list was, but not anymore. The time I invest in making the list is worth it. I buy exactly what I need—no more, no less.

- *Never without my coupons.* All the time I spent clipping is out the window if I forget the coupons. Besides, I've made part of that list based on what's on sale and what I have a coupon for, right? (See Our Best Coupon Advice, page 466.)

- *Never without my cooler in the back of the car,* if I'm not heading straight home. The expiration dates on dairy items, especially, do not take into account a 30-minute trip in a hot car to pick the kids up at school or to drop someone off at tennis practice. Since we count on the shelf life for extended value, we don't want to do anything to compromise it.

- *Never without a plan.* Short of taking a certain comedienne's advice to grab someone else's cart when they're halfway through shopping, I have to have a plan to get me through the store in a timely manner. I always write my shopping lists in the order the store is laid out, so I'm not going back to produce four times because the onions, potatoes, bananas, and apples are written in four different places on my list.

"Have a snack before you go."

From Beverly:

I count myself lucky to know many gardeners who are willing to share their summer bounty. Until the peak hits. When bounty turns to glut, my gardening buddies get a desperate look in their eyes.

"My squash are doubling in size overnight—you must take a few more," my next-door neighbor orders.

My brother's prolific string beans are driving him bananas. The bulging bags he was passing out at the family reunion guaranteed beans daily for at least a week, for all of us.

My mother summed up the situation as she stood stirring four pots at once: "When you have it, you've got to cook it."

Hey, it's free food, right?

This quick, low-fat recipe was born out of just such a situation. It's designed to use up a lot of vegetables without bogging you down in front of the stove. Feel free to add any extra beans, corn, or peas you might be forced to have on hand. The stew is also delicious when garnished with a sprinkling of Parmesan cheese or over a bed of rice.

SUMMER STEW

SERVES: 4 GENEROUSLY START TO FINISH: UNDER 25 MINUTES

1 can (about 14 ounces) vegetable broth or fat-free chicken broth, or 2 cups homemade vegetable stock or homemade chicken stock (see pages 38 and 10)

1¾ cups couscous

1 tablespoon olive oil

1 large sweet onion (for about 1½ cups chopped)

1 pound (2 medium-size) zucchini

2 cloves fresh garlic, minced, or 2 teaspoons bottled minced garlic

1 pound (2 medium) yellow squash

1 pound (2 medium or 1 large) tomatoes

1 cup packed fresh basil leaves (optional)

¼ teaspoon salt, or to taste

⅛ teaspoon black pepper, or to taste

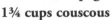
SUPER-CHEAP!

1. Pour 1 cup of the broth and 1¼ cups water into a 2-quart or larger saucepan and bring to a boil. Stir in the couscous, cover the pot, and remove it from the heat. Let it stand until the liquid is absorbed, about 5 minutes.

2. Meanwhile, heat the oil in an extra-deep 12-inch skillet over medium heat. Peel and coarsely chop the onion, adding it to the skillet as you chop. Stir the onions occasionally, while you rinse the zucchini, trim off the ends, and cut them into slices about ¼ inch thick. Add the zucchini, the remaining stock, and the garlic to the skillet.

3. Stirring the vegetables from time to time, rinse the yellow squash, trim off the ends, and cut them into slices about ¼ inch thick, adding them to the pan as you slice.

4. Core the tomatoes and cut them into bite-size pieces, adding them to the pan as you cut. Cover the skillet. Rinse the basil (if using) and coarsely chop the leaves. Add them to the skillet. Add the salt and black pepper.

5. Cover the skillet and cook, uncovering to stir from time to time, until the squash is tender but not mushy, about 5 minutes. Serve the stew at once, over a bed of hot couscous, in bowls or soup plates.

MIXED BEAN MEATLESS CASSOULET

SERVES: 4 GENEROUSLY START TO FINISH: UNDER 25 MINUTES

2 teaspoons vegetable oil
2 medium-size carrots (for about 1 cup sliced)
2 ribs celery (for about 1 cup chopped)
1 large onion (for about 1 cup chopped)
3 cans (15 ounces each) red, white, or black beans, or
    3 cups mixed homemade (see page 368), defrosted if frozen
1 can (14½ ounces) diced tomatoes seasoned with garlic
    and onion
1 clove fresh garlic, minced, or 1 teaspoon bottled
    minced garlic
1½ teaspoons dried herbes de Provence (see Note)
1 tablespoon extra-virgin olive oil
1 cup plain or lightly buttered croutons (see page 281)

1. Heat the oil in a 4½-quart Dutch oven or soup pot over medium heat. Meanwhile, cut the carrots into ¼-inch-thick slices, adding them to the pot as you slice. Chop the celery into bite-size pieces, adding them to the pot as you chop. Peel and coarsely chop the onion, adding it to the pot as you chop. Raise the heat to medium-high and cook until the vegetables are tender, about 3 minutes.

2. Drain and rinse the beans and add them to the pot. Add the tomatoes and their juice. Stir in the garlic and herbs. Continue to

A meatless cassoulet? Isn't meat what a cassoulet is all about? It's true: A traditional cassoulet combines white beans and various meats. Depending on the region as well as the cook, an old-fashioned cassoulet might contain sausages, duck, goose, or pork, or a combination of all four. But this recipe for a mixed bean cassoulet is just as filling as the traditional French dish—and ten times easier, to boot.

If you have already-cooked beans in your refrigerator or freezer, by all means throw them in in place of the canned beans. We round out this simple and satisfying bean stew with a crisp green salad and French rolls.

cook, stirring occasionally, until steaming hot and slightly thick, about 3 minutes. Remove the pot from the heat and drizzle the olive oil over the beans. Stir to mix well.

3. To serve, ladle the cassoulet into four soup bowls and top each serving with ¼ cup croutons.

NOTE: If you can't find herbes de Provence seasoning blend, use ½ teaspoon dried rosemary, ½ teaspoon dried oregano, ¼ teaspoon dried sage, and ¼ teaspoon dried marjoram.

Even dedicated carnivores will be satisfied with such a thick, rich chili. The texture is similar to "regular" chili, and the flavors are bold enough to transform the inexpensive lentil into a real feast. We always like to serve steaming bowls of chili garnished with a generous sprinkling of shredded Cheddar cheese and a dollop of sour cream. The chili would also be delicious garnished with Super Sofrito (page 338).

VERY VEGGIE LENTIL CHILI

SERVES: 6 GENEROUSLY   START TO FINISH: UNDER 1 HOUR

2 cans (about 14 ounces each) vegetable broth,
   or 4 cups homemade vegetable stock (see page 38)
1 pound (about 2⅓ cups) brown lentils
1 can (14½ ounces) diced tomatoes
1 large onion (for about 1 cup chopped)
4 cloves fresh garlic, minced, or 4 teaspoons bottled
   minced garlic
1 can (6 ounces) tomato paste
2 tablespoons ketchup
1 tablespoon chili powder
1½ teaspoons ground cumin
½ teaspoon dried thyme
½ teaspoon salt, or to taste
½ teaspoon black pepper, or to taste
2 tablespoons olive oil, preferably extra-virgin
1 tablespoon balsamic vinegar
Hot pepper sauce to taste (optional)
Shredded Cheddar cheese, for serving
Sour cream, for serving

1. Combine the broth and 1½ cups water (see Note) in a 4½-quart Dutch oven or soup pot and bring to a boil over high heat. Meanwhile, pick through the lentils, checking for stones or debris. Rinse the lentils and drain them. When the broth comes to a boil, add the lentils and bring the mixture back to a boil. Reduce the heat to low, cover, and cook at a very slow boil for 20 minutes. (Partially uncover the pot if the contents threaten to boil over.)

2. Add the tomatoes with their juice. Peel and coarsely chop the onion and add it to the pot. Add the garlic to the pot. Add the tomato paste, ketchup, chili powder, cumin, thyme, salt, and black pepper. Stir to mix well. Simmer, covered, stirring frequently, for 15 minutes. Add a little more water or vegetable stock if all of the moisture evaporates.

3. Remove the pot from the heat and stir in the oil and vinegar. Add hot pepper sauce to taste, if desired. Serve at once, topped with cheese and sour cream.

NOTE: The water can be replaced with 1½ cups vegetable broth (canned or homemade) if you have enough on hand.

CHAPTER TWO

EVERYDAY ENTRÉES

"Our strategy is simple: We try to buy meat when it's on sale, and when we find a good price, we buy enough to stock the freezer."

There seems to be one in every family, and it tends to be a man. We're talking about meat-and-potatoes guys—those wonderful men who'd eat steak and french fries every night if they could. Gotta love 'em, but we've gotta feed 'em, too! Thick slabs of meat are about the most expensive foods you can prepare, so keeping those carnivores happy can be a budget-minded cook's biggest challenge. But the fact that you're not grilling steak and steaming lobster several nights a week does not mean your family won't enjoy what they're eating. In fact, they very much will thank you!

When it comes to meat-centered entrées, our strategy is simple: We try to buy meat when it's on sale, and when we find a good price, we buy enough to stock the freezer. We've also spent a lot of time experimenting with the traditional thrifty (generally tougher) cuts of meat, finding ways to coax them into tender submission. Debbie's Autumn Pork Chops, Corned Beef and Cabbage Dinner, and Gayle's Country-Style Steak come immediately to mind.

Poultry, of course, plays a key role in the thrifty meat category, and although chicken chunks appear often in our recipes, sometimes you want a whole chicken cutlet—or even a whole chicken. From roasted chicken to baked turkey breast to chicken stew, this chapter includes our favorites. And any budget cookbook worth its salt must contain some recipes for drumsticks and thighs. We've got that covered, too!

It's never too late to start training those carnivores to branch out, and if the dinner is dazzling, the job is much easier. Test the waters with Canadian Bacon with Apples and Onions, Country Cabbage Bowls, Super Stuffed Potatoes, Enchanting Enchiladas, and Texas Cowboy's Pie.

Carnivores or not, there's no dispute that we all need to be eating more fish. Again, we like to buy whatever is on sale, so we've tried to keep our recipes flexible enough to accommodate a range of fish. Golden Broiled Fillets are successful using a host of different varieties, and even our Catfish with Pecan Crust works well with any type of thin white fish.

With recipes like these, dinner is never boring, and you'll still get a lot of bang for the buck.

Like any good country girl, my mom learned how to make country-style steak when she was a tiny thing. After she was married with children, she served this tender, gravy-smothered steak often, and it was my distinct pleasure to wolf it down.

The secret to the fall-apart-in-your-mouth tender steak was *s-l-o-w* cooking in the gravy. This is not hard to do, but it does take patience and time. I've simplified the process by using packaged brown gravy mix. Simmering the beef in the gravy is the secret to elevating this convenience item to something I'm proud to serve to my mom.

Round steak is one of the least expensive cuts of beef and needs to be cooked slowly to tenderize it, so it's perfect for this recipe. You can also use cubed steak. We love to serve Gayle's Country-Style Steak over rice or Gayle's Creamed Potatoes.

GAYLE'S COUNTRY-STYLE STEAK

SERVES: 4 PREP TIME: 5 MINUTES

½ cup all-purpose flour
½ teaspoon salt
¼ teaspoon black pepper
1 tablespoon vegetable oil
1½ pounds round steak
1 envelope (about 1 ounce) brown gravy mix
Gayle's Creamed Potatoes (page 332), for serving (optional)

1. Place the flour, salt, and black pepper in a medium-size brown paper bag, fold the top over to close it, and shake to mix well.

2. Heat the oil in an extra-deep 12-inch skillet over medium heat.

3. While the oil is heating, trim any excess fat from the steak and cut it into 3- to 4-inch-wide pieces. Place the steak pieces in the bag, refold the top, and shake vigorously to coat the steak well.

4. Place the steak in the skillet and cook until the meat is lightly browned around the edges, 4 to 5 minutes. Turn and cook until the second side is lightly browned around the edges, 4 to 5 minutes.

5. While the steak cooks, pour the gravy mix into a 2-cup or larger glass measure. Add the amount of water called for on the package and whisk well. Set aside.

6. When the steak is lightly browned on both sides, pour the gravy mix over it. Reduce the heat to medium-low and cover the skillet. Simmer, stirring and turning the steak occasionally, until it falls apart when pierced with a fork, 1 to 1½ hours. (If the gravy gets too thick, add water, ¼ cup at a time. Just pour the water directly into the skillet beside the steak and stir gently until it is mixed in.)

7. Serve immediately, with Gayle's Creamed Potatoes, if desired.

TEXAS COWBOY'S PIE

SERVES: 4 START TO FINISH: UNDER 15 MINUTES

3 cups shredded already-cooked beef (see page 348),
   defrosted if frozen
1 cup bottled mild salsa
1 cup frozen yellow corn kernels
½ cup regular, reduced-fat, or fat-free sour cream
2½ cups leftover mashed potatoes, or 1 package
   (1 pound, 4 ounces) refrigerated mashed potatoes
¼ teaspoon salt
1 tablespoon butter or margarine
½ cup shredded cheese, such as Colby-Jack or taco blend

1. Turn the broiler to high.

2. Combine the beef, salsa, corn, and sour cream in an 8-inch square microwave-safe baking dish. Stir until well mixed. Cover the dish and microwave on high power for 4 minutes, stirring once halfway through. Remove the dish from the microwave oven.

3. Season the potatoes with the salt and butter. Place the potatoes in a microwave-safe dish, cover, and microwave until heated through, 3 to 4 minutes on high power; or microwave refrigerated potatoes according to the package directions.

4. Spoon the potatoes over the beef mixture, spreading them to within 1 inch of the sides of the dish. Sprinkle the cheese over the potatoes. Broil until the cheese is bubbly and lightly toasted, about 2 minutes. Serve at once.

From Alicia:

When I was a kid, my mom always turned leftovers from the Sunday roast into shepherd's pie. Every Monday night, we knew we could count on those homey flavors.

Mom's shepherd's pie goes spicy with this delicious variation. Salsa takes the place of the gravy Mom used. We add corn to make it a one-dish meal, although a salad or additional vegetable alongside is always welcome.

Many of us tend to use our microwave ovens just to warm leftovers. Here's a recipe that uses this major appliance effectively. A quick run under the broiler browns the cheese to a perfectly golden hue.

63

These enchiladas are great on nights when dinner needs to be *now* and you don't have a lot of food in the house. Flour tortillas make wonderful blankets for wrapping bits of leftovers. Here we use our Flexible Mexican Filling, leftover rice, and refried beans (you can use the fat-free variety, if you'd like). You can also use leftover cooked black beans or any canned beans. If your tortillas have been refrigerated, microwave each one for 10 to 15 seconds before assembling so they'll be pliable enough to fold easily.

ENCHANTING ENCHILADAS

SERVES: 4 PREP TIME: 10 MINUTES

Cooking oil spray
1 cup Flexible Mexican Filling (page 352), defrosted
    if frozen
4 large (10- to 12-inch) flour tortillas
1 can (16 ounces) refried black beans or
    regular refried beans
½ cup already-cooked rice (optional)
1 jar (16 ounces) mild or hot Mexican-style salsa
⅓ cup regular or reduced-fat sour cream
2 tablespoons regular or reduced-fat mayonnaise
½ cup shredded taco-style, Mexican-blend, or
    Cheddar cheese

1. Preheat the oven to 350°F. Spray a 13- x 9-inch glass or ceramic baking dish with cooking oil spray.

2. Place the Flexible Mexican Filling in a small microwave-safe bowl and cover it with a paper towel. Microwave on high power until just warm, about 2 minutes. Remove the dish from the microwave oven and set aside.

3. Assemble the enchiladas by placing one fourth of the filling in the center of each flour tortilla, and then spooning one fourth of the refried beans and 2 tablespoons of the rice (if using) over the meat mixture. As you fill each tortilla, fold it up, tucking in one end burrito-style, and place it, seam side down, in the prepared baking dish.

4. Stir the salsa, sour cream, and mayonnaise together in a bowl and pour this sauce evenly over the enchiladas. Cover the pan with aluminum foil and bake until the sauce bubbles, about 25 minutes.

5. Remove the pan from the oven, uncover it, and sprinkle the cheese evenly over the enchiladas. Bake, uncovered, until the cheese melts, about 3 minutes. To serve, use a spatula to place an enchilada on each plate.

BEEFED-UP CHINESE BURRITOS

SERVES: 6 START TO FINISH: UNDER 25 MINUTES

1 pound ground beef, fresh or frozen
   (see Notes)
8 ounces fresh button mushrooms
1 small head green cabbage, or ½ large head
   (about 1¼ pounds; see Notes)
2 medium-size carrots
1 tablespoon peanut oil or other vegetable oil
¼ cup hoisin sauce
2 teaspoons Asian (dark) sesame oil
12 small (7-inch) flour tortillas
Extra hoisin sauce, for the tortillas (optional)

1. If the beef is frozen, run it under hot water so you can remove the packaging. Place the beef on a microwave-safe plate and microwave, uncovered, on high power for 3 minutes to partially defrost.

2. Meanwhile, rinse, pat dry, and coarsely chop the mushrooms, removing any tough stems. Set aside. Cut the cabbage in half. Cut away and discard the tough core. Using a sharp chef's or slicing knife, cut the cabbage into thin shreds. Set aside. Peel the carrots and grate them using the large holes of a box grater. Set aside.

3. Heat the peanut oil in an extra-deep 12-inch skillet over medium heat for 1 minute. Add the beef (fresh or partially defrosted) to the skillet and cook, turning and breaking up the meat, until it is completely browned, about 8 minutes. Drain any accumulated fat from the skillet, if necessary.

4. Add the mushrooms to the skillet and cook, stirring occasionally, until they just begin to release their liquid, about 3 minutes. Meanwhile, mix the hoisin sauce, sesame oil, and ¼ cup water in a 1-cup measure or small bowl.

With this recipe, your family can enjoy the exotic flavors of the East without ever having to leave the kitchen.

Hoisin sauce is a sweet and spicy condiment often used in Chinese dishes. It is sold in the supermarket alongside other Asian condiments. For a more intense flavor, spread about ½ teaspoon hoisin sauce on each tortilla before filling it. The dish is reminiscent of Chinese mu-shu dishes, and the tortillas make a great substitute for the pancakes. You can also serve the filling over rice.

5. Add the hoisin sauce mixture, the cabbage, and the carrots to the skillet. Stir well, cover the skillet, and cook, lifting the lid to stir from time to time, until the cabbage is tender, about 3 minutes.

6. While the cabbage steams, stack the tortillas on a microwave-safe plate and microwave until warm, following the package directions, 3 to 5 minutes.

7. If desired, spread a little extra hoisin sauce in the center of each tortilla. Using a slotted spoon, place about ½ cup of the beef mixture in the center of each tortilla. Tuck in one end, roll up the tortillas burrito-style, and serve.

NOTES: You can use 3 cups Basic Beef (page 347), defrosted if frozen. Add once the oil is heated in Step 3.

■ Instead of the cabbage and carrots, you can use 1 package (16 ounces) cabbage coleslaw mix. We often buy these bags of ready-to-go slaw when they are on a buy-one-get-one-free special. Most grocery stores carry 8- and 16-ounce bags. Warehouse club stores usually carry larger bags at extremely reduced prices.

Buying a Freezer

To take full advantage of great supermarket sales on meat, seafood, and other perishable items, you need to have the freezer space to store the food once you get it home. Even large, side-by-side refrigerator-freezers don't offer a lot of freezer room when you take into consideration the size of ice cream cartons and loaves of bread. It may be time to consider buying a stand-alone freezer.

The smallest freezers are usually chest-style (with a door that lifts open from the top) and measure about 5.3 cubic feet. They often go on sale for about $100 (the regular prices start at about $130). Depending on how much meat you buy (and how cheap the sale price), a freezer can easily pay for itself in a year.

Even the smallest chest freezers hold a surprising amount of food, yet they are compact enough to be kept in a small basement, the garage, or even in a large closet. (Beverly's first freezer lived in the corner of her apartment kitchen, and she threw a tablecloth over it as camouflage.)

If you have the room and want a bigger freezer, the newspaper classified ads are a good place to look. People who are moving often sell their freezers secondhand at a fraction of the original price, and a well-maintained secondhand freezer in good condition can easily last a decade or longer. (Remember, a freezer works most efficiently if fairly well filled, and it wastes a lot of energy if keeping an empty area cold. So it's important to buy the right size for your family.) If you can't find a secondhand freezer, consider buying a used refrigerator. You'll get the extra freezer compartment along with extra refrigerator space, which comes in very handy for holidays and entertaining.

If you're willing to pay a bit more than $150, you can get a new upright-style freezer (with a door that swings open to the side). If you're buying a larger freezer, it's smart to pay just a few more dollars for a frost-free model. (Defrosting a small chest-style freezer isn't a lot of work, but it's a mammoth chore when the freezer is large.)

All in all, an extra freezer is a luxury—but it's a luxury you may not be able to afford to pass up.

"People who are moving often sell their freezers secondhand at a fraction of the original price."

From Alicia:

One of my favorite restaurant treats is potato skins. They are usually served as an appetizer, but I often can't resist and order them as my meal. Why, then, couldn't I prepare them for the whole family at home? To save calories, I bake my potato skins instead of deep-frying them.

Check out our Amazing Baked Potatoes and bake extra with this recipe in mind. The scooped-out centers will be perfect for Loaded Baked Potato Soup or August Vichyssoise (pages 30 and 31).

For these potato skins, we throw together a spicy chili that will warm the weariest soul. Spoon the meaty concoction into the spud bowls, then top with cheese and sour cream. Mmm . . . dinner is served.

CHILI IN SPUD BOWLS

SERVES: 6 START TO FINISH: UNDER 25 MINUTES

6 already-baked Russet baking potatoes (see page 366)
12 ounces ground beef, fresh or frozen
1 tablespoon vegetable oil
1 large onion (for about 1 cup chopped)
1 can (15 ounces) kidney beans, or 1 cup homemade (see page 368), defrosted if frozen
1 jar (16 ounces) mild or hot Mexican picante sauce
1 tablespoon chili powder
1 clove fresh garlic, minced, or 1 teaspoon bottled minced garlic
6 tablespoons shredded Cheddar cheese, or more to taste
Sour cream to taste (optional)

1. Preheat the oven to 400°F.

2. Cut the baked potatoes in half lengthwise and carefully scoop out the pulp, leaving a good ¼ inch of potato pulp on all sides. Set the pulp aside for another use. Place the skins, cut side up, on a baking sheet.

3. Bake the skins, uncovered, until just heated through, 5 to 10 minutes.

4. Meanwhile, if the beef is frozen, run it under hot water so you can remove the packaging. Place the beef on a microwave-safe plate and microwave, uncovered, on high power for 3 minutes to partially defrost.

5. Heat the oil in an extra-deep 12-inch skillet over medium heat. Peel and coarsely chop the onion, adding it to the skillet as you chop.

6. Add the beef (fresh or partially defrosted) to the skillet. Cook, turning and breaking up the meat, until it is crumbled and browned, 8 to 10 minutes.

7. While the beef browns, rinse and drain the beans. Set them aside.

8. When the beef is no longer pink, drain any accumulated fat from the skillet. Add the picante sauce, beans, chili powder, and garlic. Stir well. Cook until heated through, 3 to 5 minutes.

9. When the potato skins are warmed through, remove them from the oven. To serve, place 2 potato skins on each plate and spoon the chili into each spud bowl. Sprinkle 1 tablespoon of the cheese (or more to taste) over each "bowl" of chili. Garnish with a dollop of sour cream, if desired.

About:
FRESH GARLIC AND BOTTLED MINCED GARLIC

It's hard to beat the convenience of bottled minced garlic, and in most recipes, we can't tell the difference between bottled and fresh. But there are times when you want the bright flavor that only comes from peeling and mincing a clove of fresh garlic.

To forestall any confusion, here's how we decide when to use what:

As a general rule, you can always substitute fresh garlic for bottled minced garlic. For recipes in which the food remains uncooked, however, we prefer to use only fresh. This includes salads and salad dressings, no-cook pasta sauces, salsas, and dips. So fresh garlic is called for in the ingredients list for all "no-cook" recipes.

In "cooked" recipes throughout this book, we give you the choice of using either fresh or bottled minced garlic for greater flexibility and convenience. One clove of fresh garlic equals 1 teaspoon of bottled already-minced garlic and vice versa.

As for price, unless you find a special deal on one or the other, there's generally not a significant difference between fresh and bottled.

Freezing and the Single Cook

W hen you're cooking for one person, you have to be especially careful about buying too much and then letting food go to waste. After all, groceries you don't eat are the most expensive ones you buy! The freezer can be the single cook's best friend. Today's leftovers can be tomorrow's (or next week's) feast.

Here are a few tips:

"The freezer can be the single cook's best friend."

- Stock up on appropriate freezer supplies. This expense will pay for itself by eliminating wasted food. Pint-size freezer-weight plastic bags work well for single servings. Some companies, such as Tupperware, now make plastic containers designed especially for the freezer.

- Some people prefer storage boxes because they stack better than bags. Label the side of the container facing the front so you can read it without removing the box from the freezer shelf.

- If you don't need to use a whole pound of hamburger in a recipe, make 4-ounce patties of the leftovers and wrap them individually. Freeze the patties in a marked, gallon-size freezer bag.

- To freeze cooked rice, portion 1½ cups for an entrée serving, or ½ to ¾ cups for a side dish, into a freezer-weight plastic box or bag. Lay the bags flat to freeze. When you are ready to use the rice, run hot tap water over the bag, remove the rice from the bag, and then microwave on high power until heated through, about 3 minutes. Fluff the rice with a fork before serving.

With a stash of goodies in your freezer, eating alone can feel just like a banquet.

MY S-T-R-E-T-C-H-E-D MEAT LOAF WITH A CHOICE OF TOPPINGS

SERVES: 8 PREP TIME: 15 MINUTES

2 large eggs

½ cup tomato juice or tomato-vegetable juice, such as V8

¼ cup ketchup

1 tablespoon Worcestershire sauce

½ teaspoon salt

½ teaspoon black pepper

1 cup packaged or homemade dry bread crumbs (see page 235)

½ cup quick-cooking (not instant) oats

6 cloves fresh garlic, or 2 tablespoons bottled minced garlic

½ cup fresh parsley leaves, or 2 tablespoons dried parsley (optional)

1 medium-size carrot

2 ribs celery

½ medium-size green bell pepper

1 large onion

1 pound lean ground beef (see Note), defrosted if frozen

Cooking oil spray

Mustard–Brown Sugar Topping or Ketchup Topping (recipes follow)

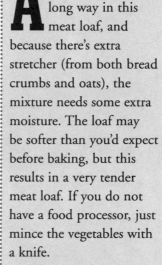

1. Preheat the oven to 350°F.

2. Break the eggs into a large mixing bowl. Add the tomato juice, ketchup, Worcestershire sauce, salt, and black pepper. Stir well. Stir in the bread crumbs and oats. Set aside.

3. Peel the garlic cloves, if using fresh. Turn on a food processor and drop the garlic cloves, one at a time, through the feed tube.

A little meat goes a long way in this meat loaf, and because there's extra stretcher (from both bread crumbs and oats), the mixture needs some extra moisture. The loaf may be softer than you'd expect before baking, but this results in a very tender meat loaf. If you do not have a food processor, just mince the vegetables with a knife.

When our friend Marietta Wynands made this, she was surprised by her twelve-year-old son's reaction. "Mom, if I ate more of this, would you let me play for five more minutes on the computer?" he asked. "Can't fool me—he liked it," Marietta said. She chunked up some of the leftover meat loaf and added it to plain bottled spaghetti sauce. "It really enlivens it," Marietta said.

Process until finely minced. Then drop the fresh parsley leaves (if using) through the feed tube and finely mince.

4. Peel the carrot and cut it into roughly 2-inch pieces. Cut the celery into roughly 2-inch pieces. Core and seed the bell pepper half and cut it into roughly 2-inch pieces. Add the carrot, celery, and bell pepper pieces to the processor bowl and pulse until the vegetables are cut into very small pieces (but not soupy). Transfer the vegetable mixture to the mixing bowl, along with the bottled minced garlic and dried parsley (if using).

5. Peel and quarter the onion and place the quarters in the processor bowl. Pulse until the onion is cut into very small pieces (but not soupy). Add the onions to the mixing bowl and stir to mix well.

6. Add the beef to the bowl and, using your hands, thoroughly combine the meat with the vegetable mixture.

7. Spray a large loaf pan (about 10 x 6 x 3 inches) with cooking oil spray. Spread the meat mixture evenly in the pan. Use the back of a spoon to spread the topping of choice evenly over the meat. Bake, uncovered, until cooked through, about 1 hour and 10 minutes. Let rest at room temperature for 10 minutes before slicing and serving.

NOTE: Because the fat is not drained off in this recipe, we suggest using ground beef that is at least 85 percent lean.

MUSTARD–BROWN SUGAR TOPPING

MAKES: ABOUT ¼ CUP **START TO FINISH:** UNDER 5 MINUTES

**2 tablespoons light or
dark brown sugar, packed**
¼ cup prepared mustard

Stir the brown sugar and mustard
together in a small bowl until smooth.

This topping is at
once sweet and tangy.
You can use any kind
of mustard, from yellow
to Dijon to spicy brown.
Mustard-lovers are sure
to swoon.

KETCHUP TOPPING

MAKES: ABOUT ¼ CUP **START TO FINISH:** UNDER 5 MINUTES

¼ cup ketchup
1 tablespoon red wine vinegar

Pour the ketchup into a small bowl and
add the vinegar. Stir until well blended.

This more traditional
meat loaf topping is
especially kid-friendly.
The hint of vinegar gives a
nice balance to the ketchup.
If you don't have any red
wine vinegar, use any other
type of vinegar (except fruit
flavored) you have on hand.

The Miracle of Menu Planning

We're not sure about you, but we'd never consider embarking on a weeklong road trip without consulting a map. That's what a menu really is—a road map that helps you navigate the potentially treacherous week of meals ahead. Need convincing?

- How many times are you forced into a restaurant or to get take-out because you walked in the door from work only to realize that your groceries ran out yesterday? If you took a bit of time to make menus, you'd have shopped with a plan and been totally stocked.

- Speaking of shopping, a menu is a map for that, too. You'll be less tempted to buy items you don't need and won't use if you're shopping with a definite meal plan in mind. You'll also shop less often. This saves money, pure and simple.

- Menu planning lets you take the best advantage of super-market sales and save big (especially on meat and seafood).

- Knowing ahead what you're going to cook all week is a miraculous stress-reducer. Gone is the walk-through-the-door-now-what panic. With a menu plan, you can just cook on automatic pilot.

- Menus help prevent the "Meatloaf Again?" syndrome. If you save your menus or write them on your calendar, you can refer back to them and see that it's time to work something new into the rotation.

Here are some of our favorite tips for making menu planning easy and efficient:

- Read the grocery ads before you plan (to take advantage of those sales). The day the ads appear will dictate when you plan and shop.

- A grocery list is obviously essential. We suggest sitting down with two pieces of paper—one for the list and another for your daily menus. Many people we know generate a master grocery list on their computer and print it out each week. You can always add items and cross them off, but a set list provides a jump start.

- Make photocopies of recipes you know your family will want to eat more than once a month and stash them in a folder. (Or type the recipes into your computer for easy printouts.) This will cut down on time spent searching through cookbooks and helps you stay organized. You can quickly refer to the recipes to make out your grocery list. (Some people even paper clip all the chicken recipes together, all of the dessert recipes together, and so on.) The file also helps you decide what to cook when you're feeling brain-dead.

- If you come across a really good sale item in the newspaper but it's not something you typically cook, take the time to look for a recipe before you go shopping. This will cut down on later emergency trips to the store for the missing ingredients. (And think of how many "extra" items go into your cart with every trip to the store!)

- Think about freshness when menu planning. Fresh fish should be served either the day you shop or the next. Always check use-by dates on fresh meat. Most packages of chicken and ground beef can hold in the refrigerator for several days (and can always be frozen). The further away you get from your shopping date, the less fresh food you'll have on hand. That's when it becomes a good idea to schedule meals centered on cured meat such as kielbasa, frozen fish or frozen meats, beans and rice, or other pantry-based staples. Likewise, perishable produce needs to be eaten early in the cycle. Rely on frozen and canned vegetables and fruits later in the week.

- Check the use-by date when you purchase dairy items: The older milk will be at the front of the shelf. The milk cartons at the back may have a later use-by date—and thus will last several days longer in your refrigerator.

"Menu planning lets you take the best advantage of supermarket sales."

"Menu planning is a miraculous stress-reducer."

- Post your menu in an obvious place in the kitchen. This helps you keep track of the food you have on hand—especially at first, when you may be buying more at one time than you're accustomed to. If a night brings an unexpected detour on your road map, you can always freeze perishable meats, and your posted menu will serve as a reminder of what you have stashed away. Posted menus also announce to the rest of the family what's on tap for dinner and cuts down on the pre-dinner questions and statements of "I had that for lunch."

- Once you've done a month or two of menus, you can simply reuse a lot of them with minor modifications. Supermarket sales tend to repeat themselves fairly frequently.

After a month or two of menu planning, you'll wonder how you made it down the dinnertime path any other way.

ONION CHOPPED STEAK WITH EASY GRAVY

SERVES: 4 START TO FINISH: UNDER 25 MINUTES

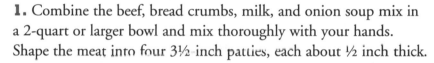

1 pound ground beef, defrosted
   if frozen

½ cup fine bread crumbs (see Notes)

¼ cup whole, low-fat, or skim milk

½ envelope (1½ tablespoons) dry onion
   soup mix (see Notes)

1 envelope (about 1 ounce) brown gravy mix (see Notes)

1. Combine the beef, bread crumbs, milk, and onion soup mix in a 2-quart or larger bowl and mix thoroughly with your hands. Shape the meat into four 3½-inch patties, each about ½ inch thick.

2. Place an extra-deep 12-inch skillet over medium heat and add the meat patties. Cook, uncovered, for 5 minutes. (Reduce the heat if the meat begins to brown too quickly.)

3. Meanwhile, place the brown gravy mix in a 2-cup or larger measure. Add the amount of tap water called for on the envelope and whisk until well blended. Set aside.

4. Turn the patties over, cover the skillet, and cook for 5 minutes. (Drain any excess fat, if necessary.)

5. Uncover the skillet, reduce the heat to low, and add the gravy mix. Cook until the gravy reaches the desired consistency and the patties are no longer pink in the center, about 5 minutes. Serve at once or allow to simmer until ready to serve.

NOTES: For tips on making your own bread crumbs, see page 235.
■ Store the remaining onion soup mix in a zipper-top plastic bag at room temperature for up to 6 months.
■ The actual weight of gravy mix varies slightly from brand to brand, but it won't matter in this recipe as long as the envelope indicates roughly 1 ounce.

During our childhood, this simple dish— (frequently called Salisbury Steak in the North)—was a standard on the menu in all old-fashioned Southern diners, although sometimes it would be called "hamburger steak." (This is to be distinguished from "country-style steak," which in the South is made with round steak rather than ground beef. See page 62 for our recipe.) Never mind that our mothers served this at least once a week when we were growing up—we'd still order it at the diner every chance we got. And we still love it today.

Corned beef can be snagged at a reasonable cost almost any time of the year, but around St. Patrick's Day, this is a gotta-have dinner. Not just because it's traditional, but because, in March, the stores seem to practically give corned beef away. And if your supermarket happens to overestimate corned beef's popularity, the prices will be even lower *after* the holiday. (The bonus: Corned beef stays fresh in its package for weeks and even can be frozen in its package.)

A boiled corned beef dinner is a hearty, easy, one-pot affair that most people love. It's humble fare that takes on a delicious twist as the beef cooks and produces a rich, assertive broth that then flavors the vegetables. This is one recipe that may never turn out quite the same way twice because much of the flavor depends on how the corned beef was seasoned by the manufacturer. Sometimes the seasonings are enclosed in a separate packet, and sometimes the spices are directly on the meat. Either way, you'll have a meal that's sure to please.

CORNED BEEF AND CABBAGE DINNER

SERVES: 4 PREP TIME: UNDER 30 MINUTES

1 corned beef (about 2½ pounds)
4 medium-size potatoes
1 large onion
4 medium-size carrots
½ small head green cabbage, or ¼ large head (about 12 ounces)

1. Place the corned beef, along with any seasonings from the package, in a 6-quart soup pot. Add cold water to cover by about 2 inches. Bring the water to a boil over high heat, then reduce the heat to the lowest setting and simmer the beef, covered, for 2½ hours. (You may have to add water to the pot halfway through the cooking time to keep the beef covered by 2 inches.)

2. Remove the pot from the heat and transfer the beef to a cutting board, leaving the broth in the pot. Cover the beef loosely with aluminum foil and set it aside.

3. Peel and quarter the potatoes and the onion and set the pieces aside. Peel the carrots, cut them into 1-inch pieces, and set aside. Cut away and discard the tough core from the cabbage. Cut it into 4 pieces and set aside.

4. Place the pot of broth over high heat and bring to a boil. Reduce the heat to medium and skim off any fat that rises to the surface. Add the potato, onion, and carrot pieces. Cook, uncovered, at a moderate boil for 10 minutes. Then add the cabbage pieces and continue to boil until all the vegetables are tender, about 10 minutes more. (Depending on the size of the pot, you may need to cover it during the final cooking if the cabbage is not completely submerged in the broth. Adjust the heat to maintain a moderate boil but make sure the heat isn't so high that the pot boils over.) Remove the pot from the heat.

5. To serve, trim away and discard the fat from the beef and slice it thinly across the grain. Place the slices in the center of a serving platter. Using a slotted spoon, remove the vegetables from the broth and arrange them around the meat. (If you like, coarsely chop the cabbage first.) Spoon a little broth over the meat to moisten it and serve.

NOTE: Any leftover corned beef makes great sandwiches for lunch the next day.

PAN-FRIED PORK CHOPS WITH PEPPER MEDLEY

SERVES: 4 START TO FINISH: UNDER 25 MINUTES

4 teaspoons vegetable oil

4 thin-sliced pork loin chops
(each about ⅓ inch thick, about
1¼ pounds total)

Salt and black pepper to taste

1 large onion (for about 1 cup chopped)

1 medium-size green bell pepper
(for about 1 cup chopped)

1 medium-size red bell pepper
(for about 1 cup chopped; see Note)

2 cloves fresh garlic, minced, or 2 teaspoons bottled
minced garlic

1 tablespoon Worcestershire sauce

1. Heat 3 teaspoons of the oil in an extra-deep 12-inch skillet over medium heat. Lightly sprinkle the pork chops with salt and black pepper and add them to the skillet.

When you're craving meat but not the hefty grocery bill that can come with it, think thin. Thin-sliced pork chops, to be exact. Many supermarkets now regularly stock pork chops that are only about a third of an inch thick. Because thin-sliced chops look like regular pork chops, your family might not even notice that they're eating less meat! It doesn't matter whether the chops come with a bone or without. The boneless variety simply weighs a bit less and costs a bit more per pound.

MoneySaver

Thinking about buying a new piece of kitchen equipment? Borrow it from a friend and test it out before you make the investment. You may discover that its strengths aren't going to help you that much and that you're better off not making the purchase. There's nothing more annoying than seeing an appliance just sitting around and not earning its keep in your kitchen. (For more on our take on gadgets, see page 442.)

2. Cook the pork chops until they are light brown on the first side, about 5 minutes. Meanwhile, peel and coarsely chop the onion. Set aside. Stem, seed, and coarsely chop the bell peppers and set aside.

3. Turn the chops and cook them until they are brown on the second side and no longer pink in the center, about 4 minutes. Remove the skillet from the heat. Place the chops on a plate and set aside.

4. Return the skillet to medium heat and add the remaining 1 teaspoon oil. Add the onion and cook, stirring, for 2 minutes. (The onion will turn brown because of the brown bits in the pan.) Add the bell peppers, garlic, and Worcestershire sauce and cook, stirring frequently, until the peppers are tender, about 3 minutes.

5. Serve the pork chops topped with the peppers and onions.

NOTE: You can use a second green pepper in place of the red, if you prefer.

Buying a Cheap Ham

When you find a ham at a low price, it would be a crime not to buy it. Here are some of our tried-and-true tips:

First, realize that the sell-by date on a fully cooked smoked ham can be nearly two months after you first see it in the store. As you shop from week to week, notice what those dates are. As the date draws nearer, many supermarkets will drastically reduce the price.

Second, note that most supermarkets load up on hams just before Easter, and often again just before Christmas—almost always stocking more than they'll sell by the holiday. A week after the holiday, the price of those unsold hams will plummet, even though the use-by date is still weeks away.

If you'd like a ham and it's not the week after Easter, the best bet is to buy a bone-in ham that has not been glazed or spiral-sliced. Also, in general, the bigger the ham you buy, the less it costs per pound. Unless we're having a party, however, we prefer to buy only half a ham. Since a bone-in ham will yield 2 to 3 servings per pound, a typical half will serve 16 to 24 people. That's simply all the ham we are likely to use in a reasonable time, and all the leftovers we have room to freeze.

There are two types of bone-in half hams: the shank and the butt portion. There's more meat in the butt portion because the bone is smaller than in the shank half, so it serves closer to 3 people per pound. The shank portion, with the larger bone, yields about 2 servings per pound.

Almost all of the pink hams you find in the supermarket are smoked and fully cooked. Although these cooked hams are safe to eat right out of the package, we think baking the ham and serving it warm brings out the flavor and allows you to add a yummy glaze for that gourmet touch. (See our recipe on page 82.)

"The bigger the ham, the less it costs per pound."

We make a sport out of seeing how little we can pay per pound of ham. It's worth the hunt because, in our experience, the delectability of a ham does not depend on its price. A very inexpensive ham can taste just as wonderful as a very expensive one—especially if you bake the ham with this marvelous marmalade glaze. The glaze is so wonderful, in fact, that we prefer to buy an unglazed, unsliced ham. (We've even been known to wash the glaze off a spiral-sliced ham we bought at a rock-bottom sale in order to use this glaze instead!) Slicing a ham isn't difficult.

Some cooks like to score the fat on the outside of the ham and insert cloves into the spaces of the cross-hatch pattern. This does make for a pretty presentation and good flavor, but jars of whole cloves are very expensive. We get the same flavor by stirring a little ground cloves into the glaze. However, if you already have whole cloves that you want to use, go ahead and stud the ham with them.

MARMALADE-GLAZED HAM

SERVES: 15 TO 24   PREP TIME: 10 MINUTES

1 cup firmly packed light brown sugar
½ cup orange marmalade (see Notes)
¼ cup Dijon mustard
3 tablespoons cider vinegar
½ teaspoon ground cloves
Cooking oil spray
1 bone-in, fully cooked smoked ham half
   (7½ to 8½ pounds)

SUPER-CHEAP!

1. Position the oven rack in the middle of the oven and preheat the oven to 325°F.

2. Combine the brown sugar, marmalade, mustard, vinegar, and cloves in a small microwave-safe mixing bowl. Stir well. Microwave, uncovered, on high power to melt the marmalade slightly, so the mixture will spread easily, 1 minute. Remove the glaze from the microwave and stir. Set aside.

3. Line a roasting pan or a large casserole with aluminum foil and spray the foil with cooking oil spray. Cut the skin off the ham (it's dark-colored and rough), if necessary. Trim away any excess fat. Place the ham on the foil, flat side down, and spoon some of the glaze over the ham to coat it. Rub the glaze into the ham with the back of a spoon to make sure all areas are covered.

4. Place the ham in the oven and bake until an instant-read meat thermometer registers 140°F when inserted in the center (do not touch the bone), about 2 hours for an 8-pound ham (see Notes). While the ham is baking, baste it three more times with the remaining glaze. (Do not rub the glaze into the ham as you did the first time or you will rub off the glaze that has begun to bake on. Just spoon the glaze over the ham—it will spread easily over the hot ham.) If the ham begins to get too brown in the final minutes of baking, tent the top with foil.

5. Remove the ham from the oven and let it stand for 15 minutes before slicing and serving. (If you expect to have leftover ham, slice only as much as you'll serve at this meal. See the box below for information on storing leftovers and page 242 for ideas on how to use them.)

NOTES: If your orange marmalade is the fruit-only type, reduce the amount of vinegar to 2 tablespoons.

■ To determine how long to bake the ham, multiply the number of pounds by 15 minutes, then round off the cooking time to the nearest 5-minute point. For example, a ham weighing 7½ pounds will cook for about 1 hour and 50 minutes. An 8-pound ham will reach an internal temperature of 140°F in about 2 hours.

MoneySaver

Don't ever throw out a ham bone. Put it in a large pot, cover it with water, and cook it at a very slow boil for about 2 hours. The resulting broth is great to use in soups or for cooking dried beans.

About:
FREEZING A HAM

It's easy to freeze extra ham—which is what you should do with any ham you don't plan to eat within 4 days of cooking. Freezing ham will change its texture somewhat, but if you use it cubed in casseroles and other dishes, you can't tell the difference. Just cut the ham into bite-size cubes, wrap them tightly in plastic wrap, and place them in freezer-weight zipper-top plastic bags or other airtight containers. We like to divide the ham into 1-cup portions to make it easier to use in individual recipes. (If you like to cook your own dried beans, you may also want to freeze some ham in smaller portions to use as seasoning.) The ham will freeze this way for up to 3 months. Thaw frozen ham cubes overnight in the refrigerator.

From Alicia:

It's not often that I can pull a favorite child-hood dinner into my hectic adult schedule. But Canadian bacon is one exception. I remember warm fall dinners with stacks of Canadian bacon, steaming baked apples, and hot rolls dripping with butter.

My streamlined recipe makes use of crisp fresh apples, so it's perfect for fall when the new crop comes in—or any time of year when you find apples on special. Canadian bacon is sold with the refrigerated packaged meats at the supermarket. We find it to be an economical choice in our sections of the country, but if it's expensive where you live, substitute a ham steak.

You'll find that kids love the mild bacon and sweet apples, while adults revel in the complexity that onions and garlic bring to the mix. Pardon us while we take a savory trip back to childhood!

CANADIAN BACON WITH APPLES AND ONIONS

SERVES: 4 START TO FINISH: UNDER 20 MINUTES

1 large onion (for about 1 cup sliced)
1 tablespoon vegetable oil
3 large Granny Smith or other tart cooking apples (for about 4 cups sliced)
2 cloves fresh garlic, minced, or 2 teaspoons bottled minced garlic
1 tablespoon butter
8 ounces (about 16 slices) Canadian bacon, or 1 center-cut ham steak (about 1 pound), cut into 4 portions

1. Peel the onion, cut it in half, and then cut the halves into crescent-shaped slices about ¼ inch thick. Heat the oil in an extra-deep 12-inch skillet over medium heat. Add the onion to the skillet and cook, stirring occasionally.

2. Meanwhile, cut the apples into quarters (but do not peel them), remove the cores, and then cut the quarters into ¼-inch-thick slices. Add the apples to the skillet and cook, stirring frequently, until they begin to soften, 2 to 3 minutes.

3. Add the garlic to the skillet. Cook, stirring, for 1 minute, then remove the skillet from the heat.

4. Pour the apple mixture into a serving bowl. Cut the butter into small pieces and scatter them over the apples. Stir until the butter melts. Set aside.

5. Place the same skillet over medium heat and add half the Canadian bacon. Cook until it is lightly browned on the first side, about 1 minute. Then turn the pieces over and cook until lightly browned on the second side and heated through, 1 to 2 minutes. Remove the Canadian bacon from the skillet and place it on a serving plate. Repeat with the remaining bacon.

6. To serve, divide the Canadian bacon among four dinner plates and spoon the apple mixture alongside.

DEBBIE'S AUTUMN PORK CHOPS

SERVES: 6 START TO FINISH: UNDER 1 HOUR

6 boneless pork loin chops (about 6 ounces each),
   or 6 bone-in pork loin chops
Garlic powder to taste
Salt and black pepper to taste
2 tablespoons vegetable oil
½ to ¾ cup apple juice, or more as needed

1. Generously season the pork chops with garlic powder, salt, and black pepper.

2. Heat the oil in an extra-deep 12-inch skillet over medium heat. Place the seasoned pork chops in the hot oil and brown them on both sides, 4 to 5 minutes on each side.

3. Remove the chops from the skillet and pour off any accumulated drippings. Return the chops to the skillet and pour in enough of the apple juice to almost cover the chops.

4. Reduce the heat to low, cover the skillet, and simmer until the chops are fork-tender, 30 to 40 minutes.

5. To serve, divide the pork chops among six dinner plates. Spoon a little of the apple juice over each one.

Debbie Schoeppey, one of the readers of our online Desperation Dinners newsletter, sent this recipe to us in response to another reader's request for the best way to cook pork chops. "The way I cook pork chops, they always are tender, juicy, and taste wonderful," Debbie says.

We liked Debbie's recipe for its simplicity as well as the delicious combination of pork and apple juice. She used garlic salt, but because we don't usually have it on hand, we use garlic powder and salt. If you do have garlic salt, feel free to use it in place of the garlic powder and salt.

Making Your Own Convenience Items

"All you need is a sharp knife and some zipper-top bags."

Grocery stores are packed with products designed to make your life easier—everything from sliced mushrooms to shredded cheese—all at a price. And whether we're willing to pay the extra cost boils down to that familiar compromise between time and money.

To be perfectly honest, when life gets crazy, we tend to buy more convenience items because time itself is so valuable. We'll pay ourselves back later on when we have a free half hour or so to make our own convenience items for the hectic days that are sure to follow. This is really, really easy to do! All you need is a sharp knife (or a food processor) and some zipper-top plastic bags (or refrigerator storage boxes).

Here are some ideas for making your own convenience items:

- **"Baby" carrots.** Okay, you're not going to get the cute "baby" shape, but you can make a small carrot stick that will taste exactly the same. Peel the carrots and trim away the ends. Cut the carrots in half lengthwise and cut the pieces into sticks. (Larger carrots may need to be cut in half again toward the top.) The size of the sticks is up to you. Store the pieces in zipper-top plastic bags in the vegetable bin for up to a week.

- **Celery sticks.** Rinse and dry the celery ribs. Cut them in half (or thirds) lengthwise. Cut into "sticks" of the length of your choice. Store the pieces in zipper-top plastic bags in the vegetable bin for up to a week.

- **Sliced mushrooms.** Cut away any tough stems. If the mushrooms are very dirty, use a soft brush or a paper towel to brush away the dirt. If you rinse the mushrooms, they'll probably need to be used within 1 day. Slice the mushrooms and wrap the slices in a paper towel. (Mushrooms that touch plastic don't store as long.) Place the towel-wrapped package in a zipper-top plastic bag. Store in the vegetable bin for 3 to 4 days.

- **Shredded green or red cabbage.** Cut the cabbage into quarters and discard the tough core. Using a long, sharp knife, cut the cabbage into thin shreds. Store the cabbage shreds in a gallon-size zipper-top plastic bag in the vegetable bin for up to 4 days.

- **Chopped onions.** Peel the onions and chop them. Refrigerate in zipper-top plastic bags or containers with airtight lids. Store them in the vegetable bin for up to 4 days. Chopped onions can also be frozen for up to 1 month. (Lay the bag flat until frozen so the onions won't freeze in a clump.)

- **Shredded cheese.** Use a food processor to shred the cheese. (Be aware that soft and semi-soft cheeses like mozzarella won't work in a processor; use a hand-held grater for them.) Store the shreds in heavy-duty plastic bags in the refrigerator (up to 1 week) or freezer (up to 1 month). Sometimes very large bags (2 pounds or more) of already-shredded cheese at the supermarket are cheaper than buying a large block, so do cost comparisons.

From Beverly:

Every fall, just like clockwork, I crave cabbage. This obsession stretches back more than three decades and finds it roots in my mother's search for an economical fresh vegetable to feed the family at this time of year. My mother could do wonders with a humble cabbage, an art that has been neglected in an age of frozen entrées and fast-food french fries.

What a shame. There's nothing easier than steaming a head of cabbage, so long as you don't overdo it. Cooking it too long is what breaks down the molecular composition of the cabbage and what causes it to stink up the kitchen, which is probably the main reason why cabbage is so often ignored.

One of the convenient things about cabbage is that it will happily wait for at least a week in the refrigerator. That means you can pull it out on one of those nights when you don't feel like going to the store. When I'm in a real hurry for a side dish, I whack a cabbage into four wedges, throw them into inch-deep

COUNTRY CABBAGE BOWLS

SERVES: 4 START TO FINISH: UNDER 25 MINUTES

Salt for cooking the rice
1 cup long-grain rice
1 large head (about 2½ pounds) cabbage (see Notes)
12 ounces reduced-fat turkey-pork sausage (see Notes)
1 large onion (for about 1 cup chopped)
1 can (14½ ounces) Italian-style stewed tomatoes or diced tomatoes seasoned with onion, garlic, and basil (see Notes)
1 can (8 ounces) tomato sauce (see Notes)

SUPER-CHEAP!

1. Bring 2 cups lightly salted water to a boil in a covered medium-size saucepan. Add the rice, stir, and reduce the heat to low. Cover the pot and simmer until the rice is tender, about 20 minutes.

2. Meanwhile, remove 2 outer leaves from the cabbage, snapping them off at the stem end and being careful not to tear them. Set aside. Remove the next 2 outer leaves by slicing across the stem at the core and lifting from the stem end, again being careful not to tear the leaves. Rinse the 4 leaves with cool water but do not dry them. Set the remaining whole cabbage aside.

3. Stack the cabbage leaves loosely inside one another and place them in a deep 1½-quart microwave-safe casserole (with sides about 3 inches high). Pour ½ cup water into the dish and seal it with a sheet of microwave-safe plastic wrap. Cut a small vent hole in the center of the plastic wrap. Microwave on high power until the leaves are crisp-tender but still retain their bowl shape, 1½ to 2 minutes. Uncover the dish and set the leaves aside to cool.

4. If your sausage is in links, remove the meat from the casings. While the cabbage microwaves, place the sausage meat in an extra-deep 12-inch skillet and cook over medium heat, stirring and turning to break the chunks into bite-size pieces, about 2 minutes. Continue cooking the sausage, stirring from time to time.

5. Meanwhile, peel and coarsely chop the onion, adding it to the skillet as you chop. Cut the reserved cabbage in half. Reserve half of the cabbage for another purpose. Cut away and discard the tough core. Slice the remaining half into ¼-inch-wide strips and chop the strips into bite-size pieces. Add the cabbage to the skillet and stir. Cook until the sausage is completely cooked through, 8 to 9 minutes.

6. Add the tomatoes and their juice and the tomato sauce to the skillet. Stir to mix, reduce the heat to low, and let the mixture simmer.

7. When the rice is done, add it to the skillet and stir it thoroughly into the sausage mixture. Cook for 1 minute to blend the flavors. To serve, drain the cabbage leaves, then place one on each plate and spoon the sausage-rice mixture into the cabbage bowl.

NOTES: If you're not going to use the large outer leaves of the cabbage as serving bowls, you could probably get away with a smaller cabbage (1 pound or so), using the whole head for this dish.
■ Regular, full-fat sausage can be used. You'll just need to drain off any extra fat from the pan before adding the cabbage.
■ If you don't have Italian-style or seasoned tomatoes, use plain diced tomatoes and add 1 teaspoon each of minced garlic and dried Italian seasoning.
■ If you don't have tomato sauce, substitute 1 cup bottled spaghetti sauce.

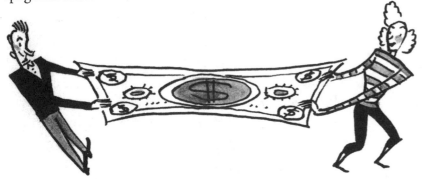

boiling water, and steam until a poke with a knife finds them crisp-tender, 5 to 7 minutes. Then I chop the wedges up right in the serving bowl, dot them with a little butter, and stir in a good squirt of Dijon mustard and a sprinkling of black pepper. (This is a good trick for the cabbage half that you won't use in this recipe.)

For a super-quick supper that's as pleasing to the eye as it is to the palate, try this modern version of my mother's original recipe. Serving this meal in cabbage "bowls" is completely optional, but it does make it attractive and involves minimal extra work. If you want to make the bowls, look for a cabbage with outer leaves that are whole and not torn.

If you can't find bulk sausage, buy breakfast-style links and remove the casing. We like to use reduced-fat turkey-pork blend sausage for this recipe because the result is just 7 grams of fat per serving; if you can't find it, just be sure to drain off any accumulated fat after browning the sausage.

When summer's bounty provides a multitude of green bell peppers, we like to eat them as frequently as possible. We grew up on our mothers' baked stuffed peppers, but the main problem with those old recipes was that the peppers cooked for an hour, turning them into army-green blobs. Our tastes have changed over the years, and now we find those overcooked peppers unappetizing. Steaming the peppers in the microwave while the stuffing cooks on the stovetop solves the problem. The result is a crisp-tender pepper that retains the fresh flavor and brilliant green of the raw vegetable. This stuffing is our twist on the traditional as well—it's packed with veggies, kielbasa sausage, and Cajun spices. Altogether it is an easy, delicious dish.

STUFFED PEPPERS WITH KIELBASA RICE

SERVES: 6 START TO FINISH: UNDER 25 MINUTES

Salt for cooking the rice
1 cup long-grain rice
3 large green bell peppers
1 tablespoon olive oil
1 large onion (for about 1 cup chopped)
1 clove fresh garlic, minced, or 1 teaspoon bottled minced garlic
1 teaspoon Cajun spice blend
8 ounces kielbasa sausage (see Note)
2 cans (14½ ounces each) stewed tomatoes
¼ teaspoon Tabasco sauce, or to taste (optional)
1 can (15 ounces) red kidney beans, or 1 cup homemade (see page 368), defrosted if frozen

1. Bring 2 cups lightly salted water to a boil in a covered medium-size saucepan. Add the rice, stir, and reduce the heat to low. Cover the pot and simmer until the rice is tender, about 20 minutes.

2. While the rice is cooking, rinse the peppers and cut them in half lengthwise. Remove the seeds and membranes. Place the pepper boats, cut side up, in a microwave-safe baking dish. Pour 2 cups cool water into the dish, taking care not to get any water inside the pepper cavities. Cover the dish with plastic wrap, turning up one corner or cutting a small slit in the center, and microwave on high power until the peppers are just crisp-tender, 4 to 6 minutes.

3. Meanwhile, heat the oil in an extra-deep 12-inch skillet over medium heat. Peel and coarsely chop the onion, adding it to the skillet as you chop. Cook the onion for 2 to 3 minutes. Add the garlic and Cajun spice blend to the skillet. Cut the sausage link into quarters to make 4 long strips and then cut each strip into ¼-inch-thick slices. Add the sausage to the skillet.

4. Add the tomatoes with their juice and the Tabasco sauce to the skillet. Rinse and drain the beans and add them to the skillet. Stir to mix. Reduce the heat to low and let the sauce simmer.

5. When the rice is done, add it to the skillet and stir until it is thoroughly coated with the sauce.

6. Remove the peppers from the baking dish with a slotted spoon, draining off any water. Place a pepper half on each plate and fill the cavities with the rice mixture. Spoon the remaining rice mixture around the outside of the peppers and serve.

NOTE: Reduced-fat turkey-blend kielbasa can be used.

SUPER STUFFED POTATOES

SERVES: 4 START TO FINISH: UNDER 10 MINUTES

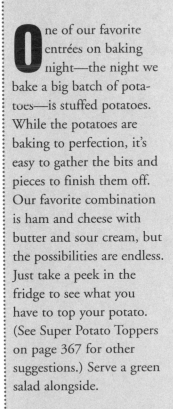

4 large already-baked Russet
    baking potatoes (see page 366)
4 tablespoons (½ stick) butter or
    margarine
¼ cup shredded cheese of choice
½ cup chopped ham
¼ cup regular or low-fat sour cream
Other optional toppings: chopped steamed broccoli,
    chopped scallions, or chopped chives

1. If the potatoes are not hot, slice them in half and place them on a microwave-safe plate. Place a paper towel loosely over the potatoes and microwave on high power until heated through, 3 to 5 minutes. If the potatoes are hot, simply cut them in half.

2. Fluff the potato pulp with a fork and top each half with ½ tablespoon of the butter, ½ tablespoon of the cheese, 1 tablespoon of the ham, and ½ tablespoon of the sour cream. Add other optional ingredients as desired, and serve.

One of our favorite entrées on baking night—the night we bake a big batch of potatoes—is stuffed potatoes. While the potatoes are baking to perfection, it's easy to gather the bits and pieces to finish them off. Our favorite combination is ham and cheese with butter and sour cream, but the possibilities are endless. Just take a peek in the fridge to see what you have to top your potato. (See Super Potato Toppers on page 367 for other suggestions.) Serve a green salad alongside.

There's nothing like comfort food that's comforting to the checkbook as well as to the soul. This hearty, homey casserole stretches a pound of chicken so effortlessly, nobody will ever know it doesn't cost a king's ransom. This is especially kid-friendly, but people of all ages will love it.

OLD-FASHIONED CHICKEN AND RICE CASSEROLE

SERVES: 6 GENEROUSLY   PREP TIME: 20 MINUTES

Salt for cooking the rice
1⅓ cups long-grain rice
1 pound skinless, boneless chicken breast halves, fresh or frozen (see Notes)
1 tablespoon vegetable oil
1 large onion (for about 1 cup chopped)
2 large ribs celery (for about 1 cup chopped)
Cooking oil spray
1 can (10¾ ounces) regular or reduced-fat condensed cream of mushroom soup
1 cup regular, low-fat, or skim milk
½ teaspoon black pepper
½ teaspoon garlic powder
½ teaspoon dried basil (optional)
2 tablespoons butter or margarine
2 cups corn flakes (see Notes)

1. Preheat the oven to 375°F.

2. Bring 2⅔ cups lightly salted water to a boil in a covered medium-size saucepan. Add the rice, cover, and reduce the heat to low. Simmer until the rice is tender, about 20 minutes.

3. Meanwhile, if the chicken is frozen, run it under hot water so you can remove the packaging. Microwave, uncovered, on high power for 3 minutes to partially defrost.

4. While the chicken defrosts, heat the oil in a 10-inch or larger skillet over medium heat. Peel and coarsely chop the onion, adding it to the skillet as you chop. Continue to cook, stirring occasionally, while you cut the chicken (fresh or partially defrosted) into bite-size chunks. Add the chicken to the skillet as you cut and cook, stirring frequently, until it turns white on the outside, 4 minutes.

5. While the chicken cooks, cut the celery into bite-size pieces and set aside. Add the celery to the skillet and cook, stirring occasionally, until it is tender, about 2 minutes. Remove the skillet from the heat and set it aside.

6. Spray a 13- x 9-inch glass or ceramic baking dish with cooking oil spray. Pour the cream of mushroom soup and the milk into the dish and stir gently until they are thoroughly mixed. Add the chicken-vegetable mixture and sprinkle with the black pepper, garlic powder, and basil (if using). Stir until the mixture is well combined. Set aside.

7. Place the butter in a microwave-safe dish and cover it with a paper towel. Microwave on high power until melted, about 1 minute. Place the corn flakes in a 1-pint or larger zipper-top plastic bag, seal the bag, and press it with your hands until the corn flakes are crushed. Pour the melted butter into the bag, close it, and shake until the flakes are coated with butter. Set aside.

8. When the rice is done, stir it into the chicken mixture in the baking dish, making sure the rice is evenly coated with sauce. Using the back of a spoon, spread the mixture evenly in the dish. Sprinkle the buttered corn flakes evenly over the ingredients. Bake, uncovered, until the mixture is bubbling at the edges and the top is lightly browned, about 30 minutes. Serve at once.

NOTES: You can use 2 cups Chunky Seasoned Chicken (page 358), Perfect Poached Chicken (page 362), or Poached Chicken Thighs (page 364), defrosted if frozen. Add with the celery in Step 5.
■ To top the casserole, any unsweetened cereal flakes or cracker crumbs can be used. Or substitute 1½ cups soft (not toasted) bread crumbs. You can also use crushed potato chips, but in that case leave out the butter.

Chew on This

In 2005, Americans spent about $476 billion in restaurants, the National Restaurant Association reported, a 4.9 percent increase over 2004.

Motivate Yourself to Real Savings!

"Target ideas that sound realistic."

I f you're like us, saving money on food sounds like a good idea, but unless we can see real results, and fast, we're likely to give up before we've barely started. So how do we psyche ourselves up and stick with a workable program?

For starters, it helps to set a goal. How much money would it take to get you excited about making even the slightest effort to save? (If you're having trouble deciding, it might help to put a dollar value on your time.) For us, a goal of $100 a month provides that motivation. That's $1,200 a year—enough for a family vacation, a wardrobe update, a down payment on a car, or a respectable chunk of retirement/college savings.

Now that we've got your attention, let's face the facts. Saving money on your food budget—and yet still eating nutritious meals that taste great—will take some degree of thought, planning, and effort. Some steps are easier and faster than others. So why not start with easier and faster?

Here's our list of kitchen-savings how-tos, more or less in easiest-first order. Scan through the list, target ideas that sound immediately realistic, and go for it. Our best advice is to wait until after you score some success on at least one of the easiest tips before progressing to the next one. They don't call it positive reinforcement for nothing.

1. Eating out is expensive, but addictive. So if you're hooked, trying to go cold turkey is probably futile. It's best to wean yourself gradually. For starters, simply choose less expensive restaurants. Or go out for lunch instead of dinner; it generally costs less. Then gradually work toward giving up the habit, cutting out one restaurant meal a month, then one every two weeks, then one a week, until you get that restaurant beast under control. When you want a restaurant-quality meal at home, look for our recipes marked with the "Cheap and Elegant" icon. (See the index for a complete listing.)

Stick-to-It Tip If you want real motivation, look back at several charge-card bills and add up your restaurant tab. Then add in the cash you spent on fast food. Ouch!

2. Junk food is expensive and fattening, not to mention nutritionally null and void. Again, give it up gradually. Cut back on (or cut out) soda first, then move on to chips. Talk to your kids about making choices for healthy living, and let them keep some of the cash. Depending on the scope of your habit, you could easily save $40 a month. Not much, you say? Hey, that's $480 a year.

Stick-to-It Tip Take an empty jar and make a colorful label for it. Every time you pass up a can of soda or a bag of chips, plunk the corresponding cash into the jar. The color of money is a beautiful sight. If that doesn't do it, tally up the fat grams and calories you've avoided.

3. Before ever setting foot in a grocery store, make friends with the newspaper supermarket ads. Most stores advertise deeply discounted specials in hopes of luring you in. Some stores use circulars inserted in the middle of the newspaper, while other stores' ads might be printed within the newspaper pages. So keep looking until you find all of the ads for all of the supermarkets. Pay particular attention to the meat and seafood specials. Buy and eat (or freeze) the meat or seafood that's on sale, and shop at the store with the best deal. The more time you're willing to spend with the ads, the more you're likely to save. And if you're willing to drive to two stores, you'll save even more. Because meat and seafood are among the most expensive items, this is the place to start.

Stick-to-It Tip There's nothing like the exhilaration of getting a really good deal, so pay attention to the regular prices of meat and seafood so you can feel great about how much you're saving by shopping the ads.

4. Using manufacturer's coupons runs the gamut from one-paragraph simple to so complex that entire books are devoted to the sport. The easiest way to start is to clip coupons only for items you already buy. If Pillsbury is your favorite flour

"An occasional splurge can make the goal more realistic."

and you spot a 25-cents-off coupon, well that's a quarter saved. (For more details on our own experiences with coupon shopping, see page 466.)

Stick-to-It Tip **Clip coupons while you're watching TV. At least you'll be getting paid (sort of) for being a couch potato.**

5. Save all of your grocery receipts for a month. (We stuff them into the bill slot of our wallets.) At the end of the month, you'll have a wealth of information at your fingertips. Pull out a calculator and run the numbers. Not only can you easily determine how much your typical monthly grocery bill runs, but you can see how much you're spending on various food categories. Is the grand total a shock? Want to save money fast? Think about eating one meatless meal a week. Want to save even faster? Make a grocery list and stick to it. Impulse buys tend to be those expensive items you could easily have lived without.

Stick-to-It Tip **Compare the next month's grocery receipts (the month when you used a list or cut back on meat), and calculate your savings. The numbers don't lie.**

6. Want to find the most expensive food in your house? Look in the garbage can. Food you buy but never get around to eating is waste, pure and simple. Wasted food is wasted money—cash you could have saved. But how do you control the waste? For starters, take stock of what's in your refrigerator and pantry before you go to the supermarket. (There's no reason to buy perishable items like milk if you don't need them.) Next, consider mapping out menus. If you know what you're cooking next week, you'll know exactly what to buy (and what not to buy). Finally, designate one meal every few days to eat all of your leftovers and to use up the fruits and vegetables that are languishing in the refrigerator. (Call it a smorgasbord and you won't feel deprived.) Or recycle leftovers as brown bag lunches. It's all money in the bank.

Stick-to-It Tip **As Mom used to say, think of all those starving children in Africa. The money you save on food you don't waste each month could be enough to support an orphan through one of the many sponsor agencies.**

"Food you buy but never eat is waste, pure and simple."

ZESTY CHICKEN SAUTÉ

SERVES: 4 START TO FINISH: UNDER 15 MINUTES

1 teaspoon chili powder
1 teaspoon garlic powder
1 teaspoon onion powder
½ teaspoon ground cumin
½ teaspoon salt
¼ teaspoon ground allspice (optional)
4 skinless, boneless chicken breast halves
   (about 6 ounces each), defrosted if frozen
1 tablespoon vegetable oil

1. Place the chili powder, garlic powder, onion powder, cumin, salt, and allspice (if using) in a gallon-size zipper-top bag and seal the bag. Shake the bag to combine the spices thoroughly.

2. Place the chicken breast halves, one at a time, between two sheets of waxed paper or plastic wrap and pound them with several whacks of a meat mallet or rolling pin so they are an even ½ inch thick. Peel off the paper. (Each serving should be about 6 ounces, so if the breast halves are large, cut them in half lengthwise.)

3. Place the chicken pieces in the bag with the spices, seal it, and shake until the chicken is coated with the spice mixture. Set the bag aside.

4. Heat the oil in an extra-deep 12-inch skillet over medium heat. Add the chicken pieces and cook until lightly browned on the first side, 4 to 5 minutes. Turn the chicken and cook until no longer pink in the center, another 4 to 5 minutes.

5. Transfer the chicken to a platter and serve.

Getting bored with chicken, the old reliable? Try this flavorful sauté. The allspice contributes a Caribbean accent, but if you don't have any, just leave it out. This dish is mild enough for children, but if you want to spice it up, add a pinch or two of cayenne pepper in Step 1. If you have a strong companion in the kitchen whom you need to put to work, follow the example of our friend Ann Mendenhall: "My husband found that the best thing to use to pound the chicken was his fist," she said. She also found it easy to prepare the dish in an electric skillet set at 375°F.

This recipe comes from Karen Barker, pastry chef and co-proprietor with her husband, Ben, of the award-winning Magnolia Grill in Durham, North Carolina. Although these burritos are worthy of a spot on the Magnolia Grill menu, this is actually a meal Karen often cooks at home for her son.

Good-old barbecue sauce is the secret ingredient in Karen's ingenious recipe for a Tex-Mex–meets–North Carolina burrito. Your favorite brand of barbecue sauce will do, or try our own Fred's Red. If you like spicy food, add a minced jalapeño in Step 3. And feel free to garnish the burritos with sour cream, if desired. These burritos are true to form for a pastry chef—slightly sweet.

"BARBECUED" CHICKEN AND BLACK BEAN BURRITOS

SERVES: 4 START TO FINISH: UNDER 25 MINUTES

1 pound skinless, boneless chicken breast halves, fresh or frozen (see Note)

1 small onion (for about ½ cup chopped)

1 tablespoon vegetable oil

1 clove fresh garlic, minced, or 1 teaspoon bottled minced garlic

1 can (15 ounces) black beans, or 1 cup homemade (see page 368), defrosted if frozen

⅓ cup Fred's Red Barbecue Sauce (page 387) or purchased barbecue sauce

½ cup finely shredded Cheddar cheese, or more to taste

4 large (10- to 12-inch) flour tortillas

About ¼ cup regular or low-fat sour cream (optional)

1. If the chicken is frozen, run it under hot water so you can remove the packaging. Place the chicken on a microwave-safe plate and microwave, uncovered, on high power for 3 minutes to partially defrost.

2. Meanwhile, peel and dice the onion and set it aside.

3. Heat the oil in a 12-inch skillet over medium heat. While the oil is heating, cut the chicken (fresh or partially defrosted) into bite-size pieces, adding them to the pan as you cut. When all of the chicken has been added, cook, stirring occasionally, for 2 minutes.

4. Add the garlic and onion to the skillet. Continue cooking, stirring frequently, until the chicken is no longer pink in the center, 3 to 4 minutes more.

5. Meanwhile, rinse and drain the beans.

6. When the chicken is cooked through, add the beans and barbecue sauce to the skillet and stir well to coat the chicken with the sauce. Sprinkle the cheese evenly over the mixture and continue to cook, without stirring, until the cheese melts, 2 to 3 minutes.

7. Meanwhile, stack the tortillas on a microwave-safe plate and microwave until warm, following the package directions, 3 to 5 minutes.

8. To serve, spoon some of the chicken mixture onto the center of each tortilla and add a dollop of sour cream, if desired. Tuck in one end and roll up the tortillas burrito-style.

NOTE: You can use 2 cups Perfect Poached Chicken (page 362), Poached Chicken Thighs (page 364), or Great Grilled Chicken Breasts (page 360), defrosted if frozen. Add in Step 6. Or use 2 cups Chunky Seasoned Chicken (page 358), defrosted if frozen. Omit the onion, oil, and garlic. Begin the recipe at Step 5, adding the Chunky Seasoned Chicken with the beans and barbecue sauce in Step 6; cook until heated through.

MoneySaver

By law, products that are advertised at a sale price must be available or the store must give you a rain check. The only exception is when the advertisement states clearly that quantities are limited.

There's nothing like an old-fashioned camping trip to polish your kitchen survival skills. Cooking while camping always seems to require doing without something—whether it's a favorite knife or a forgotten ingredient. This can cause frustration when you're at home, but on a picnic table and over the open flame, it becomes an exhilarating challenge. When cooking on a budget starts to get old (and sometimes it does), it helps us to do an attitude shift into that camping state of mind. Okay, so we don't have all of the ingredients and maybe even the energy that we'd like, but what can we cook anyway?

One of our favorite flexible recipes for times like these—whether that flame is from the campfire or just the trusty kitchen stove—hails back to our Girl Scout days. Take a bit of meat, top it with whatever vegetables happen to be on hand, add a bit of sauce, and wrap the whole shebang in foil. We use onion, potato, and bell pepper here, but you could use sliced mushrooms, asparagus spears, tomato slices, or sliced carrots.

CAMPER'S CHICKEN POCKETS

SERVES: 4 START TO FINISH: UNDER 1 HOUR

1 pound skinless, boneless chicken breast halves,
    defrosted if frozen
1 small onion (for 4 slices)
½ large green bell pepper (for 12 strips; optional)
1 large white potato (for 24 thin slices)
¾ cup Fred's Red Barbecue Sauce (page 387) or purchased
    barbecue sauce, plus more for serving (optional)
Salt and black pepper to taste (optional)

1. Preheat the oven to 450°F.

2. Tear off 4 large (14-inch) squares of aluminum foil. Cut the chicken lengthwise into strips that are roughly ½ inch wide. Divide the chicken strips among the pieces of foil. Peel the onion and cut it into 4 slices about ¼ inch thick. Place 1 slice in each packet, separating it into rings.

3. If using the bell pepper, stem, seed, and cut it into 12 thin strips. Place 3 strips over the onion in each packet.

4. Rinse the potato but do not peel it. Cut the potato into very thin slices, about ¹⁄₁₆ inch wide. (If the slices are too thick, they won't cook in the short time needed for the chicken.) Place an equal number of slices (about 6) in each packet. Spoon 3 tablespoons of the barbecue sauce over each packet.

5. Fold the aluminum foil across the middle and roll up the ends to seal the packets tightly. Place them on a baking sheet and bake until the vegetables are soft and the chicken is no longer pink in the center, 20 to 25 minutes.

6. Serve at once, passing additional barbecue sauce at the table, if desired. Season with salt and pepper at the table, if desired.

OVEN-FRIED DRUMSTICKS

SERVES: 4 TO 6 PREP TIME: UNDER 15 MINUTES

Cooking oil spray

4 tablespoons (½ stick) butter

1 cup coating of choice:
  dry bread crumbs;
  fine cracker crumbs; crushed
  unsweetened flaked cereal; or
  ¾ cup dry bread crumbs mixed
  with ¼ cup grated Parmesan cheese (see Note)

8 chicken drumsticks (about 2 pounds), skinned if
  desired, defrosted completely if frozen

Salt and black pepper to taste

SUPER-CHEAP!

1. Preheat the oven to 350°F. Spray a 13- x 9-inch baking dish with cooking oil spray and set aside.

2. Place the butter in a shallow microwave-safe dish and cover it with a paper towel. Microwave on high power until completely melted, about 45 seconds to 1 minute. Set aside.

3. Prepare the coating of choice and place it in a shallow bowl. Set aside.

4. Rinse the drumsticks and dry them with paper towels. Roll the drumsticks, one at a time, in the melted butter and then in the coating. Place them in the prepared baking dish. Liberally season the drumsticks with salt and black pepper.

5. Bake, uncovered, until the meat is extremely tender and the coating is golden brown, about 1 hour. Remove from the oven and serve.

NOTE: Commercial bread crumbs are very fine and almost disappear on the drumstick. We prefer homemade dry bread crumbs (see page 235), not only because they're basically free, but also because their coarser texture stands up to the drumsticks.

From Alicia:

When Beverly and I talked about including a recipe for drumsticks in this chapter, the first thing that came to mind was my grandmother's southern-fried chicken drumsticks that I gobbled up every chance I got. But deep-fried foods are not the healthiest choice, and no matter what the food budget, you shouldn't compromise your family's health.

That's when we started talking about "oven-fried" drumsticks. After trying several different "moisture" mixtures for getting the coating to stick, I settled on butter. (You can use margarine if you prefer.) Just 4 tablespoons of butter for 8 drumsticks adds the touch of richness I remembered from the fried drumsticks, and the butter does a bang-up job of getting the coating to stick.

You can remove the skins from the drumsticks or not—that's up to you. The only difference is that those cooked with the skin will be a bit moister. But they're higher in fat, too.

Cutting up a Whole Cooked Chicken

We find using kitchen shears (or other sturdy utility scissors) to be the easiest way to cut a cooked chicken into 4 serving pieces. Here's how:

1. Place the chicken, breast side down, on a large cutting board or plate.

2. Starting at the tailbone, use kitchen shears to cut straight along both sides of the backbone to the neck. (The backbone is about an inch wide, and the connecting bones on either side of it are very thin.) Remove and set the backbone aside to flavor stock or soup (or discard it).

3. Turn the chicken over. Use the scissors to cut straight between both halves of the breast. The breast is held together mostly by cartilage, which is easy to cut. There is one bony spot, which you can cut around with the shears; or you can use a sharp knife to cut through the bone.

4. Next, separate the leg portion (thigh and drumstick together) from each breast half: Lift the drumstick away from the breast. It will be easy to spot where the skin lifts away from the meat between the thigh and the breast. While still lifting up on the drumstick, cut along that skin with the scissors, following the contour of the thigh. You will be cutting more or less in a semicircle, and as you cut, the thigh will just continue to lift away from the breast. (If you wish to serve the wings and drumsticks separately, use a sharp knife to cut them off at the joint. Likewise, you can now easily slice the breast meat if you prefer to serve it that way.)

5. If you are making gravy, add any juices released while cutting to the pan juices. (See page 107 for our Pan Gravy recipe.) Or pour the juices over the carved chicken.

Voilà! You're done.

Oven-Baked BBQ Chicken Thighs

SERVES: 4 PREP TIME: 10 MINUTES

Cooking oil spray
8 chicken thighs
 (about 2⅔ pounds total;
 see headnote)
½ cup all-purpose flour
1 cup Fred's Red Barbecue Sauce
 (page 387) or purchased barbecue
 sauce, plus more for serving (optional)

1. Preheat the oven to 350°F. Spray a 13- x 9-inch baking dish or casserole dish with cooking oil spray. Set aside.

2. Remove the skin from the chicken, if desired. Pour the flour into a large brown paper bag. Place half the chicken in the bag, fold the top over to close it, and shake to coat the chicken with flour. Remove the chicken pieces from the bag, shaking any excess flour back into the bag. Place the chicken in the prepared baking dish. Repeat with the remaining chicken.

3. Pour the barbecue sauce evenly over the chicken. (Not all of the chicken will be coated with sauce at this point.) Cover the pan with aluminum foil and bake for 1 hour.

4. Remove the pan from the oven and discard the foil. Spoon the pan juices over the chicken. Return the pan to the oven and bake, uncovered, basting with the pan juices every 15 minutes, until the chicken reaches 180°F on an instant-read meat thermometer, 40 to 45 minutes. (If you do not have a meat thermometer, cut into one of the pieces to test for doneness.)

5. Remove the chicken from the oven and serve, passing extra barbecue sauce at the table, if desired.

From Beverly:

How do you know you've landed in a real barbecue joint? For starters, you'll be in the South. Second, none of the furniture in the dining room matches, and the tines of your fork are most likely bent. Third, the menu is full of barbecued items—but it's all spelled BBQ. Finally, the food is cheap, and it's terrific!

When it comes to BBQ chicken, I like it the way I ate it growing up: in the small-town "joints" that were scattered all across eastern North Carolina in the days before drive-through fast food. That would be baked BBQ chicken with sweet barbecue sauce. I also happen to prefer the dark meat because it's so moist. The fact that thighs are usually the least expensive part of the chicken? That just makes my day! But, if you prefer, you can use all drumsticks. Simply use the quantity of drumsticks you want per person, and adjust the amount of barbecue sauce accordingly.

When my friend Susan Umstead told me about her family's favorite chicken dinner, I was a bit dubious. It sounded way too easy to be as fantastic as she promised. Then when I got the flu one winter, Susan appeared at my door bearing her signature chicken. My family couldn't stop raving. Indeed, this is one of those "less is more" recipes, and once you try it, you may never cook chicken any other way. The simple flavors of the chicken and vegetables yield pure, unadulterated bliss.

Whole chickens go on sale frequently in most markets, and it's easy to buy one for tonight and an extra one to freeze for later. Just thaw the chicken in the refrigerator for two days before cooking.

A CHICKEN IN EVERY POT

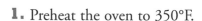

SERVES: 4 PREP TIME: UNDER 20 MINUTES

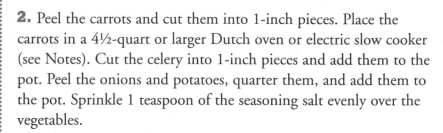

SUPER-CHEAP!

3 medium-size carrots
2 medium-size ribs celery
2 large onions
4 medium-size potatoes
2 teaspoons seasoning salt, such as Lawry's
1 whole chicken (about 3½ pounds), defrosted if frozen

1. Preheat the oven to 350°F.

2. Peel the carrots and cut them into 1-inch pieces. Place the carrots in a 4½-quart or larger Dutch oven or electric slow cooker (see Notes). Cut the celery into 1-inch pieces and add them to the pot. Peel the onions and potatoes, quarter them, and add them to the pot. Sprinkle 1 teaspoon of the seasoning salt evenly over the vegetables.

3. Remove the neck and any giblets that may be in the cavity of the chicken. (Reserve them for another use or discard them.) Rinse the chicken inside and out with cold tap water, removing and discarding any excess fat. Place the chicken, breast side up, in the pot on top of the vegetables. Rearrange the vegetables, if necessary, to make sure the pot lid closes tightly. Sprinkle the remaining 1 teaspoon seasoning salt evenly over the chicken. Pour ½ cup water into the pot alongside the chicken (taking care not to pour it over the chicken) and cover the pot.

4. Bake the chicken until an instant-read meat thermometer registers 180°F when inserted into a thigh (do not touch the bone), about 1½ hours.

5. Lift the chicken from the pot and place it, breast side down, on a large cutting board or serving platter. Use kitchen shears to cut through the chicken along both sides of the backbone. Remove and discard the backbone. Cut around each leg to separate it. Using a sharp knife, cut the breast in half down the middle. Arrange the 4 pieces of chicken on the platter. (See Notes.)

6. Using a slotted spoon, remove the vegetables from the pot or slow cooker and arrange them around the chicken. Spoon a little of the chicken broth over the platter and serve.

NOTES: Alternative cooking method: The chicken can be cooked in a slow cooker. Follow Steps 1 through 3 above, then cook in a covered slow cooker on low for 7 to 8 hours. The chicken is done when it registers 180°F on an instant-read meat thermometer in the thigh portion. Follow Step 5 above to serve.

■ The easiest way to serve the chicken is to cut it into 4 pieces. If you're serving children who eat drumsticks and nothing else, however, cut the drumsticks and thighs apart. Likewise, if the breast portions are large, cut them in half to make smaller servings.

Chew on This

Always wash your hands with soap after handling raw meat or poultry, and clean the sink and any affected surfaces well.

Even though there are almost as many ways to roast a chicken as there are cooks, it's so easy, any novice can do it. The lovely smells that will waft through your kitchen make everybody think you're slaving for sure.

Over the years we've tried out lots of ways to roast chicken, the major differences in them being (1) how high the heat should be, and therefore how long the bird should cook, (2) what should be placed inside the chicken cavity, and (3) what should be sprinkled on the skin.

We've come to favor the high-heat method and find that roasting at 450°F produces a golden brown bird that's still very moist. (Warning: If your oven is even a tiny bit dirty, you may have to temporarily disarm your smoke detector while the chicken is roasting. Definitely run the exhaust fan.)

As for the inside, a simple mix of lemon, garlic, onion, and fresh herbs, if you have any in the garden, does the trick to help flavor the chicken—and adds to that wonderful wafting aroma. We like a simple

BEST-EVER ROASTED CHICKEN

SERVES: 4 GENEROUSLY PREP TIME: UNDER 10 MINUTES

Cooking oil spray
1 whole chicken
    (about 3½ pounds),
    defrosted if frozen (see Notes)
¼ small onion
3 cloves fresh garlic
1 sprig fresh rosemary or fresh sage, or 1 teaspoon dried
    rosemary, dried sage, or poultry seasoning
½ lemon
1 tablespoon olive oil
Salt, preferably coarse, to taste
Black pepper to taste
Pan Gravy (recipe follows; optional)

1. Place an oven rack at the second-lowest position and preheat the oven to 450°F. Spray a chicken roasting rack and a roasting pan (bottom and sides) with cooking oil spray (see Notes). Set aside.

2. Remove the package of neck and giblets that may be in the cavity of the chicken. (Reserve them for another use or discard them.) Rinse the chicken inside and out with cold tap water, removing and discarding any excess fat. Pat the outside of the chicken dry with paper towels.

3. Place the onion quarter in the cavity of the chicken. Peel the garlic cloves and place them inside the cavity. Add the rosemary (if using dried, sprinkle it into the cavity). Squeeze the juice from the lemon half over the outside of the chicken and then place the lemon half inside the cavity. (You may have to cut the lemon into pieces to make it fit.) Place the chicken on the prepared roasting rack and place the rack inside the roasting pan. Rub the outside of the chicken with the oil and sprinkle it lightly with salt and black pepper.

4. Place the pan in the oven and roast until an instant-read meat thermometer registers 180°F when inserted in a thigh (don't touch the bone), 50 to 60 minutes.

5. Remove the chicken from the oven and let it stand for 10 minutes before cutting it into serving pieces. (See page 102 for cutting instructions.)

6. While the chicken is resting, make the pan gravy, if desired.

NOTES: Smaller chickens (no larger than 3½ pounds) roast more evenly and yield moister breast meat.

■ We prefer to use the type of roasting rack that holds the bird upright for even browning (see page 109 for details on roasting racks). If you don't have a vertical roasting rack, just lay the chicken, breast side down, in the roasting pan on a flat or V-shaped rack (sprayed with cooking oil spray). Turn the chicken over halfway through cooking.

PAN GRAVY

MAKES: ABOUT 1¼ CUPS START TO FINISH: UNDER 10 MINUTES

Pan drippings from 1 roasted chicken
3 tablespoons all-purpose flour
¼ cup cold water
1 cup fat-free chicken broth or
    homemade chicken stock
    (see page 10)
3 tablespoons Madeira, Marsala, Port,
    or sherry wine (optional)
Salt and black pepper, to taste

SUPER-CHEAP!

1. Pour the pan drippings into a 1-cup or larger glass measure. Let it stand until the clear grease separates from the darker juices. Discard all but about 3 tablespoons of the grease and pour the remaining drippings into an 8-inch or larger skillet. (Scrape any brown bits from the roasting pan into the skillet as well. Loosen them with a bit of boiling water if necessary.) Begin heating the

rub of olive oil, salt, and pepper to finish off the skin.

One especially handy tool is an inexpensive chicken roasting rack that allows the bird to cook standing up for even browning (see page 109 for information). You can make wonderful gravy from the pan drippings (see below).

Rich, homemade gravy is a wonderful bonus from roasting a chicken. You can serve the gravy alongside the chicken with rice or mashed potatoes, and any leftovers can be refrigerated for up to two days (reheat in the microwave oven, thinning gravy with a little chicken broth or water if it gets too thick). If you happen to have any, the wine adds a sophisticated touch.

drippings over medium heat. Meanwhile, put the flour and cold water in a small jar that has a lid, cover the jar, and shake until no lumps remain. Set aside.

2. Add the chicken broth and the wine (if using) to the drippings. Bring the mixture to a slow boil. Shake the flour mixture again and add a little at a time, stirring constantly, until the gravy is at the desired thickness. (You may not use all the flour mixture.) Season with salt and black pepper to taste.

HERB-ROASTED TURKEY BREAST

SERVES: 8 PREP TIME: 10 MINUTES

1 tablespoon all-purpose flour
1 large oven roasting bag, such as Reynolds Oven Bags (see Note)
1 turkey breast (6 to 6½ pounds), defrosted if frozen
1 tablespoon vegetable oil
2 teaspoons Italian seasoning blend
Salt and black pepper to taste
1 medium-size onion
4 cloves fresh garlic

1. Preheat the oven to 350°F.

2. Place the flour in the roasting bag, close it, and shake to coat the bag well. Place the bag in a 13- x 9-inch baking dish and fold the edge back to keep the bag open. Set the pan aside.

3. Remove any packaging from the turkey. Rinse the turkey breast inside and out and pat it dry with paper towels. Rub the oil all over the breast. Sprinkle the Italian seasoning and salt and black pepper over the skin. Place the breast, meaty side up, in the prepared roasting bag.

You don't have to wait until Thanksgiving to enjoy the delicious flavors of oven-roasted turkey. Look for turkey breasts on sale and pop them in the freezer. (Also check the freezer case, because they're often sold frozen.)

Cooking the turkey in an oven-roasting bag ensures a perfectly browned and moist breast every time—no more drier-than-dust turkey on our tables! If there are leftovers, you can store them in the refrigerator for up to two days (remove the skin first) or remove the meat from the bones and freeze it in zipper-top freezer bags for up to 2 months.

Beautifully Browned Chicken, the Easy Way

If you want to serve the most gorgeous roasted chicken ever (one that looks like it just came off a professional rotisserie), then you need to cook it so the heat hits the bird constantly and evenly from all sides. To accomplish this feat, you need a vertical chicken roasting rack or a plain beer can.

First, let's cover the rack: This handy piece of equipment is actually more stand than rack. It's composed of a wire cone-shaped dome that fits into the cavity of the chicken, allowing the bird to go into the oven in an upright position. The rack has a small metal pan underneath the wire that collects the pan juices during cooking. (We like to set the chicken and rack in a larger pan to make it easier to grab when taking the hot chicken out of the oven.)

Vertical roasting racks for chicken cost between $6 and $10, and they're available in kitchenware shops and most mart-type stores. We like to use the kind that allows the upper wires to disconnect from the pan for easier cleanup. If you use a vertical roasting rack, the oven rack must be at the lowest position in the oven so the chicken will fit in an upright position.

It is possible to accomplish this same cooking technique without using a purchased rack. Perhaps you've heard of beer-can chicken? This is a grilling method whereby a half-full can of beer (or soda) is inserted into the chicken cavity, causing the bird to stand upright during cooking. (To cook a chicken on a can in the oven, first make several openings around the top lid of the can and pour out half the liquid. Sit the chicken on the can and place it in a roasting pan. Make sure the legs are positioned to help balance the chicken. Place the oven rack at the lowest position in the oven so the chicken will fit.) During roasting, the liquid in the can bubbles up and "bastes" the interior of the bird for a moist result.

With a rack or a can, roasted chicken is a self-browning operation. No rotating required!

"You don't need to open the oven and rotate the chicken during roasting."

4. Peel and quarter the onion and place the pieces in the bag, around the turkey. Peel the garlic cloves and place them with the onion pieces. Seal the bag with the tie provided and cut six ½-inch slits in the top of the bag.

5. Bake the turkey until an instant-read meat thermometer registers 170°F when inserted in the thickest part of the breast (do not touch the bone), about 1½ hours (15 minutes per pound). Remove the turkey breast from the oven and let it stand in the bag for at least 10 minutes. (The internal temperature will rise to 180°F while the bird is standing.)

6. Carefully open the roasting bag and transfer the turkey to a platter. Discard the vegetables with the bag. Slice the breast and serve.

NOTE: We tested this recipe with large (up to 12 pounds) Reynolds Oven Bags. If you use another brand, check the instructions on the package. You may need to adjust the oven temperature or prepare the bag in a different way than we have described here.

From Beverly:

Salmon is my favorite fish, but it's often the most expensive option in the fish display at the supermarket. Even if I can't have my preferred variety, it's easy to create something delicious: I simply spice it up! One of my favorite fish toppers comes from my friend Herschel Freeman, who served this Mediterranean-inspired sauce over a whole red snapper at a dinner party.

CHEAP & ELEGANT

HERSCHEL'S SPANISH FISH

SERVES: 4 START TO FINISH: UNDER 20 MINUTES

2 tablespoons olive oil

1 pound thin fish fillets, such as tilapia or trout, defrosted if frozen

2 pinches black pepper

1 can (14½ ounces) diced tomatoes seasoned with onion and spices (see Notes)

½ cup (3 ounces) sliced or whole green olives

½ lemon

¼ cup dry white wine, such as Chardonnay (see Notes)

1. Heat the oil in an extra-deep 12-inch skillet over medium heat. Sprinkle the fish with the black pepper. Add the fish to the skillet and cook until it begins to brown on the first side, about 4 minutes. Turn the fillets over and cook until the fillets are lightly browned on the second side, 3 to 4 minutes; the fish should be opaque and should flake easily with a fork.

2. While the fish cooks, drain the tomatoes well and put them in a 2-quart bowl. Drain the olives; if they are whole, coarsely chop them. Add the olives to the bowl. Squeeze the juice from the lemon half through a strainer into the bowl. Stir well and set aside.

3. When the fish is done, transfer the fillets to a serving plate. Pour the wine into the skillet and stir to remove any brown bits from the bottom of the skillet. Cook for 2 minutes. Stir in the tomato-olive mixture and cook at a moderate boil until the sauce thickens slightly, 4 to 5 minutes.

4. To serve, place the fillets on individual plates and spoon the sauce over them.

NOTES: Canned tomatoes seasoned with garlic and other herbs such as oregano are widely available in most supermarkets. Any combination of flavorings will work here. If you don't have seasoned tomatoes, use plain diced tomatoes and add 1 teaspoon minced garlic and ¼ teaspoon dried oregano.

■ If you don't have any white wine, substitute chicken broth or water.

In fact, his tomato-olive combination is wonderful over whatever the supermarket is offering and lets you serve an impressive weeknight dinner without robbing the family piggy bank.

Eating Healthy on a Budget

From Beverly:

Long before the curative powers of food became a hot media topic, my mother was extolling the benefits of a high-quality diet: "You pay for your health one place or the other—at the grocery store or at the doctor's office. You choose."

The idea that some foods might cost a bit more but are worth it because of their health benefits is more widely discussed today than ever before. With the government's revamping of the food pyramid, new discoveries about the threats of obesity and diabetes, and conflicting advice from experts as to how much carbohydrates, fat, protein, and overall calories constitute a healthy diet, it's easy to throw up your hands in confusion. Add trying to control your food bills to the mix, and you've got a recipe for frustration.

But counting pennies while counting calories—and consuming the healthiest possible diet at the same time—isn't impossible. Here are some ideas:

- For starters, realize it's all about choices. If typical Americans counted up how much they are spending on junk food and then funneled those dollars into fresh fruits, olive oil, and vegetables instead, their overall grocery bills probably wouldn't rise a penny. Their health, however, would improve.

- Educate yourself. The media is constantly reporting the latest research on diet and health. Books and magazines on the topic abound. Just a little reading goes a long way in helping you focus on the diet/health issues that pertain to your particular situation. If reading doesn't help, talk with your health care provider.

- Use common sense. Never eat chicken skin, and if you have high cholesterol, stick with the breast meat and wings. Eat more fish, especially canned salmon (see page 290). Use olive oil whenever possible. Season vegetables with herbs and lemon juice instead of butter.

- Stock up on the more expensive healthier foods when they're on sale. Lean hamburger does go on sale periodically at most supermarkets, for example, and buying extra at a low price makes good use of your freezer space. Likewise, eat fresh fruits and vegetables in season to get the best prices.

- Practice portion control. It has become common knowledge that the super-sizing of portions in restaurants has been no help to America's waistline. As we grew accustomed to eating more in restaurants, we carried that habit home. According to the food pyramid, a portion of cooked meat is 2 to 3 ounces. That's not much! (The good news is that eating less meat is also easier on the budget.)

- Exercise. But wait, that's not about eating, is it?

- Avoid trans fats. Since these artery-hardening fats are found mostly in processed foods and in many commercially baked and fried foods, they're probably among the most unhealthy and most expensive food choices. Avoiding trans fats can lower your food budget and improve your health.

- Get more fiber. Research has shown that eating a diet rich in fiber helps reduce the risk of heart disease, stroke, high blood pressure, obesity, diabetes, and cancer. Vegetables, beans, and whole grains are the best sources of fiber. Replacing white bread with 100 percent whole wheat, white rice with brown, and instant oatmeal with old-fashioned rolled oats are easy and relatively inexpensive ways to boost the fiber in your diet.

- Limit sugar. It just isn't a body-friendly food. And cutting it out doesn't cost anything. Need we say more?

"Conflicting advice from experts as to what's healthy can cause confusion."

There's nothing easier than taking a simple piece of fish and broiling it. Adding a bit of onion and lemon juice makes for fish with lots of flavor. Although we often serve the fish plain, it's fun to dress things up a bit: Try topping the baked fish with any of our Quick Herb Butter Sauce (page 380), flavored mayonnaises (see pages 384 and 385), or Almost Rémoulade (page 386).

GOLDEN BROILED FILLETS

SERVES: 4 START TO FINISH: UNDER 15 MINUTES

1 tablespoon butter or margarine
2 teaspoons grated onion
Juice of ½ lemon
¼ teaspoon dried tarragon (optional)
Cooking oil spray
4 thin skinless, boneless fish fillets (about 6 ounces each), such as catfish, tilapia, or trout (see Note)
Salt and black pepper to taste
Paprika to taste

1. Place an oven rack about 4 inches from the broiler heating element and turn the broiler to high.

2. Put the butter in a 2-cup glass measure, cover with a paper towel, and microwave on high power until just melted, about 15 seconds. Stir in the onion, lemon juice, and tarragon (if using).

3. Line the inside of a broiler pan with aluminum foil. Spray the broiler pan rack with cooking oil spray. Place the fish fillets, skinned side down, on the broiler rack. Using a pastry brush, brush the tops of the fillets with the butter mixture, using about half of it. Sprinkle the fish lightly with salt, black pepper, and paprika.

4. Broil the fish for 4 minutes. Remove the pan from the oven and brush the fillets again with the remaining butter mixture (but do not turn them). Continue to broil until the fish is opaque and flakes easily with a fork, 2 to 3 minutes. Serve at once.

NOTE: If the only available fillets are large, cut 2 fillets in half to make 4 servings.

CATFISH WITH PECAN CRUST

SERVES: 4 START TO FINISH: UNDER 25 MINUTES

Cooking oil spray
¼ cup fine dry bread crumbs (see Notes)
2 teaspoons Cajun seafood seasoning,
  such as Paul Prudhomme's Seafood Magic
4 boneless skinned catfish fillets (about 6 ounces each),
  thawed if frozen (see Notes)
¼ cup pecan pieces
1 tablespoon butter
1 lemon, cut in half

1. Preheat the oven to 450°F. Spray a 13- x 9-inch baking dish with cooking oil spray and set it aside.

2. Put the bread crumbs and Cajun seasoning in a 1-gallon zipper-top plastic bag and shake well to combine. Add the fish fillets to the bag and shake vigorously until they are coated with the crumb mixture. Place the fillets in the prepared baking dish.

3. Use a chef's knife to finely chop the pecans. Use your fingertips to lightly press the chopped pecans onto the top side of the fish fillets.

4. Place the butter in a microwave-safe dish, cover it with a paper towel, and microwave on high power until melted, about 30 seconds. Meanwhile, squeeze the juice from the lemon halves through a strainer over the fish. Spoon the melted butter evenly over the fillets.

5. Bake, uncovered, until the fish is opaque throughout and flakes easily with a fork, 12 to 14 minutes. Serve at once.

NOTES: For tips on making your own bread crumbs, see page 235. ■ Any thin white fish fillets, such as tilapia, flounder, or trout, can be used in place of the catfish.

From Beverly:

When I was a new bride, I wanted to make a meal that would utterly astound my husband. I had received a Cajun cookbook as a wedding present, and there it was, a picture-perfect fillet of fish swimming in not one but two delicate butter sauces and studded with toasted pecans.

While my husband's taste buds were indeed spinning, I was the one in a near coma after an entire day sweating in the kitchen over that darn fish.

So, when Alicia told me about an incredible entrée she'd eaten, "Nut-Encrusted Fish," I thought, "Oh no. Here we go again."

Alicia convinced me that our recipe would be different. No fancy sauces, just a quick spice blend and a drizzle of butter. But what about the pecans?

"We will have to chop the pecans," she said. "But how long can it take?"

I'm here to report that this time, I was the one celebrating after the first bite of our 25-minute catfish. I only wish I had known back then just how easy Cajun fish could be.

CHAPTER THREE

SUMPTUOUS SKILLET MEALS

"Short on time? Short on cash? Grab your skillet."

It's almost like magic. All you need is a little meat and a few vegetables (and sometimes only veggies), a starch (usually rice), and a bit of seasoning. A quick sizzle on the stovetop, and dinner is done.

Not only is it quick and flavorful, but it is economical too: By their very nature, skillet meals are meat-stretchers.

Another boon to the budget: Because the entrée is filling and balanced, there's really no need to serve anything else. We'll often dish up a skillet meal, add some crusty bread, and head straight for the table. If we're feeling extravagant, we might serve a simple side salad or some sliced fruit. However, with the hearty recipes in this chapter, nobody seems to mind if dinner is a one-dish affair.

Skillet meals may be economical, but you're the only one who needs to know that. Recipes like Chicken and Apples with Dijon Cream and Orange Marmalade–Glazed Chicken over Rice are fancy enough to serve for company. You'll find recipes, like Island Chicken and Moroccan Meatballs over Couscous, that run slightly toward the exotic, and our favorite Cajun-inspired recipes, such as Fisherman's Seafood Creole. We've even adapted some of the comfort foods from our childhood to the skillet—Chicken and Green Bean "Casserole" leads the way. Craving Chinese food? Our Mu-shu Pork at Home, Grown-up Sweet and Sour Chicken, and Confetti Fried Rice will satisfy your desire for Asian food at a fraction of restaurant prices.

The next time you're short on time and short on cash, grab your skillet. Pull these recipes out of your top hat, and dinner is indeed just like magic.

Dinner Insurance: How Hamburger Can Save the Day

A pound of ground beef in the freezer is like an insurance policy for dinner. Even if it's frozen solid, you can walk in from work and transform this safety net into dinner in no time. There are just a few simple guidelines:

1. Buy what's on sale. If your ground beef is already in 1-pound packages, great. Otherwise, divide the meat into 1-pound sections and flatten them out. Do not leave the meat in big hunks, as this prevents quick defrosting. (A kitchen scale helps with this. For more information on scales, see page 212.)

2. Wrap each portion of meat in plastic wrap, pop them into freezer-weight plastic bags, and label and date them. Or wrap them in plastic wrap and then in a layer of aluminum foil, and use freezer tape to label the contents. (The plastic wrap keeps out the air and prevents freezer burn.)

3. Always wash your hands well after handling raw meat. Spray any surfaces the raw meat has touched with antibacterial spray.

4. When it's time to cook, run the frozen beef under hot tap water to make it easier to remove the packaging.

5. A quick zap in the microwave, about 3 minutes, defrosts the meat just enough so that it will brown quickly in a skillet. (As it cooks, scrape the browned meat from the block and turn it over frequently to speed the process.)

Now you're ready for a host of skillet meals. The easiest quick meals are skillet dinners with the vegetables and starch included. Try Salsa-Cheese Beef and Rice (page 124), Cinco de Mayo Skillet (page 126), Shipwreck Skillet Dinner (page 129), and Beefy Asian Rice (page 130).

LYNNE'S MOM'S MINCE

SERVES: 4 START TO FINISH: UNDER 25 MINUTES

Salt for cooking the rice
1⅓ cups long-grain rice
1 pound ground beef, fresh or frozen (see Note)
1 tablespoon vegetable oil
1 large onion (for about 1 cup chopped)
1 clove fresh garlic, minced, or 1 teaspoon bottled
   minced garlic
1 tablespoon Worcestershire sauce
1 envelope (about 1 ounce) brown gravy mix

1. Bring 2⅔ cups lightly salted water to a boil in a covered medium-size saucepan. Add the rice, stir, and reduce the heat to low. Cover the pan and simmer until the rice is tender, about 20 minutes.

2. Meanwhile, if the beef is frozen, run it under hot water so you can remove the packaging. Place the beef on a microwave-safe plate and microwave, uncovered, on high power for 3 minutes to partially defrost.

3. While the ground beef defrosts, heat the oil in a 12-inch skillet over medium heat. Peel and coarsely chop the onion, adding it to the skillet as you chop. Cook until the onion begins to soften, about 2 minutes. Add the garlic to the skillet.

4. Add the ground beef (fresh or partially defrosted) and cook, stirring often, until the meat is crumbled and cooked through, 7 to 8 minutes more. Stir in the Worcestershire sauce.

5. While the beef cooks, pour the gravy mix into a 2-cup or larger glass measure. Add the amount of water called for on the package and whisk well. Set aside.

6. When the beef has cooked, add the gravy mixture to the skillet and stir well. When the mixture starts to boil, reduce the heat to low and simmer, stirring occasionally, for about 5 minutes, or until ready to serve. To serve, spoon about ¾ cup over each serving of hot rice.

From Alicia:

My kids have a new most-favorite comfort dinner thanks to Lynne Soltis, a reader of our Desperation Dinners newspaper column.

"We had three daughters in four years, and I was a working mom," Lynne wrote. "Thirty years ago it was hard to find recipes that kids and spouses both liked and didn't take too long to prepare."

Lynne's mom, originally from Scotland, came to her rescue with a homey, budget-minded ground beef dish she called Mince. Over the years, Lynn streamlined her mom's recipe, using extra-lean ground beef and packaged gravy mix. (Don't feel you have to choose an expensive gravy mix—the cheapest store brand works great. A little garlic and Worcestershire sauce are the perfect fix-up.) For additional flexibility, Basic Beef can also be used.

Lynne always served her mince over mashed potatoes with a vegetable, such as frozen peas. We love that combination too, but

(continued)

119

(continued)

have branched out to serve mince over rice, baked potatoes, and even egg noodles. Just about any simple vegetable will round out your menu.

This dish is sweet enough to please children, but also appeals to adults, with the fresh taste of ginger and the tart hint from the vinegar. It's yet another wonderful way to use homemade meatballs, or you could substitute the frozen kind from the supermarket. Combined with vegetables and sauce, and served over rice, a few meatballs go a long way.

NOTE: You can use 3 cups Basic Beef (page 347), defrosted if frozen. Omit the oil, onion, garlic, and 2 teaspoons of the Worcestershire sauce. Add the Basic Beef with the remaining 1 teaspoon Worcestershire sauce in Step 4 and cook until the beef is heated through. Then proceed with the recipe.

HAWAIIAN MEATBALLS

SERVES: 4 START TO FINISH: UNDER 25 MINUTES

Salt for cooking the rice
1⅓ cups long-grain rice
2 bunches scallions (for about 1 cup pieces)
2 teaspoons vegetable oil
2 medium-size carrots (for about 1 cup sliced)
24 already-cooked meatballs (see Notes), defrosted if frozen
1 cup fat-free chicken broth or homemade chicken stock (see page 10)
1 can (20 ounces) pineapple chunks packed in heavy syrup (see Notes)
2 tablespoons red wine vinegar or cider vinegar
2 tablespoons regular or reduced-sodium soy sauce
1 tablespoon finely minced fresh ginger or bottled minced ginger
2 cloves fresh garlic, minced, or 2 teaspoons bottled minced garlic
2 tablespoons cornstarch
3 tablespoons cold water

1. Bring 2⅔ cups lightly salted water to a boil in a covered medium-size saucepan. Add the rice, stir, and reduce the heat to low. Cover the pan and simmer until the rice is tender, about 20 minutes.

2. Meanwhile, cut the scallions into pieces about 1 inch long, including enough tender green tops to make 1 cup. Set aside.

3. Heat the oil in an extra-deep 12-inch skillet over medium heat. Peel the carrots and cut them into ¼-inch slices, adding them to the skillet as you cut. Add the meatballs to the skillet. Cook, stirring frequently, until the carrots are almost tender and the meatballs begin to heat through, about 3 minutes.

4. Add the scallions, broth, pineapple chunks with their syrup, vinegar, soy sauce, ginger, and garlic to the skillet. Raise the heat to medium-high and bring the mixture to a boil.

5. Combine the cornstarch with the cold water in a small jar that has a lid. Cover and shake until the lumps dissolve. Add the cornstarch mixture to the skillet. Cook, stirring, until thick and bubbly, 1 to 2 minutes. Remove the skillet from the heat and serve at once over the hot rice.

NOTES: You can use Marvelous Meatballs (page 353) or purchased frozen meatballs (plain or traditional style).

■ We don't recommend pineapple packed in its own juice for this recipe—it isn't sweet enough.

Chew on This

According to the market research firm NPD Group, when Americans eat beef at home, the dish contains ground beef 60 percent of the time.

Easy Couscous

A staple of North Africa, couscous (rhymes with goose-goose) is ground semolina—the wheat that is used for good-quality pasta. Light and fluffy when cooked, it has a slightly nutty flavor. The couscous we usually find in this country is pre-cooked and is sometimes referred to as "quick-cooking" in recipes and on packaging.

Look for couscous displayed next to the rice (one widely available brand is Near East) or in the international foods section. Sometimes you'll find it in bulk bins at supermarkets, specialty markets, and health food stores. Flavored couscous is sold with foil seasoning pouches in the boxes. The plain variety in bulk is usually the cheapest way to go.

The exact cooking instructions and the amount of water needed for couscous can vary from one brand to another. We've noticed that the cooked yield can vary slightly as well, but in general, ⅓ cup of dry couscous makes between ¾ cup and 1 cup prepared. If you buy couscous in bulk, check the bin for the cooking instructions. (If you don't see them, ask a manager.) Don't fret if you can't get an exact water-to-couscous ratio, as couscous is forgiving and very easy to cook.

A basic cooking method to make four servings calls for combining 1¼ cups of couscous and 1 teaspoon of vegetable oil with 1½ cups of boiling water or broth. After stirring in the couscous, remove the pot from the heat, cover the pot, and let it stand until all of the water is absorbed, 5 to 8 minutes. Fluff the couscous with a fork before serving.

"*Light, fluffy, and nutty flavored.*"

MOROCCAN MEATBALLS OVER COUSCOUS

SERVES: 6 START TO FINISH: UNDER 25 MINUTES

3 teaspoons vegetable oil

1⅔ cups (10 ounces) plain couscous

36 already-cooked meatballs, fresh or frozen (see Notes)

2 large onions (for about 2 cups chopped)

1 large can (28 ounces) diced tomatoes

2 cloves fresh garlic, minced, or 2 teaspoons bottled minced garlic

1½ teaspoons sugar

1 fresh jalapeño pepper (for 2 tablespoons minced)

3 tablespoons chopped fresh cilantro (optional)

3 tablespoons chopped fresh parsley (optional)

½ teaspoon ground cumin

½ teaspoon ground cinnamon

¼ teaspoon ground (dried) ginger

1. Bring 2 cups water and 1 teaspoon of the vegetable oil to a boil in a covered medium-size saucepan. When the water boils, remove the pan from the heat and stir in the couscous. Cover the pan and let it stand until the meatballs are ready to serve. Just before serving, fluff the couscous lightly with a fork.

2. If the meatballs are frozen, run them under hot water so you can remove the packaging. Place the meatballs on a microwave-safe plate and microwave, uncovered, on high power for 2 minutes to partially defrost.

3. Meanwhile, heat the remaining 2 teaspoons oil in a 12-inch skillet over medium heat (or use a 4½-quart soup pot). Peel and coarsely chop the onions, adding them to the skillet as you chop. Cook, stirring, until the onions begin to soften, about 3 minutes.

4. Add the tomatoes and their juice. Add the garlic and sugar to the skillet.

One of our goals is to find recipes that are interesting for adults but not too weird for kids. This recipe fits that category. Yes, it does sound exotic—and indeed it is full of flavor. But this is still just meatballs, and aren't meatballs one of the most kid-friendly foods around? That's what we thought, but we wanted to be sure. So we asked our friend Elizabeth Voiers to test the recipe with her two children, ages nine and five. Moroccan Meatballs scored a "big thumbs-up" from both.

If you know your kids won't eat spicy food, hold off on the jalapeño until after you serve their portions.

We've made the fresh parsley and cilantro optional, but we do encourage you to try the dish with the fresh herbs. They can be expensive, but the leftovers needn't go to waste: Chopped cilantro adds pizzazz to purchased salsas, and sprinkled into salads. Parsley can dress up sauces, soups, and stews. Add a tablespoon here and

(continued)

(continued)

there, and before you know it, you've used the whole bunch. (To keep the herbs fresh, shake off any excess water, wrap the whole bunch in a paper towel, and place in a zipper-top bag. Refrigerated, the bunch will keep for over a week.)

We love the meatballs served over couscous for its authentic texture and taste, but the meatballs are also good over steamed rice.

Our friend Debi Williams describes this skillet meal as the perfect hearty fall or winter dinner. When she first cooked up this dish, her husband walked straight through the front door and into the kitchen to see what smelled so heavenly.

The salsa-cheese sauce is available at the supermarket, but if this becomes a favorite at your house, you can save money by picking up a three-pack at a warehouse club store. Even at the regular price, this dish costs only about $1 per serving.

5. Seed and finely chop the jalapeño (see Notes). Add it to the sauce. Cook, stirring occasionally, while you rinse and chop the cilantro and parsley (if using). Add them to the skillet. Then add the cumin, cinnamon, ginger, and meatballs (fresh or partially defrosted). Cover the skillet and cook until the meatballs are heated through and are beginning to absorb the sauce, about 10 minutes. Serve immediately over the hot couscous.

NOTES: You can use Marvelous Meatballs (page 353) or purchased frozen meatballs (plain or traditional style).

■ Wear rubber gloves when mincing the jalapeño, or else wash your hands thoroughly afterward, and do not touch your eyes for at least 24 hours.

SALSA-CHEESE BEEF AND RICE

SERVES: 6 START TO FINISH: UNDER 25 MINUTES

Salt for cooking the rice
1 cup long-grain rice
1 pound ground beef, fresh or frozen (see Notes)
1 tablespoon vegetable oil
1 large onion (for about 1 cup chopped)
1 medium-size green, red, or yellow bell pepper (for about 1 cup chopped)
2 cloves fresh garlic, minced, or 2 teaspoons bottled minced garlic
2 cups frozen yellow corn kernels
1 can (15 ounces) diced tomatoes
1 jar (15 ounces) salsa-cheese sauce (see Notes)

1. Bring 2 cups lightly salted water to a boil in a covered medium-size saucepan. Add the rice, stir, and reduce the heat to low. Cover the pan and simmer until the rice is tender, about 20 minutes.

2. If the beef is frozen, run it under hot water so you can remove the packaging. Place the beef on a microwave-safe plate and microwave, uncovered, on high power for 3 minutes to partially defrost.

3. Meanwhile, heat the oil in an extra-deep 12-inch skillet over medium heat. Peel and coarsely chop the onion, adding it to the skillet as you chop.

4. Add the beef (fresh or partially defrosted) to the skillet and cook, turning and breaking up the meat occasionally, while you stem, seed, and coarsely chop the bell pepper. Add it to the skillet as you chop. Then add the garlic. Continue to cook, stirring frequently, until the meat is crumbled and browned, 7 to 8 minutes in all.

5. Drain any accumulated fat from the beef, if necessary. Add the corn and the tomatoes with their juice to the skillet. Stir to mix well. Reduce the heat to low and simmer the beef mixture for about 5 minutes (until the rice is done).

6. Add the cooked rice and the salsa-cheese sauce to the skillet and stir well. Cook until heated through completely, about 2 minutes. Serve at once.

NOTES: You can use 3 cups Basic Beef (page 347), defrosted if frozen. Add it before the bell pepper in Step 4.

■ Salsa-cheese sauce is sold under several different brands, such as Pace and Old El Paso, in the Mexican food section or near the chips. It comes in "mild," "medium," and "hot" versions. Any variety will work in this recipe—choose the spice level that suits your preference.

Debi serves this skillet dish with a loaf of warm garlic bread, to a chorus of "Yum!" all around the table. It serves six generously, and any leftovers will warm beautifully in the microwave oven.

CINCO DE MAYO SKILLET

SERVES: 6 START TO FINISH: UNDER 25 MINUTES

Our friends Tony and Elizabeth Voiers tried this recipe and reported that it was a great weekday family dinner. They liked the fact that it's easy to have the ingredients on hand. It seems beef, sour cream, cheese, and canned tomatoes are always on sale somewhere in town, so it's easy to stock up at good prices. Elizabeth used frozen beef she'd purchased on sale the week before. The only item she had to add to her weekly grocery list was the fresh lime—which is worth it, because the juice makes the tomato sauce distinct and lively.

Because they wanted a bit of crunch with their meal, the Voierses served tortilla chips alongside. The adults added a few pickled jalapeños as a garnish, while the kids ate their skillet dinner plain.

Salt for cooking the rice
1 cup long-grain rice
1 pound ground beef, fresh or frozen (see Note)
1 tablespoon vegetable oil
1 large onion (for about 1 cup chopped)
2 cloves fresh garlic
2 cans (14 ounces each) Mexican-style stewed tomatoes
Juice of 1 lime
1 can (15 ounces) black beans, or 1 cup homemade (see page 368), defrosted if frozen
1 large ripe tomato (for about 2 cups diced)
1 small head iceberg lettuce (for about 3 cups shredded)
¾ cup shredded Mexican-blend or Cheddar cheese
Sour cream, for serving (optional)

1. Bring 2 cups lightly salted water to a boil in a covered medium-size saucepan. Add the rice, stir, and reduce the heat to low. Cover the pan and simmer until the rice is tender, about 20 minutes.

2. If the beef is frozen, run it under hot water so you can remove the packaging. Place the beef on a microwave-safe plate and microwave, uncovered, on high power for 3 minutes to partially defrost.

3. Heat the oil in an extra-deep 12-inch skillet over medium heat. Peel and coarsely chop the onion, adding it to the skillet as you chop.

4. Add the beef (fresh or partially defrosted) to the skillet and cook, turning and breaking up the meat, until it is crumbled and brown, 7 to 8 minutes.

5. While the beef cooks, make a Mexican tomato sauce: Peel the garlic cloves. Turn a blender to high and drop the garlic cloves through the hole in the lid. Process until finely chopped. Turn off the motor and add the tomatoes with their juice and the lime juice. Cover and pulse to finely chop the tomatoes. Set aside.

6. When the beef is cooked through, reduce the heat to low. Drain any accumulated fat from the skillet, if necessary. Rinse and drain the beans and add them to the skillet. Add about half of the tomato sauce, stir well, and simmer for about 10 minutes (until the rice is done). Meanwhile, core and dice the tomato, and set it aside. Shred the lettuce and set it aside.

7. Add the cooked rice to the skillet and stir well. For each serving, top 1 cup of the beef mixture with 2 tablespoons of the cheese, ½ cup of the shredded lettuce, ⅓ cup of the diced tomato, 3 tablespoons of the reserved tomato sauce (or more to taste), and sour cream to taste, if desired.

NOTE: You can use 3 cups Basic Beef (page 347), defrosted if frozen. Prepare the Mexican tomato sauce in Step 5 and add the beef to it before adding the beans in Step 6. Stir and cook until the beef is heated through, 3 minutes. Proceed with the recipe.

About:
THE BREAD RUT

Back when we first started writing our Desperation Dinners newspaper column, our readers asked us to suggest menus to go with our recipes. We started to notice a pattern: Nearly every Desperate entrée cried out for bread to serve alongside it. But even with rolls, it's easy to fall into a rut. Supermarket shelves abound with rolls, croissants, frozen biscuits, refrigerated dough, and more, but sometimes we find ourselves repeating the same-old, same-old without really meaning to. It's a shame to ignore the potential for thrifty side dishes to bring our meals out of the doldrums. Especially when the main dish has vegetables built in, all you really need to round out the meal is some interesting bread. Here are three suggestions: Flexible Cheese Crescents, Quesadilla Roll-Ups, and Parmesan English Muffins (pages 308 and 309).

Draining Ground Beef

When you cook ground beef, you will probably need to drain the excess fat from the skillet before finishing the dish. This is not a huge chore, but there is a way to do it correctly, to avoid clogging the drain with congealed grease.

1. Line a pie plate or other shallow dish with paper towels (used ones, even if they are damp, are fine).

2. Set a colander over the paper towels in the dish.

3. Slowly and carefully pour the ground beef into the colander. The fat will drain onto the paper towels.

4. Return the beef to the skillet and continue with the recipe. Set the pie plate aside until the fat solidifies on the paper towel.

5. Throw away the paper towels, and the fat goes with them. Give the pie plate a quick wash, and you're done.

SHIPWRECK SKILLET DINNER

SERVES: 4 START TO FINISH: UNDER 25 MINUTES

1 can (14 ounces) fat-free
   beef broth
1 cup long-grain rice
1 pound ground beef, fresh
   or frozen (see Note)
1 tablespoon vegetable oil
1 large onion (for about 1 cup chopped)
1 clove fresh garlic, minced,
   or 1 teaspoon bottled minced garlic
1 tablespoon Worcestershire sauce
½ teaspoon seasoning salt, such as Lawry's,
   or plain salt
1 medium-size green bell pepper
   (for about 1 cup chopped)
1 cup frozen yellow corn kernels
Black pepper to taste

1. Pour the broth and ¼ cup water into a covered medium-size saucepan and bring to a boil. Add the rice, stir, and reduce the heat to low. Cover the pan and simmer until the rice is tender, about 20 minutes.

2. Meanwhile, if the beef is frozen, run it under hot water so you can remove the packaging. Place the beef on a microwave-safe plate and microwave, uncovered, on high power for 3 minutes to partially defrost.

3. Heat the oil in an extra-deep 12-inch skillet over medium heat. Peel and coarsely chop the onion, adding it to the skillet as you chop.

4. Add the beef (fresh or partially defrosted) to the skillet and cook, turning and breaking up the meat, until the beef is crumbled and browned, 7 to 8 minutes.

A reader of our Desperation Dinners newspaper column shared this inventive skillet meal with us several years ago. She and her husband had created it one evening from bits and pieces they found in the refrigerator and freezer. She said that at first she had felt "shipwrecked" with such limited supplies, but feasted instead on this simple yet satisfying—and truly inexpensive—beefy skillet dinner. You can vary the vegetables according to your own preference or what you may have on hand: Half a cup of frozen green peas can be substituted for the green pepper, or you could use a frozen vegetable medley. Mushrooms can be thrown in, too.

5. While the meat cooks, add the garlic to the skillet. Add the Worcestershire sauce and seasoning salt. Stem, seed, and cut the bell pepper into bite-size pieces, adding them to the skillet as you chop. Add the corn and stir well.

6. Continue to cook until the green pepper is tender, about 2 minutes more. Remove the skillet from the heat and set it aside until the rice is done, if necessary.

7. Stir the rice into the beef mixture and season with black pepper. Serve at once.

NOTE: You can use 3 cups Basic Beef (page 347), defrosted if frozen. Omit the oil, onion, garlic, and Worcestershire sauce. Add the Basic Beef with the corn in Step 5. Cook, stirring, until the beef is heated through, 3 minutes. Proceed with the recipe.

"Beefed-up" rice adds tons of flavor to this quick-and-easy skillet dish. Stretching the most expensive item is one of the quickest ways to add up savings. In this case, it's the beef. No one will ever know you used only 1 pound of beef to feed six in this hearty dinner. Leftovers will warm up beautifully in the microwave.

BEEFY ASIAN RICE

SERVES: 6 START TO FINISH: UNDER 25 MINUTES

2 cans (14 ounces each) fat-free beef broth

1 cup long-grain rice

1 pound ground beef, fresh or frozen (see Note)

1 tablespoon vegetable oil

1 large onion (for about 1 cup chopped)

2 carrots (for about 1 cup sliced)

8 ounces fresh button mushrooms

5 cloves fresh garlic, minced, or 1½ tablespoons bottled minced garlic

¼ cup regular or reduced-sodium soy sauce, plus more for serving (optional)

2 tablespoons ketchup

2 tablespoons rice vinegar or distilled white vinegar

1 tablespoon finely minced fresh ginger or bottled minced ginger

½ cup frozen green peas (optional)

2 teaspoons Asian (dark) sesame oil

1. Pour the broth into a covered medium-size saucepan and bring it to a boil. Add the rice, stir, and reduce the heat to low. Cover the pan and simmer until the rice is tender, about 20 minutes. (Don't worry if the rice is very moist.)

2. Meanwhile, if the beef is frozen, run it under hot water so you can remove the packaging. Place the beef on a microwave-safe plate and microwave, uncovered, on high power for 3 minutes to partially defrost.

3. While the beef defrosts, heat the oil in an extra-deep 12-inch skillet over medium heat. Peel and coarsely chop the onion, adding it to the skillet as you chop. Peel the carrots and, holding the knife at a 45-degree angle, cut them into ½-inch-thick slices. Add the carrots to the skillet.

4. Rinse, pat dry, and coarsely chop the mushrooms, removing any tough stems and adding the mushrooms to the skillet as you chop. Add the beef (fresh or partially defrosted) to the skillet and cook, turning and breaking up the meat, until it is crumbled and browned, 7 to 8 minutes. Drain any accumulated fat from the beef, if necessary.

5. Add the garlic to the skillet, along with the soy sauce, ketchup, vinegar, and ginger. Stir well and reduce the heat to low. Add the peas (if using) and sesame oil and stir. Add the cooked rice to the skillet and stir until it is thoroughly combined. Serve at once, passing additional soy sauce at the table, if desired.

NOTE: You can use 3 cups Basic Beef (page 347), defrosted if frozen. Add it with the soy sauce and ketchup in Step 5 and cook, stirring, over medium heat, until the beef is heated through, about 3 minutes. Proceed with the recipe.

MoneySaver

Make sure your Asian (dark) sesame oil stays fresh to the very last drop by storing it in the refrigerator. If kept refrigerated, a bottle will stay fresh for up to 1 year.

Since hash is the quintessential economy comfort food, it's no surprise that many cultures have put their own stamp on this budget-stretcher. Along Calle Ocho, Little Havana's main street in Miami, you'd most likely find a more classic version of this Cuban dish, called picadillo and made with ground beef and served over rice. We've devised a similar hash to make use of leftover Savory Pork Pot Roast. The potatoes add heft, and the exotic result is hearty enough to make dinner all on its own, with no side dishes required.

If you find you are making this hash on a regular basis, here's a time-saving hint: Cook three extra potatoes along with the Savory Pork Pot Roast, and save them to use for the hash. It won't change the pot roast recipe, and the flavorful potatoes will add even more depth.

CALLE OCHO CUBAN HASH

SERVES: 4   START TO FINISH: UNDER 25 MINUTES

Salt for cooking the rice
1 cup long-grain rice
2 teaspoons vegetable oil
1 large onion (for about 1 cup chopped)
2 cloves fresh garlic, minced, or 2 teaspoons bottled minced garlic
2 cups diced cooked potatoes (see Note)
1 teaspoon ground cumin
½ teaspoon black pepper
¼ teaspoon ground cinnamon
⅛ teaspoon ground cloves (optional)
2 cans (14½ ounces each) diced tomatoes seasoned with mild green chiles
⅓ cup sliced pimiento-stuffed green olives, drained
1¼ cups cubed Savory Pork Pot Roast (page 356), defrosted if frozen
⅓ cup raisins

1. Bring 2 cups lightly salted water to a boil in a covered medium-size saucepan. Add the rice, stir, and reduce the heat to low. Cover the pan and simmer until the rice is just tender, about 20 minutes.

2. Meanwhile, heat the oil in an extra-deep 12-inch skillet over medium heat. Peel and coarsely chop the onion, adding it to the skillet as you chop. Add the garlic to the skillet. Cook, stirring occasionally, until the onion begins to soften, about 1 minute. If using refrigerated diced potatoes, add them now. Add the cumin, black pepper, cinnamon, and cloves (if using). Cook, stirring often, until the potatoes are tender, 5 to 6 minutes. (If using home-cooked potatoes, add them with the pork in Step 3.)

3. Add the tomatoes with their juices, along with ⅓ cup water. Add the olives and stir well. Add the pork and raisins. If using home-cooked potatoes, add them now. Cook, stirring frequently (gently so the potatoes don't fall apart), just until the mixture is heated through, 2 to 3 minutes. Remove the skillet from the heat, cover, and set aside until the rice is done. Add the cooked rice to the skillet and stir until it is thoroughly mixed into the dish. Serve at once.

NOTE: For the potatoes, you can boil 1 pound of diced peeled raw potatoes until tender, about 10 minutes. Drain well and proceed with the recipe. Or use peeled and diced Amazing Baked Potatoes (page 366). Or 1 package (1 pound, 4 ounces) refrigerated diced potatoes with onion, such as Simply Potatoes.

SAVORY PORK WITH MEXICAN FLAVORS

SERVES: 4 START TO FINISH: UNDER 25 MINUTES

Salt for cooking the rice
⅔ cup long-grain rice
1 cup frozen yellow or white corn kernels
1 can (15 ounces) black beans, or 1 cup homemade
    (see page 368), defrosted if frozen
2 teaspoons vegetable oil
1 medium-size green or red bell pepper
    (for about 1 cup chopped)
2 cloves fresh garlic, minced, or 2 teaspoons bottled
    minced garlic
1 teaspoon ground cumin (optional)
1 teaspoon chili powder
1 can (14½ ounces) diced tomatoes seasoned with
    jalapeños or with mild green chiles
¾ to 1¼ cups cubed Savory Pork Pot Roast (page 356)
1 cup finely shredded Cheddar or Mexican-blend cheese
½ cup regular or reduced-fat sour cream

From Beverly:

If you cook our Savory Pork Pot Roast, one of the big advantages is that you're bound to have some meat left over. Mixing the pork with beans and rice and some Mexican spices transforms those leftovers into an entirely new meal.

1. Bring 1⅓ cups lightly salted water to a boil in a covered medium-size saucepan. Add the rice, stir, and reduce the heat to low. Cover the pan and simmer until the rice is just tender, about 20 minutes.

2. Meanwhile, place the corn in a colander and rinse it under warm water for 30 seconds to partially defrost it. Pour the beans in with the corn and rinse them. Set aside to drain.

3. Heat the oil in an extra-deep 12-inch skillet over medium heat. Stem, seed, and coarsely chop the bell pepper. Add the pieces to the skillet. Stir in the garlic, along with the cumin (if using) and chili powder.

4. Add the tomatoes with their juices, the drained corn, and the black beans. Then add the pork and stir to mix well. Cover the skillet and cook, stirring occasionally, until heated through, about 3 minutes.

5. Remove the skillet from the heat. Add the cooked rice, cheese, and sour cream and stir until well combined. Serve at once.

"TWICE-COOKED" PORK STIR-FRY

SERVES: 4 START TO FINISH: UNDER 25 MINUTES

Salt for cooking the rice
1⅓ cups long-grain rice
1 cup fresh button mushrooms
2 teaspoons vegetable oil
½ large green bell pepper
  (for about ¾ cup chopped; optional)
1 bunch scallions (for about 1 cup sliced)
1 can (8 ounces) bamboo shoots (optional)
1¼ cups cubed Savory Pork Pot Roast (page 356),
  defrosted if frozen
1 can (14 ounces) fat-free beef broth
¼ cup hoisin sauce

From Beverly:

My husband and I were invited to join the "Gourmet Club" just after we moved into our new neighborhood. While I was a little apprehensive about belonging to such a serious-sounding group, we figured it'd be a great way to meet the neighbors. Our cordial host couple called to announce the theme for the evening: a Chinese buffet.

"Bring one of your favorite Chinese dishes to share" were the only instructions.

1 tablespoon regular or reduced-sodium soy sauce

3 cloves fresh garlic, minced, or 1 tablespoon bottled
    minced garlic

1 teaspoon finely minced fresh ginger or
    bottled minced ginger

1 teaspoon Asian (dark) sesame oil (optional)

2 tablespoons cornstarch

2 tablespoons cold water

Unsalted or lightly salted cashew pieces, roasted peanuts,
    or walnuts, coarsely chopped, for serving (optional)

1. Bring 2⅔ cups lightly salted water to a boil in a covered
medium-size saucepan. Add the rice, stir, and reduce the heat
to low. Cover the pan and simmer until the rice is tender, about
20 minutes.

2. Meanwhile, rinse, pat dry, and slice the mushrooms, removing
any tough stems. Set aside.

3. Heat the oil in an extra-deep 12-inch skillet over medium heat
for 30 seconds. Add the sliced mushrooms and cook, stirring occasionally, for 1 minute. If using the bell pepper, stem, seed, and
cut it into bite-size pieces; add them to the skillet and cook for
1 minute, stirring from time to time.

4. While the vegetables cook, cut the scallions into pieces about
1 inch long, including any tender green tops. Set aside. If using
the bamboo shoots, drain them and add them to the skillet.
Add the cubed pork and cook for 1 minute.

5. Add the broth, hoisin sauce, soy sauce, garlic, ginger, sesame oil
(if using), and the scallions. Cook, stirring, for 1 minute. Mix the
cornstarch and the cold water in a small jar that has a lid. Cover
and shake until the lumps dissolve. Add the cornstarch mixture to
the skillet. Cook, stirring, until thick and bubbly, about 1 minute.
Serve at once over the hot rice. Garnish each serving with nuts to
taste, if desired.

It just so happened that
the Gourmet Club was
meeting the same Saturday
I had planned to test this
recipe. Oh well, I figured,
if it didn't taste like a gourmet treat, I could always
sneak down to the local
Chinese restaurant and put
some take-out into one of
my own serving dishes.
(Hey, I'm not above faking
when all else fails!)

Not to worry. Thanks to
my stash of leftover Savory
Pork Pot Roast, my quick-
and-easy pork stir-fry really
hit the mark—all of the
folks at the Gourmet Club
seemed to think so.

oisin sauce is a Chinese condiment that gives the signature flavor to mu-shu. Hoisin stores safely in the refrigerator for up to a year. It's found with the other Asian ingredients in the supermarket, and it's well worth seeking out because once you taste our home-made mu-shu, you can kiss that Chinese take-out bill good-bye!

MU-SHU PORK AT HOME

SERVES: 6 START TO FINISH: UNDER 25 MINUTES

1 small head (about 1¼ pounds) green
    cabbage (see Notes)
2 medium-size carrots (see Notes)
1 pound boneless pork loin chops
    (about 1½ inches thick), defrosted if frozen (see Notes)
2 tablespoons peanut oil or other vegetable oil
1 small onion (for about ½ cup sliced)
8 ounces fresh button mushrooms
1 small clove fresh garlic, minced, or ½ teaspoon
    bottled minced garlic
½ teaspoon finely minced fresh ginger or bottled
    minced ginger
1 bunch scallions (for about ½ cup sliced; optional)
¼ cup dry sherry, white wine, or apple juice
2 teaspoons cornstarch
¼ cup regular or reduced-sodium soy sauce
2 teaspoons Asian (dark) sesame oil
8 small (7-inch) flour tortillas
2 tablespoons hoisin sauce, or more to taste

1. Cut the cabbage in half and remove and discard the tough core. Using a very sharp knife, cut the cabbage into thin shreds. Set aside.

2. Peel the carrots, and shred them on the largest holes of a box grater. Set aside.

3. Trim any visible fat from the pork chops. Cut the chops lengthwise into thin strips about ⅛ inch wide. Set aside.

4. Heat the oil in an extra-deep 12-inch skillet over medium heat. Peel the onion and cut it in half. Cut each half into ¼-inch-thick crescent-shaped slices, adding them to the skillet as you cut. Rinse, pat dry, and slice the mushrooms, removing any tough stems.

Add the mushrooms to the skillet as you slice. Add the pork strips and cook, tossing and stirring, until the mushrooms just begin to release their liquid, about 2 minutes.

5. Add the garlic, ginger, cabbage, and carrots to the skillet. Cook, stirring occasionally, until the pork is no longer pink in the center, 5 to 6 minutes. Meanwhile, if using the scallions, slice them, using all of the whites and enough of the tender green tops to make about ½ cup. Add them to the skillet.

6. When the pork is cooked through, combine the sherry and the cornstarch in a small container that has a lid, cover, and shake until the lumps dissolve. Add the mixture to the skillet, along with the soy sauce and sesame oil. Cook just until the mixture thickens, about 1 minute.

7. Just before serving, put the tortillas on a microwave-safe plate, cover with waxed paper, and microwave on high power for 1½ minutes to warm through.

8. To serve, spread ½ teaspoon hoisin sauce (or more to taste) on each tortilla, then top with ½ cup of the pork filling. Roll up burrito-style (one end tucked in) and serve at once.

NOTES: You can use a 1-pound bag of coleslaw mix instead of the cabbage and carrots. Warehouse club stores usually carry larger bags at much lower prices than the smaller supermarket bags.
■ You can use pork chops with the bone in—just cut around the bone and discard it.

I love steamed cabbage, but no one else in my family could muster enthusiasm for this classic and inexpensive vegetable. To me, this just doesn't make sense. Cooked cabbage is just warm slaw, I reason, and they love slaw. But they refused to even sample it, so I decided to try pairing cabbage with another family favorite in hopes that they'd fall for the ruse.

Sure enough, it worked. Now I get to enjoy the taste of the cabbage while sharing it with everyone else at the table. The depth of flavor contributed by the sausage and mustard sauce is just a bonus.

Any sausage will work well in this recipe—just be sure to cook it thoroughly before adding the cabbage. I have enjoyed turkey kielbasa, traditional kielbasa, Italian sausages, bratwurst, and even all-beef hot dogs. Any brand or style of grainy mustard will also work. I always seem to have country Dijon mustard on hand, so that's what I use.

FALL SAUSAGE AND CABBAGE SAUTÉ

SERVES: 4 START TO FINISH: UNDER 20 MINUTES

1 tablespoon vegetable oil
1 pound smoked or fresh sausage, such as kielbasa or bratwurst (see Note)
4 tablespoons (½ stick) butter
⅔ cup grainy mustard, such as country Dijon
1 medium-size head (about 1¾ pounds) green cabbage

SUPER-CHEAP!

1. Heat the oil in a 12-inch skillet over medium heat. Cut the sausage into ¼-inch-thick slices. Cook the sausage, turning and stirring it frequently, until it is lightly browned and cooked through, 7 to 8 minutes.

2. Meanwhile, place the butter and mustard in a small microwave-safe bowl and microwave on high power for 1 minute. Remove the bowl from the microwave oven and stir until the butter is melted and the sauce is well blended. Set aside.

3. Cut the cabbage in half and remove and discard the tough core. Coarsely chop the cabbage.

4. Add 1 cup water to the skillet and spread the chopped cabbage over the cooked sausage. Cover the skillet and steam until the cabbage is crisp-tender, 5 to 7 minutes.

5. Using a slotted spoon, divide the sausage-cabbage mixture equally among four dinner plates. Drizzle 2 tablespoons of the mustard sauce over each serving. Serve immediately.

NOTE: If you are using sausage that has a casing, you can remove the casing and crumble the sausage meat into the skillet. Do not use the oil with this type of sausage.

CAJUN SKILLET WITH SAUSAGE

SERVES: 4 START TO FINISH: UNDER 25 MINUTES

Salt for cooking the rice
1⅓ cups long-grain rice
1 tablespoon vegetable oil
1 large onion (for about 1 cup chopped)
1 large green bell pepper (for about 1½ cups chopped)
8 ounces regular or reduced-fat kielbasa sausage
2 cloves fresh garlic, minced, or 2 teaspoons bottled
    minced garlic
1 teaspoon Cajun-style seasoning blend
1 can (14½ ounces) diced tomatoes (see headnote)
1 small can (8 ounces) tomato sauce
1 can (15 ounces) red kidney beans, or 1 cup homemade
    (see page 368), defrosted if frozen

1. Bring 2⅔ cups lightly salted water to a boil in a covered medium-size saucepan. Add the rice, stir, and reduce the heat to low. Cover the pan and simmer until the rice is tender, about 20 minutes.

2. Meanwhile, heat the oil in an extra-deep 12-inch skillet over medium heat. Peel and coarsely chop the onion, adding it to the skillet as you chop. Seed, stem, and cut the bell pepper into bite-size pieces. Add them to the skillet.

3. Cut the kielbasa in half lengthwise. Cut each half into ¼-inch-thick slices, adding them to the skillet as you cut. Add the garlic and Cajun seasoning to the skillet. Cook, stirring frequently, until the onion is tender and beginning to brown, about 3 minutes.

4. Stir in the tomatoes with their juice and the tomato sauce. Rinse and drain the beans and add them to the skillet. Stir to mix well. Simmer until the beans are heated through, 2 to 3 minutes. Serve at once over a bed of hot rice.

Cajun-style seasoning blends abound on grocery store shelves these days. As with any spice blend, you are paying for the manufacturer to mix and measure the spices for you. Blends may appear expensive at first, but most spice blends have serving suggestions on the package, and we recommend studying them before purchasing to make sure the one you choose can be used with a variety of dishes. We love to sprinkle Cajun-style seasoning over grilled fish and chicken, as well as steamed veggies and mashed potatoes. We also use it in vegetable soups. We don't add so much that the soup tastes Cajun; just enough to give it a flavor boost.

For this recipe you may choose plain diced tomatoes or one of the many seasoned variations—with onions, garlic, basil, and/or oregano.

ORANGE MARMALADE— GLAZED CHICKEN OVER RICE

SERVES: 4 START TO FINISH: UNDER 25 MINUTES

While marmalade and white wine are a bit expensive, our friend Jeff Strickland, who tested this recipe, said it certainly doesn't cost any more than most of the ones he clips from the Sunday newspaper. "This is similar to a Patricia Wells recipe we've tried, but she makes hers with rabbit," Jeff said.

3 chicken bouillon cubes
1⅓ cups long-grain rice
1 pound skinless, boneless chicken breast halves, fresh or frozen (see Notes)
1 tablespoon vegetable oil
1 large onion (for about 1 cup chopped)
⅓ cup fruit-only orange marmalade (see Notes)
2 tablespoons smooth or grainy Dijon mustard
¾ cup dry white wine, such as Chardonnay (see Notes)

1. Place the bouillon cubes in 2⅔ cups water in a covered medium-size saucepan and bring to a boil. When the water boils, add the rice, stir, and reduce the heat to low. Cover the pan and simmer until the rice is tender, about 20 minutes.

2. Meanwhile, if the chicken is frozen, run it under hot water so you can remove the packaging. Place the chicken on a microwave-safe plate and microwave, uncovered, on high power for 3 minutes to partially defrost.

3. While the chicken defrosts, heat the oil in an extra-deep 12-inch skillet over medium heat. Peel and coarsely chop the onion, adding it to the skillet as you chop. Cook, stirring occasionally, until the onion begins to soften, about 3 minutes.

4. Cut the chicken (fresh or partially defrosted) into bite-size pieces, adding them to the skillet as you cut. Cook, stirring frequently, until the chicken is no longer pink in the center, 5 to 6 minutes.

5. Meanwhile, stir the marmalade and mustard together in a small bowl and set aside.

6. As soon as the chicken is done, add the wine to the skillet and raise the heat to medium-high. Boil, stirring to loosen any brown bits from the bottom of the pan, until the wine evaporates slightly, about 2 minutes. Then reduce the heat to medium and add the marmalade-mustard mixture. Stir until the ingredients are well mixed and the chicken is coated with sauce. Serve the chicken over the hot rice.

NOTES: You can use 2 cups Perfect Poached Chicken (page 362) or Poached Chicken Thighs (page 364), defrosted if frozen. Add with the wine in Step 6. Or use 2 cups Chunky Seasoned Chicken (page 358), defrosted if frozen. Omit the oil and onion. Skip Steps 2, 3, and 4. Add the Chunky Seasoned Chicken with the wine in Step 6.

■ We prefer all-fruit orange marmalade because it is less sweet, but any kind will work.

■ If you don't have any white wine, or for a nonalcoholic dish, substitute ¾ cup orange juice or chicken broth for the Chardonnay.

MoneySaver

If you have trouble getting excited about small savings, such as a 20-cents-off coupon, play the "percentage game." It's a mind game, really: Just think of that coupon savings as a 20 percent "investment return" on a dollar. Likewise, if using coupons saves you $20 on your grocery bill, it's like a 20 percent "investment return" on $100. Getting a 20 percent return is nothing to sneeze at!

What Keeps You Out of the Kitchen? Or, Kitchen Psychology 101

From Beverly:

Want to cut a chunk out of the family food budget? If you're really serious about trimming costs, the first thing to eliminate is pizza delivery, take-out Chinese, and those panic trips to the fast-food drive-through.

Say what? Forgo the easiest way to feed your family on the fly? It's true that before you're ready to take the plunge, you'll probably need to do some soul-searching. I found that until I'd gotten a grip on what keeps me out of the kitchen in the first place, it was difficult to get back in—and get dinner on the table.

For starters, I realized that often cooking is as much about psychology as it is about physical effort. I'm talking neuroses here—guilt trips (if I buy those already-sliced mushrooms, my mother would surely frown) and illogical assumptions (if I just wait a little longer to start dinner, my fairy godmother is bound to appear and cook it for me).

The list that prevented me from cooking was long, but the top entries included exhaustion, fear of failure, and disorganization. Once I identified the problems, it seemed I was halfway to solving them.

As for exhaustion: I've learned to glance at the calendar to gauge the *next* day's schedule at the end of each workday. If it's a killer, I know I won't feel like cooking an elaborate meal that night. So before I head to bed, I grab one of my already-cooked "batches" out of the freezer and throw it in the refrigerator to defrost. (Budget-Minded Batch Cooking starts on page 344.) When I finish work, making dinner goes a lot faster because part of the recipe is already cooked.

As for fear of failure: I used to figure that my kids would hate whatever I cooked, so why bother? I came to understand that young kids, by definition, tend to frown on anything nutritious, and it wasn't my fault. Several new tricks helped. I cut back on the kids' late afternoon snacks, especially juice. I started cooking meals to suit the adults but left some of the noodles and/or meat plain for the kids. I adopted a new rule that kids must try one bite of everything, but they're allowed to spit it back out. (The spit-back clause was the key to cooperation.) Funny how often my kids were surprised, finding they did like something after all.

If you're new to cooking, the fear of failure may be more acute. Start by asking good friends for their easiest favorite recipes (or pick almost anything from this book), and practice these recipes when you're not tired. Stick with a few until you've got them mastered, and your kitchen confidence will soon soar. Many community centers and technical colleges offer beginning cooking courses.

As for disorganization: I realized that I had a tendency to wander the supermarket in a daze. I've been known to circle the aisles for 30 minutes without putting any food into the cart. In such trances I had no recipes in mind—and no clue what was in the fridge at home. To solve that problem, I keep a running list for the grocery staples I need, and before shopping, I grab my easiest recipes and update the list. I also play it safe and put some items in the cart that will keep for a while, such as kielbasa, canned beans, canned tomatoes, and ultra-pasteurized dairy products. If there's something in the house that's versatile to cook, I'm less likely to head for a restaurant.

One final trick: I keep my favorite, fastest pantry-based recipe taped inside the door of the cabinet nearest the stove, and I always keep the ingredients on hand. So when I'm time-starved and exhausted, there's at least one no-brainer that I can always fix for dinner.

So the next time you're tempted to pick up the phone for pizza delivery, ask yourself one question: "Why am I really doing this?" Be honest. Your answers, like mine, could help you cook up some creative solutions, and save you a wad of cash to boot.

"I used to figure that my kids would hate whatever I cooked, so why bother?"

Sweet and sour chicken is one of those kid-friendly meals that it's easy to lose a taste for as an adult. You order it with fond memories in your favorite Chinese restaurant, but what arrives is candy-coated pieces of chicken colored a shocking pink. We've updated our version for today's tastes by using unsweetened pineapple juice, a splash of vinegar, and just a hint of brown sugar. As an added bonus, this dish is lower in fat than the more expensive restaurant version—only 5 grams of fat per serving.

After making this dinner, don't be surprised if your fortune cookie reads, "You will be a famous chef someday."

GROWN-UP SWEET AND SOUR CHICKEN

SERVES: 4 START TO FINISH: UNDER 25 MINUTES

Salt for cooking the rice
1⅓ cups long-grain rice
1 pound skinless, boneless chicken breast halves, fresh or frozen (see Note)
1 tablespoon peanut oil or other vegetable oil
3 medium-size carrots (for about 1½ cup sliced)
1 large onion (for about 1 cup sliced)
1 clove fresh garlic, minced, or 1 teaspoon bottled minced garlic
1 teaspoon finely minced fresh ginger or bottled minced ginger
1 large green bell pepper (for about 1½ cups sliced)
1 can (15¼ ounces) pineapple chunks packed in juice
2 tablespoons rice vinegar or white wine vinegar
1 tablespoon regular or reduced-sodium soy sauce, plus more for serving
1 tablespoon packed light brown sugar
2 tablespoons cornstarch
2 tablespoons cold water

1. Bring 2⅔ cups lightly salted water to a boil in a covered medium-size saucepan. Add the rice, stir, and reduce the heat to low. Cover the pan and simmer until the rice is tender, about 20 minutes.

2. Meanwhile, if the chicken is frozen, run it under hot water so you can remove the packaging. Place the chicken on a microwave-safe plate and microwave, uncovered, on high power for 3 minutes to partially defrost.

3. While the chicken defrosts, place the oil in an extra-deep 12-inch skillet over medium heat. Peel the carrots and, holding the knife at a 45-degree angle, cut them into ½-inch-thick slices.

Add the carrots to the skillet. Stir from time to time while you peel the onion, cut it in half, and cut each half into ½-inch-wide crescent-shaped slices. Add them to the skillet as you slice. Stir to mix well and cook until the carrot softens slightly, about 2 minutes.

4. Cut the chicken (fresh or partially defrosted) into bite-size pieces, adding them to the skillet as you cut. Add the garlic and ginger to the skillet and stir well. Cook, stirring occasionally, until the chicken is no longer pink in the center, 5 to 6 minutes.

5. While the chicken cooks, stem, seed, and cut the bell pepper into ½-inch strips, adding them to the skillet as you cut. Drain the pineapple juice from the can into a 1-cup or larger measure, reserving the pineapple chunks. Add enough water to the juice to make 1 cup liquid.

6. As soon as the chicken is done, add the juice mixture to the skillet and bring to a boil, raising the heat to medium-high, if necessary. Then add the vinegar, soy sauce, and brown sugar. Stir well to mix in the seasonings.

7. Mix the cornstarch with the cold water in a small container that has a lid. Cover, and shake until the lumps dissolve. Add the cornstarch mixture to the skillet a little at a time, stirring constantly. Stir roughly half of the reserved pineapple chunks into the skillet, saving the rest for another use. Cook, stirring constantly, until the sauce thickens slightly, 1 to 2 minutes. Remove the skillet from the heat and serve at once over the hot rice. Pass additional soy sauce at the table.

NOTE: You can use 2 cups Perfect Poached Chicken (page 362), Poached Chicken Thighs (page 364), Chunky Seasoned Chicken (page 358), or Great Grilled Chicken Breasts (page 360), defrosted if frozen. Add along with the bell pepper in Step 5 and cook until the chicken is heated through.

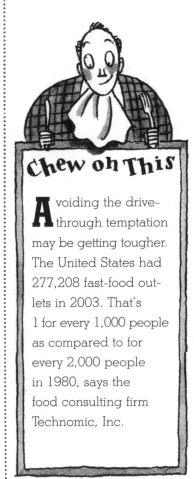

Chew oh This

Avoiding the drive-through temptation may be getting tougher. The United States had 277,208 fast-food outlets in 2003. That's 1 for every 1,000 people as compared to for every 2,000 people in 1980, says the food consulting firm Technomic, Inc.

Skin and Bone Your Own Chicken Breasts

"The truly essential thing is to use a very sharp knife."

As a general rule, the more cut up a chicken is when you buy it, the more it will cost per pound. So when regular chicken breasts go on sale at the supermarket, turn them into do-it-yourself skinless, boneless breasts. It takes only about 10 minutes to skin and bone six average-size breast halves. (Whole chicken breasts consist of two lobes, connected in the center by a small piece of cartilage. Often bone-in breasts are sold already halved.)

The skinning part is especially quick and easy. Simply slide your fingers between the skin and the chicken meat and pull. With just a few tugs, the skin comes right off.

Boning is a bit more involved, but comes easily with a little practice. The truly essential thing is to use a very sharp knife—don't even bother if your knife is dull. Here's how:

Starting at the ribs, slip a boning knife between the rib bones and the meat. Using a short sawing motion, cut the meat away from the ribs a little at a time, keeping the knife as close to the bones as you can. (Don't worry if a little meat is left behind. Until you become experienced, you won't be able to get all of it.) Once the ribs are detached, it's just a matter of cutting the meat away as best you can.

Check the meat for any stray cartilage, and if you find any, just trim it off.

To freeze the chicken, wrap each breast half in plastic wrap or waxed paper, then place the breasts flat in a zipper-top plastic bag. (This allows you to pull out only what you need at any one time.) Lay the bag flat in the freezer, so the chicken pieces will freeze flat (they will defrost faster when the time comes). You can use the leftover bones and skin to make chicken stock (see page 10).

Once the job is done, be sure to wash your hands well with hot soapy water, and thoroughly clean any surfaces that might have come into contact with raw chicken.

FIERY CHICKEN WITH VEGETABLES

SERVES: 4 START TO FINISH: UNDER 25 MINUTES

1 can (14 ounces) fat-free chicken broth,
   or 1¾ cups homemade chicken stock
   (see page 10)

1 cup long-grain rice

1 pound skinless, boneless chicken breast halves,
   fresh or frozen (see Notes)

1 tablespoon vegetable oil

1 bag (16 ounces) frozen broccoli stir-fry vegetable
   mixture (without sauce)

2 cloves fresh garlic, minced, or 2 teaspoons bottled
   minced garlic

1 tablespoon regular or reduced-sodium soy sauce

2 teaspoons finely minced fresh ginger or
   bottled minced ginger

1 teaspoon sugar

½ teaspoon red pepper flakes

2 tablespoons cornstarch

1. Combine 1 cup of the broth (reserving the rest) and 1 cup water in a covered medium-size saucepan and bring to a boil. Add the rice, stir, and reduce the heat to low. Cover the pan and simmer until the rice is tender, about 20 minutes.

2. Meanwhile, if the chicken is frozen, run it under hot water to remove the packaging. Microwave the chicken, uncovered, on high power for 3 minutes to partially defrost.

3. While the chicken defrosts, heat the oil over medium heat in an extra-deep 12-inch skillet. Add the frozen broccoli mixture and stir occasionally.

4. Meanwhile, cut the chicken (fresh or partially defrosted) into bite-size pieces, adding them to the skillet as you cut. Cook, stirring frequently, until the chicken is no longer pink in the center,

From Alicia:

I've always been drawn to the Asian dishes with the little red pepper symbol beside them on the menus—the hot ones! This dish definitely qualifies. If you aren't used to red pepper, start with ¼ teaspoon red pepper flakes. Omit them if you are serving children; or serve the children first and then add the red pepper for the adults.

This stir-fry goes together even quicker if you use a stash of already-cooked chicken. See the note on page 148 for all of the options.

5 to 6 minutes. Add the garlic to the pan. Stir well. Add the soy sauce, ginger, sugar, and red pepper flakes. Stir well and cook to blend the flavors, 2 minutes.

5. Combine the cornstarch and remaining ¾ cup chicken broth in a small container that has a lid. Cover and shake until the lumps dissolve. Drizzle the mixture over the chicken. Stir continuously until the sauce thickens, about 1 minute. Remove the skillet from the heat and set it aside until the rice is done. Serve the chicken mixture over a bed of hot rice.

NOTE: You can use 2 cups Chunky Seasoned Chicken (page 358), Perfect Poached Chicken (page 362), Poached Chicken Thighs (page 364), or Great Grilled Chicken Breasts (page 360), defrosted if frozen. Add it with the soy sauce in Step 4.

Remember Chicken Divan? That was one of those casseroles from our childhood, something easy Mom could make when she ran short of ideas and ingredients. Our mothers used to bake this dish in the oven, but we've transferred it to the skillet for the sake of speed. This is comfort food—simple, inexpensive, and hearty, stretching a pound of chicken to what seems way beyond the capacity of a mere 16 ounces.

THRIFTY CHICKEN WITH BROCCOLI

SERVES: 4 START TO FINISH: UNDER 25 MINUTES

1 can (14 ounces) fat-free chicken broth,
    or 2 cups homemade chicken stock (see page 10)

1⅓ cups long-grain rice

1 pound skinless, boneless chicken breast halves,
    fresh or frozen (see Note)

1 tablespoon vegetable oil

1 large onion (for about 1 cup chopped)

¼ teaspoon black pepper

1 clove fresh garlic, minced, or 1 teaspoon bottled
    minced garlic

1 can (10¾ ounces) cream of chicken soup

1 bag (16 ounces) frozen broccoli pieces

½ cup shredded Cheddar or Swiss cheese

1. Pour ¾ cup of the broth and 2 cups water into a covered medium-size saucepan and bring to a boil over high heat. Add the rice, stir, and reduce the heat to low. Cover the pan and simmer until the rice is tender, about 20 minutes.

2. Meanwhile, if the chicken is frozen, run it under hot water so you can remove the packaging. Place the chicken on a microwave-safe plate and microwave, uncovered, on high power for 3 minutes to partially defrost.

3. While the chicken defrosts, heat the oil in an extra-deep 12-inch skillet over medium heat. Peel and coarsely chop the onion, adding it to the skillet as you chop. Cut the chicken (fresh or partially defrosted) into bite-size pieces and add them to the skillet as you cut. Sprinkle the black pepper over the chicken and cook, stirring often. While the chicken cooks, add the garlic to the skillet.

4. When the chicken is no longer pink in the center, after 5 to 6 minutes, add the cream of chicken soup and the remaining 1¼ cups broth to the skillet. Stir until the soup is thoroughly blended and the sauce is smooth. Sprinkle the broccoli pieces evenly over the ingredients. Cover the skillet and cook until heated through, about 3 minutes.

5. Sprinkle the cheese evenly over the mixture and reduce the heat to low. Cook, covered, until the cheese melts, 1 to 2 minutes. Serve the chicken and sauce over the hot rice.

NOTE: You can use 2 cups Perfect Poached Chicken (page 362) or Poached Chicken Thighs (page 364), defrosted if frozen. Add in Step 4. Or use 2 cups Chunky Seasoned Chicken (page 358), defrosted if frozen. Omit the onion, oil, and garlic. Skip Steps 2 and 3, and add the Chunky Seasoned Chicken with the soup in Step 4. Also add the black pepper in Step 4. Cook until heated through.

When fall's new apple crop starts rolling into the market, we welcome the lower prices almost as much as the fresh taste. Apples keep well in the refrigerator for weeks, so they're convenient to keep on hand—plus they cook surprisingly fast. If you want a complete meal and something slightly more sophisticated than applesauce, this is your recipe. It's elegant, but it still goes together quickly enough for a regular family dinner. Every year the variety of cooking apples grows— don't hesitate to experiment. You can't go wrong with Granny Smith, but any tart cooking apple that happens to be on sale will work well in this recipe.

CHICKEN AND APPLES WITH DIJON CREAM

SERVES: 4 START TO FINISH: UNDER 25 MINUTES

Salt for cooking the rice
1⅓ cups long-grain rice
1 pound skinless, boneless chicken breast halves, fresh or frozen (see Notes)
8 ounces fresh button mushrooms
1 tablespoon vegetable oil
1 teaspoon butter
1 small onion (for about ½ cup chopped)
2 large tart cooking apples, such as Granny Smith or McIntosh
¾ cup apple juice
½ cup dry white wine, such as Chardonnay (see Notes)
1½ teaspoons sugar
1 chicken bouillon cube
1 tablespoon Dijon mustard
¼ cup half-and-half or heavy cream

1. Bring 2⅔ cups lightly salted water to a boil in a covered medium-size saucepan. Add the rice, stir, and reduce the heat to low. Cover the pan and simmer until the rice is tender, about 20 minutes.

2. Meanwhile, if the chicken is frozen, run it under hot water so you can remove the packaging. Place the chicken on a microwave-safe plate and microwave, uncovered, on high power for 3 minutes to partially defrost.

3. While the chicken defrosts, rinse, pat dry, and slice the mushrooms, removing and discarding any tough stems. Set aside.

4. Heat the oil and butter in an extra-deep 12-inch skillet over medium heat. Peel and coarsely chop the onion, adding it to the skillet as you chop.

5. Cut the chicken (fresh or partially defrosted) into bite-size pieces, adding them to the skillet as you cut. Cook, stirring occasionally, while you cut each apple in half and remove the core. Cut the apples into ¼-inch slices (but do not peel them). When the apples are sliced, add them to the skillet along with the mushrooms. Cook, stirring, until the mushrooms just begin to soften, about 2 minutes.

6. Add the apple juice, wine, and sugar. Crush the bouillon cube between your fingers or with the back of a spoon and add it to the skillet. Stir well. Bring the mixture to a boil and cook until the sugar has dissolved and the chicken is no longer pink in the center, about 4 minutes more.

7. Stir in the mustard and half-and-half. Cook, stirring, until the mixture is warm throughout, about 2 minutes. (If using half-and-half, do not let the mixture boil.) Serve at once over the hot rice.

NOTES: You can use 2 cups Perfect Poached Chicken (page 362) or Poached Chicken Thighs (page 364), defrosted if frozen. Add with the apple juice in Step 6. Prepare the apples as directed in Step 5 before starting the recipe.

■ You can substitute ½ cup additional apple juice for the white wine, if desired.

Chew on This

Eight billion chickens are raised for food each year in the United States, *Time* magazine reports, and Americans eat 127 of them every single second.

Thanks to the sweet pineapple and the tangy tomatoes, plus a kick from the ginger and garlic, this dish offers a complex variety of flavors that's sure to wake up the taste buds. Adding the green pepper toward the end of the cooking time keeps it bright green and crisp-tender. We like to serve Island Chicken in the dead of winter, when it's almost as good as a trip to the Caribbean but a lot easier on the budget!

ISLAND CHICKEN

SERVES: 4 START TO FINISH: UNDER 25 MINUTES

Salt for cooking the rice
1⅓ cups long-grain rice
1 pound skinless, boneless chicken breast halves, fresh or frozen (see Notes)
1 tablespoon vegetable oil
1 large onion (for about 1 cup chopped)
8 ounces fresh button mushrooms
1 medium-size green bell pepper (for about 1 cup pieces)
2 cloves fresh garlic, minced, or 2 teaspoons bottled minced garlic
1 tablespoon regular or reduced-sodium soy sauce, plus more for serving (optional)
1 teaspoon finely minced fresh ginger or bottled minced ginger
1 teaspoon Worcestershire sauce
¼ teaspoon black pepper
1 can (14½ ounces) diced tomatoes
1 small can (8 ounces) crushed pineapple packed in juice
1 tablespoon cornstarch
2 tablespoons cold water

1. Bring 2⅔ cups lightly salted water to a boil in a covered medium-size saucepan. Add the rice, stir, and reduce the heat to low. Cover the pan and simmer until the rice is tender, about 20 minutes.

2. Meanwhile, if the chicken is frozen, run it under hot water so you can remove the packaging. Place the chicken on a microwave-safe plate and microwave, uncovered, on high power for 3 minutes to partially defrost.

3. While the chicken defrosts, heat the oil in an extra-deep 12-inch skillet over medium heat. Peel and coarsely chop the onion, adding it to the skillet as you chop. Rinse, pat dry, and slice the mushrooms, removing and discarding any tough stems, and add them to the skillet as you slice.

4. Cut the chicken (fresh or partially defrosted) into bite-size pieces, adding them to the skillet as you cut. Cook, stirring frequently.

5. While the chicken cooks, stem, seed, and cut the bell pepper into bite-size pieces. Set the pieces aside. Stir the garlic, soy sauce, ginger, Worcestershire sauce, and black pepper into the skillet.

6. When the chicken is no longer pink on the inside, after 5 to 6 minutes, add the tomatoes with their juice and the pineapple with its juice. Add the bell pepper. Stir to mix well and cook, stirring frequently, until the bell pepper is crisp-tender, about 3 minutes.

7. Meanwhile, combine the cornstarch with the cold water in a small container that has a lid. Cover and shake until the lumps dissolve. Add the cornstarch mixture to the skillet a little at a time and cook, stirring constantly, until the mixture thickens slightly, 1 to 2 minutes. Serve at once over the hot rice, passing more soy sauce at the table, if desired.

NOTE: You can use 2 cups Chunky Seasoned Chicken (page 358), Perfect Poached Chicken (page 362), or Poached Chicken Thighs (page 364), defrosted if frozen. Add with the tomatoes in Step 6 and cook until heated through.

From Alicia:

A s I rushed in to pick up the children from dance class one day, a friend asked me if I had any ideas for a dinner that wouldn't cost a fortune. She said she was tired of high-priced take-out and high-calorie fast food—her solutions when she wasn't boiling up spaghetti.

"What's in your pantry?" I asked.

"Oh, the usual—a can or two of beans, maybe some tomatoes, and pasta, pasta and more pasta," she replied. "We can't eat pasta again. We've had it for the last three nights."

"Do you have any rice and salsa?" I asked.

"Sure, I think I can scrounge some up."

"Any chicken?"

"Only frozen."

"That's okay," I assured her as my brain started to formulate the recipe. "How about a Mexican chicken skillet dinner?"

"Sounds great, but whose house are we eating at—yours?"

MEXI-CHICKEN SKILLET

SERVES: 4 GENEROUSLY START TO FINISH: UNDER 25 MINUTES

1 jar (26 ounces, about 2½ cups)
   chunky salsa (see Notes)
1⅓ cups long-grain rice
1 pound skinless, boneless chicken breast halves,
   fresh or frozen (see Notes)
1 tablespoon olive oil
1 large onion (for about 1 cup chopped)
1 clove fresh garlic, chopped, or 1 teaspoon bottled
   minced garlic
2 cans (11 ounces each) corn with bell peppers (see Notes)
1 can (15 ounces) black beans, or 1 cup homemade
   (see page 368), defrosted if frozen
Regular or reduced-fat sour cream, for serving
Shredded Cheddar cheese, for serving

1. Combine 2⅔ cups water with ½ cup of the salsa in a covered medium-size saucepan and bring to a boil. Add the rice, stir, and reduce the heat to low. Cover the pan and simmer until the rice is tender, about 20 minutes.

2. Meanwhile, if the chicken is frozen, run it under hot water so you can remove the packaging. Place the chicken on a microwave-safe plate and microwave, uncovered, on high power for 3 minutes to partially defrost.

3. While the chicken defrosts, heat the oil in an extra-deep 12-inch skillet over medium heat. Peel and coarsely chop the onion, adding it to the skillet as you chop. Stir in the garlic.

4. Cut the chicken (fresh or partially defrosted) into bite-size pieces, adding them to the skillet as you cut. Cook, stirring occasionally.

5. While the chicken cooks, pour the corn and beans into a colander. Rinse with water and set aside to drain well. When all of the chicken has turned white on the outside, about 4 minutes, add the corn, beans, and remaining salsa (about 2 cups) to the skillet. Stir until the chicken and vegetables are coated with sauce. Reduce the heat to low, cover the skillet, and simmer until the chicken is no longer pink in the center, about 2 minutes more.

6. To serve, spoon the chicken mixture over a bed of hot rice. Top each serving with a dollop of sour cream and a little cheese.

NOTES: Choose the salsa according to the level of spiciness your family prefers. If your salsa is very acidic, add sugar to taste, starting with ½ teaspoon.

■ You can use 2 cups Perfect Poached Chicken (page 362) or Poached Chicken Thighs (page 364), defrosted if frozen. Add with the corn and beans in Step 5. Or use 2 cups Chunky Seasoned Chicken (page 358), defrosted if frozen. Omit the oil, onion, and garlic. Skip Steps 2, 3, and 4. Combine the chicken with the corn, beans, and salsa in Step 5 and cook until heated through.

■ Look for canned corn with bell peppers under the brand name Mexicorn. You can substitute plain canned corn.

I assured her she had all the makings of a delicious dinner right at home, without having to cook a single noodle. By this time I was thinking the same dinner sounded pretty terrific for my hungry family, too. And so it was!

About:
CAN SIZES

Canned products come in a variety of weights and sizes, and often vary according to the brand. For example, chicken broth cans range from 10 ounces to 16 ounces. Canned beans are found in 12-ounce cans, 15-ounce cans, 19-ounce cans—and just about everything in between.

When you are shopping, look for the size that's closest to the one called for in the ingredients lists. Don't fret if your store stocks a brand that is 15 ounces, not 14½, or if the 16-ounce brand is on sale and the recipe calls for a 15-ounce can. These slight differences will not matter one iota in our recipes.

Cream soups play a vital role in our pantries. They're such a budget queen's staple, we practically take them for granted. But a conversation with one of our food journalist colleagues made us stop and think.

"I'd never make a recipe that called for cream soup," she declared.

Why not, we asked.

"I just wouldn't."

The pained look on her face said it all. No food snob worth her Cuisinart would lower herself to use cream of mushroom soup in a recipe. For a couple of years after that conversation, we found ourselves second-guessing our cream soup instincts. Finally we decided to test the waters by printing a favorite skillet dinner that included a can of cream of mushroom soup in our Desperation Dinners newspaper column.

Our readers raved. The cheers came pouring in via letters and e-mail from harried mothers, busy retired couples, and budget-conscious graduate students. And that's what we find every time we feature a recipe with a

CHICKEN AND GREEN BEAN "CASSEROLE"

SERVES: 4 START TO FINISH: UNDER 25 MINUTES

1 small can (2.8 ounces) French fried onions (optional)
Salt for cooking the rice
1⅓ cups long-grain rice
1 pound skinless, boneless chicken breast halves, fresh or frozen (see Note)
1 tablespoon vegetable oil
1 large onion (for about 1 cup chopped)
2 teaspoons Worcestershire sauce
½ teaspoon garlic powder
¼ teaspoon black pepper
1 can (14½ ounces) French-style green beans
1 can (5 ounces) sliced water chestnuts (optional)
1 can (10¾ ounces) regular or reduced-fat condensed cream of mushroom soup
¼ cup whole, low-fat, or skim milk

1. Place the fried onions (if using) in a toaster oven and set it at 350°F. Bake until golden brown, about 5 minutes. Set aside until ready to serve.

2. Bring 2⅔ cups lightly salted water to a boil in a covered medium-size saucepan. Add the rice, stir, and reduce the heat to low. Cover the pan and simmer until the rice is tender, about 20 minutes.

3. Meanwhile, if the chicken is frozen, run it under hot water so you can remove the packaging. Place the chicken on a microwave-safe plate and microwave, uncovered, on high power for 3 minutes to partially defrost.

4. While the chicken defrosts, heat the oil in an extra-deep 12-inch skillet over medium heat. Peel the onion and coarsely chop it, adding it to the skillet as you chop and stirring occasionally.

5. Cut the chicken (fresh or partially defrosted) into bite-size pieces, adding them to the skillet as you cut. Cook, stirring occasionally.

6. While the chicken is cooking, add the Worcestershire sauce, garlic powder, and black pepper to the skillet. Pour the green beans and water chestnuts (if using) into a colander and set aside to drain well.

7. When the chicken is no longer pink in the center, after 5 to 6 minutes, add the cream of mushroom soup and the milk to the skillet. Stir well. Add the green beans and water chestnuts (if using) and stir until coated with the sauce. Cover the skillet and simmer until ready to serve.

8. When the rice is done, serve the chicken mixture over a bed of the hot rice. Garnish each plate with a generous sprinkling of toasted French fried onions, if desired.

NOTE: You can use 2 cups Perfect Poached Chicken (page 362), Poached Chicken Thighs (page 364), or Chunky Seasoned Chicken (page 358), defrosted if frozen. Add with the soup and milk in Step 7.

"cream of" soup. Most people love them.

The reasons are simple. Using cream soup as a sauce base is far easier than making a traditional roux with butter and flour, then adding milk and cooking until thick. Heavy cream, the other quick alternative, contains too much fat for most people's weekday diets. Canned soups go on sale practically once a month, so it's easy to stay stocked up at the cheapest price, too.

This recipe is based on one of the most famous and best-loved cream of mushroom soup recipes on the planet: green been casserole with French fried onions. Our version adds chicken and rice for a mid-week meal and moves it from the oven to the skillet for a quick fix. The casserole's traditional fried onions, which can be pricey when not on sale and pack a lot of extra calories, are optional.

Finding the Lowest-Ever Prices

When items go on sale at the supermarket—particularly items you use a lot—you'll save more money if you buy extra for later. However, not all sales are created equal. Sometimes the store knocks off just a few pennies, in which case it's not the best use of refrigerator, freezer, and pantry space to buy massive quantities. But when an item hits its lowest-ever, rock-bottom price, go all out and stock up. (We've been known to store really, really cheap canned goods under the bed.)

The only way you can know if it's time to stock up is to recognize a lowest-ever price when you see it. And the only way you can be sure (unless you have a photographic memory) is to make a price chart.

Making a price chart isn't hard—but it does take some time. You can put the chart on your computer or on a piece of notebook paper. Divide your chart into two wide columns and label them at the top: "regular price" and "sale price." Down the side, list the items, ideally in alphabetical order, that you use most frequently. (You can always add more items as you develop the chart.)

Here's the first phase of using the chart: Put it on a clipboard and take it with you on your next few shopping trips. As you shop for an item on the chart, write its regular price in pencil. If the item happens to be on sale, mark that price in the "sale price" column. (It's a good idea to note the size of the item so you can be sure you're comparing apples to apples later.)

For the second phase: As you read the supermarket ads each week, look for items on sale and write down those sale prices on the chart in pencil. Update your chart each time you read the ads—different items go on sale at different times, and not all sale prices are the same. This will give you a record of the lowest prices you've seen for each item.

Once your chart is filled with prices, you can use it as a handy guide for deciding which items, and how many of them, to buy. Let's say bacon goes on sale for less than $2 a pound. If you've been following the ads and noting the prices, you'll realize that this is a pretty good deal, and you should buy as much as you can use before the expiration date.

When we first started getting serious about saving money on food, we resisted the idea of a price chart—we were sure we could spot a good deal when it rolled around. But we quickly realized that, sure, we could remember the price of one or two items, but keeping fifty to a hundred prices in mind was impossible. With a price chart, you can be sure to get the best deals without having to turn your brain into a walking grocery ad.

"When an item hits its lowest-ever, rock-bottom price, go all out and stock up."

Having a dinner routine can be a good thing, because a stash of reliable recipes means one less thing to think about when you're tired and pressed for time. But after a few months, if your routine veers toward boring, you can find yourself more tempted than ever to head to the restaurant. That's when it's time to jolt those taste buds out of complacency, and this recipe is just the ticket.

A blend of curry, ginger, garlic, and chutney takes chicken and spinach and spins them into an exotic dance of flavors that is sure to wow everyone at the table. Because the tender spinach leaves are steamed so briefly, they retain their lovely bright green color. If you can't find baby spinach, regular spinach is fine; just be sure to discard any tough stems.

Chutney is a slightly chunky Indian condiment containing fruit, vinegar, sugar, and spices ranging from mild to hot. It's found in the supermarket with the imported foods or condiments. Major Grey's is a common mild chutney, but any type of sweet mango

CURRIED CHICKEN WITH SPINACH AND TOMATOES

SERVES: 4 START TO FINISH: UNDER 25 MINUTES

Salt for cooking the rice

1⅓ cups long-grain rice

1 pound skinless, boneless chicken breast halves, fresh or frozen (see Notes)

1 tablespoon vegetable oil

1 large onion (for about 1 cup chopped)

2 cloves fresh garlic, minced, or 2 teaspoons bottled minced garlic

1 can (14½ ounces) diced tomatoes (see Notes)

1 teaspoon finely minced fresh ginger or bottled minced ginger

¼ cup mango chutney

2 teaspoons curry powder

9 cups (9 to 10 ounces) fresh spinach, washed and tough stems removed, if necessary

½ cup sour cream (see Notes)

Black pepper to taste

1. Bring 2⅔ cups lightly salted water to a boil in a covered medium-size saucepan. Add the rice, stir, and reduce the heat to low. Cover the pan and simmer until the rice is tender, about 20 minutes.

2. Meanwhile, if the chicken is frozen, run it under hot water so you can remove the packaging. Place the chicken on a microwave-safe plate and microwave, uncovered, on high power for 3 minutes to partially defrost.

3. While the chicken defrosts, heat the oil in an extra-deep, 12-inch skillet over medium heat. Peel and coarsely chop the onion, adding it to the skillet as you chop. Continue to cook, stirring occasionally, while you cut the chicken (fresh or partially defrosted) into bite-size pieces, adding the chicken to the skillet as you cut. Cook, stirring occasionally. While the chicken cooks, add the garlic to the skillet.

4. When the chicken is no longer pink in the center, after 5 to 6 minutes, add the tomatoes with their juice, the ginger, chutney, and curry powder. Stir to mix well.

5. Scatter the spinach over the chicken mixture and cover the pan. Steam just until the spinach begins to wilt, about 2 minutes. (The spinach will not be fully wilted at this point; the heat from the sauce will finish the cooking.) Remove the skillet from the heat and add the sour cream. Stir until the sour cream is fully incorporated into the sauce. Season lightly with black pepper. To serve, spoon the chicken mixture over the hot rice.

NOTES: You can use 2 cups Perfect Poached Chicken (page 362) or Poached Chicken Thighs (page 364), defrosted if frozen. Add with the tomatoes in Step 4. Or use 2 cups Chunky Seasoned Chicken (page 358), defrosted if frozen. Omit the oil, onion, and garlic. Skip Steps 2 and 3. Add the Chunky Seasoned Chicken with the tomatoes in Step 4 and cook until heated through.
■ You can use diced tomatoes seasoned with onion and garlic.
■ Do not use reduced-fat sour cream in this recipe.

chutney you happen to find can be used. You'll need only about half the jar, and the remainder will keep in the refrigerator for up to 2 months for your next batch or for use in another recipe.

From Alicia:

When the budget was running tight at my grandparents' house and they still had a large family to feed, my grandmother would turn to hash. Funny thing is, I've seen hash recipes showing up on menus at trendy restaurants lately. Whether you view hash as a "stretcher meal" or as the latest, greatest gourmet trend, this dish, loaded with potatoes and spiked with carrots, ensures that no one leaves the table feeling empty.

To my mind this type of potato-filled hash must be served with lots of ketchup. But we've seen everything from salsa to sour cream as a garnish. Get creative and enjoy.

HOMEY CHICKEN HASH

SERVES: 4 START TO FINISH: UNDER 20 MINUTES

1 tablespoon vegetable oil
1 small onion (for about ½ cup chopped)
2 medium-size carrots (for about 1 cup sliced)
4 cups diced cooked potatoes (see Notes)
2 cups cooked chicken chunks (see Notes)
Salt and black pepper to taste
1 cup (4 ounces) shredded Cheddar cheese
Ketchup, for serving (optional)

1. Heat the oil in an extra-deep 12-inch skillet over medium heat. Peel and coarsely chop the onion, adding it to the skillet as you chop. Peel and cut the carrots into ¼-inch slices, adding them to the skillet as you slice. Cook until the onion begins to brown on the edges, 3 to 5 minutes.

2. Add the potatoes to the skillet. Cook, stirring, until brown, 5 to 7 minutes. (If using refrigerated diced potatoes, cook longer if necessary, until tender.) Add the chicken and stir well to break up any pieces. Cook until the chicken is heated through, 2 to 3 minutes.

3. Season the hash liberally with salt and black pepper. Sprinkle the cheese over the hash and cover the skillet. Remove the skillet from the heat and set it aside until the cheese has melted, about 2 minutes. Serve at once, with ketchup, if desired.

NOTES: For the potatoes, you can boil 1 pound of diced peeled raw potatoes until tender, about 10 minutes. Drain well and proceed with recipe. Or use peeled and diced Amazing Baked Potatoes (page 366), or 1 package (1 pound, 4 ounces) refrigerated diced potatoes with onion, such as the Simply Potatoes brand.

■ For the chicken, you can use 2 cups Perfect Poached Chicken (page 362), Poached Chicken Thighs (page 364), Chunky Seasoned Chicken (page 358), or Great Grilled Chicken Breasts (page 360). Or cut 1 pound skinless, boneless chicken breasts into bite-size chunks and sauté in 1 tablespoon vegetable oil until cooked through, then proceed with the recipe.

About:
BUYING A BIG SKILLET

A 12-inch, extra-deep, covered skillet should claim a prime spot in every cook's cabinet. In the South we call this type of skillet a chicken fryer. Some brands label it a chef's pan, others call it a sauté pan. You'll just call it a sanity saver—particularly if you make a lot of one-pan skillet meals or need to pan-fry enough food for a family of four or more.

The feature that sets an extra-deep skillet apart from any other sauté pan is its straight 2-inch, or even 3-inch, sides. (Typical skillets have sloping sides of only about 1½ inches.) This skillet has a large surface area and a total capacity of 4½ to 6 quarts, so you can cook an entire meal without the food flying out as you stir.

Extra-deep skillets are sold in mart-type stores for about $35. Better-quality models can run $100 and up at department stores and cookware shops. Most extra-deep skillets come with a lid, but they are sometimes sold separately. The lid is perfect for finishing meals that have the rice cooked right in, for bringing sauces to a boil, and for melting cheese quickly.

So whether you by an inexpensive skillet or a pricier one, just make sure it's big!

This is one of those flexible home-style recipes that's a sure hit with the kids. The tykes won't touch mushrooms, you say? Just leave those offending 'shrooms in the fridge. Frozen biscuits are handy, but canned refrigerated biscuits, Bisquick biscuits, or homemade biscuits can also be used. Cream of chicken soup also makes a delicious base for the sauce. We like to use a frozen vegetable blend that has peas, carrots, and corn, but you can substitute leftover cooked vegetables, or any combination of frozen vegetables that measures 2 cups.

INDIVIDUAL CHICKEN COBBLERS

SERVES: 4 START TO FINISH: UNDER 30 MINUTES

4 frozen Southern-style biscuits
1 pound skinless, boneless chicken breast halves, fresh or frozen (see Notes)
1 tablespoon vegetable oil
1 large onion (for about 1 cup chopped)
8 ounces fresh button mushrooms
¼ cup sherry (not cooking sherry; see Notes)
1 can (10¾ ounces) condensed regular or reduced-fat cream of mushroom soup
½ cup whole, low-fat, or skim milk
1 teaspoon Worcestershire sauce
2 cups frozen mixed vegetables

1. Preheat the oven and bake the biscuits according to the package instructions.

2. Meanwhile, if the chicken is frozen, run it under hot water so you can remove the packaging. Place the chicken on a microwave-safe plate and microwave, uncovered, on high power for 3 minutes to partially defrost.

3. While the chicken defrosts, heat the oil in an extra-deep 12-inch skillet over medium heat. Peel and coarsely chop the onion, adding it to the skillet as you chop. Cook, stirring, for 1 minute.

4. Cut the chicken (fresh or partially defrosted) into bite-size pieces, adding them to the skillet as you cut. Cook, stirring occasionally. Meanwhile, rinse, pat dry, and slice the mushrooms, removing and discarding any tough stems. When the chicken turns white on the outside, after about 4 minutes, add the mushrooms to the skillet and cook, stirring often, until they begin to release their liquid, about 2 minutes.

5. Add the sherry and cook, stirring, for 1 minute. Then add the cream of mushroom soup, milk, and Worcestershire sauce and stir to mix well. Add the frozen vegetables and stir to mix in. Cook, stirring frequently, until the mixture is bubbly and the vegetables are heated through, about 3 minutes.

6. Reduce the heat to low and let the mixture simmer while the biscuits finish baking. To serve, split the biscuits in half and place a bottom portion in each of four bowls. Spoon the chicken mixture evenly over the biscuits and top with the other half of the biscuits.

NOTES: You can use 2 cups Perfect Poached Chicken (page 362), Poached Chicken Thighs (page 364), or Chunky Seasoned Chicken (page 358), defrosted if frozen. Add with the soup and milk in Step 5.

■ You can use Madeira, Marsala, or white wine in place of the sherry; or just use ¼ cup more milk.

Chew on This

We're shocked at how often we find mistakes on our grocery receipts. Sale items don't always ring up at the low price advertised. At other times the checker will accidentally ring up two cans of beans when we only bought one. So be sure to watch the cash register monitor as your groceries are tallied. This can be difficult to do in stores where you have to unload your own items onto the conveyor belt. If you can't watch a monitor as the checker rings up your items, go over your receipt before leaving the store.

Seafood soups and stews are a good way to enjoy the luxury of a seafood dish without the expense of buying a large quantity of fish. Although this dish contains less than a pound of fish, it packs enough seafood flavor to make you think you're dining right beside the ocean. Buy whatever fish is on special or readily available—the exact type is not important. You could even substitute shrimp or scallops in equal amounts if that's what happens to carry the best price tag. Several national food companies now carry frozen okra in plastic bags, which makes it easy to scoop out a cupful. While okra is authentic to a Creole stew, simply leave it out if you can't find any.

FISHERMAN'S SEAFOOD CREOLE

SERVES: 4 START TO FINISH: UNDER 25 MINUTES

Salt for cooking the rice
1⅓ cups long-grain rice
2 tablespoons vegetable oil
1 large onion (for about 1 cup chopped)
2 ribs celery (for about 1 cup chopped)
1 medium-size green bell pepper (for about 1 cup chopped)
2 cloves fresh garlic, minced, or 2 teaspoons bottled minced garlic
2 tablespoons real (not imitation) bacon bits (see Notes)
1 bay leaf
1 teaspoon Worcestershire sauce
¼ teaspoon black pepper
1 can (14½ ounces) stewed tomatoes
1 small can (8 ounces) tomato sauce
12 ounces firm fish fillets, boned and skinned
1 cup frozen sliced okra (optional; see Notes)
Hot pepper sauce to taste

1. Bring 2⅔ cups lightly salted water to a boil in a covered medium-size saucepan. Add the rice, stir, and reduce the heat to low. Cover the pan and simmer until the rice is tender, about 20 minutes.

2. Meanwhile, heat the oil in a 12-inch skillet over medium heat. Peel and coarsely chop the onion, adding it to the skillet as you chop. Raise the heat to medium-high. Cut the celery into bite-size pieces, adding them to the skillet as you slice. Seed, stem, and coarsely chop the bell pepper, adding it to the skillet as you chop.

3. Add the garlic, bacon bits, bay leaf, Worcestershire sauce, and black pepper to the skillet. Stir to mix. Add the tomatoes with their juice and the tomato sauce. Stir to mix. Cover the skillet and bring the sauce to a boil.

4. While the sauce is heating, cut the fish into roughly 2-inch pieces.

5. Add the fish and the okra (if using) to the skillet and stir to mix. Cover the skillet and cook until the fish is almost opaque throughout, about 4 minutes.

6. Season with hot pepper sauce to taste. Reduce the heat to low and simmer for about 2 minutes (or until the rice is done). To serve, spoon the hot rice into pasta bowls or large shallow soup bowls and top with the Seafood Creole.

NOTES: For tips on making your own bacon bits, see the box below.

■ Be sure to use sliced okra that has not been breaded.

About:
MAKING YOUR OWN BACON BITS

It's easy to make bacon bits whenever you have a slice or two of leftover breakfast bacon. Just place the bacon on a cutting board and use a sharp chef's knife to chop it finely. (Or if the bacon is crisp enough, you can crumble it with your fingers.)

Pour the bits into a freezer-weight zipper-top plastic bag, and write the date on the bag. Stored in the freezer, the bacon bits will be useable for up to 3 months. They can be stored in the refrigerator for up to 4 days.

If you frequently have leftover bacon at your house, you can just keep adding bits to the same freezer bag, as long as you use the entire bag within 3 months of the original freezing date (written on the bag). Then just start over with a new bag.

To use the bacon bits, just scoop out the amount you need and place them on a microwave-safe plate that's lined with a paper towel. Cover them with a second paper towel and microwave on high power until crisp, about 10 seconds per ¼ cup. Now they are ready for your recipe.

If you order paella in a restaurant, it will usually contain chicken, shrimp, and sometimes other shellfish in addition to sausage and clams. When you're making the dish at home on a budget, however, this array of ingredients is overkill. Besides, there's so much flavor from the sausage, clams, and spices that you don't need the extras. We've served this very economical version of paella to friends (just double it and use a 6-quart pot), and they clamor for the recipe.

PLEASING PAELLA

SERVES: 4 START TO FINISH: UNDER 30 MINUTES

2 teaspoons olive oil

1 large onion (for about 1 cup chopped)

1 can (6½ ounces) minced or chopped clams

1 chicken bouillon cube

8 ounces regular or reduced-fat kielbasa

1⅓ cups converted rice (see Note)

1 can (14½ ounces) diced tomatoes

2 bay leaves

1 teaspoon dried basil

1 teaspoon dried thyme

1 teaspoon paprika

2 teaspoons Worcestershire sauce

¼ teaspoon hot pepper sauce, such as Tabasco (optional)

1 clove fresh garlic, minced, or 1 teaspoon bottled minced garlic

1 cup frozen green peas

1. Heat the oil in a 4½-quart Dutch oven or soup pot over medium heat. Peel and coarsely chop the onion, adding it to the pot as you chop. Cook, stirring frequently, until the onion begins to soften, about 2 minutes.

2. Meanwhile, drain the juice from the clams into a 2-cup measure. Add enough water to equal 2 cups. Set the clams aside.

3. When the onion has softened, add the clam juice mixture and the bouillon cube to the pot and bring to a boil.

4. Meanwhile, cut the kielbasa in half lengthwise and cut the halves into bite-size pieces; set them aside.

5. When the liquid comes to a boil, stir to make sure the bouillon cube is dissolved. Add the rice and the tomatoes with their juice. Stir in the bay leaves, basil, thyme, paprika, Worcestershire sauce, hot pepper sauce (if using), and the sausage pieces. Then add the garlic, stir well, cover the pot, and reduce the heat to low. Simmer for 18 minutes.

6. Meanwhile, pour the frozen peas into a colander and run tap water over them for about 1 minute to defrost them slightly. Set aside to drain.

7. When the rice mixture has cooked for 18 minutes, stir in the peas and the clams. Cook until the rice is tender, about 2 more minutes. (When it is done, the paella will still be fairly moist.) Fluff and stir the paella with a fork and serve.

NOTE: We like the texture of converted rice in this recipe, but long-grain rice can be used.

oppin' John is tradi-
tionally served for
good luck on New
Year's Day in the South.
The dish originated with
African slaves, for whom
(as for us today) it was a
filling way to stretch a little
bit of meat. Packaged sliced
ham typically comes in
6-ounce pouches, and
that's how we arrived at
the amount of ham to use
in this dish. We often find
these packages on sale at
the supermarket (look near
the bacon and other cold
cuts). Because the shelf life
extends for a month or
more, this is an easy and
economical way to keep
ham on hand for recipes
where only a little is
required. Of course this is
also a wonderful way to use
up the last bits of a bigger
ham (see page 242).

OLD SOUTH HOPPIN' JOHN

SERVES: 6 START TO FINISH: UNDER 30 MINUTES

SUPER-CHEAP!

2 teaspoons olive oil

1 large onion (for about 1 cup chopped)

1 cup (about 6 ounces) chopped ham

2 cloves fresh garlic, minced,
    or 2 teaspoons bottled
    minced garlic

2 cans (14 ounces each) vegetable broth,
    or 4 cups homemade vegetable stock
    (see page 38; see Notes)

1 teaspoon Worcestershire sauce

¼ teaspoon dried basil

¼ teaspoon black pepper

1½ cups long-grain rice

2 cans (15 ounces each) black-eyed peas, or 2 cups
    homemade (see page 386), defrosted if frozen

1 can (14½ ounces) diced tomatoes (see Notes)

1. Heat the oil in an extra-deep 12-inch skillet over medium heat.
Peel and coarsely chop the onion, adding it to the skillet as you
chop. Cook for 2 minutes, stirring occasionally. Add the ham and
the garlic to the skillet and cook, stirring, for 1 minute.

2. Add the broth and raise the heat to high. (If using canned
broth, add ½ cup water.) Stir in the Worcestershire sauce, basil,
and black pepper. Cover the skillet and bring the stock to a boil.
Then add the rice, stir, and reduce the heat to low. Cover the pan
and simmer until the rice is tender, about 20 minutes.

3. While the rice cooks, drain and rinse the black-eyed peas. Set
them aside.

4. When the rice is tender, uncover the skillet. Add the black-eyed peas and the tomatoes with their juice. Cook, stirring, until the tomatoes and peas are thoroughly mixed in with the rice. Serve at once or remove the skillet from the heat and let the dish stand, covered if desired, until ready to serve, up to 5 minutes.

NOTES: Vegetable bouillon cubes dissolved in water could be used in place of the broth. Chicken broth or stock can also be used.
■ You can use seasoned tomatoes, such as those flavored with garlic and onion.

About:

SUBSTITUTING HOME-COOKED DRIED BEANS FOR CANNED

A 15-ounce can of beans contains 1¾ cups beans and liquid. Once you drain the liquid off, you have about 1 cup of beans. In most of our recipes we call for 1 cup of home-cooked dried beans as a substitute for each can of beans. Because the liquid in most canned beans is pretty salty, we usually drain the beans and rinse them well before adding them to a recipe. Rinsing home-cooked beans is not necessary.

From Beverly:

Here's a dish that appeals to the kid in everyone, yet it's a bit more sophisticated than the basic franks-and-beans. My favorite premium brand of seasoned baked beans goes on sale fairly regularly, and I always stock up. If you can't find a deal on seasoned baked beans, use the cheapest can you can find and add your own brown sugar and onion powder to taste in Step 4.

FANCY FRANKS AND BEANS

SERVES: 4 START TO FINISH: UNDER 25 MINUTES

8 ounces lean ground beef, fresh or frozen

8 ounces fully cooked sausage, such as kielbasa, smoked sausage, or bratwurst, defrosted if frozen (see Note)

2 teaspoons vegetable oil

1 can (28 ounces) baked beans seasoned with onion, bacon, and brown sugar

1 can (15 ounces) black beans, or 1 cup homemade (see page 368), defrosted if frozen

1 teaspoon garlic powder

1 teaspoon Worcestershire sauce

1. If the beef is frozen, run it under hot water so you can remove the packaging. Place the beef on a microwave-safe plate and microwave, uncovered, on high power for 2 minutes to partially defrost.

2. Meanwhile, cut the sausage into ¼-inch-thick rounds and set them aside.

3. Heat the oil in an extra-deep 12-inch skillet over medium heat. Add the beef and cook, stirring often, until the meat is crumbled and half browned. Then add the sausage pieces and cook, stirring often, until the beef and sausages have completely browned, 7 to 8 minutes total.

4. Add the baked beans with their liquid (remove and discard any large pieces of pork). Rinse and drain the black beans and add them to the skillet. Add the garlic powder and Worcestershire sauce. Stir to combine, gently so as not to break up the beans. Bring the mixture just to a boil and then reduce the heat to low. Simmer for about 5 minutes to combine the flavors. Serve at once, in shallow bowls or plates.

NOTE: Hot dogs can also be used.

GOOD OL' BEANS AND RICE

SERVES: 4 START TO FINISH: UNDER 25 MINUTES

Salt for cooking the rice
1 cup long-grain rice
2 teaspoons vegetable oil
1 large onion (for about 1 cup chopped)
1 can (15 ounces) red or white beans, or 1 cup homemade (see page 368), defrosted if frozen
1 can (15 ounces) black beans, or 1 cup homemade (see page 368), defrosted if frozen
1 can (14½ ounces) diced tomatoes seasoned with garlic and onion
1 clove fresh garlic, minced, or 1 teaspoon bottled minced garlic
1 cup frozen yellow corn kernels
1 teaspoon chili powder
½ teaspoon ground cumin
½ cup shredded Cheddar or Mexican-blend cheese

1. Bring 2 cups lightly salted water to a boil in a covered medium-size saucepan. Add the rice, stir, and reduce the heat to low. Cover the pan and simmer until the rice is tender, about 20 minutes.

2. Meanwhile, heat the oil in an extra-deep 12-inch skillet over medium heat. Peel and coarsely chop the onion, adding it to the skillet as you chop.

3. Cook the onion for 2 minutes, stirring occasionally, while you rinse and drain the red or white beans. Add them to the skillet. Add the black beans with their juice and the tomatoes with their juice. Add the garlic to the skillet. Add the corn, chili powder, and cumin. Stir to blend well. Reduce the heat to low and simmer until heated through, about 2 minutes.

4. To serve, divide the rice among four pasta bowls, and top it with the bean mixture. Sprinkle the cheese evenly over each serving.

SUPER-CHEAP!

From Beverly:

A few years ago, at a dinner with my husband's co-workers, the conversation turned to the fact that people don't cook anymore. I shared a tidbit from a press release that had recently crossed my desk: "The hottest new category at the supermarket is something called meal replacement," I said.

A chorus of "What?"s darted around the table.

"You know, food that you take home, and maybe you heat up, but food you don't really have to cook," I said.

That really got the conversation going. As we covered all the predictable laments, I sat there thinking that what people really need is more quick recipes. And then the beautiful, kind soul to my right said it better than I ever could: "Every time I make a pot of beans and rice, I think there's absolutely no reason on earth why anybody can't cook this."

Indeed. Not only is this recipe easy, easy, easy, it's cheap, cheap, cheap, too.

When you have some cooked lentils on hand, it's easy to whip up this Italian-inspired, 12-minute recipe. Not only is this dish inexpensive, it's also very low in fat. But thanks to the finish of rich olive oil, you won't feel as if you're eating a low-fat meal at all.

ITALIAN LENTILS OVER RICE

SERVES: 6 START TO FINISH: UNDER 15 MINUTES

SUPER-CHEAP!

Salt for cooking the rice
1½ cups long-grain rice
4 teaspoons extra-virgin olive oil
1 large onion (for about 1 cup chopped)
1 large green bell pepper (for about 1½ cups chopped)
2 cloves fresh garlic, minced, or 2 teaspoons bottled minced garlic
2 cans (14½ ounces each) stewed tomatoes
1 teaspoon dried Italian seasoning
3 cups already-cooked brown lentils (see page 369), defrosted if frozen
Salt and black pepper to taste

1. Bring 3 cups lightly salted water to a boil in a covered medium-size saucepan. Add the rice, stir, and reduce the heat to low. Cover the pan and simmer until the rice is tender, about 20 minutes.

2. Meanwhile, heat 2 teaspoons of the oil in an extra-deep 12-inch skillet over medium heat. Peel and coarsely chop the onion, adding it to the skillet as you chop. Cook, stirring occasionally, while you seed, stem, and coarsely chop the bell pepper. Add the bell pepper to the skillet as you chop. Cook, stirring, until the onion is tender, about 1 minute.

3. Add the garlic, tomatoes with their juice, and the Italian seasoning to the skillet. Stir well and cut the larger pieces of tomato with the side of the spoon to make bite-size pieces. Stir in the lentils and the remaining 2 teaspoons oil. Cook until the lentils are heated through, 3 to 4 minutes. Season with salt and black pepper and serve at once over a bed of hot rice.

CONFETTI FRIED RICE

SERVES: 4 START TO FINISH: UNDER 25 MINUTES

Salt for cooking the rice
1⅓ cups long-grain rice
Cooking oil spray
2 large eggs
1 large onion (for about 1 cup chopped)
2 tablespoons vegetable oil
1 large green, yellow, or red bell pepper
  (for about 1½ cups chopped)
8 ounces fresh button mushrooms
3 cloves fresh garlic, minced, or 1 tablespoon bottled
  minced garlic
¼ cup apple juice or dry sherry
3 tablespoons regular or reduced-sodium soy sauce,
  plus more for serving (optional)
1 to 2 bunches scallions (for about ¾ cup chopped)
1 can (8 ounces) chopped or sliced water chestnuts,
  drained (optional)
1 cup frozen green peas
1½ tablespoons Asian (dark) sesame oil

1. Bring 2⅔ cups lightly salted water to a boil in a covered medium-size saucepan. Add the rice, stir, and reduce the heat to low. Cover the pan and simmer until the rice is tender, about 20 minutes.

2. Meanwhile, spray an extra-deep 12-inch skillet with cooking oil spray and place it over medium heat. Beat the eggs lightly, pour them into the skillet, and cook without stirring (as you would an omelet) until they are almost dry, 2 to 3 minutes.

3. While the eggs cook, peel and coarsely chop the onion and set it aside. When the eggs are ready, transfer them to a plate and set aside. (Do not wash the skillet.)

4. Heat the oil in the same skillet used for the eggs over medium heat. Add the onion and cook, stirring occasionally, until it just begins to soften, 2 to 3 minutes.

At about a dollar per serving, this Chinese dinner beats the cost of take-out by a mile—and yet it tastes just as if it came from your favorite restaurant! You'll never miss the meat in this filling, colorful dish.

When we have leftover rice in the fridge, fried rice is never too far away on the menu. But for this easy recipe, you won't mind cooking up a fresh batch. If you'd like to use leftovers, you'll need 4 cups cooked rice.

175

5. Meanwhile, stem, seed, and cut the bell pepper into bite-size pieces and add them to the skillet. Rinse, pat dry, and coarsely chop the mushrooms, discarding any tough stems. Add the mushrooms and garlic to the skillet. Cook, stirring, for 2 minutes.

6. Add the apple juice, soy sauce, and cooked rice. Continue to cook, stirring occasionally, while you slice the scallions, using the white and enough of the tender green tops to make ¾ cup. Add them to the skillet and stir well.

7. Drain the water chestnuts (if using) and add them to the skillet. Add the peas and sesame oil. Cut the eggs into thin strips, add them to the pan, and stir. Stir-fry to heat the water chestnuts and peas and to mix in the sesame oil, 1 minute. Serve at once over the hot rice, passing extra soy sauce at the table, if desired.

Shanghai Vegetable Medley

SERVES: 4 START TO FINISH: UNDER 25 MINUTES

Salt for cooking the rice
1⅓ cups long-grain rice
2 tablespoons vegetable oil
2 medium-size carrots (for about
   1 cup chopped)
1 large onion (for about 1 cup sliced)
1 bunch fresh broccoli, or 4 cups frozen broccoli pieces
8 ounces fresh button mushrooms
1 can (8 ounces) sliced water chestnuts (optional)
Stir-Fry Sauce (recipe follows)

1. Bring 2⅔ cups lightly salted water to a boil in a covered medium-size saucepan. Add the rice, stir, and reduce the heat to low. Cover the pan and simmer until the rice is tender, about 20 minutes.

The secret to most Asian food is crisp vegetables and terrific sauces, and this dish is no exception. The Stir-Fry Sauce is sure to become a family favorite at your house, as well.

The choice of vegetables for this medley is fairly flexible, but the combination of carrots, onions, broccoli, and mushrooms is our favorite. If you decide to substitute or add additional veggies to the stir-fry, just be sure to cut them all in similar sizes. And by all means, don't overcook them.

2. Meanwhile, heat the oil in an extra-deep 12-inch skillet over medium heat. Peel the carrots and, holding the knife at a 45-degree angle, cut them into ½-inch-thick slices. Add the carrots to the skillet, stirring occasionally. Peel the onion, cut it in half, and then cut the onion halves into ¼-inch-thick crescent-shaped slices. Add the onions to the skillet.

3. Cut the broccoli florets from the stalks. (Discard the stalks.) Cut the florets into bite-size pieces, if necessary. Add the broccoli to the skillet and continue to cook while you rinse, pat dry, and slice the mushrooms, removing and discarding any tough stems. Add the mushrooms to the skillet as you slice.

4. Drain the water chestnuts (if using) and set aside. Raise the heat to high and cook, stirring, until the broccoli and carrots are crisp-tender, 4 to 5 minutes more.

5. Add the water chestnuts and Stir-Fry Sauce. Stir to mix well and cook until the sauce is slightly thick, about 1 minute. Serve at once over the hot rice.

When you're looking for a meatless dinner to stretch the budget, this satisfying medley of vegetables, served over hot steamed rice, is sure to fill the bill.

STIR-FRY SAUCE

MAKES: ABOUT ½ CUP START TO FINISH: UNDER 5 MINUTES

¼ cup regular or reduced-sodium soy sauce

3 cloves fresh garlic, minced, or 1 tablespoon bottled minced garlic

1 tablespoon rice vinegar or distilled white vinegar

1 tablespoon ketchup

2 teaspoons finely minced fresh ginger or bottled minced ginger

1 teaspoon Asian (dark) sesame oil

SUPER-CHEAP!

This sauce is delicious with the Shanghai Vegetable Medley, and we find ourselves whipping it up for many of our other quick stir-fries, as well—chicken, pork, beef, or vegetable. We prefer the reduced-sodium soy sauce, but any type is fine. For a spicy sauce, add red pepper flakes to taste.

Whisk all of the ingredients together in a small bowl. It will keep for 1 week, covered, in the refrigerator.

CHAPTER FOUR

EMPOWERING PASTAS

"Pasta doesn't have to mean Italian only."

Can you ever have too many pasta recipes? As long as we've been writing recipes (more than twenty years between the two of us), we still want more. And so do our readers.

Simply put, pasta is cheap. Dinner doesn't get much easier than boiling water and throwing in some noodles. And as for the sauce, anything goes: from fresh tomatoes and garlic in a no-cook sauce to a simmered Italian sauce with sausage and peppers.

But pasta doesn't have to mean Italian only. We've ventured into the other ethnic flavors with Not Quite Tapenade with Rigatoni, Thai Spaghetti Toss, and Tex-Mex Noodles, just to name a few. And not all pastas are hot, either, meaning we can enjoy them even when it's sweltering outside. Check out Pasta with Salami and Basil and Seashells with Tuna and Dijon Cream.

Pasta is inherently kid-friendly. If the kids won't eat the sauce, just serve their noodles plain—or with a bit of butter and a sprinkling of Parmesan cheese. Mom and Dad can still enjoy the whole dish. It's easy to keep the ingredients on hand—it seems there's always a store special on one brand of pasta or another, not to mention the bulk buys available at warehouse stores. Pasta is also flexible: Just about any long or short pasta, depending on which is specified, will do in each of the following recipes, making it easy to use whatever kind is the best deal. And with more than thirty choices in this one chapter, that's a whole month's worth of pasta options. (Even *we* don't eat that much pasta in a month.)

Pasta dishes make the novice cook feel competent, and yet pasta can be one of the most elegant dishes in your repertoire. Save you money? Oh yeah! Pasta will do it. The plainest of pasta dishes in a restaurant can start at $9 a plate. Need we say more? Want to get in and out of the kitchen and on to other important endeavors? In a jiffy, pasta will do it! Not one of the following recipes will take longer than thirty minutes. Empower you? Absolutely, pasta will do it!

So enjoy this foray into the ever-expanding world of pasta dinners. Your budget will thank you, and so will your family.

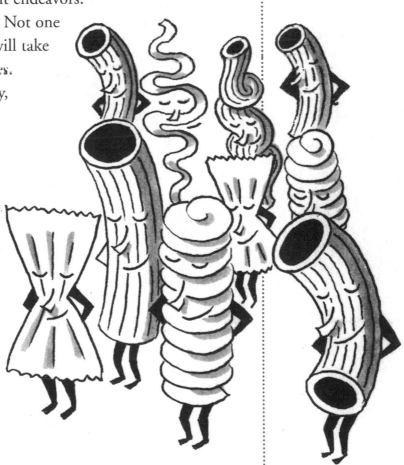

MINESTRONE CHICKEN

SERVES: 4 START TO FINISH: UNDER 25 MINUTES

All the flavors of our favorite Italian soup are present in this pleasing pasta dinner. There's so much happening here, you need only a crusty roll to complete the menu.

While this is one of our favorite meals for any time of the year, we especially love it in the summer, when bell peppers are at their peak.

Substituting half of a yellow, red, or orange pepper for half of the green pepper adds not only beauty, but also a slightly sweeter pepper flavor, too.

Salt for cooking the pasta
8 ounces short pasta, such as ziti
1 pound skinless, boneless chicken breast halves, fresh or frozen (see Note)
2 teaspoons olive oil
1 large onion (for about 1 cup chopped)
2 cloves fresh garlic, minced, or 2 teaspoons bottled minced garlic
1½ teaspoons dried Italian seasoning
1 medium-size green bell pepper (for about 1 cup chopped; see headnote)
2 cans (14½ ounces each) Italian-style stewed tomatoes
1 can (15½ ounces) chickpeas, or 1½ cups homemade (see page 368), defrosted if frozen
1 can (2¼ ounces) sliced black olives (optional)
Salt and black pepper to taste
Shredded or grated Parmesan cheese to taste (optional)

1. Bring 2½ quarts lightly salted water to a boil in a covered 4½-quart or larger pot. When the water reaches a rapid boil, add the pasta and cook, uncovered, until just tender, following the package directions.

2. Meanwhile, if the chicken is frozen, run hot water over it so you can remove the packaging. Place the chicken on a microwave-safe plate and microwave, uncovered, on high power for 3 minutes to partially defrost.

3. While the chicken defrosts, heat the oil in an extra-deep 12-inch skillet over medium heat. Peel and coarsely chop the onion, adding it to the skillet as you chop.

4. Cut the chicken (fresh or partially defrosted) into bite-size pieces, adding them to the skillet as you cut. Add the garlic to the skillet. Add the Italian seasoning. Stir occasionally while you stem, seed, and cut the bell pepper into bite-size chunks, adding them to the skillet as you cut. Continue to cook, stirring frequently, until the chicken is no longer pink in the center, 5 to 6 minutes in all.

5. Add the tomatoes with their juice. Rinse and drain the chickpeas and add them to the skillet. Drain the olives (if using) and add them to the skillet. Cook until the sauce thickens slightly, 2 to 3 minutes.

6. When the pasta is done, drain it well and add it to the skillet. Stir to coat the pasta with the sauce. Season with salt and black pepper. Serve at once, topped with Parmesan cheese, if desired.

NOTE: You can use 2 cups Perfect Poached Chicken (page 362) or Poached Chicken Thighs (page 364), defrosted if frozen. Add in Step 5 with the tomatoes. Or use 2 cups Chunky Seasoned Chicken (page 358), defrosted if frozen. Omit the onion and garlic. Skip Steps 2 and 3 and add the chicken with the Italian seasoning in Step 4. The chicken will heat through while the bell pepper cooks.

Chew on This

Warehouse clubs such as Costco and Sam's Club don't accept coupons because they often sell in multi-packs that have bar codes that don't match up with single-item coupons. The packs often contain items that are "not for individual sale."

Shopping and the Single Cook

"Invest in storage containers to keep leftovers fresh."

Buy only what you can use before it spoils—that is the mantra. But if you're the only person eating, this can be difficult indeed. Here are a few tricks:

- Lots of foods in various supermarket departments are sold by the pound. The fresh meat, seafood, deli, produce, and bakery departments are perfect places to buy the exact sizes you need without paying any more per pound than if you were buying for a family of six.

- When food sold by the pound is packaged in containers larger than you need, ask the department manager to divide the package. Stores are happy to divide packages so you can buy only what you need.

- Many stores now sell cartons that contain just six eggs. If not, ask the manager to cut a carton in half.

- The deli isn't just for sandwich meats, cheeses, and salads anymore. The deli is the new home for already-cooked everything! For convenience, supermarkets now offer more prepared foods than ever before, so if you want one burrito, one slice of pizza, one grilled chicken breast, and 2 ounces of antipasto, you can get it—all by the piece or by the pound.

- The bulk foods section of the store also allows you to buy small quantities. If you can't eat a whole box of cereal or a whole bag of nuts before they go stale, buy only the amount you need from the bulk bins.

- Invest in storage containers to keep leftovers fresh. If you're going to freeze leftovers, be sure to use bags or containers made especially for the freezer so your food won't get freezer burn.

SPINACH PESTO PASTA WITH CHICKEN

SERVES: 4 START TO FINISH: UNDER 15 MINUTES

Salt for cooking the pasta
8 ounces short pasta, such as rotini
5 plum tomatoes (for about 1⅔ cups pieces)
1 small can (2¼ ounces) sliced black olives
2 cups cooked chicken chunks (see Note), defrosted if frozen
½ cup Spinach Parsley Pesto (page 372), defrosted if frozen
Salt and black pepper to taste
Shredded or grated Parmesan cheese, for serving

1. Bring 3 quarts lightly salted water to a boil in a covered
4½-quart or larger pot. When the water reaches a rapid boil,
add the pasta and cook uncovered, until just tender, following
the package directions.

2. Meanwhile, core and chop the tomatoes into bite-size pieces.
Put the pieces in a 3-quart or larger serving bowl. Drain the olives
and add them to the bowl.

3. If any of the chicken cubes are larger than bite-size, cut them in
half. If they are cold, microwave, uncovered, on high power until
just warmed through, about 2 minutes. Add the chicken cubes to
the bowl with the vegetables.

4. When the pasta is done, drain it well and add it to the serving
bowl. Stir the pesto to mix in any oil that may have separated.
Add the pesto to the bowl and toss until the pasta is well coated.
Season lightly with salt and black pepper. Serve at once, passing
Parmesan cheese to sprinkle on top.

NOTE: You can use Chunky Seasoned Chicken (page 358), Perfect
Poached Chicken (page 362), or Great Grilled Chicken Breasts
(page 360), cut into chunks.

This recipe takes a few ingredients and showcases them in a dinner that's robust but very quick to put together—especially if you happen to have some already-cooked chicken on hand. The flavor-boosting secret is our Spinach Parsley Pesto, which is inexpensive to make. We like to keep small batches in the freezer to pull out for dinners just such as this.

We wouldn't dare call this recipe Pad Thai. To make that delectable noodle dish from Thailand, you'd need pickled radishes, dried ground shrimp, and rice noodles. While grocery stores in North America have greatly expanded their selection of Asian—and especially Thai—foods, pickled radishes are probably still a few years away. In the meantime, we offer our ultra-easy substitute. Our version combines the classic mix of sweet, salty, hot, and sour that makes Thai cuisine so intriguing. We think you'll find this noodle toss light, flavorful, and very satisfying.

THAI SPAGHETTI TOSS

SERVES: 4   START TO FINISH: UNDER 25 MINUTES

Salt for cooking the pasta
12 ounces thin pasta, such as thin spaghetti
   or angel hair
1 pound skinless, boneless chicken breast halves,
   fresh or frozen (see Note)
8 ounces fresh bean sprouts
1 to 2 bunches scallions (for about 1½ cups pieces)
¼ cup unsalted or lightly salted roasted peanuts
2 teaspoons vegetable oil
2 cups (6 ounces) fresh snow peas or sugar snap peas
   (optional)
1 cup Thai-Style Peanut Sauce (page 374), defrosted
   if frozen

1. Bring 3 quarts lightly salted water to a boil in a covered 4½-quart or larger pot. When the water reaches a rapid boil, add the pasta and cook, uncovered, until just tender, following the package directions.

2. Meanwhile, if the chicken is frozen, place it on a microwave-safe plate and microwave, uncovered, on high power for 3 minutes to partially defrost.

3. While the chicken defrosts, rinse and drain the bean sprouts, shaking the colander to remove as much water as possible. Set aside. Cut the scallions into roughly 1-inch pieces, using all of the whites and enough tender green tops to make 1½ cups. Set aside. Coarsely chop the peanuts and set them aside.

4. Heat the oil in an extra-deep 12-inch skillet over medium heat. Cut the chicken (fresh or partially defrosted) into bite-size pieces, adding them to the pan as you cut. Cook, stirring occasionally, until the chicken turns white on the outside, 4 minutes. Then add the snow peas (if using) and scallions to the skillet. Continue to cook, stirring constantly, until the chicken is no longer pink in the center and the snow peas are bright green, about 2 minutes more.

5. Add the bean sprouts and peanut sauce to the skillet and reduce the heat to low. Stir to mix well and simmer until ready to serve.

6. When the pasta is done, drain it in a colander, shaking it to remove as much water as possible. Return the drained pasta to the cooking pot. Add the chicken mixture and toss until well mixed. To serve, divide the pasta, chicken, and vegetables evenly among four plates. Sprinkle 1 tablespoon of the chopped peanuts over each plate and serve.

NOTE: You can use 2 cups Perfect Poached Chicken (page 362), Poached Chicken Thighs (page 364), or Great Grilled Chicken Breasts (page 360), defrosted if frozen. Or use 2 cups Chunky Seasoned Chicken (page 358), defrosted if frozen. Add the chicken at the end of Step 4, after cooking the snow peas and scallions.

About:
COVERING YOUR PASTA POT

We often suggest covering your pasta pot while the water comes to a boil. That's simply because it saves time. The quicker the water boils, the faster you get the pasta cooked and dinner on the table.

But, we do not suggest that you leave the pot unattended. Most of our recipes are written so that you'll start other tasks while the water heats, and our expectation is that you'll be in the kitchen with your pot as it approaches a boil. If you're forced to leave the pot, uncover it and lower the heat to medium-high. The water will still come to a boil—but it won't boil up and over your stove. Even if it takes a bit longer, you won't have to clean up the spill.

From Alicia:

I knew I was pushing the envelope when I sent this recipe to my friends Tony and Elizabeth Voiers to try. The traditional version of cacciatore was a specialty of Tony's Italian-born grandmother. How would something so quick and easy match up to the dish Tony had grown up with?

"I was impressed with how fresh and delicious this tasted," Tony reported. Elizabeth added that, because it was so easy to put together, it got a big thumbs-up from her.

QUICKIE CACCIATORE

SERVES: 4 START TO FINISH: UNDER 20 MINUTES

Salt for cooking the pasta
8 ounces thin pasta, such as thin spaghetti or angel hair
1 pound skinless, boneless chicken breast halves, fresh or frozen (see Note)
2 teaspoons olive oil
1 large onion (for about 1 cup chopped)
1 large green bell pepper (for about 1½ cups chopped)
8 ounces fresh button mushrooms
1 clove fresh garlic, minced, or 1 teaspoon bottled minced garlic
1 can (14 ounces) Italian-style stewed tomatoes
½ teaspoon dried Italian seasoning
½ teaspoon Worcestershire sauce
¼ cup regular or no-salt-added tomato paste

1. Bring 2½ quarts lightly salted water to a boil in a covered 4½-quart or larger pot. When the water reaches a rapid boil, add the pasta and cook, uncovered, until just tender, following the package directions.

2. Meanwhile, if the chicken is frozen, run hot water over it so you can remove the packaging. Place the chicken on a microwave-safe plate and microwave, uncovered, on high power for 3 minutes to partially defrost.

3. While the chicken defrosts, heat the oil in an extra-deep 12-inch skillet over medium heat. Peel and coarsely chop the onion, adding it to the skillet as you chop. Stem, seed, and cut the bell pepper into bite-size pieces, adding them to the skillet as you cut. Rinse, pat dry, and slice the mushrooms, removing and discarding any tough stems. Coarsely chop the mushrooms and add them to the skillet as you chop. Cook until the mushrooms release their liquid and are tender, 4 to 5 minutes.

4. Cut the chicken (fresh or partially defrosted) into bite-size pieces, adding them to the skillet as you cut. Add the garlic. Cook, stirring, until the vegetables are tender and the chicken is no longer pink in the center, 5 to 6 minutes.

5. Add the tomatoes with their juice, Italian seasoning, and Worcestershire sauce. Stir well. Add the tomato paste 1 tablespoon at a time, stirring after each addition. Continue to stir until the tomato paste is completely incorporated. Reduce the heat to low and simmer until ready to serve.

6. When the pasta is done, drain it well and divide it among four plates. Top it with the chicken mixture and serve right away.

NOTE: You can use 2 cups Perfect Poached Chicken (page 362) or Poached Chicken Thighs (page 364), defrosted if frozen. Add in Step 4. Or use 2 cups Chunky Seasoned Chicken (page 358), defrosted if frozen. Omit the onion and garlic. Add the Chunky Seasoned Chicken in Step 4 and cook until heated through.

About:
BUYING THE CHEAPEST PASTA

Our pasta philosophy is simple: For most of us, pasta is pasta—so you may as well buy the least expensive kind you can find. Generally our recipes allow for a choice of either short pastas or long pastas, so unless you've advertised tonight's dinner specifically as spaghetti and meatballs, use whatever similar shape you happen to have on hand.

If we don't get fixated on a particular brand, we can frequently get pasta at a reduced price. And when we do see a sale, we buy several shapes and sizes, since it keeps for months. In fact, we like varying the type of pasta we use in our recipes because it keeps everyone from getting bored.

As long as you haven't raised a houseful of future restaurant critics (and as long as your mother-in-law isn't visiting from Rome), just buy the house brand and prepare it for satisfied pasta-lovers.

Budget food for company? Absolutely. Our neighbors decided to serve this elegant pasta dish when friends came calling. "Raves around the dining room table" was the report.

They used the Chunky Seasoned Chicken they already had in the freezer, and this went together in a flash. That meant they had more time to spend with their guests.

You don't have to wait for company to come knocking to try this Greek-inspired delight. Any leftovers warm beautifully for lunch later in the week.

GREEK CHICKEN OVER ORZO

SERVES: 4 START TO FINISH: UNDER 25 MINUTES

8 ounces orzo (see Notes)
1½ pounds skinless, boneless chicken breast halves, fresh or frozen (see Notes)
2 teaspoons olive oil
1 large onion (for about 1 cup chopped)
2 cloves fresh garlic, minced, or 2 teaspoons bottled minced garlic
1 can (14½ ounces) stewed tomatoes
1 small can (8 ounces) regular or no-salt-added tomato sauce
1 can (14 ounces) quartered artichoke hearts (not marinated)
1 can (3.8 ounces) sliced black olives
½ teaspoon dried oregano
½ teaspoon dried basil
¼ cup crumbled feta cheese, or more to taste

1. Bring 2 quarts unsalted water to a boil in a covered 4½-quart or larger pot. When the water reaches a rapid boil, add the pasta and cook, uncovered, until just tender, following the package directions.

2. Meanwhile, if the chicken is frozen, run it under hot water so you can remove the packaging. Place the chicken on a microwave-safe plate and microwave, uncovered, on high power for 3 minutes to partially defrost.

3. While the chicken defrosts, heat the oil in a 12-inch skillet over medium heat. Peel and coarsely chop the onion, adding it to the skillet as you chop. Cook until the onion begins to soften, about 2 minutes.

4. Cut the chicken (fresh or partially defrosted) into bite-size pieces and add them to the skillet as you cut. Cook, stirring, until the chicken turns white on the outside, about 4 minutes. Add the garlic to the skillet. Add the tomatoes with their juice and the tomato sauce. Drain the artichoke hearts and add them to the skillet. (If the artichoke hearts are in big pieces, coarsely chop them first.) Drain the olives and add them to the skillet. Add the oregano and basil and stir to mix well.

5. Bring the mixture to a boil, stirring occasionally. Cook until the chicken is no longer pink in the center, about 5 minutes. Reduce the heat to low and simmer until ready to serve.

6. When the orzo is done, drain it well and divide it among four plates. Spoon the chicken over the hot orzo, garnishing each serving with about 1 tablespoon of the feta cheese.

NOTES: Orzo is a rice-shaped pasta that's available alongside other pastas in the supermarket.

■ You can use 3 cups Perfect Poached Chicken (page 362) or Poached Chicken Thighs (page 364), defrosted if frozen. Add in Step 4. Or use 3 cups Chunky Seasoned Chicken (page 358), defrosted if frozen. Omit the onion, oil, and garlic. Skip Steps 2 and 3. In Step 4, place the Chunky Seasoned Chicken in the skillet, add the tomatoes and tomato sauce, and proceed with the recipe.

Chew on This

Eighty percent of shoppers nationwide used coupons, saving them an average of $206 in 2003, according to figures from a coupon clearinghouse for manufacturers and retailers in Deerfield, Illinois.

Expensive Spices and Dried Herbs

Your spice cabinet can easily become the most expensive investment in your kitchen. And the spices don't even have to get exotic or extensive for the prices to start adding up to significant money. To add insult to injury, spices don't stay fresh forever.

Many books and magazines today will tell you that your spices should be replaced every six months, but we honestly don't know a soul who tosses herbs and spices after six months. In our experience, most spices continue to add flavor and body for a year or more, provided they're stored on a relatively cool, dark shelf. So you'll probably be able to use those last teaspoons of aging spices in the jar. Just give the spice a sniff, and, if it still smells the way it is supposed to (no off odors), then it should be fine to use.

Even with a full year of shelf life, spices and dried herbs present some special challenges for the budget-minded cook. Let's say you get the urge to try your hand at Indian cooking. Based on an unscientific survey of several Indian cookbooks, most recipes use between six and ten herbs and spices. If you plan to cook Indian food often, this might not be a problem because many recipes rely on the same seasonings. But if you just want to experiment with one dish and you have to buy turmeric, cumin, mustard seeds, garam marsala, saffron threads, and whole cardamom pods, your investment in spices alone can top $25. This same situation comes into play with many other ethnic cuisines.

In developing the recipes for this book, one of our top priorities was to limit the use of unusual spices and flavoring agents that most cooks wouldn't typically stock and that you would be unlikely to use up once you'd bought them. We have weighed this against the fact that herbs and spices can add immeasurably to your enjoyment of a dish. Our best advice? Buy smart. Here are some tips:

- Whenever possible, buy premixed spice blends. One jar of Italian seasoning combines a balanced blend of marjoram,

"Whenever possible, buy premixed spice blends."

thyme, rosemary, savory, sage, oregano, and basil. It's a bargain considering what each separate jar would cost. Other best-known blends include Cajun seasoning, apple pie spice, and herbes de Provence, but check the spice shelf—premixed blends are expanding all the time.

- Find a store that sells spices in bulk and buy only the amount you need for the recipe. There's no need to pay $4.50 for a jar of turmeric when you need only a pinch at a time! Many upscale specialty markets and some ethnic markets sell spices in bulk, as do some larger supermarkets.

- If you know you can't use a whole jar of a spice, shop with a friend and split the bottle (and the cost).

- The more of a spice you buy, the cheaper it is per ounce. This is particularly true if you buy a whopping lot of it. For example, warehouse club stores sell 20-ounce containers of chili powder for only a little more than it costs to buy a 2½-ounce bottle in the supermarket. The same thing is true at many ethnic grocery stores, particularly Indian and Asian ones. (See page 224 for more information on shopping at ethnic grocery stores.) To take advantage of these deals, you practically need a spice cartel: Line up several friends to share the bounty.

- If a recipe calls for a number of spices and you have all of them exccept one, just leave that spice out. If a dish is full of flavor, you'll probably never notice that it's missing ¼ teaspoon of cardamom. Considering the $5 the jar of spice will cost, that seems like a reasonable compromise.

- Keep all red spices—cayenne pepper, chili powder, paprika, and red pepper flakes—in the refrigerator or freezer to pro-long freshness.

- When you buy a spice, attach a small sticker or piece of tape to the lid and write the purchase date on it. Plan to do a spice purge once a year, and make a special effort to cook with spices that are losing freshness.

We simply adore salsa, but why should Mexican food have all the fun? Thanks to a can of seasoned stewed tomatoes, some fresh parsley, and lemon juice, this barely cooked tomato sauce packs a bright Italian flavor. At about $1 per serving, it brightens the budget as well.

MAMMA MIA SALSA CHICKEN

SERVES: 4 START TO FINISH: UNDER 20 MINUTES

SUPER-CHEAP!

Salt for cooking the pasta
8 ounces thin pasta,
   such as thin spaghetti or angel hair
1 pound skinless, boneless chicken
   breast halves, fresh or frozen
   (see Note)
2 teaspoons olive oil
1 large onion (for about 1 cup chopped)
4 cloves fresh garlic
⅓ cup fresh parsley leaves
1 can (14½ ounces) Italian-style stewed tomatoes
½ lemon (for about 2 tablespoons juice)

1. Bring 2½ quarts lightly salted water to a boil in a covered 4½-quart or larger pot. When the water reaches a rapid boil, add the pasta and cook, uncovered, until just tender, following the package directions.

2. Meanwhile, if the chicken is frozen, run it under hot water so you can remove the packaging. Place the chicken on a microwave-safe plate and microwave, uncovered, on high power for 3 minutes to partially defrost.

3. While the chicken defrosts, heat the oil in an extra-deep 12-inch skillet over medium heat. Peel and coarsely chop the onion, adding it to the skillet as you chop. Cook until the onion begins to soften, about 3 minutes.

4. Cut the chicken (fresh or partially defrosted) into bite-size pieces, adding them to the skillet as you cut. Cook, stirring frequently, until the chicken is no longer pink in the center, 5 to 6 minutes. Remove the skillet from the heat.

5. Peel the garlic. Turn on a food processor or blender and drop the garlic cloves, one at a time, through the feed tube. Chop it finely. Drop the parsley leaves onto the moving blade and mince them finely. Add the tomatoes and their juice to the processor bowl. Squeeze the juice from the lemon half through a strainer into the processor bowl. Pulse three times, just until the tomatoes are chopped to a salsa consistency.

6. Return the skillet to medium heat. Add the tomato salsa and stir to coat the chicken. Cook just until the sauce begins to bubble, about 3 minutes.

7. Drain the pasta and divide it among four plates. Top it with the chicken and salsa and serve at once.

NOTE: You can use 2 cups Perfect Poached Chicken (page 362), Poached Chicken Thighs (page 364), or Great Grilled Chicken Breasts (page 360), defrosted if frozen. Add in Step 4 and cook only until the chicken is heated through, about 2 minutes. Or use 2 cups Chunky Seasoned Chicken (page 358), defrosted if frozen. Omit the onion and oil. Skip Steps 2, 3, and 4. Add the Chunky Seasoned Chicken to the skillet with the salsa in Step 5. Cook until heated through.

Chew on This

Seventy-eight percent of parents feel that eating dinner together as a family is important, according to recent research conducted for General Mills by Opinion Research Corp. However, only 55 percent of those parents say they are able to eat dinner together four times each week.

CHICKEN AND BROCCOLI LO MEIN

SERVES: 4 START TO FINISH: UNDER 20 MINUTES

From Beverly:

My friends have marveled that even from the time they were just tykes, my children have loved all types of Chinese food. How did I do it, they all wanted to know. The answer was simple, really. The big trend in Chinese restaurants at the time was the all-you-can-eat buffet. Every time a new buffet restaurant would open in town, the prices would be ridiculously cheap for the first few weeks to lure new customers. Our family would be the first to line up, and we always had a simple rule for our kids: Take only a little of each dish they selected. If they didn't like it, they didn't have to eat it. If they *did* like a dish, they were encouraged to go back for more.

Because the kids felt no pressure to eat any of the new foods, they weren't afraid to try new things. And because the entire buffet was included in the price, they could try as many new dishes as they wanted. The result has been that they developed adventurous palates when it comes to Chinese food.

Salt for cooking the pasta

8 ounces long pasta, such as linguine

⅔ pound skinless, boneless chicken breast halves, fresh or frozen (see Note)

1 cup fresh button mushrooms

1 tablespoon peanut oil or other vegetable oil

1 large onion (for about 1 cup chopped)

1 bag (16 ounces) frozen broccoli pieces

3 cloves fresh garlic, minced, or 1 tablespoon bottled minced garlic

2 teaspoons finely minced fresh ginger or bottled minced ginger

3 tablespoons regular or reduced-sodium soy sauce

1 tablespoon rice vinegar or white wine vinegar

1 tablespoon ketchup

1 teaspoon Asian (dark) sesame oil

1. Bring 2½ quarts lightly salted water to a boil in a covered 4½-quart or larger pot. When the water reaches a rapid boil, add the pasta and cook, uncovered, until just tender, following the package directions.

2. Meanwhile, if the chicken is frozen, run it under hot water so you can remove the packaging. Place the chicken on a microwave-safe plate and microwave, uncovered, on high power for 2 minutes to partially defrost.

3. While the chicken defrosts, rinse, pat dry, and slice the mushrooms, removing and discarding any tough stems. Set aside.

4. Heat the oil in an extra-deep 12-inch skillet over medium heat. Peel and coarsely chop the onion, adding it to the skillet as you chop. Stirring the onion occasionally, cut the chicken (fresh or partially defrosted) into bite-size pieces. When all of the chicken is cut, add it to the skillet.

5. Add the mushrooms, broccoli, and garlic to the skillet. Add the ginger. Cook, stirring frequently, until the mushrooms release their liquid and the chicken is no longer pink in the center, 5 to 6 minutes.

6. Add the soy sauce, vinegar, ketchup, and sesame oil to the skillet. Stir well to blend. Remove the skillet from the heat.

7. When the pasta is done, drain it well and add it to the skillet. Stir until it is coated with the sauce and combined with the vegetables. Serve at once.

NOTE: You can use 1 cup Perfect Poached Chicken (page 362) or Poached Chicken Thighs (page 364), defrosted if frozen. Add in Step 5 after the mushrooms have cooked for about 3 minutes. Or use 1 cup Chunky Seasoned Chicken (page 358), defrosted if frozen. Omit the onion. Begin the recipe at Step 5, having heated the oil in the skillet. Add the Chunky Seasoned Chicken after the mushrooms have cooked for about 3 minutes.

One of my daughter Grey's favorite Chinese dishes is lo mein, and so I decided to learn to make it at home. Since lo mein relies on lots of noodles and little meat, it's an economical dish.

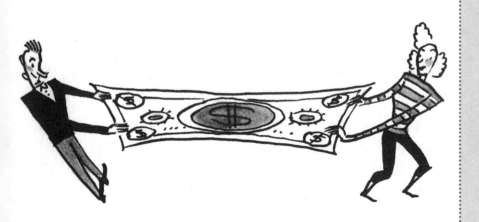

Canned soup has been a pantry backbone for years, providing an inexpensive way to make a quick sauce. Only now we have more choices: It's not just tomato and plain cream of mushroom anymore. Take this bold and flavorful chicken Stroganoff. Everyone will think you slaved over it, but the secret (if you want to share it) is in the soup: cream of mushroom flavored with roasted garlic. The mellow piquancy of roasted garlic blends beautifully with the creamy smoothness of the mushroom soup we have all relied on for so many years. We also get depth of flavor by adding a shot of a robust wine. Sherry, Madeira, Marsala, and Port are all fortified wines, and because of their higher alcohol content, they remain suitable for cooking for several months after opening. Pick up one of the less expensive California varieties; they work well for cooking.

SOUPED-UP CHICKEN STROGANOFF

SERVES: 4 START TO FINISH: UNDER 25 MINUTES:

Salt fro cooking the pasta
1 pound long pasta, such as fettuccine
1 pound skinless, boneless chicken breast halves, fresh or frozen (see Notes)
2 teaspoons olive oil
1 large onion (for about 1 cup chopped)
8 ounces fresh button mushrooms
1 clove fresh garlic, minced, or 1 teaspoon bottled minced garlic
1 bag (16 ounces) frozen broccoli spears or pieces (see Notes)
2 tablespoons dry sherry, Madeira, Marsala, or Port wine
1 can (10¾ ounces) condensed cream of mushroom soup seasoned with roasted garlic (see Notes)
1 teaspoon Worcestershire sauce
⅔ cup regular or reduced-fat sour cream
Black pepper to taste

1. Bring 2½ quarts lightly salted water to a boil in a covered 4½-quart or larger pot. When the water reaches a rapid boil, add the pasta and cook, uncovered, for 7 minutes.

2. Meanwhile, if the chicken is frozen, run it under hot water so you can remove the packaging. Place the chicken on a microwave-safe plate and microwave, uncovered, on high power for 3 minutes to partially defrost.

3. While the chicken defrosts, heat the oil in an extra-deep 12-inch skillet over medium heat. Peel and coarsely chop the onion, adding it to the skillet as you chop. Rinse, pat dry, and slice the mushrooms, removing and discarding any tough stems. Add the mushrooms and garlic to the skillet and stir.

4. Cut the chicken (fresh or partially defrosted) into bite-size pieces and add them to the skillet as you cut. Raise the heat to medium-high. Cook, stirring occasionally, until the chicken is no longer pink in the center, 5 to 6 minutes.

5. Meanwhile, when the pasta has cooked for 7 minutes, add the broccoli to the boiling water. Bring back to a boil and continue to cook until the pasta is tender, 4 to 5 minutes.

6. When the chicken is cooked through, add the sherry and cook for 1 minute. Add the cream of mushroom soup, reduce the heat to medium-low, and stir until well combined. Add the Worcestershire sauce and sour cream and stir until well combined. (If using reduced-fat sour cream, do not let the sauce boil once it has been added.) Season with black pepper.

7. Drain the pasta and broccoli. Place some pasta on each plate, and arrange the broccoli spears over the pasta. Top each serving with chicken and sauce and serve.

NOTES: You can use 2 cups Perfect Poached Chicken (page 362), Poached Chicken Thighs (page 364), or Great Grilled Chicken Breasts (page 360), defrosted if frozen. Add in Step 6. Or use 2 cups Chunky Seasoned Chicken (page 358), defrosted if frozen. Omit the onion and garlic. Add the wine, then the Chunky Seasoned Chicken in Step 6.

■ Many companies are now packaging frozen broccoli spears in bags, which defrost faster than spears packed in boxes. If you can't find spears in a bag, use broccoli pieces, sometimes called broccoli "cuts."

■ If you can't find mushroom soup seasoned with roasted garlic, substitute plain cream of mushroom soup for a milder, but still delicious, dish.

Any time there's one less pot to wash, that's cause for celebration. So we wondered, does cooking the pasta in the same pot along with the sauce really work? In many cases, the answer is yes.

The challenge is to avoid having the starch from the pasta overpower the sauce, changing the texture and flavor. The answer for that, we've found, is to avoid thick pasta and instead use small, quick-cooking pasta such as elbow macaroni, egg noodles, or orzo.

The other secret is to get the amount of liquid right: There must be enough to cook the pasta without watering down the sauce. This recipe combines water, wine, and chicken broth, but you can replace the wine with water if you don't happen to have any available.

ONE-POT PASTA WITH ITALIAN CHICKEN

SERVES: 4 START TO FINISH: UNDER 25 MINUTES

1 pound skinless, boneless chicken breast halves, fresh or frozen

2 teaspoons olive oil

1 large onion (for about 1 cup chopped)

8 ounces fresh button mushrooms

1 clove fresh garlic, minced, or 1 teaspoon bottled minced garlic

1 teaspoon dried Italian seasoning

½ cup dry white wine, such as Chardonnay (see Note)

1 can (14½ ounces) Italian-style stewed tomatoes

1 can (14 ounces) fat-free chicken broth, or 2 cups homemade chicken stock (see page 10)

8 ounces quick-cooking pasta, such as egg noodles, elbow macaroni, or orzo

Salt to taste

1. If the chicken is frozen, run it under hot water so you can remove the packaging. Place the chicken on a microwave-safe plate and microwave, uncovered, on high power for 3 minutes to partially defrost.

2. While the chicken defrosts, heat the oil in an extra-deep 12-inch skillet over medium heat. Peel and coarsely chop the onion, adding it to the skillet as you chop. Rinse, pat dry, and slice the mushrooms, removing and discarding any tough stems. Add the mushrooms to the skillet as you slice, then add the garlic.

3. Cut the chicken (fresh or partially defrosted) into bite-size pieces, adding them to the skillet as you cut. Add the Italian seasoning. Cook, stirring frequently, for 3 minutes. Then add the wine and cook, stirring constantly, for 1 minute.

4. Add the tomatoes with their juice, the broth, ½ cup water, and pasta. Bring the mixture to a boil and press the pasta down into the liquid. Cover the skillet and cook at a moderate boil until the pasta is tender and the chicken is no longer pink in the center, 7 to 9 minutes. Stir once halfway through cooking. Season with salt and serve.

NOTE: An extra ½ cup water can be used instead of the wine.

About:
SAVING WINE FOR LATER

From Alicia:

What do you do when there's wine left over from a recipe or from serving? I never cook with anything I wouldn't drink, so the answer's obvious—recork the bottle.

Air causes wine to mature, so an unopened bottle matures very slowly, with only the smallest amount of air able to move through the cork. Once you've removed the cork, the air speeds the wine through its life.

That's why we love our handy-dandy wine saver. The vacuum action of this gadget slows the process again, by sucking out the air left in the bottle. It's nothing more complicated than a rubber stopper and a suction device that pulls out most of the extra air, resealing the wine.

The first vacuum-seal wine saver to hit the market was Vacu-Vin, manufactured in Holland and priced at about $15. Other brands are also available at most wine shops and kitchen stores. Extra stoppers are sold separately.

Investing in one of these handy gadgets makes it more economical to cook with wine in the first place, because not one drop will be wasted.

O ur kids are of an age that they occasionally make plans of their own, and my husband and I find ourselves "kid-free" for an evening. At first, when it was just the two of us, we often found ourselves heading out to a restaurant to grab a quick bite. We noticed, however, that these little bonus nights without the kids were starting to add up. A typical out-to-eat meal for us includes two plates of pasta with salad, a glass of wine each, and a shared dessert. Before tip, our tab easily comes to more than $50. Wow!

Elegant pasta dishes can be prepared at home at a fraction of the cost. And a glass of wine in a restaurant often costs $7 to $10. For $7, I can buy a whole bottle.

A bottle of wine contains a little over 3 cups. If you select a $7 Chardonnay, you're using only about $2 worth of wine for this recipe. The flavor the wine imparts, however, is worth a whole lot more! And you can pour a couple of glasses to enjoy with dinner tonight.

CHICKEN WITH MUSHROOM WINE SAUCE

SERVES: 4 START TO FINISH: UNDER 25 MINUTES

Salt for cooking the pasta
8 ounces thin pasta, such as thin spaghetti or angel hair
1 pound skinless, boneless chicken breast halves, fresh or frozen (see Note)
2 teaspoons olive oil
1 large onion (for about 1 cup chopped)
8 ounces fresh button mushrooms
1 clove fresh garlic, minced, or 1 teaspoon bottled minced garlic
1 cup dry white wine, such as Chardonnay
Fresh parsley leaves (for 2 tablespoons chopped; optional)
3 tablespoons half-and-half
Salt and black pepper to taste

1. Bring 2½ quarts lightly salted water to a boil in a covered 4½-quart or larger pot. When the water reaches a rapid boil, add the pasta and cook, uncovered, until just tender, following the package directions.

2. Meanwhile, if the chicken is frozen, run it under hot water so you can remove the packaging. Place the chicken on a microwave-safe plate and microwave, uncovered, on high power for 3 minutes to partially defrost.

3. While the chicken defrosts, heat the oil in an extra-deep 12-inch skillet over medium heat. Peel the onion and finely chop it, adding it to the skillet as you chop.

4. Cut the chicken (fresh or partially defrosted) into bite-size pieces, adding them to the skillet as you cut.

5. Rinse, pat dry, and coarsely chop the mushrooms, removing and discarding any tough stems. Add the mushrooms and garlic to the skillet. Cook stirring frequently, for 1 minute. Add the wine to the skillet and cook, stirring occasionally, until almost all the liquid has evaporated and the chicken is no longer pink in the center, 7 to 9 minutes. While the chicken cooks, chop enough parsley (if using) to make 2 tablespoons. Set it aside.

6. When the pasta is done, drain it, put it back into the pot, cover the pot, and set it aside, off the heat, to keep warm.

7. Remove the skillet from the heat and stir in the half-and-half. The sauce will be thin. Season with salt and black pepper. Sprinkle the parsley (if using) over the chicken. To serve, divide the pasta among four plates and top with the sauce.

NOTE: You can use 2 cups Chunky Seasoned Chicken (page 358), defrosted if frozen. Omit the onion and garlic. Skip steps 2, 3, and 4. Heat the oil in the skillet, add the mushrooms, and cook until they release their liquid, 2 to 3 minutes. Add the chicken and continue with the recipe, cooking just until the Chunky Seasoned Chicken is heated through, about 3 minutes.

This is a beautiful pasta dish that flies together in no time at all. It's perfect fare for summertime, when zucchini is fresh, abundant, and, best of all, cheap.

If you're not serving children, you can turn up the volume on the flavor by adding red pepper flakes to taste before you add the cheese in Step 6.

CORKSCREWS WITH CHICKEN AND ZUCCHINI

SERVES: 4 START TO FINISH: UNDER 25 MINUTES

Salt for cooking the pasta
8 ounces rotini or other short pasta
1 pound skinless, boneless chicken breast halves, fresh or frozen (see Notes)
2 teaspoons olive oil
1 large onion (for about 1 cup chopped)
8 ounces fresh button mushrooms
2 cloves fresh garlic, minced, or 2 teaspoons bottled minced garlic
1 teaspoon dried Italian seasoning
2 medium (about 1¼ pounds) zucchini (see Notes)
1 medium-size tomato, or 3 medium-size plum tomatoes (for about 1 cup chopped)
¼ cup fresh parsley or basil leaves, loosely packed (optional)
¼ cup shredded or grated Parmesan cheese
Salt and black pepper to taste

1. Bring 2½ quarts lightly salted water to a boil in a covered 4½-quart or larger pot. When the water reaches a rapid boil, add the pasta and cook, uncovered, until just tender, following the package directions.

2. Meanwhile, if the chicken is frozen, run it under hot water so you can remove the packaging. Place the chicken on a microwave-safe plate and microwave, uncovered, on high power for 3 minutes to partially defrost.

3. While the chicken defrosts, heat the oil in an extra-deep 12-inch skillet over medium heat. Peel and chop the onion, adding it to the skillet as you chop. Cut the chicken (fresh or partially defrosted) into ½-inch cubes, adding them to the skillet as you cut and stirring occasionally. Rinse, pat dry, and coarsely

chop the mushrooms, removing and discarding any tough stems. Add the mushrooms, garlic, and Italian seasoning to the skillet.

4. Slice the zucchini into ¼-inch-thick rounds and stir them into the pan. Cover the pan and cook, stirring occasionally, until the chicken is no longer pink in the center, 5 to 6 minutes.

5. Meanwhile, core and chop the tomato into bite-size cubes and set them aside. Finely chop the parsley (if using) and set it aside.

6. When the zucchini is crisp-tender, remove the pan from the heat. Stir in the tomatoes and parsley and cover the pan. Drain the pasta well and add it to the skillet. Add the cheese and stir until it melts. Season with salt and black pepper and serve at once.

NOTES: You can use 2 cups Perfect Poached Chicken (page 362), Poached Chicken Thighs (page 364), or Great Grilled Chicken Breasts (page 360), defrosted if frozen. Add in Step 4. Or use 2 cups Chunky Seasoned Chicken (page 358), defrosted if frozen. Omit the onion and garlic. Begin the recipe at Step 3. Add the Chunky Seasoned Chicken with the zucchini in Step 4.

■ If you prefer soft zucchini, add 1 to 2 minutes to the cooking time in Step 4. Two cups of broccoli florets can be used in place of the zucchini.

MoneySaver

If you currently have spices that have been in your cabinet too long, don't throw them away! It's easy to turn them into scents for your home. Simply pour a spice into a saucepan and fill it with water. Bring the water to a boil, then reduce the heat to simmer. Simmer the spice for as long as you like, refilling the water every hour. Although this works especially well with cinnamon and cloves, other spices such as rosemary, bay leaves, and basil make welcoming scents too.

For us, Thanksgiving wouldn't be Thanksgiving without leftover turkey for tetrazzini. This family favorite never seems to turn out the same way twice. Some years there's more turkey than other years, sometimes we leave out the green pepper and add pimento, and occasionally we vary the kind of cheese. But we had never experimented with the noodles until we received a letter from Mary McEwen, a reader of our Desperation Dinners newspaper column. Mary makes an "Instant Tetrazzini" using the ramen noodles from the little packages of flavored ramen noodle soup found beside the canned soups at the supermarket. Those noodles are fast, tasty, and very cheap, so we thought we'd give them a try. After some experimenting, we came up with this convenient twist to our yearly ritual. Our children loved the curly noodle shapes. Our thanks to Mary for a new take on an old favorite!

LAST-OF-THE-TURKEY TETRAZZINI

SERVES: 4 START TO FINISH: UNDER 25 MINUTES

SUPER-CHEAP!

2 teaspoons vegetable oil
1 large onion (for about 1 cup chopped)
8 ounces fresh button mushrooms
1 medium-size green bell pepper (for about 1 cup chopped)
1 clove fresh garlic, minced, or 1 teaspoon bottled minced garlic
1 teaspoon Worcestershire sauce
¼ teaspoon black pepper
3 cups cooked turkey or chicken, skin removed (see Note)
1 can (10¾ ounces) regular or reduced-fat condensed cream of mushroom soup
½ cup whole, low-fat, or skim milk
½ cup regular or reduced-fat sour cream
3 packages (3 ounces each) chicken-flavor ramen soup
1 cup (4 ounces) shredded Cheddar cheese, or more to taste

1. Bring 6 cups unsalted water to a boil in a covered 3-quart or larger pot.

2. While the water is heating, heat the oil in an extra-deep 12-inch skillet over medium heat. Peel and coarsely chop the onion, adding it to the skillet as you chop. Cook the onion for 1 minute. Rinse, pat dry, and slice the mushrooms, discarding any tough stems. Add the mushrooms to the skillet as you slice. Cook the mushrooms and onions, stirring occasionally, while you stem, seed, and coarsely chop the bell pepper. Add it to the skillet. Add the garlic to the skillet. Add the Worcestershire sauce and black pepper. Cook the vegetables, stirring occasionally, until the mushrooms release their liquid, about 5 minutes.

3. While the vegetables cook, cut the turkey into bite-size chunks. Set aside.

4. Add the cream of mushroom soup, milk, sour cream, and turkey chunks to the skillet. Stir until well blended. Cook, stirring frequently, until heated through, about 2 minutes. (Do not boil the sauce.) Reduce the heat to low.

5. While the sauce simmers in the skillet, add the ramen noodles to the boiling water along with one of the seasoning packets. (Reserve the remaining 2 seasoning packets for another use.) Boil, stirring occasionally, until soft, 3 minutes (do not overcook). Immediately drain the noodles well. Gently stir the noodles into the turkey mixture until just coated with the sauce. (Vigorous stirring will break the tender noodles.) Sprinkle the cheese over the noodle mixture, cover the skillet, and cook just until the cheese melts, about 2 minutes. Serve at once.

NOTE: Instead of turkey, you can use 2 cups Perfect Poached Chicken (page 362), Poached Chicken Thighs (page 364), or Chunky Seasoned Chicken (page 358). Or cut 1 pound skinless, boneless chicken breasts into bite-size chunks and sauté until cooked through, then proceed with the recipe.

This is one of those one-pan meals that's economical and keeps cleanup to the bare minimum: Just assemble everything in a skillet—including the macaroni—slam on the lid, and simmer until tender. This dish is equally kid-friendly and hungry-man-filling, so if you're like us, that combination makes it a prime candidate for the "favorite dinners" list. If you've got anybody around who doesn't appreciate green pepper, just leave it out.

If you need dinner really fast, make use of your stash of frozen Basic Beef.

HUNGRY MAN'S MACARONI

SERVES: 4 START TO FINISH: UNDER 25 MINUTES

1 pound ground beef, fresh or frozen (see Notes)
2 teaspoons olive oil
1 large onion (for about 1 cup chopped)
1 medium-size green bell pepper (for about 1 cup chopped)
2 cloves fresh garlic, minced, or 2 teaspoons bottled minced garlic
1 can (14 ounces) fat-free chicken broth, or 2 cups homemade chicken stock (see page 10)
2 cups bottled spaghetti sauce (see Notes)
8 ounces short pasta, such as elbow macaroni
¼ cup shredded or grated Parmesan cheese, or more to taste

1. If the beef is frozen, run it under hot water so you can remove the packaging. Place the beef on a microwave-safe plate and microwave, uncovered, on high power for 3 minutes to partially defrost.

2. Meanwhile, heat the oil in an extra-deep 12-inch skillet over medium heat. Peel and coarsely chop the onion, adding it to the skillet as you chop. Add the beef (fresh or partially defrosted) and cook, turning and breaking up the meat, until it begins to crumble and brown, 5 to 6 minutes. Drain any accumulated fat from the beef, if necessary.

3. Stem, seed, and coarsely chop the bell pepper, adding it to the skillet as you chop. Add the garlic to the skillet.

4. Add the broth, spaghetti sauce, and pasta. Stir until well mixed. Cover the skillet and bring the mixture to a boil. Cook at a moderate boil, stirring occasionally, until the pasta is just tender, about 10 minutes. (Cook 2 minutes more for softer pasta.) Serve at once, sprinkling each serving with about 1 tablespoon Parmesan cheese.

NOTES: You can use 3 cups Basic Beef (page 317), defrosted if frozen. Omit the onion and add the ground beef in Step 3 after you add the bell pepper.

■ Use your favorite spaghetti sauce. We like a smooth marinara-style sauce, such as Ragù Traditional.

WILD WEST WAGON TRAIN SUPPER

SERVES: 4 START TO FINISH: UNDER 25 MINUTES

Salt for cooking the pasta
12 to 16 ounces wagon wheels (rotelle) or
    other short pasta
1 pound ground beef, fresh or frozen (see Note)
2 teaspoons olive oil
1 large onion (for about 1 cup chopped)
1½ teaspoons chili powder, or to taste
½ teaspoon garlic powder
2 cups mild or hot bottled salsa
1 can (10¾ ounces) condensed Cheddar cheese soup

1. Bring 3 quarts lightly salted water to a boil in a covered 4½-quart or larger pot. When the water reaches a rapid boil, add the pasta and cook, uncovered, until just tender, following the package directions.

2. Meanwhile, if the beef is frozen, run it under hot water so you can remove the packaging. Place the beef on a microwave-safe plate and microwave, uncovered, on high power for 3 minutes to partially defrost.

We had great fun with a recipe challenge from a fourteen-year-old reader of our Desperation Dinners newspaper column.

"I am really impressed with your ability to spice up recipes and create your own," wrote Gerling, who described himself as an aspiring cook who enjoys making meals for his family. "My brothers love my recipe for Hamburger Casserole (hamburger, cheese soup, an onion, milk, and macaroni), but I am getting bored with it. I thought perhaps you would administer some taste to this child-pleaser of a dish."

When it comes to pleasing children, sometimes a fun pasta shape makes the difference. Wagon wheels

(continued)

3. While the beef defrosts, heat the oil in an extra-deep 12-inch skillet over medium heat. Peel and coarsely chop the onion, adding it to the skillet as you chop. Cook until the onion begins to soften, about 2 minutes.

4. Add the beef (fresh or partially defrosted) to the skillet. Add the chili powder and garlic powder. Cook, turning and breaking up the meat, until it is crumbled and browned, 7 to 8 minutes. Drain any accumulated fat from the beef, if necessary.

5. Add the salsa and the cheese soup and stir well to combine.

6. When the pasta is done, drain it well and add it to the skillet. Stir until the pasta is coated with the sauce. Serve at once.

NOTE: You can use 3 cups Basic Beef (page 347), defrosted if frozen. Omit the oil, onion, and garlic powder and add the beef in Step 4 with the chili powder.

TEX-MEX NOODLES

SERVES: 6 START TO FINISH: UNDER 25 MINUTES

Salt for cooking the pasta
1 pound thin pasta, such as thin spaghetti or angel hair
1 pound ground beef, fresh or frozen (see Note)
2 teaspoons vegetable oil
1 large onion (for about 1 cup chopped)
3 cloves fresh garlic, minced, or 1 tablespoon bottled minced garlic
1 tablespoon chili powder
1 teaspoon ground cumin
1 can (14½ ounces) Mexican-style stewed tomatoes or chopped tomatoes seasoned with jalapeños
1 can (8 ounces) tomato sauce
1 cup frozen yellow or white corn kernels
Salt to taste (optional)
Hot pepper sauce to taste (optional)

(continued)

(rotelle to the Italians) immediately came to mind. Next, the trick is to spice things up without overdoing it for the kids. Most youngsters like Mexican food, as long as it's not too spicy. So we threw in a jar of mild salsa, a little chili powder, and some garlic and really started those wagon wheels rolling.

From Alicia:

My family is crazy about the flavors of mild Mexican and Tex-Mex foods. They'd eat south-of-the-border cuisine every night if I'd fix it for them. But I'm a pasta nut and can't get enough of any and every kind of pasta. This recipe solves these conflicting cravings: All the flavors of our favorite Mexican-inspired dishes are here, and it's served as a pasta sauce over thin spaghetti. My oldest daughter, Hannah, adds shredded taco cheese and sour cream to hers!

1. Bring 3 quarts lightly salted water to a boil in a covered 4½-quart or larger pot. When the water reaches a rapid boil, add the pasta and cook, uncovered, until just tender, following the package directions.

2. Meanwhile, if the beef is frozen, run it under hot water so you can remove the packaging. Place the beef on a microwave-safe plate and microwave, uncovered, on high power for 3 minutes to partially defrost.

3. Heat the oil in an extra-deep 12-inch skillet over medium heat. Peel and coarsely chop the onion, adding it to the skillet as you chop. Add the garlic to the skillet.

4. Add the meat (fresh or partially defrosted) to the skillet. Cook, turning and breaking up the meat, until it begins to crumble and brown, 7 to 8 minutes. Drain any accumulated fat from the beef, if necessary.

5. Add the chili powder, cumin, tomatoes with their juice, tomato sauce, and corn. Bring the sauce to a boil. Season with salt and hot pepper sauce (if using). Reduce the heat to low and let the sauce simmer, uncovered, until ready to serve.

6. When the pasta is done, drain it well and serve it on individual plates, topped with the sauce.

NOTE: You can use 3 cups Basic Beef (page 347), defrosted if frozen. Omit the oil, onion, and garlic. Skip Steps 2, 3, and 4. Add the beef with the other ingredients in Step 5.

From Beverly:

Dinner scores three runs—fast, economical, and kid-friendly —when you start with pasta and a hefty shot of Flexible Mexican Filling. "Wow, Mom, I really like this" were the first words out of my son's mouth when he took a taste. He didn't say much more for quite a few minutes—as he was too busy chewing and heading back for a second helping. Okay, so this meal doesn't encourage teenagers to engage in a lot of stimulating dinner conversation, but you can't have everything!

TACO TWISTS

SERVES: 6 START TO FINISH: UNDER 15 MINUTES

Salt for cooking the pasta
1 pound short pasta, such as rotini
2 teaspoons vegetable oil
1 large onion (for about 1 cup chopped)
2 cans (14½ ounces each) Mexican-style stewed tomatoes (see Note)
2 cups Flexible Mexican Filling (page 352), defrosted if frozen
¼ cup shredded cheese, such as Cheddar, taco blend, Colby, or Monterey Jack

1. Bring 3 quarts lightly salted water to a boil in a covered 4½-quart or larger pot. When the water reaches a rapid boil, add the pasta and cook, uncovered, until just tender, following the package directions.

2. Meanwhile, heat the oil in an extra-deep 12-inch skillet over medium heat. Peel and coarsely chop the onion, adding it to the skillet as you chop. Cook until the onion is soft, about 2 minutes.

3. Add the tomatoes with their juice. Cook, stirring, until the mixture comes to a boil. Add the Flexible Mexican Filling and stir until well combined.

4. When the mixture returns to a boil, reduce the heat to low and simmer, stirring occasionally, until ready to serve.

5. When the pasta is done, drain it well and divide it among six plates. Spoon the sauce over the hot pasta, topping each serving with 1 tablespoon of the cheese.

NOTE: You can use plain stewed tomatoes, but don't substitute diced tomatoes. The sauce does not simmer long enough to eliminate the raw taste of diced tomatoes.

SAM'S SWEDISH MEATBALLS

SERVES: 4 START TO FINISH: UNDER 25 MINUTES

8 ounces medium or wide egg noodles

2 cups (about 6 ounces) broccoli florets,
    fresh or frozen

1 can (14½ ounces) fat-free beef broth

24 already-cooked meatballs (see Notes),
    defrosted if frozen

3 tablespoons dry sherry or apple juice

1 cup sour cream (see Notes)

2 tablespoons cornstarch

3 tablespoons cold water

Salt and black pepper to taste

1. Bring 2½ quarts unsalted water to a boil in a covered 4½-quart
or larger pot. When the water reaches a rapid boil, add the noodles and cook, uncovered, for 4 minutes. Then place the broccoli
on top of the noodles and continue to cook until the noodles and
broccoli are just tender, about 3 minutes.

2. Meanwhile, pour the broth into a 12-inch skillet, cover the
skillet, and bring the broth to a boil over medium heat. Add the
meatballs and sherry and cook, uncovered, stirring occasionally,
until the meatballs are heated through, 5 to 6 minutes. Reduce
the heat to low.

3. Move the meatballs over to one side of the skillet and add the
sour cream on the other side of the skillet. Stir with a whisk until
the sour cream is incorporated into the broth. (A few lumps of
sour cream are okay.) Add the meatballs. Mix the cornstarch and
cold water in a small jar that has a lid. Cover, and shake well to
break up any lumps. Add the cornstarch mixture to the skillet
and stir until thickened to the consistency of heavy cream, about
1 minute.

From Beverly:

I'd been sick with the flu
for a week when
my son Sam delivered
the news. "Remember that
social studies project?" he
said. "It's due tomorrow."

"That social studies
project" consisted of cooking Swedish meatballs for
a smorgasbord to be served
to his entire class, and I'd
totally forgotten that I was
going to help Sam with the
recipe. Just how long does
it take to make Swedish
meatballs, anyway? Time
to find out. I thought
we'd be slaving for hours,
but thanks to a batch of
Marvelous Meatballs
(page 353) in my freezer,
the dish we devised was
a snap.

For dinner at home, we
add some broccoli for color
and to round out the meal.
Sam's Swedish Meatballs
make a fine, inexpensive
dinner for the social studies
class—or anybody else.

4. Drain the noodles and broccoli in a colander, shaking the colander to remove as much water as possible. Pour the noodles and broccoli into the skillet and stir to coat the noodles with the sauce. Season with salt and black pepper to taste. Serve at once.

NOTES: You can use Marvelous Meatballs (page 353) or purchased frozen meatballs (plain or traditional style).

■ Reduced-fat sour cream should *not* be used in this recipe.

About:
THE KITCHEN SCALE

Investing in an inexpensive kitchen scale can save you money. The best example of kitchen scale savings has to do with meat and portion size. Controlling the amount of meat you use in each recipe can quickly add up to real savings.

Take ground beef, for example. We often buy the "family size" packages because they're cheaper per pound. When we get home, we need a reliable way to divide the meat into usable portions. If a recipe is filling and tastes great with just 1 pound of ground beef, then why use 1¼ pounds? (If we just try to eyeball a pound of beef, we find it's easy to be ¼ pound off!)

Kitchen scales are easy to use and easy to clean, so there's no worry about food contamination. There are a variety of styles to choose from in kitchen equipment and mart-type stores. Just be sure to purchase one with a removable tray for efficient cleaning.

While we don't pull our scales out every day, they are handy to have around for weights and measures when we need them. Then we confidently mark our divided meats and other food items with the actual weight.

HAM AND BROCCOLI PASTA TOSS

SERVES: 6 START TO FINISH: UNDER 20 MINUTES

Salt for cooking the pasta
1 pound short pasta, such as rotini
1½ cups fresh broccoli florets or frozen
    broccoli pieces
6 ounces ham (for about 1 cup pieces)
1½ cups grape or cherry tomatoes
2 cloves fresh garlic
½ teaspoon dried basil
½ cup shredded or grated Parmesan cheese
2 tablespoons olive oil
Salt and black pepper to taste

1. Bring 3 quarts lightly salted water to a boil in a covered 4½-quart or larger pot. When the water reaches a rapid boil, add the pasta and cook, uncovered, until just tender, following the package directions. Three minutes before the pasta is done, add the broccoli to the boiling water.

2. Meanwhile, cut the ham into bite-size pieces. Put the pieces in a 3-quart or larger serving bowl. Cut the tomatoes in half and add the pieces to the bowl.

3. Peel and mince the garlic and add it to the bowl. Add the basil. Stir to mix well.

4. When the pasta and broccoli are done, drain them in a colander, shaking the colander to remove as much water as possible. Add the pasta and broccoli to the serving bowl and sprinkle the Parmesan cheese and drizzle the oil evenly over the pasta. Toss until the cheese melts. Season with salt and black pepper and serve at once.

From Beverly:

"Pasta tosses" are one of our favorite ways to stretch meat and veggies, because the main star is the pasta itself. I created this after getting a good deal on ham, but you can use left-over chicken or cooked sausages, and even salami or other deli meats. If you happen to have fresh basil or other fresh herbs on hand, throw in a couple of tablespoons of chopped leaves for a real taste treat.

This extremely simple meal uses an often-overlooked ingredient: Canadian bacon. Found with the cured and packaged meats in most grocery stores (look near the packaged pepperoni), Canadian bacon now comes in not only "sandwich size" but also pizza size, which is about the size of traditional pepperoni. Either product works well here.

Adding sour cream yields a tasty twist to traditional sauces.

PASTA WITH A TWIST

SERVES: 6 START TO FINISH: UNDER 25 MINUTES

Salt for cooking the pasta
1 pound short pasta, such as rotini
2 teaspoons olive oil
5 to 6 ounces sliced Canadian bacon or ham
1 clove fresh garlic, minced, or 1 teaspoon bottled minced garlic
1 large onion (for about 1 cup chopped)
½ teaspoon dried basil
1 can (14½ ounces) pasta-style chopped tomatoes or chopped tomatoes seasoned with onion and herbs
1 cup smooth-style bottled spaghetti sauce
½ cup frozen green peas (optional)
½ cup regular or reduced-fat sour cream

1. Bring 2½ quarts lightly salted water to a boil in a covered 4½-quart or larger pot. When the water reaches a rapid boil, add the pasta and cook, uncovered, until just tender, following the package directions.

2. Meanwhile, heat the oil in a 12-inch skillet over medium heat. While the oil heats, coarsely chop the Canadian bacon into bite-size pieces.

3. Add the Canadian bacon to the skillet, and stir to separate the pieces. Add the garlic to the skillet. Peel and coarsely chop the onion, adding it to the skillet as you chop. Cook, stirring, until the onion is tender, about 3 minutes.

4. Add the basil, tomatoes with their juice, and spaghetti sauce and stir. Cook until the sauce comes to a boil, then reduce the heat to low and simmer until ready to serve. If you are using the green peas, add them to the skillet in the last 2 minutes of simmering, then stir.

5. When the pasta is done, drain it well and place it in a 3-quart or larger serving bowl. Toss the sour cream with the hot pasta until the pasta is well coated. Add the sauce mixture to the pasta bowl, stir well, and serve at once.

MARY'S GREEK-INSPIRED PASTA

SERVES: 4 START TO FINISH: UNDER 20 MINUTES

Salt for cooking the pasta
8 ounces short pasta, such as penne
2 ounces (about 25 slices) pepperoni
3 medium-size plum tomatoes (for about 1 cup chopped)
2 cloves fresh garlic
1 can (2¼ ounces) sliced black olives
1 can (13¾ ounces) quartered artichoke hearts, packed in water
1 teaspoon onion powder
¼ cup crumbled feta cheese
1 tablespoon extra-virgin olive oil
Black pepper to taste

1. Bring 2½ quarts lightly salted water to a boil in a covered 4½-quart or larger pot. When the water reaches a rapid boil, add the pasta and cook, uncovered, until just tender, following the package directions.

2. Meanwhile, line a microwave-safe plate with paper towels and place the pepperoni in a single layer on the plate. Cover the plate with another paper towel and microwave the pepperoni on high power until the slices release some of their oil but are still tender, about 45 seconds. Set aside.

3. Core and chop the tomatoes into bite-size pieces and place them in a 3-quart or larger serving bowl. Peel and finely mince the garlic and add it to the bowl. Drain the olives and add them to the bowl. Drain the artichokes, coarsely chop them, and add them to the bowl. Chop the pepperoni slices roughly into quarters and add them to the bowl. Stir in the onion powder.

4. When the pasta is done, drain it well and add it to the bowl. Add the feta cheese. Drizzle the oil over the ingredients and toss to mix well. Season with black pepper and serve at once.

Mary DeSilva, a reader of our Desperation Dinners newspaper column, shared this recipe for an out-of-the-ordinary pasta dish featuring artichoke hearts, black olives, and feta cheese.

"Having grown up in southern Louisiana, my cooking roots were firmly planted in the Cajun style," Mary said. "At twenty-two, I moved to the 'big' city, New Orleans. It was there I discovered cuisine from all over the world."

One of Mary's favorite activities was the annual Greek Festival. "This pasta recipe was influenced by dishes I tasted there," Mary said, and it has since become one of her family's favorites. We think you'll like this pasta as much for its assertive Mediterranean flavors as for the fact that it is elegant enough for company!

Radiatore means "little radiators," and that's exactly what this short pasta looks like, with its rippled edges. Not too long ago, *radiatore* was found only in specialty stores; now it's even sold under the house brand at our local supermarket. But if you can't find it, any short pasta will do.

We make this dish with either Italian pork sausage or Italian turkey sausage. (Italian turkey sausage is usually found alongside the Italian pork sausage.) Since turkey sausage is much leaner than pork, it sometimes sticks to the pan while cooking. If this happens, add a teaspoon, or so, of olive oil or a little water. Fans of spicy foods may want to use hot sausage.

This dish is especially nice when made with two colors of peppers, but red bell peppers can cost twice as much as green ones. If red peppers are not in season, use all green. It will still be delicious.

SAUSAGE AND PEPPER PASTA

SERVES: 6 GENEROUSLY   START TO FINISH: UNDER 25 MINUTES

Salt for cooking the pasta
1 pound short pasta, such as radiatore
1 pound sweet or hot Italian-style pork
   or turkey sausage
1 large onion (for about 1 cup chopped)
3 large red or green bell peppers, or any combination
   (for about 4½ cups chopped)
2 cloves fresh garlic, minced, or 2 teaspoons bottled
   minced garlic
½ cup shredded or grated Parmesan cheese

1. Bring 3 quarts lightly salted water to a boil in a covered 4½-quart or larger pot. When the water reaches a rapid boil, add the pasta and cook, uncovered, until just tender, following the package directions.

2. Meanwhile, use kitchen shears or a sharp knife to cut the casing off the sausage links. Discard the casings. Place the sausage in an extra-deep 12-inch skillet over medium heat. Stir to break up the links.

3. While the sausage cooks, peel and coarsely chop the onion, adding it to the pan as you chop. Continue to stir and break up the sausage meat from time to time. Cook the sausage until it is no longer pink, 8 to 9 minutes. If using pork sausage, pour it into a colander to drain away any accumulated fat, then return the meat mixture to the skillet.

4. Stem, seed, and cut the bell peppers into bite-size pieces. Add them to the skillet. Add the garlic to the skillet. Stir well.

5. When the pasta is done, drain it well, pour it back into the cooking pot or into a large serving bowl, and toss with the sausage mixture. Sprinkle the Parmesan cheese on top, stir to mix well, and serve.

PASTA WITH SALAMI AND BASIL

SERVES: 4 START TO FINISH: UNDER 20 MINUTES

Salt for cooking the pasta
8 ounces short pasta, such as rotini
4 ounces thinly sliced hard salami
1 large tomato (for about 1½ cups chopped)
2 cloves fresh garlic
Fresh basil leaves (for ¼ cup chopped)
2 tablespoons extra-virgin olive oil
1 tablespoon Dijon mustard
¾ cup shredded or grated Parmesan cheese
Black pepper to taste

1. Bring 2½ quarts lightly salted water to a boil in a covered 4½-quart or larger pot. When the water reaches a rapid boil, add the pasta and cook, uncovered, until just tender, following the package directions.

2. Meanwhile, stack the salami slices, cut them into ¼-inch-wide strips, and place the strips in a 3-quart or larger serving bowl. Core and chop the tomato into bite-size pieces and add the pieces and any juice to the serving bowl.

3. Peel and mince the garlic and add it to the bowl. Chop the basil leaves and add them to the bowl. Add the oil and mustard and stir well.

4. When the pasta is done, drain it well and add it to the bowl. Sprinkle with the Parmesan cheese, tossing to melt the cheese. Season with black pepper. When all of the cheese has melted and the pasta is mixed well with the sauce, serve at once.

This has all the flavors of a deli-style salami and cheese sandwich, folded into an elegant pasta dish. *Yum!* Prepare it when basil is at its seasonal peak, or plant a few small basil plants in pots each spring. Before you know it, you'll be looking for creative ways to use your bounty—and this recipe fits the bill. You could even double the amount of fresh basil and enjoy the bright summer-fresh taste in every bite. Salami from the deli and the packaged kind work equally well.

When you're a health-conscious and busy retiree living on a fixed income, it's especially nice when a dish is good for you, easy to fix, and frugal to boot.

"I am trying to add more salmon to our diet because it is so good for your heart," Beverly's aunt Flo Strickland told us, "and I'm constantly looking for ways to prepare canned salmon because it's less expensive than fresh."

When we got wind of Aunt Flo's salmon quest, we knew she'd be the perfect candidate to try this recipe. So how did it rate? "We thought this dish was excellent, and we're definitely going to add it to our recipe rotation," she said.

SALMON PASTA WITH TOMATOES AND DILL

SERVES: 4 START TO FINISH: UNDER 20 MINUTES

Salt for cooking the pasta
8 ounces short pasta, such as shells
½ cup frozen green peas
5 medium-size plum tomatoes
    (for about 1⅔ cups chopped)
1 cup whole, low-fat, or skim milk
1 can (10¾ ounces) condensed cream of celery soup
1 tablespoon butter
½ cup shredded or grated Parmesan cheese
2 teaspoons dried onion flakes
1 teaspoon garlic powder
1 teaspoon Worcestershire sauce
¼ teaspoon Tabasco sauce
¼ teaspoon dried dill
1 foil pouch (7.1 ounces) premium skinless, boneless pink
    salmon, or 2 cans (6 ounces each) salmon, drained well
Salt and black pepper to taste

1. Bring 2½ quarts lightly salted water to a boil in a covered 4½-quart or larger pot. When the water reaches a rapid boil, add the pasta and cook, uncovered, until just tender, following the package directions.

2. Meanwhile, place the peas in a colander and run warm tap water over them for 30 seconds to partially defrost them. Set aside to drain well. Core and chop the tomatoes into bite-size pieces. Set aside.

3. Combine the milk and celery soup in a saucepan over low heat and whisk until most of the lumps dissolve. Cut the butter into 3 pieces and add them to the pan. Add the Parmesan cheese, onion flakes, garlic powder, Worcestershire sauce, Tabasco sauce, and dill. Raise the heat to medium-high and bring the mixture just to the boiling point, stirring until the butter and cheese melt.

4. Reduce the heat to low. If using canned salmon, remove and discard any skin and bones. Add the salmon to the pan, along with the peas and tomatoes. Flake the chunks of salmon with a wooden spoon. Season with salt and black pepper and remove the sauce from the heat.

5. Drain the pasta and place some on each serving plate. Top with the sauce and serve.

NOT QUITE TAPENADE WITH RIGATONI

SERVES: 6 START TO FINISH: UNDER 20 MINUTES

Salt for cooking the pasta
1 pound rigatoni or
    other short tubular pasta
2 cloves fresh garlic
¼ cup raisins
1 can (6 ounces) pitted black olives
1 can (6 ounces) tuna
1 lemon
3 tablespoons extra-virgin olive oil
Black pepper to taste
1 large tomato (for about 1½ cups chopped)
Fresh parsley leaves (for 2 tablespoons chopped; optional)
¼ cup shredded or grated Parmesan cheese (optional)

1. Bring 2½ quarts lightly salted water to a boil in a covered 4½-quart or larger pot. When the water reaches a rapid boil, add the pasta and cook, uncovered, until just tender, following the package directions.

2. Meanwhile, peel the garlic. Turn on a food processor and drop the garlic cloves through the feed tube. Process until finely

When is a classic recipe not classic? When you're too stressed out to care or when the budget doesn't allow for fancy foods. Take tapenade, a classic French caper and olive paste that's a cinch to throw together in the food processor and makes a terrific spread or pasta sauce. The problem is the defining ingredient: capers. (In the Provençal language, capers are called *tapeno*—thus the name.) While the other ingredients are pantry staples, capers are one of those specialty items that can be very expensive and only occasionally find their way into our grocery cart. The good news is that tapenade without capers, while no longer a true tapenade, is still wonderful.

(continued)

(continued)

With apologies to the French, we left out the capers, chose tuna over anchovies, and added raisins for a slightly sweet twist. What we discovered was a classically inspired pasta toss that fits our daily desperation, our pantries, and our budgets.

Don't be intimidated when you can't turn out the classics. Be inspired by them instead.

Any type of tuna, canned or the new pouch version, will work in this recipe, which comes from our friend Liz Cilem, who used to cook for a catering company. Liz relies on this dish for emergency nights when she faces an empty refrigerator. "I've always got some tuna, pasta, and canned tomatoes," she says.

So far, Liz is sticking with chunk light tuna, packed in spring water. "It falls apart better for the sauce," she says.

minced. Add the raisins and process until finely chopped. Drain the olives and tuna. (Check over the olives to be sure they're all pitted.) Add the olives and tuna to the processor bowl and pulse until the olives are coarsely chopped, about six times.

3. Squeeze the juice from the lemon through a strainer into the processor bowl. Add the oil and process until well blended, about 15 seconds. Season with black pepper.

4. Cut the tomato into bite-size pieces and place them, with any juice, in a 3-quart or larger serving bowl. Chop enough parsley (if using) for 2 tablespoons and add it to the tomatoes. Add the tuna mixture to the bowl.

5. When the pasta is done, drain it well and add it to the bowl. Stir and toss until the pasta is well coated with the sauce. Serve at once, topping each serving with 1 tablespoon Parmesan cheese, if desired.

LIZ'S TUNA TOSS

SERVES: 6 START TO FINISH: UNDER 20 MINUTES

Salt for cooking the pasta
1 pound short pasta, such as penne
3 tablespoons olive oil
3 cloves fresh garlic, minced, or 1 tablespoon bottled minced garlic
1 can (6 ounces) tuna
1 large can (28 ounces) diced tomatoes
1 tablespoon anchovy paste (see Notes; optional)
2 tablespoons tomato paste (see Notes)
1 teaspoon sugar
⅛ teaspoon black pepper, or more to taste
⅓ cup fresh parsley leaves (see Notes; optional)

1. Bring 3 quarts lightly salted water to a boil in a covered 4½-quart or larger pot. When the water reaches a rapid boil, add the pasta and cook, uncovered, until just tender, following the package directions.

2. Meanwhile, heat the oil in a 12-inch skillet over medium heat. Add the garlic to the pan and cook to soften, 1 minute. Drain the tuna well, add it to the skillet, and stir to flake the tuna chunks. Add the tomatoes with their juice.

3. Stir in the anchovy paste (if using), tomato paste, sugar, and black pepper. Cook, stirring occasionally, until the sauce thickens, 5 minutes. While the sauce is cooking, chop the parsley (if using) and add it to the skillet. If the sauce starts to stick, reduce the heat to low.

4. Drain the pasta in a colander, then pour it back into the cooking pot (off the heat). Pour the sauce into the pot and toss to coat the pasta with the sauce. Serve at once.

NOTES: Anchovy paste adds depth, but if you don't have any (or if you're watching your sodium), leave it out. Anchovy paste is sold in a tube; it's usually shelved with the imported foods at the supermarket.

■ Tomato paste is also available in tubes alongside foods imported from Italy. If you use a can of tomato paste, refrigerate the leftover in an airtight container for up to 5 days.

■ Parsley adds color and zing, but if you're without, just omit it.

Since many of our readers are interested in cutting back on sodium, we tested the low-salt tuna and were pleased with the results. No matter which tuna you choose, you'll like the convenience of keeping these ingredients on hand for this low-fat, 20-minute, money-saving recipe.

Tuna Time

From Beverly:

The last time I tried to zoom down the tuna aisle, I was forced to screech my cart to a halt. What in the world were all those cans? For me, tuna fish had always been a no-brainer—and an obvious choice for desperate pantry dinners at home. But these days it's not so mindless.

You can choose from chunk light or chunk white tuna, solid white Albacore or premium albacore. To confuse matters, there's now select-prime light fillets and "gourmet's choice" light fillets. You'll find chunk white or light tuna that's reduced in sodium and also happens to be slightly lower in fat. (All of these variations are packed in spring water, but there's also tuna packed in oil.) And most of these various configurations are offered by every company.

Just looking at the can doesn't help much. It wasn't until we opened the cans side-by-side that Alicia and I discovered that there *is* a difference in taste and texture. If you don't want fishy-tasting tuna, go with either the solid white or premium albacore. If you want a minced texture, choose chunk light. Our can of select-prime light fillets was more on the mushy side, while the "gourmet's choice" fillets were quite firm.

The differences in taste and texture are dictated by the type of tuna in the can and what the fish is mixed with when it's cooked, said Michael Mullen, a spokesman for Starkist Tuna. Gourmet tunas tend to be yellowfin; all-white tunas are albacore; and the least expensive are usually skipjack tuna.

For many shoppers, price may be the variable that sways. Comparing tunas packed in spring water, the standard chunk light is the most economical and the low-sodium is the most expensive.

Not to confuse matters, but there's yet another variety: tuna sold in pouches that don't require draining. Because this tuna is cooked in half the time of canned, it has a fresher taste and firmer texture.

(One note: Because canned tuna contains mercury, pregnant women should consult their doctors before eating it.)

"We prefer tuna packed in water because of the savings in calories."

SEASHELLS WITH TUNA AND DIJON CREAM

SERVES: 4 **START TO FINISH:** UNDER 20 MINUTES

Salt for cooking the pasta
8 ounces shells or other short pasta
1 large can (12 ounces) tuna
1 bunch scallions (for about ½ cup sliced)
1 clove fresh garlic
½ cup regular or reduced-fat sour cream
½ cup regular or reduced-fat mayonnaise
4 teaspoons Dijon mustard
1 teaspoon lemon juice, fresh or from frozen concentrate
15 cherry tomatoes (for about 1 cup sliced)
¼ cup chopped fresh parsley (optional)
Black pepper to taste
Lettuce leaves (optional)

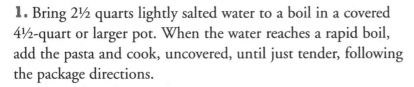
SUPER-CHEAP!

This delicious dinner is our own twist on a traditional tuna salad. It transforms a simple can of tuna into a no-cook pasta sauce that makes quick work of dinner. Serve it either at room temperature or slightly chilled.

1. Bring 2½ quarts lightly salted water to a boil in a covered 4½-quart or larger pot. When the water reaches a rapid boil, add the pasta and cook, uncovered, until just tender, following the package directions.

2. Meanwhile, drain the tuna and put it in a 3-quart or larger bowl. Using a fork, flake the tuna into bite-size pieces. Slice the scallions, using all of the whites and enough tender green tops to make ½ cup. Add them to the bowl. Peel and finely mince the garlic and add it to the bowl. Add the sour cream, mayonnaise, mustard, and lemon juice. Stir well to mix and set aside.

3. Slice the tomatoes in half and set aside.

4. When the pasta is done, drain it in a colander and rinse it under cool tap water for 1 minute. Drain well, shaking the colander to eliminate as much water as possible. Add the pasta, tomatoes, parsley (if using) and black pepper to the tuna and toss gently until coated with the sauce. Serve at once over lettuce leaves (if using) or refrigerate until ready to serve.

Other Places to Shop

Finding the best dollar value for high-quality food is a challenge. But the good news is that there are more and more places to discover reasonably priced foods every day. Included here are just a few of our favorites. Most of these businesses are close enough to our homes that we're able to frequent them on a monthly basis. Because most do not advertise, the easiest way to discover the values inside is by word of mouth and by popping in when you have some extra time.

▪ **Ethnic grocery stores.** "It's a small world after all" means good news for the budget shopper. Even in small towns, ethnic grocery stores are opening in record numbers. Our favorites are the Hispanic grocery store for terrific prices on avocados, limes, tomatoes, peppers, and tortillas; the Asian grocery for sesame seeds and Asian seasonings such as soy sauce, hoisin sauce, fish sauce, and sesame oil; and Indian grocery stores for spices such as whole cloves, curry powders, ground cumin, and chutneys.

▪ **Co-op grocery stores.** Especially if you prefer to buy organically grown produce, you'll find big savings at a co-op. Most stores are open to the whole community, but the large savings come when you become a member or volunteer worker. There's also the benefit of investing in your community and buying locally. Check out www.localharvest.org/food-coops to find a co-op near you.

▪ **Alternative grocery stores.** Nontraditional grocery stores, or as one friend calls them, "bare-bones basic stores," are popping up everywhere. One store in Alicia's area is called Aldi. A company that started in Germany over forty years ago, Aldi doesn't advertise and doesn't provide grocery bags, and you must "rent" your shopping cart. (You get your quarter back when you return the cart to the holding bin.) Aldi offers limited items (only about 13,000 items compared to the 25,000 most stores carry), and many items are the store brand. The benefit is "insane" savings. Most of these stores are "warehouse" in nature, without displays or shelving. But it's easy to shop here, as everything is marked clearly and the aisles are wide.

In Beverly's neighborhood, the Cub Food Stores, which do advertise and are not quite as bare-bones as Aldi, often have the lowest prices in the area on staples.

▪ **Outlets for boutique and gourmet items.** As we are exposed to so many different types of food, our palates have become much more discriminating. But when we check out that ten-year-old balsamic vinegar and see the hefty price tag, we're reluctant to splurge. For those boutique items we decide we can't do without, there seem to be more and more specialty markets that offer quality at cheaper prices. Stores such as Trader Joe's are spreading through the country with a philosophy of offering "hard-to-find, boutique domestic and imported wines (where the store is allowed to sell them), and gourmet food items at outstanding prices." Alicia goes so far as putting in an order when a friend travels to Virginia (the closest store). Her best buy? A mixed case of Merlot and Chardonnay, boutique-quality table wines, for $3.29 a bottle.

▪ **Farmer's markets and fruit and vegetable stands.** The ultimate in freshness comes with the gratifying knowledge that you are supporting local farmers. The only caution: This produce is super-fresh and usually perfectly ripe, and must be used fairly quickly to prevent spoilage and waste. Nothing is more pitiful than half a bag of precious peaches that have turned to mush. So don't buy more than you can use within a day or two.

▪ **Warehouse shopping.** Sam's Club, Costco, and other ware-house-style, membership-only stores offer good buys. See page 282 for details.

"There are more and more specialty markets offering quality at cheaper prices."

Roasted garlic has a distinctively mellow and almost sweet flavor, so recipes usually call for a lot of it. Roasted Garlic Pasta Toss is a good example: Although two whole heads might appear to be too much, it balances the noodles and broccoli perfectly. This recipe flies together with just seven ingredients, and because there's no meat, it is easy on the pocketbook too.

ROASTED GARLIC PASTA TOSS

SERVES: 4 START TO FINISH: UNDER 15 MINUTES

Salt for cooking the pasta
8 ounces short pasta, such as wagon wheels (rotelle)
4 cups fresh broccoli florets or frozen broccoli pieces
2 heads roasted garlic (for about ½ cup chopped cloves; see page 391)
1 can (2¼ ounces) sliced black olives
2 tablespoons extra-virgin olive oil
¾ cup shredded or grated Parmesan cheese

1. Bring 2½ quarts lightly salted water to a boil in a covered 4½-quart or larger pot. When the water reaches a rapid boil, add the pasta and cook, uncovered, until just tender, following the package directions. About halfway through the pasta cooking time, add the broccoli and bring the water back to a boil. (The broccoli should cook for 4 to 5 minutes.)

2. Meanwhile, remove the peel from the roasted garlic and coarsely chop the cloves. Set aside. Drain the olives and set aside.

3. When the pasta and broccoli are done, drain them well, then pour them into a 3-quart or larger serving bowl. Add the garlic and black olives. Drizzle the olive oil over the pasta and sprinkle the cheese over it. Toss until the cheese has melted. Serve at once.

NOODLES AND VEGETABLES WITH PEANUT SAUCE

SERVES: 4 START TO FINISH: UNDER 20 MINUTES

Salt for cooking the pasta
12 ounces thin pasta, such as thin spaghetti or angel hair
2 teaspoons vegetable oil
1 large onion (for about 1 cup chopped)
2 medium-size carrots (for about 1 cup sliced)
1 medium-size red or green bell pepper
   (for about 1 cup chopped)
1 cup broccoli florets, or 4 ounces asparagus spears
4 scallions (for about 1 cup pieces)
½ cup dry white wine, such as Chardonnay
1 cup Thai-Style Peanut Sauce (page 374),
   defrosted if frozen
Unsalted roasted peanuts, for serving (optional)

1. Bring 3 quarts lightly salted water to a boil in a covered 4½-quart or larger pot. When the water reaches a rapid boil, add the pasta and cook, uncovered, until just tender, following the package directions.

2. Meanwhile, heat the oil in an extra-deep 12-inch skillet over medium heat. Peel and coarsely chop the onion, adding it to the skillet as you chop. Stir the onion from time to time while you peel the carrots and cut them into thin slices. Add the carrots to the skillet as you slice them. Continue to cook, stirring frequently, while you stem, seed, and cut the bell pepper into bite-size pieces. Add them to the pan.

3. If you are using broccoli, add the florets to the skillet. If you are using asparagus, discard any tough portions at the bottom of the spears and cut the spears into roughly 1-inch pieces. Add them to the pan. Continue to cook, stirring frequently.

4. Cut the scallions into roughly ½-inch pieces, using the whites and enough tender green tops to make about 1 cup. Add them to

When we aren't serving meat for dinner, we figure we can splurge a bit on the ingredients. This recipe combines a colorful array of vegetables and a splash of white wine. Don't feel you have to buy a break-the-bank bottle of wine. The recipe requires only half a cup, so the rest of the wine is available to drink with dinner. Just buy a bottle that you're happy to consume—there are a myriad of inexpensive, delicious choices. If you want to skip the wine altogether, substitute chicken or vegetable stock.

We use thin noodles because their quick cooking time coincides well with finishing the veggies, but if you start cooking them a few minutes ahead, you could use other types of pasta that take a bit longer to cook. Our friend Denise Deen says this dish is also great with rice noodles, which are found alongside other Asian foods in larger supermarkets.

the skillet. Add the wine. Cook until the vegetables are just crisp-tender, 2 to 3 minutes, and then remove the skillet from the heat. Add the peanut sauce to the skillet and stir to combine it with the wine and to coat the vegetables with the sauce.

5. When the pasta is done, drain it in a colander. To serve, divide the pasta evenly among four plates and top with vegetables and sauce. Garnish each serving with chopped peanuts, if desired.

BALSAMIC-GLAZED VEGETABLES WITH PASTA

SERVES: 4 START TO FINISH: UNDER 20 MINUTES

Salt for cooking the pasta
8 ounces short pasta, such as corkscrews (rotini)
2 teaspoons olive oil
1 large onion (for about 1 cup chopped)
8 ounces fresh button mushrooms
2 cloves fresh garlic, minced, or 2 teaspoons bottled
    minced garlic
½ cup balsamic vinegar
½ teaspoon dried thyme
3 medium-size plum tomatoes
    (for about 1 cup chopped)
½ cup fresh parsley leaves (optional)
¼ cup shredded or grated Parmesan cheese,
    plus additional, for serving (optional)
Salt and black pepper to taste

1. Bring 2½ quarts lightly salted water to a boil in a covered 4½-quart or larger pot. When the water reaches a rapid boil, add the pasta and cook, uncovered, until just tender, following the package directions.

Warning: Balsamic vinegar can become addictive. The good news is that this habit is good for your taste buds, and maybe even for your health. Balsamic vinegar is a deep brown Italian brew that has the power to transform almost any food it touches. It is so rich that it is often described in wine terms, and in Italy, many wine shops reserve one corner for glass carafes of balsamic vinegar, some of them a century old. The aging process requires the vinegar to pass through a series of wooden barrels, which makes balsamic vinegar slightly sweet and less acidic than other vinegar. Balsamic's resulting complex flavor lends depth and distinction when added to other foods. If all you have to do to lend a gourmet

2. Meanwhile, heat the oil in a 12-inch skillet over medium heat. Peel and coarsely chop the onion, adding it to the skillet as you chop. Cook until the onion begins to soften, about 2 minutes.

3. Rinse, pat dry, and slice the mushrooms, removing and discarding any tough stems. Add the mushrooms to the skillet as you slice. Add the garlic to the skillet. Cook, stirring frequently, until the mushrooms release their liquid, about 4 minutes.

4. Reduce the heat to low, add the vinegar and thyme, and simmer to blend the flavors, 4 to 5 minutes.

5. Meanwhile, core and coarsely chop the tomatoes and place them a 3-quart or larger serving bowl. If using the parsley, coarsely chop it and add it to the bowl. Set aside.

6. Pour the mushroom-onion mixture into the serving bowl. Drain the pasta and add it to the bowl along with the Parmesan cheese. Stir to coat the pasta with the sauce and melt the cheese. Season with salt and black pepper and serve at once, passing extra cheese at the table, if desired.

touch to sauces and salad dressings is splash in a little vinegar, well, how easy is that?

More good news: Balsamic vinegar doesn't have to cost as much as fine wine. It's now available in most supermarkets, and we've even found imported balsamic vinegars in discount stores that sell clothes and housewares along with gourmet foods. Most bottles of balsamic vinegar in grocery and discount stores cost no more than $5 a bottle, but they vary greatly in quality. Watch out for vinegars that have other additives, mainly sugar. The slightly sweet flavor should come from the aging process, not from additives. When you find an inexpensive brand that you like, you'll have a delicious, useful item in your pantry.

When the dog days of summer hit, our thoughts turn to wiltless cooking—which means that the cook gets a meal on the table without melting into the middle of the kitchen floor. Salads and sandwiches work, but sometimes we just have to have Mexican. One of our favorite wiltless cooking tricks is a no-cook pasta sauce, so we decided to combine flavorful, room-temperature Mexican ingredients in a big bowl, and then toss them with hot noodles. The heat from the pasta melts the cheese and brings the entire dish to warm room temperature—perfect for an August swelter.

ZITI MEXI-CALI

SERVES: 4 START TO FINISH: UNDER 20 MINUTES

Salt for cooking the pasta
8 ounces ziti or other short pasta
1 can (14½ ounces) Mexican-style
    stewed tomatoes or diced tomatoes
    seasoned with jalapeños
1 can (11 ounces) yellow corn kernels, or
    1 cup frozen corn kernels (see Note)
1 can (15 ounces) black beans, or 1 cup homemade
    (see page 368) defrosted if frozen
1 bunch scallions (for about ½ cup sliced)
Fresh cilantro leaves (to make 2 tablespoons; optional)
¼ cup (1 ounce) shredded Mexican-blend cheese or
    Cheddar cheese

1. Bring 2½ quarts lightly salted water to a boil in a 4½-quart or larger pot. When the water reaches a rapid boil, add the pasta and cook, uncovered, until just tender, following the package directions.

2. Meanwhile, pour the tomatoes with their juice into a 3-quart or larger bowl. Cut up any chunks that are larger than bite-size. Drain the corn and add it to the bowl. Rinse and drain the black beans and add them to the bowl. Thinly slice the scallions, using the whites and enough of the tender green tops to make ½ cup. Add them to the bowl.

3. Chop enough of the cilantro leaves (if using) to make 2 tablespoons and add them to the bowl. Stir to mix well.

4. When the pasta is done, drain it well and add it to the bowl. Toss to mix well. To serve, divide the mixture evenly among four plates and sprinkle 1 tablespoon of the cheese over each serving.

NOTE: If using frozen corn kernels, rinse them in a colander under warm tap water to defrost them before adding them to the dish.

PASTA WITH CREAMY TOMATO SAUCE

SERVES: 4 START TO FINISH: UNDER 20 MINUTES

Salt for cooking the pasta
8 ounces short pasta, such as penne
2 teaspoons olive oil
1 large onion (for about 1 cup chopped)
8 ounces fresh button mushrooms
1 clove fresh garlic, minced, or 1 teaspoon bottled
   minced garlic
1½ cups bottled spaghetti sauce
¼ cup heavy or whipping cream
Shredded or grated Parmesan cheese, for serving (optional)

1. Bring 2½ quarts lightly salted water to a boil in a covered 4½-quart or larger pot. When the water reaches a rapid boil, add the pasta and cook, uncovered, until just tender, following the package directions.

2. Meanwhile, heat the oil in a 12-inch skillet over medium heat. Peel and coarsely chop the onion, adding it to the skillet as you chop, stirring occasionally. Rinse, pat dry, and coarsely chop the mushrooms, removing and discarding any tough stems. Add the mushrooms to the skillet as you chop. Cook, stirring occasionally, until the onions and mushrooms are soft and the liquid from the mushrooms has evaporated, 6 to 7 minutes. Then add the garlic to the skillet.

3. While the vegetables cook, pour the spaghetti sauce into a 1-quart measure or a mixing bowl. Add the cream and stir to mix. When the mushrooms are cooked, add the spaghetti sauce mixture, reduce the heat to low, and simmer until ready to serve.

4. When the pasta is done, drain it well and divide it among four plates. Serve the sauce over the pasta, topped with Parmesan cheese, if desired.

F ood fads, just like fashion, repeat themselves. We can honestly say there are some food fashion moments we'd rather not see again. But we were thrilled when we started to see cream, used in moderation, appearing in recipes again.

Back in the '80s, recipes with creamy textures were either "light" (made with low-fat milk products) or "splurge" (throwing caution to the wind and calling for as much as 1 cup of cream per serving). We had under-indulgence and over-indulgence, but no real middle ground.

But why not compromise? A touch of cream is just the ticket for depth, fullness of flavor, and natural goodness. Cream has long been one of our dairy staples, and we'd rather not feel guilty about it. Moderation is the key. In this case, a hint of cream is what makes this simple low-fat pasta sauce so special and rich.

There comes a day when we find ourselves gazing at a cupboard shelf full of odds and ends of pasta shapes: a bag with a few penne, a quarter of a cup of elbow macaroni, some stray *rotelle*, a few bow-ties. . . . It seems a waste to throw away perfectly good pasta, so here's a solution. Your family will get a kick out of this mixed-up dish, and the kids will eat their veggies while trying to see how many pasta shapes you've included. Just choose short pasta shapes that are somewhat the same size—medium or large shells, rotini, and ziti, for example. Cooking times vary for the different shapes and from one brand to another, so the shells might be a bit softer than the ziti—but that just adds to the interest.

To turn this into a more substantial dish, you can add any of the following cooked meats, cut into bite-size pieces and stirred into the sauce with the garlic in Step 3: chicken, turkey, roast beef or steak, or pot roast or pork chops.

MIXED PASTA WITH CARAMELIZED VEGETABLES

SERVES: 4 **START TO FINISH:** UNDER 20 MINUTES

Salt for cooking the pasta, plus more to taste
8 ounces mixed short pasta (see headnote)
3 tablespoons extra-virgin olive oil
2 large onions (for about 2 cups chopped)
2 large green or red bell peppers, or 1 of each
    (for about 3 cups chopped)
2 cloves fresh garlic, minced, or 2 teaspoons bottled
    minced garlic
2 tablespoons shredded or grated Parmesan cheese,
    or more to taste

1. Bring 2½ quarts lightly salted water to a boil in a covered 4½-quart or larger pot. When the water reaches a rapid boil, add the pasta and cook, uncovered, until just tender, following the package directions.

2. Meanwhile, heat the oil in an extra-deep 12-inch skillet over medium-high heat. Peel and coarsely chop the onions, adding them to the skillet as you chop. Stem, seed, and coarsely chop the bell peppers, adding them to the skillet as you chop. Cook the vegetables, stirring frequently, until the onions begin to turn golden brown, about 6 minutes.

3. Add the garlic to the skillet. Cook, stirring, for 2 minutes. Remove the skillet from the heat.

4. Drain the pasta well and add it to the skillet. Toss well to distribute the vegetables. (Or pour the pasta and vegetables into a 3-quart or larger serving bowl and toss.) Season with salt, sprinkle the Parmesan cheese over the dish, and serve.

ZITI WITH GARLIC AND TOMATO NO-COOK SAUCE

SERVES: 4 START TO FINISH: UNDER 20 MINUTES

Salt for cooking the pasta
8 ounces ziti or other short pasta
2 cloves fresh garlic
2 tablespoons extra-virgin olive oil
½ teaspoon dried Italian seasoning
4 medium-size plum tomatoes (for about 1⅓ cups chopped)
2 tablespoons chopped ripe olives (see Note)
¼ cup shredded or grated Parmesan cheese
Salt and black pepper to taste

SUPER-CHEAP!

1. Bring 2½ quarts lightly salted water to a boil in a covered 4½-quart or larger pot. When the water reaches a rapid boil, add the pasta and cook, uncovered, until just tender, following the package directions.

2. Meanwhile, peel and finely chop the garlic and place it in a 4-quart or larger bowl. Add the oil and Italian seasoning. Core and chop the tomatoes into bite-size pieces and add them to the bowl. Stir to coat with the oil. Drain the olives and add them to the bowl.

3. Drain the pasta well and add it to the bowl. Scatter the Parmesan cheese on top, and toss to melt the cheese. Season with salt and black pepper and serve at once.

NOTE: Buy the ripe olives already chopped if you can find them. Otherwise buy sliced olives and chop them finely. Refrigerate the leftover chopped olives in an airtight container, and sprinkle them over a salad later in the week.

From Alicia:

E asy doesn't begin to describe this pasta dish. One of my good friends, Rhett Holladay, is not a confident cook. So when I asked her to try this recipe, she replied that if she could do it, anyone could. Guess what? She did it—and in no time flat, with 1½- and 2½-year-old little boys wrapped around her legs.

Rhett and her husband loved the fresh taste of this pasta dish and said that it was so summery, they decided to eat it out on the screened porch.

When tomatoes are at their abundant peak, this is the perfect gourmet budget dish.

"This is my new most favorite recipe," my husband declared after first tasting penne mixed with a bit of cheese and buttery seasoned bread crumbs. It's one of those dishes you have to experience to believe—it just seems too simple. I know, because I almost didn't try it myself, but after making a huge batch of bread crumbs, I ran across a variation on this age-old Italian recipe. So I whipped up a batch and fell in love.

There's actually a lot to love about this recipe. It's incredibly inexpensive. While it's an obvious side dish, it is hearty enough for a main course. It's also wonderful for using up bits of leftover meat or vegetables. Just cut the leftovers into bite-size pieces, warm them in the microwave, then stir them in with the cheese in Step 3.

Coarse bread crumbs, such as crumbs made from whole-grain or European-style breads, work best in this recipe.

PASTA WITH BREAD CRUMBS

SERVES: 6 AS A SIDE DISH, 4 AS A MAIN
START TO FINISH: UNDER 20 MINUTES

Salt for cooking the pasta
8 ounces short pasta, such as penne
2 tablespoons butter
2 teaspoons olive oil
3 cloves fresh garlic, minced, or 1 heaping tablespoon bottled minced garlic
1 cup coarse soft bread crumbs (see opposite page)
½ teaspoon dried Italian seasoning, oregano, or basil
¼ teaspoon salt, or to taste
⅓ cup shredded or grated Parmesan cheese

1. Bring 2½ quarts lightly salted water to a boil in a covered 4½-quart or larger pot. When the water reaches a rapid boil, add the pasta and cook, uncovered, until just tender, following the package directions.

2. While the pasta is cooking, melt the butter in a 12-inch skillet over medium heat. Add 1 teaspoon of the oil and the garlic to the skillet. Cook for 1 minute, stirring frequently. Then add the bread crumbs, Italian seasoning, and salt and stir to coat the crumbs with the butter mixture. Cook, stirring frequently, until the crumbs are crisp and golden brown, 6 to 10 minutes. (Each time after stirring, shake the skillet to distribute the crumbs evenly over the bottom.) Remove the skillet from the heat and set it aside until ready to serve.

3. Drain the pasta well and pour it into a serving bowl. Drizzle the remaining 1 teaspoon oil over the pasta. Add the Parmesan cheese and toss well. Just before serving, add the bread crumbs and toss well. Serve at once.

The Last Slice: Making Your Own Bread Crumbs

Bread crumbs and bread cubes are great ways to use up the last slice or two of bread that's in danger of going stale and getting tossed. Making bread crumbs can be as simple as whirring a few slices in a food processor or blender for just a few seconds. Any type of bread will work—from white sandwich bread to seven-grain bread to bagels to leftover French rolls. To make crumbs, tear the bread into pieces and place them in the processor bowl or blender and process on high until the bread becomes fine-textured crumbs, stopping the motor to stir if necessary. (Exactly how long this will take depends how much bread you're using and the capacity of your blender or processor.)

You'll get beautiful, fine crumbs like magic that are perfect for topping casseroles or adding to meat loaf (see page 71), Marvelous Meatballs (page 353), Salmon Cake Sandwiches (page 252), Magically Modern "Croquette" Sandwiches (page 250), and the like. Pasta with Bread Crumbs (opposite) makes bread crumbs the star of the show.

Store-bought bread crumbs are dry. To duplicate this texture, you simply need to bake your soft homemade crumbs until the moisture in the bread evaporates. It's easy: Spread the crumbs out on a rimmed baking sheet and bake them at 350°F, stirring every 10 minutes. Exactly how long it will take depends on the moisture content of the bread and the depth of the layer of crumbs. But 20 to 30 minutes is usually plenty of time. You can make Italian-style seasoned bread crumbs by adding 1 teaspoon dried Italian seasoning blend to every 2 cups of crumbs before baking.

There's nothing like "found food," and saving those stray slices of bread will serve you well come dinnertime.

"There's nothing like found food."

CHAPTER FIVE

FAST AND FRUGAL "SANDWICHES"

From Alicia:

Ask just about anyone to name the cheapest meal they can make, and they'll mention some type of sandwich. I'm a bit embarrassed to admit how often those sandwiches are PB&J specials at my house. While grabbing the peanut butter and jelly is easy and cheap, it does get a bit boring—at least for the adults.

Sandwiches are simply food on (or in) bread. It doesn't matter what shape the bread is or what the filling contains. To be considered dinner, a sandwich doesn't have to involve fancy gourmet concoctions. The goal is to find the middle ground between plain (dull) and ridiculous (too fancy to eat).

In this chapter you'll find creative ways to look at the sandwich, from Ham and Cheese Turnovers with Dipping Sauce to Mini Mexican Pizzas. We've included Magically Modern "Croquette" Sandwiches and "New-Fashioned" Grilled Cheese Sandwiches, both of which put a new spin on a traditional favorite.

Hungry for a trip down Memory Lane? Try Your Egg Salad just as it is, or with our updated additions. Or our Best BLT Melts or the Salmon Cake Sandwiches with Terrific

Tartar Sauce. You might think you're sitting at your grandmother's table.

From the trendy Ultra-Easy Veggie Quesadillas to Shrimp Po' Boys, you'll find what you need to inspire an imaginative sandwich night at your house. It's as easy on the cook as it is on the budget.

Whenever our kids start begging for a trip to the fast-food drive-through, we just whip up these sandwiches. Funny how our amazing Sloppy Joes can stop a fast-food craving in its tracks—for adults and kids alike.

Some supermarkets sell tomato paste in tubes, which makes it easy to squirt out just as much as you need and refrigerate the rest for future use. If you're using tomato paste from a can, which is what we usually do, refrigerate the leftover paste in an airtight storage container for up to 5 days. It will last longer if you cover the surface with a layer of olive oil. You can just mix in the oil when you use the paste.

SIMPLE JOE'S OPEN-FACE SANDWICHES

SERVES: 4 START TO FINISH: UNDER 20 MINUTES

SUPER-CHEAP!

1 pound ground beef, fresh or frozen (see Note)
2 teaspoons vegetable oil
1 large onion (for about 1 cup chopped)
2 cloves fresh garlic, minced, or 2 teaspoons bottled minced garlic
½ cup ketchup
3 tablespoons tomato paste
2 teaspoons Worcestershire sauce
1 tablespoon chili powder
½ teaspoon salt
¼ teaspoon black pepper
4 hamburger or sandwich buns

1. If the beef is frozen, run it under hot water so you can remove the packaging. Place the beef on a microwave-safe plate and microwave, uncovered, on high power for 3 minutes to partially defrost.

2. While the beef defrosts, heat the oil in an extra-deep 12-inch skillet over medium heat. Peel and coarsely chop the onion, adding it to the skillet as you chop.

3. Add the beef (fresh or partially defrosted) to the skillet. Cook, turning and breaking up the meat, until it is crumbled and browned, 7 to 8 minutes. While the meat cooks, add the garlic to the skillet.

4. In a small bowl, whisk the ketchup, tomato paste, Worcestershire sauce, chili powder, salt, and black pepper with ½ cup water. When the meat has browned, add this mixture to the skillet and bring it to a boil. Then reduce the heat to low and simmer for 5 minutes.

5. Meanwhile, toast the buns, if desired. Place the buns, open, on four plates, and spoon the beef mixture over them, open-face style. Serve right away.

NOTE: You can use 3 cups Basic Beef (page 347), defrosted if frozen. Omit the oil, onion, garlic, and Worcestershire sauce. Heat the Basic Beef with the sauce mixture in Step 4.

BARBECUED BEEF ON A BUN

SERVES: 4 START TO FINISH: UNDER 10 MINUTES

SUPER-CHEAP!

4 hamburger or
   sandwich buns
2 cups shredded cooked beef roast
   (see page 348), defrosted if frozen
1 cup Fred's Red Barbecue Sauce
   (page 387) or bottled barbecue sauce
Coleslaw, for serving (optional)

1. Split the buns and lightly toast them in a toaster oven. Set aside.

2. Place the beef and the barbecue sauce in a small saucepan and place it over medium heat. Stir well and cook until the beef is heated through, 3 to 4 minutes. Spoon the barbecue beef over the buns and top with coleslaw, if desired. Serve immediately.

From Alicia:

When there's leftover beef roast in the refrigerator or freezer, it's going to end up in sandwiches at my house. That may sound boring, but it's not. These juicy beef barbecue sandwiches are everything a hungry family could want.

Being rooted in my Southern barbecue traditions, I can't imagine my sandwich without coleslaw. There's a terrific recipe for Coleslaw Good Enough for Company on page 319, or you can try our Simply Southern Coleslaw on page 318.

Commercial barbecue sauces abound, but my favorite still remains Fred's Red. With a bottle of Fred's Red on the refrigerator shelf, I'm in business!

Shopping the Discount Bread Stores

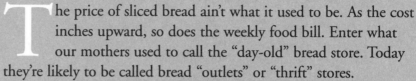

T he price of sliced bread ain't what it used to be. As the cost inches upward, so does the weekly food bill. Enter what our mothers used to call the "day-old" bread store. Today they're likely to be called bread "outlets" or "thrift" stores.

In the old days, bakeries sold only bread that was made that morning, and it was delivered to houses just as milk was. The bread that wasn't sold that day was sold cheaply the next day and became known as "day-old bread." Today, supermarkets don't replace all of their bread every day, but if commercial bread hasn't sold in a few days, the distributor takes it back from the supermarket. It frequently shows up at what are known as bread "outlet" or "thrift" stores. Although it is more than one day old, it is still frequently referred to as "day-old bread."

Sometimes you'll find coffee cake, doughnuts, fruit pies, and snack cakes in addition to bread at these stores. Prices vary by region, but they're usually half of full retail. Be aware of what you normally pay at your local supermarket—it's easy to get drawn in by a really low price on, say, hamburger buns and then fall for a loaf of sandwich bread that's actually more than the sale price at your local supermarket. Local groceries must compete with each other by offering good prices. The outlets are all run and stocked by the same manufacturer. So be an informed shopper.

To find the store nearest you, check the Yellow Pages under "bakers." If nothing jumps out, call the larger wholesale bakeries and ask where their "day-old" outlet is located. There doesn't seem to be a particular day that is best to shop at our local outlets—it's basically hit-or-miss. But ask the outlet employees what days the shelves are stocked and when your favorite items are most likely to be available.

Even though the low prices will astonish you, buy only what you can use within 3 days unless you have the space to freeze the loaves for later. Even cheap bread is expensive once it's moldy.

"Ask outlet employees when your favorite items are likely to be available."

THE KIDS' FAVORITE MEATBALL HOAGIES

SERVES: 4 GENEROUSLY START TO FINISH: UNDER 15 MINUTES

24 already-cooked meatballs,
  defrosted if frozen (see Notes)
1½ cups bottled smooth-style spaghetti sauce
4 hoagie rolls
1 cup finely shredded mozzarella cheese (see Notes)

1. Preheat the broiler to high.

2. Place the meatballs in a microwave-safe container, cover them with a paper towel, and microwave on high power until heated through, 3 to 4 minutes. Set aside.

3. Pour the spaghetti sauce into a microwave-safe container, cover with a paper towel, and microwave on high power until heated through, about 4 minutes, stirring once halfway through. Set aside.

4. Cut the hoagie rolls in half and lightly toast them under the broiler, 1 to 2 minutes.

5. Place both halves of a roll, toasted side up, on each of four plates, and arrange 6 meatballs on one of the halves. Spoon some sauce over the meatballs and then sprinkle ¼ cup of the cheese evenly over the sauce. (The heat from the sauce will melt the cheese.) Close the sandwiches and serve.

NOTES: You can use Marvelous Meatballs (page 353) or purchased frozen meatballs (Italian, plain, or traditional style).
■ Some brands refer to finely shredded mozzarella cheese as "fancy" or "chef's style." Part-skim mozzarella is fine here.
■ Meatball hoagies can be decked out with any number of add-ins. Some of our favorites include: sautéed sliced mushrooms and green peppers, reconstituted sun-dried tomato strips, caramelized onions, and shredded fresh basil leaves.

From Alicia:

I often trick myself into believing that my mom was never hard-pressed to produce dinner. How did she do it? She had two kids and a full-time job and did her share of volunteer work as well. But the truth is, she felt as if she was at the end of her rope at times, just as I do. I can remember that there were months when we ate spaghetti with a simple red sauce at least once a week. Even as a child I yearned for just a small twist on the same-old same-old.

Now I know Mom wasn't trying to bore us— she was just trying to get through the week. Maybe her stress was budget-related, or maybe too much was going on for her to slave over dinner. I know this because it happens to me, too. Only now, thanks to having a stash of home-made meatballs on hand, I can expand on Mom's theme of cheap and easy Italian-inspired dinners with hot meatball sandwiches.

How to Use up a Big Hunk of Ham

From Alicia:

There's always leftover ham at my house after Easter. That's because ham tends to be less expensive at this time of year, so I can't resist buying a big one. But then the ham lingers in the fridge, slowly being transformed into sandwiches. The truth is that in the past I often ended up throwing a good portion away, which is not only sad but also wasteful. Then one year I vowed that things would be different and set about to transform my leftover ham from a big daunting hunk into a form that would be more useful. So I coarsely chopped the ham, divided it into portions, and froze them. (See page 83 for more on freezing ham.) That way, I figured, when I needed a rescue meal in a week or two, my chopped ham would be just the ticket.

So here's what to do: Chop the ham into bite-size chunks (about ½ inch), and freeze it in 1-cup portions in heavy-duty freezer bags. The texture will change, but the ham is still fine for many dishes. If the ham is frozen within a day or two of cooking, it will keep for up to 3 months.

Here are some ways you can use a bounty of chopped ham:

- As a pizza topper, such as on Pizza Cordon Bleu (page 260).

- Scattered over garden salads.

- Mixed with cheese and extra veggies on a chef salad.

- In Black-Eyed Pea Salad with Ham (page 288).

- Stirred into pasta salads.

- Tossed with hot pasta, as in Ham and Broccoli Pasta Toss (page 213).

- Sprinkled over baked potatoes.

- Tucked inside an omelet, frittata, or quiche. See our Back-to-Barcelona Tortilla (page 399).

- Half a cup of ham chunks can also be added to either the Zucchini Frittata (page 398) or the Mushroom-Swiss Frittata (page 395).

- Mixed with hash browns.

- Stirred into macaroni and cheese.

- Added to potatoes gratin or a rice casserole, or as the star of a ham-and-noodle casserole.

- Added to jambalaya.

- Added to almost any soup, such as Good Luck Soup (page 29).

- Stirred into Old South Hoppin' John (page 170).

- Baked in Ham and Cheese Turnovers with Dipping Sauce (page 245).

- And of course there's always the trusty ham sandwich, which makes a great midweek dinner with just a little boost, as in our Ham and Asparagus Crostini (page 244) or "New-Fashioned" Grilled Cheese Sandwiches (page 255).

Once you get used to relying on ham leftovers, you may find yourself buying more than you need on purpose. (Conventional wisdom says each pound of bone-in ham yields two to three servings.) More and more, we're finding that good prices on ham aren't limited to springtime. So look for deals at other times of the year and stock up. (See page 81 for more on buying inexpensive hams.)

"Transform a daunting hunk of ham into a more useful form."

s crostini have become all the rage in restaurants, the definition has expanded. In this country, crostini used to be limited to appetizer-size bites of something yummy on toast. But if a little is good, a lot must be better, and now it's not uncommon to see crostini make the meal. We usually turn to this recipe in the spring, when the price of asparagus falls and we need to use up the last bits of the Easter ham.

If you don't have left-over ham, look for deli ham on sale and substitute that. Be sure to enjoy these crostini often when asparagus is at its peak.

HAM AND ASPARAGUS CROSTINI

SERVES: 4 START TO FINISH: UNDER 20 MINUTES

8 ounces fresh pencil-thin asparagus spears
8 slices (1 inch thick) French
  country-style bread
1 cup ham chunks (about ½-inch chunks)
2 tablespoons regular or reduced-fat mayonnaise
1 tablespoon grainy Dijon mustard
4 slices (4 ounces) provolone or Swiss cheese

1. Preheat the oven to 450°F.

2. Rinse the asparagus and snap off the tough ends. Place the spears in a glass pie plate or other shallow microwave-safe dish. Cover the dish with plastic wrap and cut a 1-inch slit in the top for a vent. Microwave on high power until the spears are crisp-tender, 2 to 3 minutes. Set aside.

3. Place the bread slices in a single layer on a baking sheet, place it in the regular oven, and bake until lightly toasted, about 5 minutes. Meanwhile, mix the ham, mayonnaise, and mustard together in a small bowl.

4. Carefully spread the ham mixture over the hot toasted bread on the baking sheet, dividing it evenly. Place 3 or 4 asparagus spears on top of the ham mixture on each sandwich. Cut the cheese slices in half and place half a slice over the asparagus on each sandwich.

5. Return the baking sheet to the oven and bake just until the cheese melts, about 2 minutes. Serve at once, placing 2 open-face sandwiches on each plate.

HAM AND CHEESE TURNOVERS WITH DIPPING SAUCE

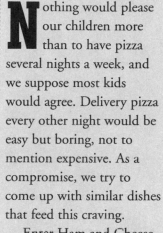

SERVES: 4 START TO FINISH: UNDER 25 MINUTES

1 cup fresh button mushrooms

8 ounces thinly sliced or
    chopped ham

1 tube (16 ounces) refrigerated
    biscuit dough, for 8 extra-large
    biscuits (see Note)

¼ cup shredded part-skim mozzarella cheese

1 cup smooth-style bottled spaghetti sauce

1. Preheat the oven to 400°F.

2. Rinse, pat dry, and coarsely chop the mushrooms, removing and discarding any tough stems. Place the mushrooms in a microwave-safe container. Cover the dish with plastic wrap and cut a 1-inch slit in the top for a vent. Microwave on high power until they release their liquid, about 2 minutes.

3. Meanwhile, coarsely chop the ham and set it aside. Using a rolling pin, roll 4 of the biscuits to flatten them to 4 inches in diameter. Place the flattened biscuits on an ungreased baking sheet.

4. Drain the mushrooms well. Divide the mushrooms, ham, and cheese among the flattened biscuits, spreading them evenly to within ¼ inch of the edge.

5. Roll out the remaining 4 biscuits to about a 4-inch diameter. Place a one over each filled turnover bottom and press the edges together firmly to seal well.

6. Bake until the turnovers are golden brown, about 9 minutes.

Nothing would please our children more than to have pizza several nights a week, and we suppose most kids would agree. Delivery pizza every other night would be easy but boring, not to mention expensive. As a compromise, we try to come up with similar dishes that feed this craving.

Enter Ham and Cheese Turnovers with Dipping Sauce. Made from biscuit dough, it's based on a traditional calzone, which is a turnover stuffed with pizza ingredients. These are a great way to use up the last bits of that ham you bought on sale. Sometimes we like to get creative with the turnover fillings, using up leftovers—instead of mushrooms, try steamed broccoli, asparagus, or carrots. Just be sure not to overstuff the dough or the filling will spill out.

7. While the turnovers are baking, place the spaghetti sauce in a microwave-safe container. (You can use the same container you used for the mushrooms.) Microwave, covered, on high power until heated through, 1 to 1½ minutes.

8. Remove the turnovers from the oven and serve at once, with the spaghetti sauce on the side for dipping.

NOTE: If you are accustomed to the taste of reduced-fat refrigerated biscuits, feel free to substitute them.

BEST BLT MELTS

MAKES: 6 SANDWICHES START TO FINISH: UNDER 25 MINUTES

18 slices bacon (see Notes)
6 English muffins
2 large ripe tomatoes (for 6 slices; see Notes)
Condiments of choice, such as mayonnaise
  and mustard
6 slices (about 6 ounces) Swiss cheese
6 lettuce leaves

1. Line a microwave-safe plate with paper towels. Place half the bacon slices in a single layer on the plate, cover with a paper towel, and microwave on high power until crisp, 3 to 4 minutes. Set the cooked bacon aside and repeat with the remaining slices. (Or you can fry the bacon in a skillet until crisp, 5 to 6 minutes.)

2. Place the oven rack 3 to 4 inches from the heating element of your broiler. Turn the broiler to high.

3. Cut the English muffins in half and place them, cut side up, on a baking sheet. Toast the muffins under the broiler until lightly browned, 2 to 3 minutes. Toast the other side, if desired.

4. Core the tomatoes and slice them, setting aside the 6 nicest slices for the sandwiches. Save the remaining tomato for another use.

Our families love bacon. And when it's the height of tomato season, we crave crisp, smoky bacon paired with juicy, plump tomatoes. What better way to enjoy them both than with a hearty bacon, lettuce, and tomato sandwich? We've put a twist on the traditional here by adding Swiss cheese and switching from regular toast to English muffins. The muffins stand up to the juicyness of a thick slice of tomato better than traditional loaf bread does, but you could certainly make the BLTs with slices of a hearty wheat loaf.

It's easy to find sale prices on all of these ingredients, especially in the summer, when the tomato crop is overflowing. (If you're especially lucky, you or your neighbors might

5. Remove the muffins from the oven (leave the oven on) and, if using, spread the condiments over the bottom halves. Cut the bacon slices in half and arrange them over the bottom halves. Place a tomato then a cheese slice over the bacon.

6. Remove the top halves of the muffins from the baking sheet and set aside. Return the baking sheet to the oven and broil until the cheese melts, about 1 minute. Remove the sandwiches from the oven. Place a lettuce leaf on each sandwich, cover with the top halves, and serve.

NOTES: For tips on buying already-cooked bacon, see the box below. For tips on cooking the cheapest bacon ahead of time and storing it, see page 248.

■ You need 6 good-size tomato slices for these sandwiches. Save end pieces and smaller slices to chop up for salads and salsas.

have an abundance in the garden.) Look for deals on the cheese at the deli case, and also in the packaged cheese section of the grocery store. Some English muffins are located in the refrigerated section, others in the bread and deli sections. Your best deals will often be the supermarket brand. The muffins can be purchased on sale and frozen for up to a month. Even cheese slices can be frozen—just thaw them overnight in the refrigerator.

About:
ALREADY-COOKED BACON

Cooking bacon can make a mess! We almost quit buying it until we discovered precooked bacon at the supermarket, in the refrigerated section right alongside traditional bacon.

While at first glance already-cooked bacon appears to be vastly more expensive than regular uncooked bacon, when we did a more thorough price comparison we realized we were comparing uncooked weight to cooked. As more brands begin to appear (and therefore competition arises), the already-cooked bacon is starting to go on sale occasionally. Coupons are also available, meaning that true savings are ready for the taking.

So for a consistent savings of time and money, we buy already-cooked bacon when it's on sale, and then we freeze it. We use it as a cheap, quick, and easy flavor-booster or as the main event, such as in Best BLT Melts (opposite).

When regular bacon is featured at a sale price we buy several packages and make our own already-cooked (see page 248).

Buying the Cheapest Bacon

From Beverly:

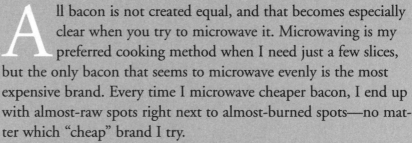

All bacon is not created equal, and that becomes especially clear when you try to microwave it. Microwaving is my preferred cooking method when I need just a few slices, but the only bacon that seems to microwave evenly is the most expensive brand. Every time I microwave cheaper bacon, I end up with almost-raw spots right next to almost-burned spots—no matter which "cheap" brand I try.

However, I can't always justify paying top dollar for bacon when there are brands that cost half that much (or even less). My solution is to bite the bullet and cook the bacon the old-fashioned way. And to make this chore less painful, I've learned a few tricks.

For starters, if I'm going to the trouble of spattering up the stove, it's just as easy in the long run to go ahead and fry the whole package. This takes a bit longer, but after all, I have to clean the pan and the stove only once. And the big bonus is that if you fry some of the bacon just slightly less crisp than you normally like it, you can refrigerate or freeze the almost-cooked strips and then crisp them to perfection later in the microwave. (The cheap bacon actually does fine with just this final crisping in the microwave.) This initial time investment actually pays big dividends on future mornings when I'm rushed and my bacon is just a zap away from the plate.

Unfortunately, the microwave issue isn't the only drawback to buying the least expensive brands of bacon. Really cheap bacon, in general, contains more fat. Since you'll lose a good percentage of that fat in cooking, the actual price per pound isn't quite as cheap as it seems. (To determine the exact price per pound, you'd have to compare the cooked weight of the cheap bacon against a cooked version of a leaner brand.)

Cheap bacon slices also are not uniform in thickness, so it's sometimes impossible to pry the slices apart without tearing them

"Once cheap bacon is fried, it tastes pretty much the same as expensive bacon."

to shreds. I get around this by making sure the bacon sits at room temperature for 10 to 15 minutes before I cook it. (Or I microwave the whole pound for about 30 seconds to warm it up a bit and make it more pliable.) If the slices still won't separate, I pull off several pieces at once and put the whole clump into the skillet. Once the bacon begins to soften in cooking, you can pull the slices apart fairly easily with tongs or a fork.

The good news is that once cheap bacon is fried, it tastes pretty much the same as expensive bacon. If you don't mind a bit more fat than lean on a slice of bacon—and if you don't mind frying—cheap brands are a good option.

From Alicia:

Beverly and I brainstorm ideas weekly. Sometimes I'll start things going with a recipe, then Beverly will suggest using a particular herb or seasoning. That makes me think of another ingredient to add or prep step to try. Before long we head into the kitchen to try out our latest concoction. That's where the idea can change again—several times, maybe—until we're excited about the finished dish.

This recipe is a prime example. We started out discussing crab cakes, which we both love. But they're expensive. So one of us suggested using chicken instead. Into the kitchen we went, armed with a plan to make old-fashioned chicken croquettes. But where we ended up is so far from where we started, and yet so wonderful, that we suspect there must be a little magic in the process. We think you'll love this modern version of "croquettes" as much as we do. The recipe makes five croquettes; leftovers make great sandwiches the next day.

MAGICALLY MODERN "CROQUETTE" SANDWICHES

SERVES: 5 START TO FINISH: UNDER 25 MINUTES

1 cup already-cooked chicken chunks, defrosted if frozen (see Notes)

½ small onion (for about ¼ cup chopped)

½ small green bell pepper

1 large egg

½ cup regular or reduced-fat mayonnaise

¼ teaspoon black pepper

¾ cup plain bread crumbs (see Notes)

2 tablespoons vegetable oil

5 Kaiser rolls or sturdy hamburger buns

Condiments of choice, such as Thousand Island dressing, mayonnaise, or Dijon mustard

5 lettuce leaves, for serving (optional)

5 tomato slices, for serving (optional)

1. Place the chicken in a food processor and process until it is finely shredded. Remove the chicken from the bowl and set it aside.

2. Peel the onion half and, with the processor running, drop it through the feed tube. Process until finely chopped. (There's no need to wash the processor bowl first.) Stem, seed, and halve the bell pepper half and drop it through the feed tube. Process until finely chopped.

3. Break the egg into the processor bowl. Pour the reserved shredded chicken into the bowl. Add the mayonnaise and black pepper. Pulse, scraping down the sides of the bowl if necessary, just to combine the ingredients. Spoon the mixture into a medium-size mixing bowl.

4. Add the bread crumbs and stir until they are completely combined with the chicken mixture.

5. Heat the oil in an extra-deep 12-inch skillet over medium heat for 1 minute. Using your hands, shape the chicken mixture into five 3-inch patties that are about ½ inch thick, adding the patties to the skillet as you shape them.

6. Fry the patties until they are golden brown on one side, 3 to 4 minutes. Turn the patties and fry until they are golden brown on the second side, 3 to 4 minutes more.

7. While the patties cook, toast the rolls, if desired, and spread them with the condiments of your choice.

8. Place a patty on each roll, top with a lettuce leaf and a tomato slice (if using), and serve at once.

NOTES: You can use 1 cup Perfect Poached Chicken (page 362), Poached Chicken Thighs (page 364), or Chunky Seasoned Chicken (page 358). Or cut an 8-ounce skinless, boneless chicken breast half into bite-size chunks and sauté until cooked through; then proceed with the recipe.

■ For tips on making your own bread crumbs, see page 235. Dry or soft crumbs will work in this recipe.

Chew on This

Children in the United States have eaten an average of 1,500 peanut butter and jelly sandwiches by the time they graduate from high school, *Time* magazine reports. Americans eat enough peanut butter every year to spread across the floor of the entire Grand Canyon.

Here's a revisit to the salmon croquettes our mothers made when we were growing up. Our moms always kept a can or two of pink salmon in the pantry for those last-minute, end-of-the-month dinners when an inexpensive meal was doubly appreciated. Today, pink salmon also comes packed in foil pouches; this new packaging eliminates the draining step.

Working these sandwiches into the monthly mix of dinners has more than the obvious budget benefits—canned salmon is good for you, too. (For more information on salmon's health benefits and concerns, see page 290.)

These patties will seem very moist when you place them in the skillet, but don't worry. Just turn them carefully after they have completely browned on the first side, and they will hold together for a juicy, delicious end result.

SALMON CAKE SANDWICHES

SERVES: 4 START TO FINISH: UNDER 25 MINUTES

SUPER-CHEAP!

1 foil pouch (7.1 ounces) premium skinless, boneless pink salmon (see Notes)
1 small onion (for about ½ cup chopped)
2 large eggs
½ cup dry bread crumbs (see Notes)
¼ cup regular or reduced-fat mayonnaise
2 teaspoons Worcestershire sauce
¼ teaspoon black pepper
½ teaspoon salt
1 tablespoon butter or margarine
2 tablespoons vegetable oil
4 sandwich buns
4 lettuce leaves, for serving (optional)
4 tomato slices, for serving (optional)
¼ cup Terrific Tartar Sauce (page 383) or purchased tartar sauce

1. Place the salmon in a medium-size mixing bowl, flaking it with your fingers to break up any chunks. Peel and finely chop the onion and add it to the bowl.

2. Lightly beat the eggs and add them to the bowl. Add the bread crumbs, mayonnaise, Worcestershire sauce, black pepper, and salt. Stir to combine well.

3. Melt the butter in the oil in an extra-deep 12-inch skillet over medium heat. Meanwhile, using your hands, shape the mixture into 4 patties roughly 3½ inches in diameter and ½ inch thick.

4. Swirl the pan to combine the butter and oil and place the patties in the skillet. Sauté until golden brown on the first side, about 3 minutes. Carefully turn the patties over and sauté until golden brown on the second side, about 3 minutes more.

5. While the patties cook, toast the sandwich buns, if desired.

6. Place a salmon patty on the bottom half of each bun and top with a lettuce leaf and a tomato slice, if desired. Top each with 1 tablespoon of the tartar sauce, cover with the top half of the bun, and serve.

NOTES: You can also use two 6-ounce cans of skinless and boneless pink salmon. Drain it thoroughly before placing it in the bowl.
■ For information on making your own bread crumbs, see page 235.

SHRIMP PO' BOYS

SERVES: 4 START TO FINISH: UNDER 15 MINUTES

1 package (14 ounces) frozen popcorn shrimp
⅔ cup Terrific Tartar Sauce (page 383) or purchased
    tartar sauce
4 sandwich buns
4 lettuce leaves, for serving (optional)
4 tomato slices, for serving (optional)

1. Microwave or bake the shrimp according to the package directions.

2. Spread a heaping tablespoon of tartar sauce over each half of the buns. (The buns can be toasted first if you prefer.) Place 12 to 15 cooked shrimp (they're small) on the bottom half of each sandwich bun. Top with a lettuce leaf and a tomato slice, if desired, and cover with the top half of the bun. Serve at once.

From Beverly:

For the longest time, the only shrimp my children would eat were "popcorn" shrimp, fried to perfection by our local seafood restaurant. Imagine my delight when I recently discovered "popcorn" shrimp alongside the frozen fish in the supermarket and learned that some brands are even suitable for the microwave.

Shrimp Po' Boys, with our wonderful homemade tartar sauce, has become a favorite. We usually make this with the microwave-ready shrimp, but any brand of frozen popcorn shrimp will do. Just follow the cooking directions on the package.

"New-Fashioned" with Frills

We started experimenting with variations on grilled cheese after eating several "mod" versions at our favorite neighborhood sandwich shop. It almost doesn't matter what you add to a grilled cheese—if the flavors are bold, you'll have a hit. Think of the "New-Fashioned" Grilled Cheese Sandwiches recipe (opposite) as a starting point and get creative. To get you started, here are some examples: Just add any of these ingredients instead of (or in addition to) the tomato and avocado in Step 3.

- Bacon slices and fresh basil leaves (or a sprinkle of dried basil)

- Pickled jalapeños and a dollop of jarred bean dip

- A smear of hummus and some roasted red peppers

- A shake of dried Italian seasoning and a few slices of sun-dried tomato

- Deli ham and watercress leaves

- Pepperoni slices and mozzarella cheese

- Salami and provolone cheese

- Already-cooked chicken and coleslaw

- Sliced hard-cooked egg and sweet pickle relish

"New-Fashioned" Grilled Cheese Sandwiches

SERVES: 2 START TO FINISH: UNDER 10 MINUTES

1 tablespoon butter
2 teaspoons Dijon mustard
4 slices country white or hearty whole wheat bread
2 teaspoons regular or reduced-fat mayonnaise
2 slices sharp Cheddar or other cheese
2 slices Swiss or other cheese
4 thin slices tomato
6 thin slices avocado (optional)

1. Melt the butter in an extra-deep 12-inch skillet over low heat. While the butter melts, spread 1 teaspoon of the mustard on each of 2 slices of the bread. Spread 1 teaspoon of the mayonnaise on each of the remaining 2 slices of bread. Place 1 slice of Cheddar and 1 slice of Swiss cheese on each of 2 slices of the bread.

2. Place the cheese-topped bread, cheese side up, in the skillet. Cover the skillet and cook until the bread is golden brown on the bottom and the cheese is just beginning to melt, 2 to 3 minutes.

3. Arrange 2 slices of tomato and 3 slices of avocado (if using), on top of the cheese and place the top piece of bread on each sandwich. Turn the sandwiches over, pressing the top of each sandwich with a spatula to keep it together. Cook, uncovered, until the second side is golden brown, 2 to 3 minutes more. While each sandwich is cooking, press it firmly with a spatula several times so it begins to stick together.

4. Transfer the sandwiches to plates, cut them in half, and serve.

There's nothing better than an old-fashioned grilled cheese sandwich—unless it's a *new*-fashioned grilled cheese sandwich. Take your favorite hearty bread, slather on a bit of mayonnaise and mustard, then add at least two kinds of cheese (any combination that seems pleasing will do—we buy whatever's on sale) and a slice or two of red-ripe tomato. Melt a bit of butter (the real thing!), and sizzle the sandwich to a golden burnish. Pure heaven is only a bite away.

Only two sandwiches will fit in the skillet at one time, but since these sandwiches cook so quickly, it's easy to make as many batches as you need, customizing them to everyone's preference.

These meatless "burgers" are close cousins to the Middle-Eastern, deep-fried falafel. This may be inexpensive peasant fare, but our lemony garlic mayonnaise elevates the humble dish to a taste sensation. Instead of sandwich buns, you could serve them tucked into pita pockets, Middle Eastern–style.

SASSY CHICKPEA BURGERS WITH LEMON AÏOLI

SERVES: 4 START TO FINISH: UNDER 20 MINUTES

SUPER-CHEAP!

2 cloves fresh garlic
1 small onion
¼ green bell pepper
1 can (15 ounces) chickpeas, or 1 cup homemade (see page 368), defrosted if frozen
1 large egg
1¼ cups soft bread crumbs (see Note)
½ teaspoon salt
½ teaspoon black pepper
¼ cup vegetable oil
⅓ cup all-purpose flour
4 hamburger or sandwich buns, for serving
4 lettuce leaves, for serving
4 tomato slices, for serving
Lemon Aïoli (page 386), for serving

1. Peel the garlic. Turn on a food processor and drop the cloves through the feed tube. Process until finely minced.

2. Peel the onion, cut it into quarters, and place the quarters in the food processor bowl. Cut the bell pepper piece into quarters and add them to the processor bowl. Pulse until the onion and pepper are finely minced but not mushy, stopping once or twice to scrape down the sides of the bowl. Using a rubber spatula, scrape the minced vegetables into a medium-size mixing bowl.

3. Drain the liquid from the can of chickpeas into a small bowl or cup and set it aside. Pour the chickpeas into the processor bowl and add the egg. Add 2 tablespoons of the reserved chickpea liquid or water. Process just until the chickpeas are finely chopped but still have some texture. Add them to the onion mixture. Add the bread crumbs, salt, and black pepper to the bowl and stir until the ingredients are well mixed.

4. Heat the oil in an extra-deep 12-inch skillet over medium heat. While the oil is heating, shape the mixture into patties: Squeeze one fourth of the mixture in your hands to make a tight ball. Flatten the ball into a patty, making it as thin as you can without it cracking. Repeat with the remaining mixture to make 3 more patties.

5. Spread the flour on a plate and dredge the chickpea patties lightly in it. Add the patties to the hot oil and fry until golden brown, 3 to 4 minutes per side. Meanwhile, split the buns and lightly toast them in a toaster oven.

6. Serve the patties on the buns with lettuce, tomato, and a dollop of Lemon Aïoli.

NOTE: See page 235 for tips on making your own bread crumbs.

Chew on This

Need an incentive besides just saving money to pack your kids' school lunches? The number of overweight children has tripled in the past 30 years, according to the U.S. Centers for Disease Control and Prevention. And school lunches average 35 percent of calories from fat, according to a recent survey of 1,000 public schools by the U.S. Department of Agriculture. That's a good reason to pack carrot sticks and reduced-fat peanut butter on whole wheat!

People are serious about egg salad. When I casually asked several of my friends, they all had definite opinions about what it should include and how it should be served. Most reminisced about their mom's egg salad, their grandmother's delicious recipe, or happy memories of events at which egg salad was served: family reunions, summer picnics by the lake, beach vacations.

All of their recommendations sounded wonderful, but I realized that as personal as egg salad seems to be, what is needed is a basic recipe that can serve as a foundation for all the various additions.

Most children tend to like egg salad plain (mayo only). Adults' tastes vary from strictly plain to "all the way." Any way you choose to fix it, egg salad is a satisfying snack, lunch, or dinner that easily fits into the family budget.

YOUR EGG SALAD

MAKES: ABOUT 3½ CUPS (WITHOUT ADDITIONS)
START TO FINISH: UNDER 20 MINUTES

SUPER-CHEAP!

Basic egg salad
1 dozen large eggs
¾ cup regular or reduced-fat mayonnaise
Salt and black pepper to taste

Optional additions
1 tablespoon yellow, brown, or Dijon mustard
2 tablespoons sweet pickle relish (see Note)
About 1 cup finely chopped celery (2 ribs)
2 tablespoons finely chopped fresh watercress, basil,
   cilantro, or parsley leaves

White or wheat bread or crackers, for serving

1. Place the eggs in a large saucepan and fill the pan with enough cold water to just cover the tops of the eggs. Place the pan over high heat and bring to a boil. When the water comes to a boil, cook the eggs for 3 minutes. Then remove the pan from the heat, cover it, and set it aside for at least 20 minutes or up to 1 hour.

2. Crack and peel the eggs and place them in a 1½-quart or larger mixing bowl. Add the mayonnaise. Using a potato masher or a fork (if using a fork, coarsely chop the eggs after peeling them), mash the eggs and mayonnaise together, making the mixture as chunky or as smooth as you like. Season with salt and black pepper.

3. Mix in any of the additions, if desired.

4. Serve the egg salad immediately on bread, toast, or crackers; or store in a covered container in the refrigerator for up to 3 days.

NOTE: Sweet pickle relish is sometimes called "sweet salad cubes." If you can't find it, substitute any sweet pickle, drained and finely chopped.

ULTRA-EASY VEGGIE QUESADILLAS

SERVES: 6 START TO FINISH: UNDER 25 MINUTES

1 tablespoon vegetable oil

1 small onion
(for about ½ cup chopped)

2 cloves fresh garlic, minced,
or 2 teaspoons bottled
minced garlic

1 cup frozen yellow corn kernels

2 cans (15 ounces each)
black beans, or 2 cups homemade
(see page 368), defrosted if frozen

½ teaspoon ground cumin

Cooking oil spray

8 large (10- to 12-inch) flour tortillas

1 cup shredded Cheddar cheese

Condiments of your choice, such as salsa, sour cream,
chopped tomato, and/or shredded lettuce

1. Preheat the oven to 450°F.

2. Heat the oil in a 12-inch skillet over medium heat. Peel and coarsely chop the onion, adding it to the skillet as you chop. Add the garlic to the skillet. Cook until the onion is translucent, about 3 minutes, stirring from time to time.

3. While the onion cooks, put the corn in a colander and run it under cool tap water to defrost it slightly. If using canned beans, rinse and drain them.

4. When the onion is tender, add the beans and corn to the skillet. Stir to mix. Add the cumin. Cook to heat the mixture through, 1 minute. Remove the skillet from the heat.

5. Spray 2 baking sheets with cooking oil spray. Place 1 tortilla on one of the baking sheets. Spoon ½ cup of the bean mixture onto

Since quesadillas appear on so many trendy restaurant menus, you might expect them to be difficult to make. But when you scrutinize this Mexican dish, you realize it's just bread (more or less) covering up a cheesy filling. Looks like a sandwich, must be a sandwich (more or less). We can handle cooking that, even on the busiest nights. And so can you.

This meat-free recipe isn't expensive—and it simply requires frying an onion and heating some pantry ingredients in a skillet, then putting a little filling on the tortillas and popping them in the oven for 5 minutes. Baking the quesadillas is healthier than pan frying them.

Serve the quesadillas with your favorite salsa and some sour cream, and you've got dinner.

Most restaurant versions of this Mexican classic use two tortillas, one stacked on top of the other. Traditionally, quesadillas are made from one tortilla folded over, and we find this traditional method easier to fit on the baking sheets as well.

one half of the tortilla. Top the bean mixture with 2 tablespoons of the cheese. Fold the tortilla in half over the bean mixture, pressing lightly with your hands so it adheres. Repeat with 3 more tortillas and filling on the first baking sheet. Then repeat the process with the remaining 4 tortillas and filling on the second baking sheet.

6. Place both baking sheets in the oven and bake until the tortillas are crisp and the cheese has melted, 5 to 7 minutes.

7. Remove the baking sheets from the oven. Using a pizza cutter, cut each quesadilla into 3 wedges. Place 4 wedges on each plate. Serve topped with the condiments of your choice.

PIZZA CORDON BLEU

SERVES: 4 START TO FINISH: UNDER 30 MINUTES

1 refrigerated pizza dough (10 ounces), or
   1 prepared pizza crust, such as Boboli
½ small onion (for about ¼ cup sliced)
1½ cups fresh button mushrooms
2 tablespoons Dijon mustard
¼ cup regular or reduced-fat sour cream
1 cup bite-size already-cooked chicken chunks,
   defrosted if frozen (see Note)
1 cup bite-size cooked ham chunks
1 cup shredded Swiss cheese

1. Preheat the oven to the temperature specified on the pizza crust package. If using refrigerated dough, prepare the crust for baking and prebake if necessary, following the package directions.

2. Peel the onion half and slice it thinly. Place the slices in a 2-quart microwave-safe dish. Rinse and slice the mushrooms, discarding any tough stems, and add them to the dish with the onions. Cover the dish with microwave-safe plastic wrap and vent

Back when our kids were small, "pizza" always meant "cheese pizza." Period. But now that we have teenagers, we love to experiment with bolder flavors and new combinations, such as the fancy pizzas at "California-style" restaurants. Fortunately, it's a simple and inexpensive matter to make interesting pizzas at home.

This recipe replaces the traditional red sauce with a snazzy combo of mustard and sour cream that turns the same-old pizza into a Wow! If you like, add half a red or green bell pepper, thinly sliced, instead of (or in addition to) the mushrooms.

one corner. Microwave on high power until the onions are wilted and the mushrooms have released their liquid, about 3 minutes.

3. While the vegetables microwave, place the prepared pizza crust on an ungreased baking sheet. Stir the mustard and sour cream together in a small bowl and spread the mixture evenly over the crust. (A rubber spatula or the back of a spoon works well.) Sprinkle the chicken and ham pieces evenly over the crust.

4. Remove the vegetables from the microwave and drain off any liquid. Distribute the vegetables evenly over the pizza. Sprinkle the cheese evenly over the top.

5. Bake in the regular oven following the directions on the package until the cheese has melted and the crust reaches the desired crispness. Cut into wedges and serve.

NOTE: You can use 1 cup Perfect Poached Chicken (page 362), Poached Chicken Thighs (page 364), or Great Grilled Chicken Breasts (page 360). Or cut an 8-ounce skinless, boneless chicken breast half into bite-size chunks and sauté in ½ tablespoon vegetable oil until cooked through, then proceed with the recipe.

It's a snap to get a pizza on the table if you use already-prepared pizza crusts—either partially baked or refrigerated dough in a tube.

If you've been craving pizza that goes beyond the ordinary, Pizza Cordon Bleu is a sure bet.

Let Them "Cook": Having Kids in the Kitchen Means More Hands on Deck

"Children are more likely to eat what they've helped to prepare."

We never used to cook with our children except for the occasional baking spree. Decorating cookies and cupcakes was fun, but when it came time to get dinner on the table, everyone younger than six was generally banished from the kitchen. Now that they are a little older, however, we're learning how to put their energies to good use. Allowing kids to make dinner builds confidence and reinforces that they're a vital part of the family unit. We've discovered that our children need to "do" for us as much as we need to "do" for them. In fact, kids love to cook and we should have let them in the kitchen a lot sooner. They're imaginative, take their responsibilities seriously, and working together in the kitchen makes for great quality time.

The trick is to make sure they succeed—and you survive. It's a delicate balance. To find it, simply think about the menu in a slightly different way. Especially at first, choose dishes that are more "assembled" than cooked. Pizza is perfect for children of all ages (for some recipes to get you started, see pages 260 to 265). With the help of an adult to insert and remove the pizzas from the hot oven, kids can do the rest. Even the youngest tykes, with a little supervision, can smear sauce and sprinkle on the toppings they choose.

The bonus (in addition to having a few extra hands) is that children are more likely to eat what they've helped to prepare. That's reason enough to allow the kids in the kitchen!

CHICKEN AND ONION PIZZA

SERVES: 4 START TO FINISH: UNDER 30 MINUTES

1 refrigerated pizza dough (10 ounces),
   or 1 prepared pizza crust, such as Boboli
2 teaspoons olive oil
1 medium-size onion (for about ¾ cup sliced)
1 cup salsa
1 cup already-cooked chicken chunks,
   defrosted if frozen (see Note)
2 cups shredded Monterey Jack cheese

1. Preheat the oven to the temperature specified on the pizza crust package. If using refrigerated dough, prepare the crust for baking and prebake if necessary, following the package directions.

2. Meanwhile, heat the oil in an 8-inch or larger skillet over medium heat. Peel the onion and slice it into rings, adding them to the skillet as you slice. Cook, stirring, until the onion is well browned, about 7 minutes. Set aside.

3. Spread the salsa over the prepared crust. Chop the chicken into very small pieces and spread them over the salsa. Top with the onions and cheese.

4. Bake the pizza following the directions on the package until the cheese has melted and the crust reaches the desired crispness. Serve.

NOTE: You can use 1 cup Perfect Poached Chicken (page 362), Poached Chicken Thighs (page 364), Great Grilled Chicken Breasts, or Chunky Seasoned Chicken (page 358). Or cut an 8-ounce skinless, boneless chicken breast half into bite-size chunks and sauté until cooked through, then proceed with the recipe.

When we tested this "fancy" pizza by serving it to friends for an impromptu Saturday-night meal, everyone raved! The secret is the caramelized onions. The depth of flavor is unsurpassed, and it only takes a little olive oil and an onion. Not bad, huh?

Salsa replaces the traditional red pizza sauce with flair. Any bottled salsa will do—choose your favorite level of spiciness. With mild salsa, this pizza is a kid-favorite. Kids even like the onions because they are sweet.

If you have a big pizza-eating family, simply double the recipe. Depending on the crust you choose (refrigerated dough or prepared partially baked), one pizza will yield eight medium-size slices. Even with a side salad, heartier eaters might enjoy seconds. But when you're making pizza at home, you can afford to make a lot of it.

Think bean-dip pizza. That's what these little darlings resemble. The pizzas can be customized to suit each diner, and the topping options are vast. Is there a leftover chicken breast in the fridge? Throw it on! A can of refried beans in the pantry? Any variety—regular, fat-free, or black bean—is delicious. And any type of cheese you'd typically use in a Mexican-style dish tastes great.

When a recipe is this flexible, it becomes a staple. Plus it's a favorite with all of our kids, which means no extra snacking after dinner! One pizza per person is usually sufficient, but those who have larger appetites will require two. Just double or triple the recipe.

MINI MEXICAN PIZZAS

MAKES: 6 PIZZAS START TO FINISH: UNDER 25 MINUTES

SUPER-CHEAP!

6 small (7-inch) soft corn tortillas
1 can (16 ounces) refried beans
   (see Note)
6 tablespoons shredded Cheddar
   or Mexican-blend cheese
6 tablespoons frozen yellow corn kernels
1 can (4 ounces) chopped green chiles,
   mild or hot
Salsa, for serving
Sour cream, for serving (optional)

1. Preheat the oven to 450°F.

2. Place the tortillas on an ungreased 17- x 11-inch baking sheet. (The edges may overlap slightly.) Divide the beans evenly over the tortillas and, using a rubber spatula or the back of a spoon, spread them to within ½ inch of the edges.

3. Sprinkle 1 tablespoon of the cheese and 1 tablespoon of the corn over each tortilla. Drain the chiles and divide them evenly over the tortillas.

4. Bake the tortillas until they are steaming and the cheese has melted, 5 to 6 minutes. Remove the baking sheet from the oven and, using a wide spatula, transfer each tortilla to a serving plate. Serve at once, topping the tortillas with salsa and sour cream, if desired.

NOTE: Fat-free refried beans or refried black beans can be used.

PERFECT SPINACH PESTO PIZZA

SERVES: 4 START TO FINISH: UNDER 30 MINUTES

1 refrigerated pizza dough (10 ounces) or
  prepared pizza crust, such as Boboli
½ cup Spinach Parsley Pesto (page 372)
½ cup bite-size ham chunks (see Note)
¾ cup shredded part-skim mozzarella cheese
3 ripe medium-size plum tomatoes
1 tablespoon shredded or grated Parmesan cheese
  (optional)

1. Preheat the oven to the temperature specified on the pizza crust package. If using refrigerated dough, prepare the crust for baking and prebake if necessary, following the package directions.

2. Place the prepared crust on an ungreased baking sheet. Stir the pesto to mix in any oil that may have separated and spread it evenly over the crust. (It will be a very thin layer.) Sprinkle the ham evenly over the pesto. Sprinkle the mozzarella evenly over the ham.

3. Core and cut the tomatoes into roughly ¼-inch-thick slices. Layer the slices over the mozzarella. Sprinkle the Parmesan cheese (if using) evenly over the tomatoes.

4. Bake the pizza following the directions on the package until the cheese has melted and the crust reaches the desired crispness. Cut into wedges and serve.

NOTE: You can also use 2 ounces of ham from the supermarket deli, very thinly sliced. Just chop the slices into bite-size pieces.

Here's another delightfully different pizza that's easy to make at home. Pesto gives it an out-of-the-ordinary zing. We use our stash of Spinach Parsley Pesto, which we keep on hand in the freezer. You can also try it with homemade or commercially prepared basil pesto. And if you happen to have ripe tomatoes from the garden, by all means use them.

Making School Lunches Reasonable

When it comes to saving money, packing a school lunch would seem to be a no-brainer. Brown-bagging from home *has* to be cheaper, right? Not necessarily. With all the high-priced, overpackaged, snackable, and squirtable kid-targeted lunches on the market, the tab can quickly mount.

Here are our best mom-tested and kid-tested tricks for packing school lunches that will be the envy of the cafeteria, without breaking a sweat or breaking the bank:

- Create a budget target, and do the math. If you first figure out what you think is a reasonable per-day amount to spend on a school lunch, it's much easier to hit the mark. Use the shelf labels in the supermarket to help you figure out the per-unit cost of prepackaged foods and snacks. Figure out how much meat, cheese, fruit, bread, and peanut butter you'll use in a given week, then divide the total by five to see what each day's lunch costs. (You may be surprised at what a deal the cafeteria lunch turns out to be!)

- It's a fact that kids love small cups and tubes of foods like yogurt and applesauce, but these cute little packages are the most expensive way to buy food. Try making your own. Small, reusable plastic snack cups are readily available in mart-type stores, and if you scoop the applesauce from a large jar into your own snack cup, the savings are huge. Same goes for fruit such as peaches, pineapple, and raisins.

- Look for plastic sipper cups that won't leak and come with a built-in straw. You can pour juice from a large bottle into the cute cup for just pennies a serving. Older children who don't want sippy cups are just as pleased with these funky straw cups. Or go for the old standby of plastic cups with a lid.

- Invest in an insulated Thermos. Single-serving Thermos containers are perfect for keeping soup and leftovers hot until lunchtime. (Pack only leftovers you know your child likes!) A Thermos will also keep yogurt, Jell-O, and fruit salad cold.

- When you do splurge on "Lunchables" on sale, save the package. Wash the plastic tray and then fill it with your own crackers, and cold cuts and cheese that you've cut into squares. Pop the tray into a large zipper-top bag or cover it with foil. You get the pizzazz without the price. Ziploc and other brands make similar divided plastic trays that are reusable and come with a tight-fitting lid.

- If you need to send plastic spoons and forks to school, buy heavy-duty ones and ask your kids not to throw them away. Heavy plastic utensils go through the dishwasher without peril and can then be reused. (You could send stainless steel, but common sense tells you a spoon will get lost every now and then.)

- Ask for feedback about what your kids are and aren't eating in lunches packed from home. (Don't nag, or you won't get the truth!) There's no reason to send apples at 50 to 60 cents each if they're just getting thrown in the trash. We find we need to ask for this information regularly, as kids' eating habits can vary.

- Finally, as a fun addition that won't cost you a penny, write a note to your child on the napkin you tuck in the bag. They'll love hearing from you in the middle of the day. Be inspirational or funny, loving or mysterious—it's just a nice way to say hi when you're not there.

"It may turn out that cafeteria lunches are the best deal."

Tacos at home are fun for everyone, and they don't have to cost nearly as much as heading to your local fast-food outlet. Taco fixings can include everything from guacamole and sliced ripe olives to leftover sautéed green peppers. We always like to include our favorite salsa (spicy for the adults and mild for kids), diced fresh tomato, and a little shredded lettuce for crunch. Just this minimum effort (3 minutes, max!) makes for a hearty and economical meal.

Speaking of hearty, how many people this recipe feeds depends on individual appetites. Two loaded tacos will satisfy big appetites, while young children will probably be happy with just one taco containing only a couple tablespoons of filling. This version allows enough filling for 4 large tacos with ¼ cup filling per tortilla. If you are serving big eaters, increase the amount of filling by ¼ cup for each extra taco you want to make. If you have filling left over, serve it later as a snack dip with tortilla chips, warmed in the microwave.

MAKE-YOUR-OWN SOFT TACOS

SERVES: 4 START TO FINISH: UNDER 20 MINUTES

Toppings of choice, such as salsa, diced tomato, and shredded lettuce, for serving, about 1 cup each (or to taste)
1 cup Flexible Mexican Filling (page 352), defrosted if frozen
4 large (10- to 12-inch) flour tortillas

1. Prepare the toppings for serving (see headnote) and set them aside.

2. Place the Flexible Mexican Filling on a microwave-save dish, cover with a paper towel, and microwave on high power until heated through, 2 to 3 minutes. Set aside.

3. Place a paper towel on a microwave-safe plate and stack the tortillas on the paper towel. Microwave, uncovered, on high power just until warm, about 1 minute. Remove the tortillas and place them on dinner plates.

4. Build each taco according to personal preference: Place the filling and condiments in the center of the tortilla, fold one end over the filling, and roll up the tortilla, burrito-style. Serve at once.

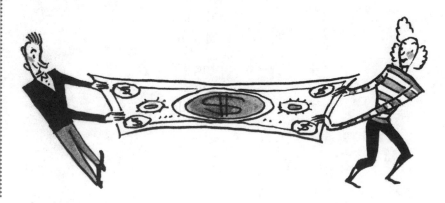

BEEF AND CHEESE QUESADILLAS

SERVES: 6 START TO FINISH: UNDER 25 MINUTES

Cooking oil spray
8 large (10- to 12-inch) flour tortillas
2 cups Flexible Mexican Filling
  (page 352), defrosted if frozen
2 large tomatoes, for serving
½ head iceberg lettuce, for serving
2 cups salsa, for serving

SUPER-CHEAP!

1. Preheat the oven to 450°F.

2. Spray a baking sheet with cooking oil spray. Place 1 tortilla on the baking sheet. Pour about ¼ cup of the Flexible Mexican Filling on half of the tortilla, spreading it to within about ½ inch of the edge. (The filling will spread out a bit during baking.) Fold the tortilla in half over the meat mixture, pressing it lightly with your hands so it adheres. Repeat with 3 more tortillas on the first baking sheet. Then repeat the process with the remaining tortillas on the second baking sheet.

3. Place both baking sheets in the oven and bake until the tortillas are crisp, 5 to 7 minutes.

4. While the quesadillas bake, core and dice the tomatoes, placing the pieces in a serving bowl. Shred the lettuce, placing the pieces in another serving bowl. Pour the salsa into a third serving bowl.

5. Remove the baking sheets from the oven and, using a pizza cutter, cut each quesadilla into 3 wedges. Place 4 wedges on each plate. Serve at once, topping each quesadilla with tomato, lettuce, and salsa, as desired.

These quesadillas make a wonderful supper or lunch. Toppings of tomato, lettuce, and salsa look impressive and provide a counterpoint to the rich, meaty filling, but you can get a bit fancier if your budget allows. Anything goes—from avocado to ripe olives to pickled jalapeños. But if you prefer yours plain or just with salsa, these quesadillas are wonderful solo, too.

Most restaurant versions of this Mexican classic use two tortillas, one stacked on top of the other. Traditionally, quesadillas are made with one tortilla folded over, and we find this traditional method easier to fit on the baking sheets.

FIESTA DINNER NACHOS

SERVES: 4 START TO FINISH: UNDER 10 MINUTES

**2 cups Flexible Mexican Filling
(page 352), defrosted if frozen**

Cooking oil spray

**4 to 5 cups tortilla chips
(see Notes)**

1 large tomato (for about 1½ cups chopped)

½ head iceberg lettuce (for about 4 cups shredded)

**½ cup shredded Monterey Jack cheese
(optional; see Notes)**

**1 can (2¼ ounces) sliced black olives, drained
(optional)**

Salsa, for serving (optional)

1. Place an oven rack 3 to 4 inches from the heating element of your broiler. Turn the broiler to high.

2. If the Flexible Mexican Filling is cold, place it in a microwave-safe bowl, cover with a paper towel, and microwave on high power, stirring it halfway through, until warmed through, about 2 minutes.

3. Spray a 17- x 11-inch baking sheet that has at least a 1-inch rim (such as a jelly roll pan) with cooking oil spray. Spread the chips evenly in the pan. (Use enough chips to cover the bottom of the pan in a single layer.) Set aside.

4. Core and dice the tomato and set aside. Cut the lettuce into ¼-inch-wide strips, and then again to make strips about 3 inches long. Set aside.

5. Remove the filling from the microwave and spoon it over the chips as evenly as possible. (Some of the chips will not have filling on them.) Sprinkle the cheese over the filling, if desired.

Most restaurants list nachos as an appetizer, but since they're filling, why not let them be your whole meal every now and then? Nothing is more fun than setting a platter of chips loaded with toppings in the middle of the table and telling the kids to dig in. Fortunately, nachos are a cinch—and cheap—to make at home. It's cause for a fiesta! Serve fresh fruit for dessert.

6. Broil until the cheese has melted and the chips are barely beginning to brown, about 1 minute. Remove the nachos from the oven and sprinkle the lettuce and tomato evenly on top. Sprinkle the olives (if using) evenly on top. Serve at once, passing salsa at the table, if desired (see Notes).

NOTES: We don't recommend reduced-fat (baked) tortilla chips for this recipe; the filling contains too much moisture for their fragile texture.

■ The filling already contains plenty of cheese and sour cream, but go ahead and sprinkle more on top if you'd like.

■ Nachos are typically eaten with your fingers, so provide plenty of napkins. Use a spatula to portion it out.

MoneySaver

If your avocados get ripe before you're ready to eat them, make a puree, add a few drops of lemon juice, and freeze it for up to 2 months.

About: FAST AND FLEXIBLE

Want your kitchen to be as versatile as the kitchen in a Mexican restaurant? If you start with our Flexible Mexican Filling (page 352) you can choose between finishing it off as tacos, dinner nachos, or hearty quesadillas—all in a flash. The filling—a blend of ground beef, onions, taco seasoning, cheese, sour cream, and tomato soup (the surprise ingredient)—is the basic building block for each recipe. It's so hearty and rich that all you really have to do is add flour tortillas or tortilla chips and a few toppings, heat, and serve. But to be precise, starting on page 268 are exact recipes for three different preparations. Once you get the hang of it, these three dinners are so easy, you probably won't need a recipe at all.

CHAPTER SIX

SIMPLY SATISFYING SALADS

"When life calls for salad, you don't have to spend a fortune."

Simple salads make great summer meals, but if you're not careful, they can end up being not so simple at all. The more complicated a salad gets, the more expensive it tends to be, so resist the urge to chop up every vegetable in your kitchen. Even when salads are dinner, they don't need to be elaborate.

It's easiest to keep things simple when you let one ingredient take center stage. If your salad includes meat—and chicken is often our budget meat of choice—let that one flavorful, hearty ingredient be the star. You'll find several examples in this chapter, including Chicken Caesar Salad, Fall Chicken Salad, Sweet and Savory Chicken Salad, and Waldorf Pasta Salad. Pasta is always a good stretcher, and we make good use of pasta not only in the Waldorf, but also in our Super Salmon Pasta Salad and Red Bean and Pasta Salad. Beans are another easy and inexpensive way to put together a hearty salad, and if beans are involved the meat can be more of a garnish—if it's included at all. We've put our best beans forward in Three-Bean Salad, Black-Eyed Pea Salad with Ham, and Easiest Taco Salad.

When it comes to salad greens there are tons of choices and ways to save, and we've got them all covered in a special box on page 274. And what salad would be complete without a wonderful dressing? Of course the supermarket shelves are lined with choices, and when we're in a hurry and see a decent bottle on sale, we're not opposed to letting someone else do the work. However, it's very easy to whip up a marvelous, inexpensive salad dressing in a matter of minutes, so we've included some of our favorites. Even though some of the dressings have been paired with specific salads (the Creamy Pseudo-Caesar and Thai Peanut dressings, for example), all of them would be equally good over a basic tossed green salad.

When life calls for salad, you don't have to spend a fortune. With these recipes you can keep it simple and still make it delicious and satisfying.

Saving on the Green Stuff

"Believe it or not, we often end up using prewashed bagged salad greens."

It never ceases to surprise us that one of the most expensive components of a salad is the lettuce. Even your basic iceberg can cost more than expected at certain times of the year. Since there are so many lettuce choices available, we do find ourselves branching out beyond iceberg. Believe it or not, we often end up using prewashed bagged salad greens. When we first encountered these bags of lettuce with hefty price tags, we thought, "No way. They're too expensive." After a while, we realized that the bags of mixed "baby" greens—such as mizuna, radicchio, arugula, baby red chard, frisée, baby spinach, and baby romaine—are actually fairly economical. You're getting a mixture that would cost up to three times as much if you bought the individual heads or bunches and put it together yourself. (Bags containing only one type of lettuce, such as iceberg and Romaine, however, are not such a bargain.) And because the bags contain only enough lettuce for one large bowl of salad at a time, you don't have the waste of left-over half-heads of lettuce wilting in your refrigerator.

Some supermarkets sell these mixed greens loose, by the pound, and we often buy just enough to sprinkle on top of a basic iceberg salad to add interest without so much cost. The only note of caution when buying loose greens is that the leaves are sometimes saturated with water from the produce section's sprinkler system. If that's the case, whir them in a salad spinner before storing the leaves in your refrigerator's vegetable bin—dry baby greens stay fresh days longer. We've also found that we can get 1-pound bags of mixed greens at warehouse club stores. That's almost a dozen cups of lettuce, and these giant bags cost a fraction of the super-market 10-ounce counterparts. Supermarkets frequently run sales on bagged salads, so you can often get them for less.

Some companies package whole salads, complete with croutons and salad dressing, but we find that adding our own toppings and dressing is the less expensive—and tastier—choice.

SWEET AND SAVORY CHICKEN SALAD

SERVES: 4 START TO FINISH: UNDER 20 MINUTES

6 to 7 cups torn mild salad greens, such as romaine

1 cup torn bitter salad greens, such as radicchio, or
½ cup sliced radishes

2 carrots (for about 1 cup sliced)

3 scallions (for ¼ cup sliced)

1 large tomato (for about 1 cup chopped)

1 cup seasonal berries or other sweet fruit, such as
blueberries or pears

¼ cup crumbled strong cheese, such as blue cheese or feta

2 cups already-grilled chicken strips (see Note)

Raspberry Vinaigrette (page 297) to taste

1. Mix the salad greens together in a large salad bowl. Peel and thinly slice the carrots, adding them to the bowl as you slice. Slice the scallions, using all of the whites and enough of the tender green parts to make ¼ cup. Add them to the bowl.

2. Core and chop the tomato into bite-size pieces, adding it to the bowl as you chop. Add the fruit and cheese. Toss the salad well to evenly distribute the ingredients.

3. Divide the salad among four dinner plates and top with the grilled chicken. Pass the dressing at the table.

NOTE: You can use 2 cups Great Grilled Chicken Breasts (page 360). Or grill 1 pound skinless, boneless chicken breasts and slice them into strips, then proceed with the recipe.

The combination of sweet and savory flavors in salads is all the rage: bitter greens with sweet berries; juicy pears with walnuts and Gorgonzola cheese; sugared pecans with tangy vinaigrette dressing. These creative combinations are easy to put together in your own kitchen.

Leave out the chicken for a delicious side salad.

We naturally think of this salad when the new crop of apples arrives in the fall—but the truth is, it's a beautiful, bountiful salad that's terrific any time of the year. The Ginger Chutney Dressing makes an exotic addition, but if you don't want to make your own, just drizzle on poppy-seed dressing, French or Russian dressing, or any other dressing that's slightly sweet.

FALL CHICKEN SALAD

SERVES: 4 START TO FINISH: UNDER 20 MINUTES

8 cups torn lettuce of choice
2 cups already-cooked chicken chunks, defrosted if frozen (see Notes)
2 medium red sweet-tart apples, such as Gala or Braeburn (for about 2 cups chopped)
1 tablespoon lemon juice
1 pint grape tomatoes
¼ cup toasted sunflower seeds (see Notes)
¼ cup crumbled blue cheese (optional)
Ginger Chutney Dressing (recipe follows) to taste

1. Place the lettuce on a large serving platter and scatter the chicken chunks over it.

2. Core the apples (not peeled) and cut them into bite-size pieces. Toss with the lemon juice, then scatter them over the chicken. Add the tomatoes to the salad. Scatter the sunflower seeds and blue cheese (if using) over the salad.

3. Serve at once, passing the dressing at the table to drizzle on top.

NOTES: You can use Perfect Poached Chicken (page 362), Poached Chicken Thighs (page 364), or Great Grilled Chicken Breasts (page 360).
■ Chopped walnuts, pecans, or unsalted peanuts can be used instead of sunflower seeds.

GINGER CHUTNEY DRESSING

MAKES: 1⅓ CUPS START TO FINISH: UNDER 10 MINUTES

1 clove fresh garlic, peeled

½ cup mango chutney

2 tablespoons Dijon mustard

1 tablespoon regular or reduced-fat
  mayonnaise

⅛ teaspoon cayenne pepper, or more to taste
  (see Note)

2 teaspoons finely minced fresh ginger or
  bottled fresh ginger

1 cup vegetable oil

1. With the food processor running, drop the garlic clove through the feed tube. Process until it is finely chopped. Add the chutney, mustard, mayonnaise, cayenne pepper, and ginger and pulse several times, until the chutney is finely chopped.

2. With the motor running, drizzle the oil in a thin stream through the feed tube and process until it is completely incorporated.

3. Serve at once or refrigerate in a covered container until ready to serve, up to 2 weeks. (Shake to recombine before serving.)

NOTE: Hot pepper sauce, such as Tabasco, or red pepper flakes can be substituted, to taste, for the cayenne pepper.

This dressing takes only 5 minutes to make, and you'll have enough left over for another salad or two. The signature ingredient is mango chutney, usually found with the ethnic or imported foods at the supermarket. It's available in hot and mild varieties, and either one will work. One jar of the chutney is enough to make two batches of the dressing, and it's so tasty, you definitely won't mind whipping up another batch.

From Beverly:

Waldorf Salad is one of my favorite side dishes, and one day when just about the only fresh thing in the house was a few apples, I started experimenting. What if I took the flavors of a Waldorf Salad and bulked it up with pasta? I also had some frozen cooked chicken. If I threw it in, wouldn't the whole salad make a nice dinner? Indeed it did! I liked the colorful combination so much that I took it to a Christmas potluck lunch. Any kind of apples you have on hand can be used; a combination of red and green apples makes for an especially colorful salad. For the Christmas party, I used tri-color rotini and added some dried cranberries to make the dish even more festive.

WALDORF PASTA SALAD

SERVES: 6 START TO FINISH: UNDER 25 MINUTES

SUPER-CHEAP!

Salt for cooking the pasta
8 ounces short pasta, such as rotini
3 medium-size apples
   (for about 3 cups chopped)
1 tablespoon lemon juice
2 ribs celery (for about ¾ cup chopped)
1 cup already-cooked chicken chunks, defrosted if frozen
   (see Notes)
½ cup raisins or other dried fruit (optional)
½ cup walnut or pecan pieces (optional; see Notes)
1 cup mayonnaise (see Notes)
½ teaspoon onion powder
¼ teaspoon garlic powder
¼ teaspoon salt, or to taste
¼ teaspoon black pepper, or to taste

1. Bring 3 quarts lightly salted water to a boil in a covered 4½-quart or larger pot. When the water reaches a rapid boil, add the pasta and cook, uncovered, just until firm-tender, following the package directions. When the pasta is done, drain it in a colander and throw in 2 handfuls of ice cubes. Rinse the pasta under cold running tap water and toss with the ice cubes until it reaches cool room temperature, about 2 minutes. Drain well, removing any unmelted ice cubes.

2. Core the apples and cut them (unpeeled) into bite-size pieces. Place the apple pieces in a large (about 3-quart) serving bowl. Toss with the lemon juice. Cut the celery into bite-size pieces and add them to the bowl. Add the chicken chunks. If using raisins and nuts, add them to the bowl. Add the pasta to the bowl.

3. Mix together the mayonnaise, onion powder, garlic powder, salt, and black pepper. Add to the bowl and stir until combined. Serve at once, or refrigerate until ready to serve, up to 3 hours.

NOTES: You can use Perfect Poached Chicken (page 362), Poached Chicken Thighs (page 364), or Great Grilled Chicken Breasts (page 360). Or cut an 8-ounce skinless, boneless chicken breast half into bite-size chunks and sauté until cooked through; allow to cool and then proceed with the recipe.

■ The nuts can be toasted in the microwave, uncovered, on high power until fragrant, 1 to 2 minutes, stirred halfway through.

■ Reduced-fat mayonnaise or a mixture of half mayonnaise and half sour cream can be used.

CHICKEN
CAESAR SALAD

SERVES: 4 START TO FINISH: UNDER 20 MINUTES

8 cups torn Romaine lettuce
½ cup grated Parmesan cheese
1 cup croutons (see page 281)
Creamy Pseudo-Caesar Dressing (recipe follows)
    or ¾ cup other Caesar-style dressing
2 cups already-cooked chicken chunks,
    defrosted if frozen (see Note)

1. Place the lettuce in a large salad bowl. Add the Parmesan cheese and croutons. Pour the dressing over the salad and toss to coat well.

2. Divide the salad among four dinner plates and top with the chicken. Serve immediately.

NOTE: You can use Perfect Poached Chicken (page 362), Poached Chicken Thighs (page 364), Chunky Seasoned Chicken (page 358), or Great Grilled Chicken Breasts (page 360). Or cut 1 pound skinless, boneless chicken breasts into bite-size chunks and sauté until cooked through, then proceed with the recipe.

We often like to add chicken to one of our favorite salads and call it dinner! Caesar salads are easy to make at home, and although you can often find bottled Caesar salad dressing on sale, we prefer our home-made version. It only takes a few minutes to whip it up.

Romaine is almost as inexpensive as iceberg lettuce, and it is definitely as easy to prepare. One large head usually yields about 8 cups torn lettuce, perfect for this scrumptious dinner salad.

Traditional Caesar dressings frequently contain anchovies and usually raw egg. We've steered clear of these two ingredients because the anchovies add expense where it's not needed and many people prefer to avoid eating raw egg. The creamy spiciness of the Dijon mustard is the perfect replacement. This dressing is so tasty that you'll never miss the traditional ingredients anyway.

CREAMY PSEUDO-CAESAR DRESSING

MAKES: ABOUT ¾ CUP   **START TO FINISH:** UNDER 10 MINUTES

1 lemon
2 tablespoons red wine vinegar
2 tablespoons Dijon mustard
¼ teaspoon black pepper
2 cloves fresh garlic
½ cup extra-virgin olive oil

1. Cut the lemon in half and squeeze the juice from both halves through a strainer into a 2-cup or larger bowl. Add the vinegar, mustard, and black pepper. Peel and finely mince the garlic cloves and add them to the bowl. Whisk until well combined.

2. Drizzle the oil into the bowl in a thin stream, whisking constantly until all the oil is added and the dressing is slightly thick. Use the dressing immediately or cover and refrigerate for up to 3 days. (Whisk the dressing to recombine, if necessary.)

CRISP HOMEMADE CROUTONS

MAKES: 4 CUPS START TO FINISH: UNDER 1 HOUR

12 bread slices
 (for about 4 cups ½-inch
 cubes, lightly packed; see Note)
¼ cup olive oil, or 4 tablespoons
 (½ stick) butter, melted
½ teaspoon garlic powder (optional)
½ teaspoon dried basil (optional)

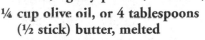

1. Preheat the oven to 325°F.

2. Trim the crusts from the bread, saving them to make bread crumbs (see page 235). Cut the bread into ½-inch cubes and place them in a single layer in a baking pan and bake, uncovered, for 10 minutes. Remove the pan from the oven, stir the cubes, and return the pan to the oven. Bake, uncovered, for 10 more minutes.

3. Remove the pan from the oven. Drizzle the oil over the cubes and sprinkle the garlic powder and basil (if using) evenly over them. Stir well.

4. Return the pan to the oven and continue to bake, uncovered, removing the pan from the oven to stir the croutons every 5 minutes, until the croutons are golden brown and crisp, 15 to 20 minutes.

5. Allow the croutons to cool to room temperature. They will stay fresh for up to 3 weeks in an airtight container at room temperature.

NOTE: Use a serrated knife and use a light sawing motion when cutting the bread into cubes so that you don't mash the bread. Bread that is still slightly frozen is easier to cut. You don't need to get the ruler out and measure. Slight variations in size are fine.

There's no reason to ever buy boxed croutons, since they are a cinch to make—and are a use for the last slices of a loaf of bread that might otherwise go to waste. (Collect the slices in the freezer until you have enough to make croutons. Combining different types of bread is fine.) The following recipe is just a guide. You can make more croutons per batch, or fewer. Just be sure the croutons rest in a single layer in the baking pan. If you have a lot of croutons, use two pans. (For even browning, rotate the pans' positions in the oven every time you stir them.)

Our general rule for seasoning is to use 1 table-spoon olive oil or melted butter and ⅛ teaspoon each of garlic powder and basil per cup of croutons. Vary the type of dried herbs and spices to add interest.

The baking time may vary somewhat from batch to batch, depending on the moisture content of the bread and the size of the cubes. You'll know the croutons are done when they are light brown and crunchy throughout.

Smart Shopping at the Club Warehouse Stores

Buying in bulk from your local members-only warehouse club can save you money—if you're smart about it. Getting a good deal really makes our day, but buying more than you need simply because an item seems cheap can add up to wasted food.

There are several ways to avoid the pitfalls of giant-size buying. One way is to form a "club" of your own: Find a friend or neighbor (or several) who frequents the same warehouse and shop together. Warehouse staples often are bundled in ways that are quite easy to split when you get home. But even if you buy a 5-pound bag of baby carrots, say, or 10 pounds of hamburger, it's still relatively easy to divide things. You didn't really want to eat carrots every night for a week, did you?

Some items come in such large quantities at the warehouse that you really will need to have several members of your "club" go in on the purchase so the items don't lose freshness before they're used. Examples include baking supplies, such as flour, sugar, chocolate chips, and spices.

Once you and a friend agree on a list of items to buy, you can take turns shopping, which cuts the chore in half. Or turn the trip into an enjoyable social outing by stopping for coffee before hitting the warehouse together.

Another trick to warehouse shopping is figuring out if you're truly getting a good deal. Some items are vastly cheaper, but some things cost the same or may even be more expensive than at your regular supermarket. The only way to know for sure is to do the math. An accurate comparison between warehouse and supermarket prices is likely to require a calculator, because the cost unit at the warehouse might not be the same unit used by the supermarket. For example, the shelf label at the warehouse may list the price of coffee per pound, while the supermarket lists the price per ounce.

One solution is to take notes on the prices of items you typically buy at the supermarket. When you get to the warehouse, jot that price down too. Then in the comfort of your own home, get out the calculator and figure it out ounce per ounce. (Or you could take along a pocket calculator and do the math standing in the warehouse aisle.) The good news is that you'll need to do this only once for the items you buy repeatedly.

While you're at the math, it might pay to figure out whether you'll be buying enough at the warehouse during the course of the year to make up for the cost of membership. Say the warehouse membership is $35 per year and you're only going to buy ground beef there. You'd have to buy 35 pounds of ground beef during the year at a savings of $1 per pound over the supermarket price just to recoup the membership investment. (Of course chances are good you'll buy more than just ground beef, so it's important to calculate your own scenario.)

Warehouse memberships typically cost between $35 and $45 per year, but check around because the prices and categories of membership vary. There is a category that allows several people to join under the same membership, and this type is cheaper if you're planning on forming the already-mentioned "shopping club." Also, if you work for a large company or government organization that purchases a group membership, chances are your individual membership is paid for or reduced under your company's umbrella.

One more membership tip: Watch for half-price or reduced membership rates every time a new warehouse location opens in your area. You may have to drive to the new warehouse to apply for the membership, but once you've secured the card, it's valid at all stores.

The final challenge is to figure out where you'll store your stash once you get it home. We've been known to cram extra rolls of toilet paper under beds and to hide the extra garbage bags in the garage. If 2 pounds of chocolate chips don't fit in the baking section of your pantry, you may find yourself repackaging staples in more manageable portions. Zipper-top plastic bags come in handy for this. (Luckily, zipper bags tend to be cheaper at the warehouse too.) If your refrigerator and freezer spaces are tight, that will limit the cold items you can buy.

"Getting a good deal really makes our day."

Here are some items we tend to buy regularly at the warehouse because the savings are significant:

- Fresh meat: This is the one category that makes membership worthwhile all by itself. All types tend to beat even the supermarket's best sales.
- Fresh salmon and other fresh fish
- Individually quick-frozen (IQF) boneless chicken breast halves
- Dried fruit, especially raisins and dried cranberries
- Nuts, especially shelled pecans and walnuts
- Peanut butter
- Condiments such as ketchup, mayonnaise, and mustard
- Chocolate, especially baking cocoa and morsels
- Microwave popcorn
- Spices and flavorings, especially pure vanilla extract, bottled minced garlic, and garlic powder. Note that the containers are huge, and spices do get stale.
- Bagged prewashed salad mixes
- Cheeses, especially already-shredded varieties
- Frozen and/or refrigerated stuffed pastas, such as tortellini
- Pure maple syrup
- Cooking oils
- Canned olives
- Bottled water
- Coffee
- Fruit juice
- Wine and beer (in states allowing such sales)
- Zipper-top plastic bags
- Aluminum foil
- Pet food
- Cat litter
- Garbage bags
- Paper products

"Watch for half-price or reduced membership rates."

EASIEST TACO SALAD

SERVES: 4 START TO FINISH: UNDER 20 MINUTES

½ head iceberg lettuce (for about 4 cups torn)

1 large ripe tomato, or 3 plum tomatoes
(for about 1 cup pieces)

2 cups Flexible Mexican Filling (page 352),
defrosted if frozen

1 can (15 ounces) black beans, or 1 cup homemade
(see page 368), defrosted if frozen

4 cups regular or reduced-fat tortilla chips

Shredded cheese, taco sauce, chopped green chiles, sliced
black olives, and/or guacamole, for serving (optional)

1. Tear the lettuce into bite-size pieces and set them aside. Core and chop the tomato into small chunks; set them aside.

2. Pour the Flexible Mexican Filling into a microwave-safe container and microwave it, covered with a paper towel, on high power until just heated through, about 2 minutes.

3. Meanwhile, rinse and drain the black beans. Divide the tortilla chips and lettuce among four plates.

4. Pour ½ cup of the Flexible Mexican Filling over the lettuce on each plate. Sprinkle the beans and tomato chunks evenly over the filling. Serve the salads, letting each person garnish his or her salad with as many toppings as desired.

It's always a challenge to find budget meals that the whole family will eat and that don't take forever to fix. This salad is perfect for feeding finicky kids and adults. (If the word "salad" results in them making faces, call it "crumbled tacos" or "layered tacos.") The toppings can be as elaborate or as simple as you like—for us, they are often dictated by items that happen to be in the fridge or pantry. By "cooking," kids take ownership of the meal and have a vested interest in seeing it consumed. The real secret to the success of this salad is the Flexible Mexican Filling, a mixture of taco-seasoned ground beef, sour cream, cheese, and tomato soup. The filling already contains enough cheese and sour cream so that you really don't need to add more. Unless you subscribe to the same philosophy we do: More cheese is always better!

From Beverly:

This hearty dinner salad is a hit at my house any season of the year. Both my husband and I enjoy the crunchy combination of cucumbers, cabbage, and romaine lettuce. And I also look at it as just another excuse to consume my favorite peanut sauce. You could use bok choy in place of the green cabbage if you happen to have it. I usually just buy the least expensive pork chops I can find for this recipe.

THAI SALAD WITH PORK

SERVES: 4 START TO FINISH: UNDER 25 MINUTES

1 pound thin boneless pork chops, defrosted if frozen
1 tablespoon vegetable oil
1 bunch scallions (for about 1 cup sliced)
1 clove fresh garlic, minced, or 1 teaspoon bottled minced garlic
4 cups torn romaine lettuce (bite-size pieces)
½ very small head (about 12 ounces) green cabbage
2 large carrots (for about 1½ cups grated)
1 medium-size seedless (hothouse) cucumber (see Notes)
Thai Peanut Salad Dressing to taste (recipe follows)
¼ cup chopped lightly salted or unsalted peanuts, for garnish (optional; see Notes)

1. Slice the pork into thin strips no more than ¼ inch wide. Trim away and discard any excess fat. Set the pork aside.

2. Heat the oil in an extra-deep 12-inch skillet over medium heat. Add the pork and cook, stirring frequently, until it is no longer pink, 4 to 5 minutes.

3. Meanwhile, cut the scallions into 1-inch pieces. Just before the pork is cooked through, add the scallions and garlic. Cook, stirring, until the scallions are crisp-tender, about 1 minute. Remove the skillet from the heat and set it aside.

4. Divide the lettuce among four dinner plates. Remove and discard any tough core from the cabbage. Thinly slice the cabbage and then cut the shreds into bite-size pieces. Scatter the cabbage evenly over the lettuce on each plate.

5. Grate the carrots on the largest holes of a box grater (or use a food processor). Scatter the grated carrots evenly over the cabbage. Thinly slice the cucumber and divide the slices evenly among the plates, scattering the slices over the carrots.

6. Arrange the pork and scallion mixture on top of each salad and drizzle with the dressing. (Or pass the dressing at the table.) Garnish each salad with 1 tablespoon chopped peanuts, if desired.

NOTES: Small Kirby (sometimes called pickling) cucumbers can be used.

■ Toasted sliced or slivered almonds or sesame seeds can be used instead of the peanuts.

THAI PEANUT SALAD DRESSING

MAKES: 1¼ CUPS START TO FINISH: UNDER 5 MINUTES

1 cup Thai-Style Peanut Sauce (page 374)
¼ cup water

Pour the peanut sauce and water into a medium-size mixing bowl. Whisk until all of the water is incorporated. Serve at once, or refrigerate in an airtight container until ready to serve, up to 1 week. (Shake the dressing to recombine before serving, if necessary.)

To double as a salad dressing, our Thai-Style Peanut Sauce simply needs to be thinned out a bit. The sauce is so flavorful, any additional ingredients would be overkill. The dressing is wonderful over a basic tossed salad, or use it to turn plain raw cabbage strips into a gourmet delight.

This salad makes a perfect addition to a potluck party when you need to take a filling dish that can be made ahead and won't necessitate a bank loan. The salad also makes a wonderful light supper or lunch. It's especially good with our Tomato Dressing, but you could substitute a bottled vinaigrette.

BLACK-EYED PEA SALAD WITH HAM

SERVES: 8 AS A SIDE DISH, 4 AS A MAIN
START TO FINISH: UNDER 20 MINUTES

**2 cans (15 ounces each) black-eyed peas,
  packed without pork, or
  2 cups homemade
  (see page 368), defrosted if frozen**
1 cup frozen yellow corn kernels
**1 medium-size green bell pepper
  (for about 1 cup chopped)**
2 ribs celery (for about ¾ cup chopped)
1 cup (about 6 ounces) ham chunks
Tomato Dressing (recipe follows) to taste

SUPER-CHEAP!

1. Rinse and drain the black-eyed peas and put them in a 2-quart or larger serving bowl. Pour the corn into a colander and rinse it under cool tap water until almost defrosted, about 2 minutes. Set aside to drain.

2. Core, seed, and cut the bell pepper into bite-size pieces. Add them to the bowl. Cut the celery into bite-size pieces and add them to the bowl. Add the corn and ham chunks and stir well.

3. Pour the dressing over the salad and stir well. Serve at once or refrigerate until ready to serve. (Leftovers can be refrigerated in an airtight container for up to 3 days.)

TOMATO DRESSING

MAKES: ABOUT ⅔ CUP **START TO FINISH:** UNDER 5 MINUTES

½ small onion
⅓ cup tomato-vegetable juice, such as V8
2 tablespoons red wine vinegar
1 tablespoon olive oil
1 teaspoon Dijon mustard
¼ teaspoon black pepper, or more to taste

1. Peel the onion half and cut it into quarters. With a food processor or blender running, drop the pieces through the feed tube and process until finely chopped, about 30 seconds. Stop the motor and scrape down the sides of the bowl.

2. Add the tomato-vegetable juice, vinegar, oil, mustard, and black pepper. Process just to mix well, about 30 seconds. Pour into a small bowl and set aside until ready to dress the salad. Stir to reblend before using.

This is a dressing that'll wake up your taste buds, thanks to the tangy vegetable juice and the raw onion. And because there's only a tablespoon of oil, it's lower in fat than most dressings. Try it on a tossed green salad for something refreshingly different. The dressing will keep in the refrigerator for up to 1 week.

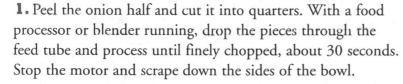

Salmon: the Good-for-You Fish

"Salmon's most famous benefit is its ability to lower cholesterol."

Salmon is a virtual medicine cabinet with fins. Not only is it a good source of protein and vitamins B_6 and B_{12}, it also contains all of the essential amino acids plus iron, niacin, riboflavin, zinc, magnesium, and phosphorus. But this is just the beginning. Salmon's most famous benefit is its ability to lower cholesterol, thanks to a high level of omega-3 fatty acids. The omega-3s also reduce the stickiness of blood platelets. This means that eating salmon can lower your risk of heart disease.

In recent years, however, the miracle fish has been the source of concern. Some environmental groups have warned against dangerous levels of cancer-causing polychlorinated biphenyls (PCBs) in farmed salmon. In 2003 the Environmental Working Group found that farmed salmon purchased in grocery stores contained sixteen times the levels of PCBs found in salmon caught in the wild. The Environmental Protection Agency considers these levels in farmed fish to be harmful, while the Food and Drug Administration, the agency responsible for fish sold in stores, considered them safe in 2003.

So what's a salmon lover to do? Eat more canned salmon! All canned salmon is caught in the wild, and the price is much cheaper than wild salmon sold fresh.

A lot of research has been dedicated to figuring out how much omega-3 fatty acids a serving of salmon has, but there's no exact answer. In farmed salmon, the levels depend on how the fish are fed. In wild salmon, the levels vary according to the time of year and the age and size of the fish. All of this is information you just don't get at the supermarket. If you're eating canned salmon, note that the water-packed and water-free pouch types contain more omega-3s than do oil-packed cans.

The bottom line is that, while salmon is really, really good medicine, it pays to watch the headlines and stay current on industry recommendations. And meanwhile, stock up on the cans.

SUPER SALMON PASTA SALAD

SERVES: 4 START TO FINISH: UNDER 25 MINUTES

Salt for cooking the pasta
8 ounces short pasta, such as medium-size shells
2 cups seedless red or green grapes
½ seedless (hothouse) cucumber, or 2 Kirby
  cucumbers (about 8 ounces)
1 foil pouch (7.1 ounces) premium skinless,
  boneless pink salmon (see Note)
1 cup bottled ranch or Green Goddess salad dressing
½ lemon
1 teaspoon snipped fresh dill, or ½ teaspoon dried dill

1. Bring 2½ quarts lightly salted water to a boil in a covered 4½-quart pot. When the water reaches a rapid boil, add the pasta and cook, uncovered, until just firm-tender, following the package directions.

2. Meanwhile, cut the grapes in half and place them in a 3-quart or larger serving bowl. Thinly slice the cucumber and add it to the bowl. Add the salmon, flaking it with a fork. Set aside.

3. Pour the salad dressing into a small mixing bowl or 2-cup glass measure. Squeeze the lemon juice through a strainer into the dressing. Add the dill and whisk until well blended.

4. When the pasta is done, drain it in a colander and throw in 2 handfuls of ice cubes. Rinse the pasta under cold running water and toss with the ice cubes until it reaches cool room temperature. Drain well, removing any unmelted ice cubes.

5. Add the cooled pasta and the salad dressing to the serving bowl, toss to mix well and to coat the pasta with the dressing, and serve.

NOTE: Two 6-ounce cans of skinless, boneless salmon can be used. (The drained weight will be about the same as that of one pouch.)

This is an easy and economical pasta salad for those times when you need a fish fix but don't happen to have fresh salmon at hand. Thanks to salmon in a foil pouch (or canned), you can make this salad any time you like. It's amazing what a little fresh lemon juice and a hint of dill can do for bottled salad dressing.

If you use a hothouse or Kirby cucumber, there's no need to peel it. Other cucumbers should be peeled.

DIVINE DEVILED EGGS ON GREENS

MAKES: 16 DEVILED EGGS **START TO FINISH:** UNDER 45 MINUTES

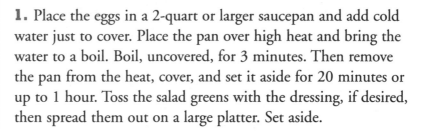

8 large eggs
8 cups torn mild salad greens,
   such as romaine
¼ cup Dot's Salad Dressing
   (page 295; optional)
5 tablespoons regular or reduced-fat mayonnaise
1 tablespoon Dijon mustard
2 teaspoons cider vinegar
⅛ teaspoon black pepper
Salt to taste
Paprika to taste

If you ever need an inexpensive dish for a potluck, deviled eggs are a sure bet. We've discreetly stood by at many a potluck table to observe what folks are most enthusiastic about, and the deviled eggs win hands-down every time. (We've never seen a deviled egg dish that didn't go home empty!) Perhaps the deviled egg's popularity lies in the fact that it is such a simple, comforting food.

In some circles, deviled eggs are strictly an appetizer, while in the South, they're most often served as a side dish. Nestled on a bed of greens, they make a very satisfying salad. If you'd like a little vinaigrette on the lettuce, try Dot's Salad Dressing. Be sure to give your eggs just a light dusting of paprika for color—too much paprika will overwhelm the delicate flavor.

1. Place the eggs in a 2-quart or larger saucepan and add cold water just to cover. Place the pan over high heat and bring the water to a boil. Boil, uncovered, for 3 minutes. Then remove the pan from the heat, cover, and set it aside for 20 minutes or up to 1 hour. Toss the salad greens with the dressing, if desired, then spread them out on a large platter. Set aside.

2. Peel the eggs and cut them in half lengthwise. Remove the egg yolks and put them in a food processor. Add the mayonnaise, mustard, vinegar, and black pepper. Process until smooth, about 30 seconds, stopping once to scrape down the bowl. Season with salt.

3. Spoon the filling into the egg whites. (Use a rubber spatula to remove all the filling from the processor.) Dust the filled eggs lightly with paprika, nestle them on the salad greens, and serve.

RED BEAN AND PASTA SALAD

SERVES: 8 AS A SIDE DISH, 4 AS A MAIN
START TO FINISH: UNDER 25 MINUTES

Salt for cooking the pasta
8 ounces short pasta, such as shells
1 pint cherry or grape tomatoes
2 cans (15 ounces each) red beans, or
    2 cups homemade (see page 368), defrosted if frozen
3 scallions (for ¼ cup chopped)
¼ cup flavored mayonnaise (see pages 384 and 385)
¼ cup regular or reduced-fat sour cream
¼ teaspoon black pepper
Salt to taste
Lettuce leaves, for serving (optional)

1. Bring 2½ quarts lightly salted water to a boil in a covered 4½-quart pot. When the water reaches a rapid boil, add the pasta and cook, uncovered, until just tender, following the package directions.

2. Meanwhile, slice the tomatoes in half and place them in a 3-quart or larger bowl. Rinse the beans, drain them well, and add them to the tomatoes. Slice the scallions, using all of the whites and enough tender green tops to make ¼ cup. Add them to the bowl.

3. When the pasta is done, drain it in a colander and throw in 2 handfuls of ice cubes. Rinse the pasta under cold running water and toss with the ice cubes until it reaches cool room temperature. Drain well, removing any unmelted ice cubes.

4. Add the pasta, mayonnaise, sour cream, and black pepper to the bean mixture and toss gently until coated with the sauce. Season with salt. Serve at once over lettuce leaves, if desired, or refrigerate until ready to serve.

We just love the creamy goodness of this versatile pasta salad. It actually can be four entirely different salads, depending on which mayonnaise you choose—Pesto, Garlic, Herbed, or Curry Mayonnaise. So get creative with this simple pasta dish. The possibilities are endless.

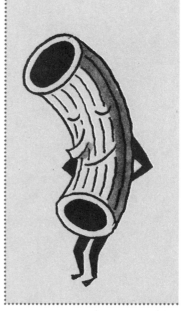

Bean salads are perfect for the hot, humid days of summer. This little beauty flics together in less than 15 minutes and makes enough to serve six. If you don't finish it off the first night, use the leftovers as a side dish later in the week. (It will keep, covered and refrigerated, for three days.)

THREE-BEAN SALAD

SERVES: 12 AS A SIDE DISH, 6 AS MAIN
START TO FINISH: UNDER 15 MINUTES

SUPER-CHEAP!

1 can (15 ounces) black beans, or
    1 cup homemade (see page 368),
    defrosted if frozen

1 can (15 ounces) red beans,
    such as kidney beans, or
    1 cup homemade (see page 368),
    defrosted if frozen

1 can (15 ounces) chickpeas, or 1 cup homemade
    (see page 368), defrosted if frozen

1 cup frozen yellow corn kernels

1 small onion (for about ½ cup chopped)

2 ribs celery (for about 1 cup sliced)

¼ cup fresh cilantro or parsley leaves (optional)

¼ cup extra-virgin olive oil

¼ cup red wine vinegar

½ teaspoon garlic powder

¼ teaspoon salt, or to taste

¼ teaspoon black pepper, or to taste

1. Place all the beans and the frozen corn in a large colander and rinse with cool tap water. Shake to drain well. Place the beans and corn in a medium-size serving bowl.

2. Peel and finely chop the onion, adding it to the bean mixture as you chop. Thinly slice the celery and add it to the bowl. Coarsely chop the cilantro (if using) and add it to the bowl. Toss gently to mix the vegetables.

3. Pour the oil into a 2-cup glass measure. Whisk in the vinegar, garlic powder, salt, and black pepper. Pour the dressing over the bean mixture and stir until well coated. Serve at once or cover and chill until ready to serve, up to 24 hours.

DOT'S SALAD DRESSING

MAKES: ABOUT ½ CUP START TO FINISH: UNDER 5 MINUTES

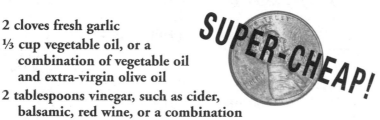

2 cloves fresh garlic

⅓ cup vegetable oil, or a combination of vegetable oil and extra-virgin olive oil

2 tablespoons vinegar, such as cider, balsamic, red wine, or a combination

2 cloves fresh garlic

1 teaspoon sugar

½ teaspoon salt

¼ teaspoon black pepper

½ teaspoon dried Italian seasoning or basil (optional)

1. Peel the garlic cloves and crush them lightly.

2. Combine all the ingredients in a small jar that has a lid. Cover and shake vigorously until the dressing is well combined and the sugar has dissolved. Use at once or store in the refrigerator for up to a week. Remove 30 minutes before serving and shake to recombine just before using.

From Beverly:

This very basic vinaigrette was my favorite salad dressing when I was growing up, and now it's my own children's favorite, too. The recipe originated with my grandmother, Zeta Mills. My mom, Dot Mills, has altered it slightly through the years. The nicest thing about the dressing is that you can whip it up in just minutes.

While my children prefer plain vegetable oil, I sometimes like to make the dressing using roughly half plain vegetable oil (such as Crisco or Wesson) and half extra-virgin olive oil. This gives you the flavor of the good olive oil, but it's not as expensive. Any type of vinegar (except distilled white) you have will be terrific, but I also like a mixture. I tend to use a tablespoon of cheap cider vinegar and a tablespoon of the more expensive balsamic or wine vinegar. The garlic, sugar, salt, and pepper are essential, but at my kids' request, I often leave out the dried herbs. If you eat salads often, double the recipe; it will keep for a week.

Every spring, my cravings veer to baby greens, and I start buying the 1-pound economy bags at my local warehouse club. Salads of tantalizing baby greens can quickly become addictive, and you soon realize that although the mixture of flavors is assertive, the texture of the greens is quite delicate. This calls for a light dressing. Our Mandarin Orange Vinaigrette is delightfully different, and Raspberry Vinaigrette is one of our favorites. Each dressing goes together in 5 minutes, and, in a pinch, the only work to make a salad is to fluff the baby greens into a bowl. When you've got a dozen different kinds of greens, additional ingredients aren't missed.

TWO FRUIT VINAIGRETTES

MANDARIN ORANGE VINAIGRETTE

MAKES: 1½ CUPS   START TO FINISH: UNDER 5 MINUTES

1 can (8 ounces) mandarin oranges
¼ cup red wine vinegar or cider vinegar
¼ teaspoon salt
¼ teaspoon black pepper
1 tablespoon honey
⅔ cup vegetable oil

Drain the oranges and put them in a blender or food processor. Add the vinegar, salt, and black pepper. With the motor running, add the honey and oil in a thin stream through the feed tube. Process until thoroughly blended. Serve at once or cover and refrigerate until ready to serve, up to 2 weeks. (If the dressing separates while standing, shake it well to recombine before serving.)

RASPBERRY VINAIGRETTE

MAKES: ABOUT 1½ CUPS   START TO FINISH: UNDER 5 MINUTES

3 tablespoons seedless all-fruit raspberry jam
⅓ cup red wine vinegar or cider vinegar
¼ teaspoon salt
¼ teaspoon black pepper
1 cup vegetable oil

Put the jam in a 2-cup glass measure and microwave, uncovered, on high power until the jam just melts, about 15 seconds. Remove the container from the microwave and add the vinegar, salt, and black pepper. Whisk until well combined. Slowly add the oil in a thin stream, whisking constantly until it is thoroughly blended. Serve at once or cover and refrigerate until ready to serve, up to 2 weeks. (If the dressing separates while standing, shake it well to recombine before serving.)

MoneySaver

Don't wash berries until just before you're ready to eat them; they'll stay fresh longer if unwashed. Wash strawberries before you remove their hulls so they don't fill with water.

CHAPTER SEVEN

MONEY-SAVING SIDES

With soups, stews, skillet meals, and pasta dishes, often the only accompaniments you need (if you need any at all) are a green salad and some bread. But when you're serving a stand-alone entrée such as barbecued chicken, meat loaf, sliced ham, pork chops, or baked fish, you want vegetables and a starch to round out the meal. And since meat and fish entrées can be pricey, we balance things out with side dishes that are especially economical.

In the starch category, rice and potatoes come immediately to mind. We're partial to rice pilaf, and we've included several of our favorites in this chapter. As for potatoes, you'll want to try Dad's Spicy Spuds, along with two types of mashed potatoes that are easy and wonderful—Garlicky Smashed Potatoes and Alicia's mom's Southern version, Gayle's Creamed Potatoes.

We've also branched out a bit with some less obvious, but equally wonderful, choices. Be sure to try our Barley and Mushroom Risotto and Southern-Style Cornbread Dressing. For a starch that's room temperature or cold, try Italian-Style Bread Salad or Spinach Pesto Pasta Salad. We're not forgetting beans; try our Dressed-up Beans and Mexican-Style Black Beans.

Unless you have a garden for growing your own, fruits and vegetables can be tricky for the budget cook. Eating what's in season is the biggest help, but even in season, some vegetables are cheaper than others. Here you'll find some of our favorite slaws to dress up the humble cabbage, and a couple of miraculous methods for transforming simple carrots into show-stoppers. For times when broccoli is abundant, we've got the how-to on blanching. We've also included our favorite ways to make the most of the annual corn and tomato crops.

European-style loaves of bread command high prices, and even basic brown-and-serve rolls aren't what we'd consider cheap. So we're adding a few of our favorite bread fix-ups to help you turn a simple tortilla or English muffin into a bread sensation. (For tips on performing some wizardry with a thrifty box of corn muffin mix, see page 310.)

With this arsenal of side dishes that don't cost a fortune, your meal will be balanced, and so will your checkbook.

"When you're serving a stand-alone entrée, you want vegetables and a starch to round out the meal."

ADULT APPLESAUCE TWO WAYS

FIRED-UP APPLESAUCE

SERVES: 4 START TO FINISH: UNDER 5 MINUTES

This "adult" applesauce is bright and intense, with just the right amount of mouth-tingling taste. Lovers of really spicy foods may want to increase the heat even a little more. Another bonus: This applesauce is fat-free and has only 54 calories per serving.

2 cups plain applesauce
1 tablespoon cider vinegar
½ teaspoon apple pie spice or ground cinnamon
⅛ teaspoon cayenne pepper, or more to taste

SUPER-CHEAP!

Pour the applesauce into a 1-quart bowl. Stir in the vinegar, apple pie spice, and cayenne pepper. Serve at once or refrigerate until ready to serve. The applesauce will keep, covered and refrigerated, for 4 days.

FRUITY APPLESAUCE WITH WALNUTS

SERVES: 6   START TO FINISH: UNDER 5 MINUTES

2 cups plain applesauce
1 can (8 ounces) crushed pineapple
**   packed in juice**
½ cup golden or black raisins (see Note)
½ cup chopped walnuts
½ teaspoon ground cinnamon

Pour the applesauce into a 1-quart bowl. Drain the pineapple, reserving the juice for another use, and add the pineapple to the bowl. Add the raisins, walnuts, and cinnamon and stir well to blend. Serve at once or refrigerate until ready to serve. The applesauce will keep, covered and refrigerated, for 3 days.

NOTE: Although any raisins will work, the color of golden raisins nicely complements this applesauce.

This slightly crunchy applesauce is so terrific that you may find it appeals to the kids (if you catch them before the inevitable no-nuts phase). With the added ingredients boosting the flavor, you can use the cheapest store brand of applesauce. This recipe can be cut in half to make 3 servings.

About:
ADULT APPLESAUCE

When your children are small, applesauce is the perfect low-cost side dish: Just open the jar and scoop out a serving. There's only one problem: adults. After months of eating plain applesauce twice a week, you couldn't blame us for getting bored, could you? The question became: How could we make applesauce more interesting without adding a lot of work or expense?

We headed to the kitchen and came up with two versions that are sophisticated enough for adults and teens but require only 5 minutes to put together. The younger kids can still have theirs right out of the jar, but we can choose from Fired-Up Applesauce and Fruity Applesauce with Walnuts.

Every once in a while we have to force ourselves to break out of the rice rut. When the moment comes, we usually turn to barley, a very economical and healthy grain that's readily available in the supermarket. Barley paired with mushrooms is a terrific complement to almost any entrée. A little half-and-half gives the dish a risotto-like texture and appearance—without all the stirring it takes to turn out the classic Italian rice dish. So step out of your rice rut. You and your family will be glad you did.

BARLEY AND MUSHROOM RISOTTO

SERVES: 4 PREP TIME: UNDER 10 MINUTES

2 teaspoons vegetable oil
1 large onion (for about 1 cup chopped)
1 heaping cup fresh button mushrooms
1 clove fresh garlic, minced, or 1 teaspoon
   bottled minced garlic
2 cans (14 ounces each) fat-free beef broth
¾ cup medium-size pearl barley
2 tablespoons half-and-half, heavy cream, or whole milk
Salt and black pepper to taste

1. Heat the oil in an extra-deep 12-inch skillet over medium-low heat. Peel and chop the onion, adding it to the skillet as you chop. Rinse, pat dry, and coarsely chop the mushrooms, removing and discarding any tough stems. Add the mushrooms to the skillet. Cook, stirring frequently, until the mushrooms just begin to soften, about 2 minutes. While the mushrooms are cooking, add the garlic to the skillet.

2. Add the broth, ½ cup water, and the barley and stir well to mix. Raise the heat to medium and bring the broth to a boil. Then reduce the heat to low, cover the skillet, and cook, stirring occasionally, until the barley is tender and most of the broth has been absorbed, 50 to 55 minutes. (If all of the broth is absorbed before the barley is tender, add ¼ cup water as often as necessary.)

3. When the barley is tender, remove the skillet from the heat and stir in the half-and-half. Season with salt and black pepper and serve at once.

INDIAN RICE PILAF

SERVES: 4 GENEROUSLY   START TO FINISH: UNDER 25 MINUTES

1 small onion (for about ½ cup chopped),
    or 2 tablespoons dehydrated minced onion
1 can (14 ounces) fat-free chicken broth, or
    2 cups homemade chicken stock (see page 10)
1 cup long-grain rice
1 teaspoon curry powder
½ teaspoon garlic powder, or ½ teaspoon bottled or fresh
    minced garlic
⅛ teaspoon ground cinnamon, or 1 small (1-inch)
    cinnamon stick
Pinch of ground cloves, or 2 whole cloves (optional)
⅓ cup raisins

1. Peel and coarsely chop the onion, if using fresh, and set it aside.

2. Combine the broth and ¼ cup water in a 2-quart or larger saucepan and bring to a boil. (If you are using 2 cups homemade stock, do not add the water.) Meanwhile, pour the rice into a 2-cup bowl or measuring cup and sprinkle the curry powder, garlic powder, cinnamon, and cloves (if using) over the rice.

3. As soon as the broth comes to a boil, add the onion and the rice mixture. Stir, cover the pan, reduce the heat to low, and simmer until the rice is tender, about 20 minutes.

4. When the rice is tender, remove the pan from the heat. If you used a cinnamon stick or whole cloves, remove and discard them. Stir in the raisins and serve at once.

It's hard to believe that just a few spices can so easily jazz up a pot of cheap-o rice. "This recipe was really easy, and I found it to be a pleasing change from our usual plain-old white rice," said our friend Julie Realon, who tried the recipe out on her husband and two sons. "I enjoyed the interesting blend of flavors and really liked the raisins, but a few in my family picked around them." Raisins do add an exotic touch, but if, like Julie, you have raisin-resisters, feel free to leave them out.

"This is a healthy and tasty side dish that is made with inexpensive ingredients that I usually have in my cupboard," said our friend Carmel Dunlop. "We had some beans left over, and I heated them up in the microwave the next night. Delicious!"

DRESSED-UP BEANS

SERVES: 6 PREP TIME: UNDER 15 MINUTES

Cooking oil spray
1 can (15 ounces) black beans, or 1 cup homemade
(see page 368), defrosted if frozen
1 can (15 ounces) white beans, such as navy or
Great Northern, or 1 cup homemade (see page 368),
defrosted if frozen
1 small onion (for about ½ cup chopped)
½ large green bell pepper (for about ¾ cup chopped;
optional)
3 tablespoons molasses (see Note)
1 tablespoon ketchup
1 tablespoon Dijon mustard
1 teaspoon Worcestershire sauce
1 teaspoon garlic powder

1. Preheat the oven to 350°F.

2. Spray a medium-size casserole dish with cooking oil spray. Pour the black beans, with their liquid, into the dish. Rinse and drain the white beans and then add them to the dish. Peel and coarsely chop the onion and add it to the dish. Stem, seed, and dice the bell pepper (if using) and add it to dish.

3. Add the molasses, ketchup, mustard, Worcestershire sauce, and garlic powder. Stir gently but thoroughly.

4. Bake the beans until the mixture is bubbling and the onion and bell pepper are tender, about 45 minutes. Serve right away.

NOTE: There are several different kinds of molasses—sulfured and unsulfured, mild and full-flavored. Any kind is fine for this dish. An equal amount of brown sugar can be substituted.

MEXICAN-STYLE BLACK BEANS

SERVES: 4 START TO FINISH: UNDER 25 MINUTES

SUPER-CHEAP!

2 teaspoons olive oil
1 medium-size onion
    (for about ¾ cup chopped)
2 cloves fresh garlic, minced, or
    2 teaspoons bottled minced garlic
1 can (15 ounces) black beans, or
    1 cup homemade (see page 368),
    defrosted if frozen
1 can (14½ ounces) diced tomatoes
1 teaspoon Worcestershire sauce
1 teaspoon chili powder
1 teaspoon sugar
½ teaspoon ground cumin (optional)

1. Heat the oil in a 2-quart or larger saucepan over medium heat. Peel the onion and coarsely chop it, adding it to the pan as you chop and stirring frequently. Add the garlic to the pan. Cook, stirring, for 1 minute.

2. Add the beans with their liquid. Add the tomatoes with their juice and the Worcestershire sauce, chili powder, sugar, and cumin (if using). Stir well and bring the mixture to a boil. Then reduce the heat to low and simmer, uncovered, stirring occasionally, until the beans have thickened slightly, about 10 to 20 minutes. Serve at once.

From Beverly:

I make these beans at least once a month—and sometimes once a week. They're a quick and easy way to add a filling component to a meal that everyone's sure to eat. The beans are versatile and forgiving. The exact simmering time will depend on personal preference and on how much liquid your beans contain. (This can vary from pot to pot or can to can.) We often like to eat the beans over plain steamed rice, and if that's the case, I might leave them on the moist side. My daughter likes hers topped with cheese, and my husband and I like ours with a dollop of Super Sofrito (page 388).

BLANCHED BROCCOLI

MAKES: ABOUT 7 CUPS FLORETS; SERVES 10 TO 12
START TO FINISH: UNDER 20 MINUTES

6 stalks fresh broccoli
(for about 7 cups florets)

1. Bring 2 quarts water to a boil in a covered 4½-quart or larger pot over high heat.

2. While the water is heating, cut the florets from the broccoli stems and set the florets aside (see Note). Pour 2 quarts cold water into a large bowl. Add 3 handfuls of ice cubes to the water and place the bowl on the counter near the sink. Place a colander in the sink.

3. When the water comes to a boil, add the broccoli florets and cook, uncovered, until they are bright green and crisp-tender, 2 to 3 minutes. (Do not overcook!)

4. Carefully drain the broccoli in the colander and then immediately pour the broccoli into the bowl of ice water. Stir the broccoli around in the cold water to make sure all the florets are submerged. Let the broccoli stand in the water until it has cooled completely, about 5 minutes.

5. Pour the broccoli back into the colander to drain and shake the colander to remove as much water as possible. If you are serving the broccoli now and want it hot, reheat the florets in the microwave oven for 2 to 3 minutes on high power. Or the florets can be refrigerated in a zipper-top plastic bag for up to 4 days.

NOTE: If you're a fan of broccoli stems, trim away the thick ends and peel the thinner pieces. Cut them into ½-inch-wide sticks and cook them separately from the florets and about 1 minute longer. Follow Steps 4 and 5 for draining and cooling.

Along with carrots, broccoli is probably one vegetable you can count on to be reasonably priced all year round.

With blanching, you can cook several meals' worth all at once—you'll have a stash of perfectly crisp-cooked florets that will stay brilliantly green and ready to use for up to 4 days. (This recipe calls for blanching 2 heads of broccoli, but for times when you don't want leftovers, just blanch 1 head using the same directions and amounts of water.)

The secret behind blanching is to cook the broccoli just until it is brilliant green and then preserve that wonderful color by plunging it into ice-cold water. This stops the cooking process and seals in the color, so you've got perfect, bright green broccoli that stays that way. You can drain and serve part of the broccoli immediately, and if you want it hot, just reheat it in the microwave. (Don't skip the cold-water step for the broccoli you're serving now.) Pop the remaining florets into the refrigerator for later.

Our Way with Broccoli

Here are some of our favorite serving ideas for using blanched broccoli:

- Warm, with melted butter and/or lemon juice

- Warm, with soy sauce and sesame seeds (toasted, if desired)

- Cold, with ranch dressing and bacon bits

- Added to stir-fries

- Added to tossed salads

- Warm, tossed with Alfredo pasta sauce or cheese sauce

- Added to any pasta salad

- As a snack, plain or with salad dressing for dipping

- Chopped, in omelets, quiches, or quesadillas

A TRIO OF BREAD FIX-UPS

PARMESAN ENGLISH MUFFINS

SERVES: 4 START TO FINISH: UNDER 10 MINUTES

Let these cheese-filled muffins transform familiar morning fare into dinnertime satisfaction.

"I usually have English muffins in my freezer, so this would be a great inexpensive emergency bread to serve for a last-minute dinner," said our friend Julie Realon. "My son said I should serve them with spaghetti next time because they'd make great dippers with marinara sauce!"

2 English muffins
2 teaspoons olive oil
1 teaspoon garlic powder
¼ cup shredded or grated
   Parmesan cheese

1. Preheat the broiler (or use a toaster oven).

2. Split the muffins in half. Place the halves on a baking sheet, split side up. Drizzle ½ teaspoon of the oil over each muffin half.

3. Sprinkle ¼ teaspoon of the garlic powder and 1 tablespoon of the Parmesan cheese over each muffin half. Spread the cheese evenly to the edges of the muffin.

4. Toast the muffins until the cheese has melted and they are beginning to brown around the edges, 3 to 5 minutes. Serve at once.

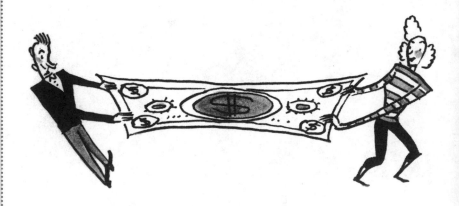

FLEXIBLE CHEESE CRESCENTS

MAKES: 8 ROLLS   PREP TIME: 5 MINUTES

1 package (8 ounces) refrigerated
   crescent roll dough
16 teaspoons (5 tablespoons plus
   1 teaspoon) shredded Cheddar cheese

1. Preheat the oven to 375°F.

2. Separate the dough into triangles and place them on a clean
work surface. Sprinkle 2 teaspoons of the cheese over each triangle. Roll each triangle up loosely, from the shortest side to the
opposite point.

3. Place the rolls, point side down, on an ungreased baking sheet.
Bake until golden brown, 11 to 13 minutes. Serve at once.

QUESADILLA ROLL-UPS

SERVES: 4   START TO FINISH: UNDER 10 MINUTES

2 large (10- to 12-inch) flour tortillas
¼ cup taco sauce
⅓ cup shredded Mexican-blend
   or Cheddar cheese

1. Place the tortillas on a clean work surface. Spread 2 tablespoons
of the taco sauce evenly over each tortilla, spreading it nearly to
the edge. Sprinkle 3 tablespoons of the cheese evenly over each
tortilla. Roll the tortillas up tightly, jelly roll–fashion.

2. Place the tortilla rolls, seam side down, on a microwave-safe
plate and microwave, uncovered, on high power until they are
heated through and the cheese has melted, about 1 minute.

3. Remove the tortillas from the microwave and cut each roll in
half. Serve at once.

Need a little dress-up for the refrigerated dough you bought on sale? Flexible Cheese Crescents make a quick rescue. This recipe calls for Cheddar, but any kind of cheese will work—from Parmesan to Swiss or even blue.

Need bread to accompany a Southwestern dish? These roll-ups make use of the leftover tortillas and salsa you're bound to have hanging around. Enchilada sauce or a smooth salsa can be substituted for the taco sauce.

Corn Muffin Add-ins

P ackages of corn muffin mix are frequently on sale at our local supermarkets, and even at the regular price we almost can't afford *not* to serve them.

We always stock up when the muffin mixes are on sale, and we do bake them quite frequently. But plain corn muffins can get boring if you serve them often. Thankfully they're just about the easiest food on earth to doctor up. Just about anything you suspect would make a flavorful addition does indeed make a flavorful addition. We've stirred in everything from jalapeños to bacon bits to blueberries, all with marvelous results. The mixes are so forgiving that exact proportions aren't mandatory, making them the perfect vehicle for using up the last little bits of vegetables, cheese, and whatever else lingers in the fridge. (Using up these bits and pieces is part of our strategy—we wouldn't want the additional ingredients to push the muffins into the expensive category!)

Muffin mixes come in 7.5-ounce boxes and in 6.5-ounce pouches. Some of the mixes call for adding an egg and milk, and others just water. Any type of corn muffin mix will work fine. Just follow the directions on the package—the stir-ins will not change the baking time, but you will get one or two more muffins, thanks to the additional ingredients.

Here are some of the combinations we like. The quantity of the stir-in doesn't have to be exact—just don't add more than we indicate. All of the dairy products can be reduced-fat, if you prefer. Have fun!

- ⅓ cup shredded Mexican-blend cheese and 2 tablespoons canned chopped green chiles (or minced fresh jalapeño peppers)

- ¼ cup sour cream and ½ onion, finely diced

- ⅓ cup shredded Swiss cheese and ¼ cup diced ham

- ⅓ cup crumbled feta cheese and ¼ cup sliced black olives

- ⅓ cup shredded Mexican-blend cheese and 3 to 4 cloves chopped roasted garlic

- ⅓ cup shredded Cheddar cheese and ¼ to ⅓ cup chopped cooked broccoli

- ⅓ cup shredded mozzarella cheese, ¼ cup chopped pepperoni slices, and ½ teaspoon dried basil or dried Italian seasoning

- ⅓ cup shredded Muenster cheese, ¼ cup bacon bits, and ¼ cup diced fresh tomato

- ⅓ cup shredded pepper Jack cheese, ¼ cup sour cream, and ¼ cup yellow corn kernels

- ¼ cup shredded or grated Parmesan cheese and ¼ cup diced green, red, or yellow (or a combination) bell pepper

- ⅓ cup shredded Cheddar cheese, 1 tablespoon minced fresh cilantro, and the juice of ½ lime

- ¼ cup finely cubed cream cheese and ¼ cup sliced or chopped green olives

- ⅓ cup cottage cheese and 3 tablespoons chopped scallions (2 scallions, including tender green parts)

- ½ cup blueberries and 3 tablespoons sugar

"You can doctor any type of corn muffin mix."

In the South, what most people think of as stuffing is called "dressing." It's baked in a casserole dish instead of being stuffed inside a turkey or chicken, and it's really, really wonderful. (It also may be safer than stuffing: In recent years many food-safety experts have frowned on cooking stuffed turkeys.) The baked dressing is served in squares. It's remotely similar in texture and appearance to fried Italian polenta.

We ate cornbread dressing only at Thanksgiving when I was growing up, and it is indeed wonderful with our Herb-Roasted Turkey Breast (page 108). But it also makes a wonderful, inexpensive side dish with roasted chicken, pork roast, or Debbie's Autumn Pork Chops (page 85).

We use a box of corn muffin mix, but if you usually make cornbread from scratch, feel free to use it. (Muffin mixes are very cheap, and the cornbread can be made up to 2 days ahead.) The cornbread is combined with bread crumbs for the stuffing, providing another way to use up bread that might otherwise go to waste.

SOUTHERN-STYLE CORNBREAD DRESSING

SERVES: 8 START TO FINISH: UNDER 1 HOUR

8 tablespoons (1 stick) butter
2 teaspoons vegetable oil
1 medium-size onion (for about ¾ cup chopped)
2 medium-size ribs celery (for about ¾ cup diced)
3 cloves fresh garlic, minced, or 1 tablespoon bottled minced garlic
2 large eggs
1 pan (8 inch square) cornbread, prepared from corn muffin mix (6.5- to 7.5-ounce box or pouch)
2 cups soft bread crumbs (see page 235)
2 teaspoons dried poultry seasoning or dried ground sage
1 teaspoon black pepper
¾ teaspoon salt
1 can (14 ounces) fat-free chicken broth, or 2 cups homemade chicken stock (see page 10)

1. Preheat the oven heat to 375°F. Lightly grease an 8-inch-square baking pan and set it aside.

2. Cut the butter into 4 pieces, place them in a microwave-safe dish, and cover with a paper towel. Microwave on high power until melted, about 1 minute. Set aside.

3. Heat the oil in an 8-inch or larger skillet over medium heat. Peel and coarsely chop the onion, adding it to the skillet as you chop. Dice the celery, adding the pieces to the skillet as you cut. Add the garlic. Cook, stirring occasionally, until the onion and celery are soft, 2 to 3 minutes. Remove the skillet from the heat, and set it aside.

4. Break the eggs into a medium-size mixing bowl and whisk until they are foamy. Finely crumble the cornbread into the bowl. Add the onion mixture, bread crumbs, poultry seasoning, black pepper, and salt. Stir to mix well. Pour the broth and the butter evenly over the mixture and stir well. (The mixture will be very moist.) Pour the dressing into the prepared baking pan and smooth it to the edges of the pan, pressing lightly with the back of a spoon.

5. Cover the pan with aluminum foil and bake for 20 minutes. Then uncover the pan and continue to bake just until the outer edges turn brown, 20 to 25 minutes. Remove from the oven and let the dressing stand for 5 to 10 minutes. Then cut it into squares and serve.

ITALIAN-STYLE BREAD SALAD

SERVES: 6 START TO FINISH: UNDER 20 MINUTES

SUPER-CHEAP!

3 large day-old bagels or other hearty
    bread (for 6 cups cubes)
3 scallions (for ⅓ cup sliced)
3 ripe large plum tomatoes
    (for about 1½ cups diced)
1 medium-size cucumber (for about 1½ cups diced)
Red Wine Vinaigrette (recipe follows), or ½ cup
    purchased vinaigrette

1. Place an oven rack about 5 inches from the broiler element. Turn the broiler to high.

2. Cut the bagels into bite-size pieces and place them on a baking sheet. Place the baking sheet in the oven and toast until the bread is just lightly brown on top, 30 seconds to 1 minute. Remove the baking sheet from the oven and toss the bread pieces. Continue to toast just until the bread is medium-brown, about 30 seconds more. Set aside.

Occasionally readers of our newspaper column will write to tell us about great dishes they prepare or sample in their favorite restaurants. Several years ago, Terry Lorbiecki described a bread salad she had enjoyed, and soon after that we started to notice bread salads ourselves. Terry told us she was going to try making bread salad at home using leftover bagels, something we always seem to have on hand. So we decided to give Terry's idea a shot.

Here's our result: a delicious little side dish that's as easy to throw together as a simple green salad. The bonus is that slightly stale

(continued)

(continued)

bread works best, so it's a great way to use up leftovers. If the main component is almost-stale bread, you know you've got a budget winner! Any kind of hearty bread works great—pita, French bread, Italian rolls, bagels. Use a mixture if you have several varieties on hand.

This vinaigrette is wonderful on Italian-Style Bread Salad—or on any green salad you happen to make.

3. Cut the scallions into ¼-inch-thick slices, including enough of the tender green tops to make ⅓ cup, and put them in a 3-quart or larger bowl. Core and cut the tomatoes into ¼-inch dice. Add the pieces to the bowl. Peel the cucumber, slice it in half lengthwise, and use a teaspoon to scoop out the seeds. Cut the cucumber into ¼-inch dice and add the pieces to the bowl.

4. Just before serving, add the bagel pieces to the bowl and toss well. Shake the vinaigrette to mix it well and drizzle ¼ cup of the dressing over the salad. Toss well. Then add the remaining ¼ cup vinaigrette and toss again. Serve at once.

RED WINE VINAIGRETTE

MAKES: ABOUT ½ CUP START TO FINISH: 5 MINUTES

⅓ cup olive oil, preferably extra-virgin
3 tablespoons red wine vinegar
1 teaspoon garlic powder
½ teaspoon sugar
¼ teaspoon salt
¼ teaspoon black pepper

Combine all the ingredients in a small jar that has a lid. Cover and shake well to combine. Serve at once or let stand at room temperature until ready to serve. The vinaigrette will keep, covered, in the refrigerator up to 7 days.

CABBAGE WITH RED WINE VINEGAR

SERVES: 4 GENEROUSLY   START TO FINISH: UNDER 20 MINUTES

1 very small head green cabbage, or
    ½ large head (about 1¼ pounds)
2 tablespoons butter or margarine
1 tablespoon red wine vinegar
¼ teaspoon salt, or to taste
¼ teaspoon black pepper, or to taste

1. Pour about 3 cups water (to a depth of 1 inch) into a 2-quart or larger saucepan, cover, and bring it to a boil over high heat.

2. While the water is heating, cut the cabbage into quarters. Remove and discard the tough core.

3. When the water reaches a boil, add the cabbage, cover the pan, and cook until the cabbage is crisp-tender, about 8 minutes. (Do not overcook.)

4. Meanwhile, place the butter in a microwave-safe serving bowl, cover it with a paper towel, and microwave on high power just until the butter melts, about 1 minute. Remove the bowl from the microwave and whisk in the vinegar. Set aside.

5. When the cabbage is done, drain it well in a colander. Shake the colander to remove as much water as possible. Add the cabbage to the serving bowl containing the butter mixture. Using two sharp knives and a sawing motion, cut the cabbage into bite-size pieces. Sprinkle the salt and black pepper over the cabbage and stir to mix well and to coat the cabbage with the butter mixture. Taste and add more salt and pepper, if desired. Serve at once.

Steamed cabbage is one of those humble fall and winter vegetable side dishes that can easily get overlooked. It's kind of like the boy next door whom you take for granted until he starts driving a new car. The "new car" in this recipe is red wine vinegar. Southerners have long known the glories of cabbage topped off with a little vinegar, but in the old days cooks would use either cider vinegar or vinegar infused with hot chile peppers. Red wine vinegar offers a touch that is slightly more refined without sacrificing the old-fashioned goodness.

Like a lot of root vegetables, carrots are inexpensive and keep a long time in the refrigerator—which is why we almost always have some on hand. When we're at a loss for what to serve alongside a roasted chicken or slices of ham, we can count on carrots to make a wonderful side dish. These carrots are packed with flavor, thanks to the chicken broth, and the slightly sweet glaze ensures that our kids will be glad to eat them. The wonderful orange color always brightens up a plate.

MAPLE-GLAZED CARROTS

SERVES: 4 START TO FINISH: UNDER 20 MINUTES

1 pound carrots (see Notes)
1 can (14 ounces) fat-free chicken broth, or 2 cups homemade chicken stock (see page 10)
¼ cup pure maple syrup (see Notes)

SUPER-CHEAP!

1. Peel the carrots and cut them into pieces about 1½ inches long. Cut the thicker pieces in half lengthwise. Set the carrots aside.

2. Pour the broth into a 12-inch skillet and bring it to a boil over medium heat. Add the carrots, cover the skillet, and cook for 5 minutes. Then uncover the skillet and continue to boil the carrots until they are crisp-tender, 8 to 9 minutes.

3. Using a slotted spoon, transfer the carrots to a serving dish. Add the maple syrup and stir until the carrots are coated. Serve hot.

NOTES: You can use a pound of already-peeled baby carrots if you like. Just cut the whole baby carrots in half lengthwise as indicated in Step 1.
■ Use only real maple syrup (not artificially flavored pancake syrup). If you don't have any, substitute ¼ cup honey.

WINTER ROASTED CARROTS

SERVES: 4 START TO FINISH: UNDER 1 HOUR

SUPER-CHEAP!

Cooking oil spray
1 pound carrots (see Notes)
2 small onions
    (for about 1¼ cups pieces)
4 to 6 cloves fresh garlic (see Notes)
1 tablespoon olive oil
½ teaspoon dried thyme
¼ teaspoon salt
Black pepper to taste
1 teaspoon balsamic vinegar

1. Preheat the oven to 475°F. Spray a 13- x 9-inch glass or ceramic baking dish with cooking oil spray and set it aside.

2. Peel the carrots and cut them crosswise into thirds. Cut the carrot pieces into matchsticks roughly 2½ to 3 inches long, ½ inch wide, and ½ inch thick. Place the carrots in the prepared baking dish.

3. Peel the onions and cut them into quarters. Cut the quarters in half crosswise and add the pieces to the dish with the carrots. Peel the garlic and add the cloves to the dish.

4. Drizzle the oil over the vegetables and then sprinkle the thyme and salt over them. Sprinkle lightly with black pepper. Stir and toss until the vegetables are coated with the oil.

5. Roast the vegetables, uncovered, for 15 minutes. Remove the pan from the oven and stir. Return the pan to the oven and continue to roast, stirring every 10 minutes, until the carrots and onions are beginning to brown and are very tender when pierced with the tip of a sharp knife, about 45 minutes in all.

From Beverly:

Winter expeditions to the produce department can be downright depressing. My family's favorites are out of season, and the fruits and vegetables shipped in from far afield are priced like gold. Plus, they often simply don't taste right. Most days I depend on salad or use frozen veggies. But every now and then, I satisfy my cravings for a fresh vegetable side dish by roasting a pan of carrots.

Alicia and I discovered the joys of roasting vegetables a few years ago when a flood of books came out on the subject. There's something about high heat that burnishes a carrot, bringing out the natural sugars in much the same way an onion caramelizes. Because the oven will be blazing at 475°F, it's important to stir frequently during the last 30 minutes of cooking so the vegetables will brown evenly.

6. Remove the pan from the oven and drizzle the vinegar over the vegetables. Stir and toss until the vinegar is well distributed. Serve immediately.

NOTES: Already-peeled baby carrots can be used, but be aware that sometimes the water sprinklers in supermarket produce sections can waterlog the bags of baby carrots. Be sure to choose a bag that has not been saturated with water, and dry the carrots with paper towels before cooking so they will brown properly.
■ The exact amount of garlic doesn't matter. If the cloves are large, use 4; if they are small, use 6. Fans of sweet roasted garlic will enjoy eating the extra cloves.

If you've only had deli coleslaw that's way too sweet and practically drowning in mayonnaise, we bet you don't like coleslaw very much. Give ours a try and you'll change your tune. This is a mild slaw that appeals to everyone—kids included. It's an easy, inexpensive way to add salad to almost any meal.

SIMPLY SOUTHERN COLESLAW

SERVES: 4 GENEROUSLY START TO FINISH: UNDER 10 MINUTES

½ cup regular or reduced-fat mayonnaise
2 teaspoons sugar
2 teaspoons cider vinegar or distilled
   white vinegar
¼ teaspoon salt, or more to taste
¼ teaspoon black pepper
1 very small head green cabbage, or ½ large head
   (about 1¼ pounds)

SUPER-CHEAP!

1. Combine the mayonnaise, sugar, vinegar, salt, and black pepper in a 3-quart serving bowl and stir well.

2. Halve the cabbage and remove and discard the core. Coarsely chop it, adding the cabbage to the bowl as you chop. Stir until the cabbage is well coated with the dressing. (At first it may not seem as if there's enough dressing. Just keep stirring—the dressing will seem to expand as the cabbage gives off moisture.)

3. Serve at once or refrigerate until ready to serve, up to 24 hours.

Coleslaw Good Enough for Company

SERVES: 6 START TO FINISH: UNDER 15 MINUTES

½ cup chopped nuts, such as walnuts,
    pecans, almonds, or unsalted peanuts
½ cup regular or reduced-fat mayonnaise
⅓ cup regular or reduced-fat sour cream
2 tablespoons whole, low-fat, or skim milk
½ teaspoon curry powder
1 very small head green cabbage, or ½ large head
    (about 1¼ pounds)
½ cup raisins
¼ teaspoon salt, or more to taste
1 teaspoon black pepper, or more to taste

1. Spread the nuts in a single layer on a microwave-safe dish. Microwave, uncovered, on high power until fragrant and lightly toasted, about 2 minutes, stirring once halfway through. (If you are using roasted peanuts, this step won't be necessary.) Set the nuts aside to cool.

2. Combine the mayonnaise, sour cream, milk, and curry powder in a 3-quart or larger bowl and whisk to blend.

3. Halve the cabbage and remove and discard the tough core. Cut it into very thin, long shreds, then cut the shreds in half and place them in the bowl. Add the raisins and nuts. (If you are making the slaw more than 1 hour ahead, wait to stir the raisins and nuts into the mixture until just before serving.) Stir until the mixture is evenly coated with the dressing. Season with the salt and black pepper. Serve at once or refrigerate, covered, until ready to serve, up to 24 hours.

oleslaw is made of cabbage, and cabbage is cheap. But coleslaw doesn't have to be dull. Add a few raisins and nuts, and suddenly you've got a side dish that will make your family feel like company. A dash of curry powder adds to the exotic flavor of this dish, but if you're not a curry fan or if you don't have any, just leave it out. Dried cranberries, dried cherries, or chopped dried apricots (or a mixture) can be used in place of the raisins to add a splash of color and additional flavor.

Think Like Your Grandmother

From Alicia:

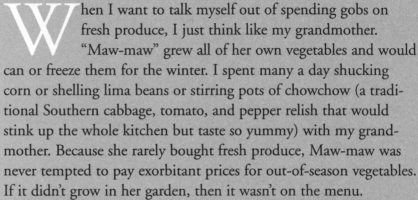

When I want to talk myself out of spending gobs on fresh produce, I just think like my grandmother. "Maw-maw" grew all of her own vegetables and would can or freeze them for the winter. I spent many a day shucking corn or shelling lima beans or stirring pots of chowchow (a traditional Southern cabbage, tomato, and pepper relish that would stink up the whole kitchen but taste so yummy) with my grandmother. Because she rarely bought fresh produce, Maw-maw was never tempted to pay exorbitant prices for out-of-season vegetables. If it didn't grow in her garden, then it wasn't on the menu.

These days we have the convenience of blueberries in February, tomatoes in December, and asparagus in October. But we pay dearly for it. Here in my hometown you can buy strawberries from some faraway land in December, but they are at their most delicious and least expensive in June, when they're in season right in our own backyard. Buying local produce is the cheapest because you're not paying for shipping. Buying in-season produce makes budget sense, too, because of simple supply and demand: The harvest is in, the supply is huge, and the price goes way down. Sure, I can buy a watermelon in March for $6.99, but in August their price is rock bottom. And waiting for in-season produce makes it taste all that much better, too.

So the next time you're tempted to buy that 1-pound bunch of fresh but out-of-season asparagus for $5.99, think like your grandmother. Would it be growing in her garden right now? Well, there's your answer.

"Waiting for in-season produce makes it taste all that much better."

BITS-OF-FRUIT SALAD WITH STRAWBERRY YOGURT DRESSING

SERVES: 4 TO 6 START TO FINISH: UNDER 15 MINUTES

1 smallest-size can of fruit, such as
    pineapple, mandarin oranges,
    or pears
1 medium-size red or green apple
1 medium-size banana (see Notes)
½ cup seedless grapes (see Notes)
Strawberry Yogurt Dressing (recipe follows)

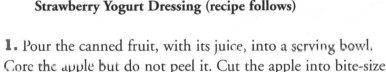

1. Pour the canned fruit, with its juice, into a serving bowl. Core the apple but do not peel it. Cut the apple into bite-size pieces and add the pieces to the bowl. Stir to coat the apples with the juice.

2. Slice the banana and add it to the bowl. Add the grapes, cutting them in half, if desired. Set the fruit aside, without stirring, until just before serving.

3. When you are ready to serve the salad, stir the fruit and serve it in small bowls. Spoon a little of the dressing on top of each bowl and pass the rest at the table.

NOTES: If you are waiting a while to serve the salad, don't peel, slice, or add the banana until right before serving. The banana can hold in the salad for only about 10 minutes before turning brown and mushy.

■ Sometimes the stem end of grapes will turn a bit brown, but that doesn't mean the entire grape is blemished. Just trim away the brown part and then cut the grape in half before adding it to the salad. Nobody will be able to tell the difference.

From Beverly:

When I got really, really tired of tossing out the last few grapes, that stray strawberry, and the apple half that my daughter didn't eat, my frustration led to fruit salad. This one recipe has cut my weekly fruit waste to almost zero. Instead of tossing out the last bits of fruit, I combine them into a delicious fruit salad that, in the end, seems decidedly more intentional than the recipe's beginnings would indicate.

This is really more of a method than a recipe. The trick is to end up with the exact amount of fruit salad that everyone will eat, so that you don't end up wasting fruit in spite of yourself. It may take a few trials to calculate this amount, but start by figuring on ¾ cup sliced fruit per serving. So to serve four, you need 3 cups of fruit. The amounts of the different fresh fruits don't matter, and neither does the exact combination. You do, however, need one type of canned fruit if you're using fresh apples or pears, because the juice is the secret to keeping apples or pears from turning dark.

This dressing adds a festive touch to fruit salad, turning it into a dish that's great for guests as well as family. It can be made with any fruit-flavored yogurt you happen to like, so you can vary it to keep things interesting.

STRAWBERRY YOGURT DRESSING

MAKES: ABOUT ½ CUP **START TO FINISH:** 5 MINUTES

½ cup strawberry yogurt
1 teaspoon grated orange zest (optional)
2 tablespoons orange juice

Pour the yogurt into a small mixing bowl. Add the orange zest (if using) and the orange juice. Stir until well combined. Spoon over fruit salad or refrigerate, covered, until ready to serve, up to 24 hours.

From Alicia:

Frozen corn is a staple in my freezer—I use it often in soups and stews, and throw it into a last-minute skillet meal, but I rarely use it as more than an add-in. Yet as I yearned for a super-quick side, I remembered the delectable flavor of the corn that escaped from the vegetable quesadillas we often enjoy. The kernels had roasted to a light brown and were terrific. Who would have thought a side dish recipe would result from a stray nibble?

A recipe this easy sounds a bit ridiculous. But after sampling our savory corn just once, you'll understand my admiration for this sweet, thrifty side dish.

SWEET ROASTED CORN

SERVES: 4 **START TO FINISH:** UNDER 25 MINUTES

1 pound frozen extra-sweet
  yellow corn kernels (see Note)
1 tablespoon vegetable oil
Salt to taste

1. Preheat the oven to 450°F.

2. Place the corn in a colander and rinse it with cool water to partially defrost. Drain well.

3. Spread the corn in a single layer on an ungreased 17- x 11-inch baking sheet that has at least a 1-inch edge (a jelly-roll pan is ideal). Drizzle with the oil. Stir to coat well and then redistribute to form a single layer. Roast until the corn kernels start to brown, about 10 minutes. Remove from the oven, season with salt, and serve.

NOTE: We especially like the yellow corn that some brands label "extra-sweet," but any yellow corn works well.

HANNAH'S CORN SAUTÉ

SERVES: 4 GENEROUSLY START TO FINISH: UNDER 20 MINUTES

2 slices bacon
3 cups frozen corn kernels (white, yellow, or a combination)
2 teaspoons olive oil
1 tablespoon butter
1 small onion (for about ½ cup chopped)
1 medium-size zucchini (for about 1 cup pieces; see Note)
1 teaspoon herbes de Provence or dried basil
Salt and black pepper, to taste

1. Cover a microwave-safe plate with paper towels. Place the bacon on the plate, cover with another paper towel, and microwave on high power until just crisp, 1 to 2 minutes. Set aside.

2. Place the corn in a colander and rinse it with warm water to partially defrost. Set aside to drain well.

3. Combine the oil and butter in a 12-inch skillet over medium heat. While the oil mixture is heating, peel and coarsely chop the onion, adding it to the skillet as you chop. Cut the zucchini into bite-size pieces. Add the zucchini to the skillet. Cook, stirring occasionally, until the onion is translucent, 4 to 5 minutes.

4. Add the corn and herbes de Provence and stir to mix well. Cover and steam until heated through, about 4 minutes.

5. Crumble the bacon over the vegetables and toss to mix well. Season with salt and black pepper. Serve at once.

NOTE: Any fresh vegetable can be substituted for the zucchini: 1 cup chopped green or red bell pepper, sliced carrots (which will take a bit longer to cook), or even chopped fresh spinach.

From Alicia:

My oldest daughter, Hannah, loves to experiment in the kitchen. While I can always use the help, sometimes her creations take on a life of their own, requiring more energy than I normally have during midweek dinner preparation. But this quick side dish is a definite exception. Inspired by a recipe she read in an old cookbook, she set out to make a quick side dish with just a few items we had in the refrigerator and freezer.

The secret ingredients are the herbes de Provence and the finish of bacon. Who would know this was so quick to prepare when it looks and tastes as if it took hours?

Cooking a Giant Pot of Summer Corn

From Beverly:

Every July since he was a boy, my father, Jay Mills, starts dreaming about eating sweet corn. The dreams, he assures me, are full-flavored and in living color. Maybe that's why my mother always prepares a giant cauldron of corn to serve on the cob and with plenty of leftovers for salads and creamy corn dishes. I absorbed this family legacy, and along about July, fresh sweet corn starts showing up at every meal. But I don't like to steam up the kitchen every night, so like my mother, I figure if you're going to the trouble to boil corn, you might as well do a huge vat and get it over with!

The best part of having this stash of already-cooked corn on hand is that it lets you get a bit more creative with your corn recipes. With a few swipes of a sharp knife, you'll have a lovely bowl of sweet corn kernels to speed you on your way to dishes like Fresh Corn and Tomato Salad (page 327), Copycat Creamed Corn (page 326), and Summer Corn Pilaf (page 340).

Here's how to cook a dozen ears of corn:

Fill an 8-quart or larger pot roughly a third of the way full with water (about 3 quarts). Place the pot over high heat, cover it, and bring to a boil. (If you don't have a pot that big, use two 4½-quart pots.) Place a large protective hot pad next to the sink, and place a large colander in the sink.

While the water is heating, shuck the 12 ears of corn. Do not obsess over this job: Three pulls (four max) should get it, and don't try to pick off every strand of silk or you'll stand there all day.

When the water reaches a rolling boil, add the corn, cover the pot, and bring it back to a boil. Cook the corn at a rolling boil until it is just tender. The time will vary according to the size of the ears and the tenderness of the kernels, but it takes only a few minutes.

Using potholders or mitts, transfer the pot to the protective hot pad next to the sink. Use tongs to transfer the ears of corn to the colander. Serve the corn you are planning to eat at once. Let the remaining ears cool (place them under cold running water to stop the cooking) and then refrigerate them in a large zipper-top plastic bag. The cooked corn will keep, refrigerated, for up to 4 days.

If you are planning to reheat the refrigerated corn on the cob, wrap the ears individually in heavy-duty microwave-safe plastic wrap and microwave on high power until heated through, 1 to 2 minutes per ear. If you are going to cut the corn kernels off the cob, do this while the corn is cold.

So strike while the summer corn is fresh, abundant, and reasonably priced. Cooking a giant stash at once makes it a snap to enjoy corn at every meal.

"Cooking a giant stash at once makes it a snap to enjoy corn at every meal."

From Alicia:

My mother-in-law makes the best Southern-style creamed corn I've ever tasted. It's expected that Betty's creamed corn will show up at any potluck party she attends—it doesn't matter if it's a church social or a family reunion. The only problem is that Betty's recipe is based on an ingredient I don't usually have: fresh corn kernels straight from the cob.

I may not always have garden-grown corn, but I do always have a bag or two of frozen corn kernels from the grocery store. Combining white and yellow frozen kernels and chopping part of the corn in my food processor mimics the "milky" quality of true Southern-style creamed corn. A little onion sautéed in butter finishes my copycat recipe.

Nothing will ever match the garden-fresh goodness that Betty stirs into her creamed corn, but this quick-and-easy version impresses even the family members who crave Betty's corn.

COPYCAT CREAMED CORN

SERVES: 4 GENEROUSLY START TO FINISH: UNDER 20 MINUTES

SUPER-CHEAP!

2 tablespoons butter
½ small onion (for about ¼ cup chopped)
2 cups frozen white corn kernels (see Note)
⅓ cup plus 3 tablespoons whole, low-fat, or skim milk
2 cups frozen yellow corn kernels (see Note)
⅛ teaspoon salt, or to taste
Black pepper, to taste

1. Melt the butter in a 2-quart or larger saucepan over low heat.

2. Meanwhile, peel and finely chop the onion. Add the onion to the pan and cook, stirring frequently, until soft, 4 to 5 minutes.

3. While the onion cooks, pour the white corn kernels into a colander and rinse them under lukewarm water for 1 minute. Drain well. Then transfer the corn to a food processor, add ⅓ cup of the milk, and process on high power until pureed, about 15 seconds. Set aside.

4. Pour the yellow corn kernels into a colander and rinse under lukewarm water for 1 minute. Drain well.

5. Add the yellow corn kernels, the white corn mixture, and the remaining 3 tablespoons milk to the saucepan. Raise the heat to medium and cook, stirring constantly, until the mixture comes to a boil. Then reduce the heat to low and continue to cook, stirring frequently, until the corn is heated through, about 2 minutes. Season with the salt and black pepper. Serve at once or simmer until ready to serve, up to 30 minutes, stirring occasionally.

NOTE: We buy frozen corn in the largest possible bags for the biggest savings. It's easy to just scoop out the amount you need and stash the rest back in the freezer.

FRESH CORN AND TOMATO SALAD

SERVES: 4 START TO FINISH: UNDER 20 MINUTES

4 ears fresh corn (for about
   2½ cups kernels)
2 medium-size (about 1 pound)
   ripe tomatoes
3 scallions (for ¼ cup chopped)
½ cup loosely packed fresh cilantro leaves
½ lime
Salt and black pepper to taste

SUPER-CHEAP!

1. Pour water to a depth of 2 inches in a large deep skillet. Place it over high heat, cover, and bring to a boil. While the water is heating, shuck the corn and remove the silks.

2. When the water reaches a boil, add the ears of corn (they don't need to be completely covered with water), cover the pot, and bring it back to a boil. Cook the corn at a rolling boil until the kernels are just tender, 4 to 5 minutes.

3. Remove the corn from the skillet and place it in a colander in the sink. Run cold water over the corn until it is cool enough to handle. Carefully slice the kernels from the corncobs into a shallow dish, such as a pie plate. Scrape the cobs with the back of the knife to remove any remaining kernels and milk, adding them to the dish as well.

4. Core and chop the tomatoes into roughly ¼-inch cubes, adding them to the dish as you chop. Chop the scallions, including enough of the tender green tops to make ¼ cup. Add the scallions to the dish. Finely chop the cilantro and add it to the dish. Squeeze the lime juice into the corn mixture and toss well to combine. Season with salt and black pepper. Serve at once or refrigerate, covered, until ready to serve, up to 2 hours.

This fresh salad features the delightful combination of summer corn and tomatoes and a bright accent of lime and cilantro. It's yet another addictive way to enjoy summer's bounty. If you happen to have leftover corn on the cob (also, see the summer corn box on page 324), this is a terrific way to recycle it.

From Beverly:

My mother loves to tell the story of my first restaurant excursion in the Deep South, when I was 3 years old. "Have you got any call-reds?" I reportedly asked the waitress, referring to collard greens, my favorite food at the time. My love of strongly flavored greens extends well beyond collards, and I like to cook several different kinds of greens together. Like many Southerners, I grew up eating greens cooked with fatback or some other type of fatty pork and topped with vinegar. When my mom's cholesterol count hit the roof several years ago, she started cooking greens in chicken bouillon. This is a wonderful substitution, still imparting lots of flavor and the much-needed salt.

Greens have many benefits. They're packed with vitamins, and they're a very economical way to get a fresh vegetable on the table in the fall and winter. Greens are not hard to cook, but you do have to be careful in the washing process—gritty greens are not good greens. If you've never cooked fresh greens

GREENS, SOUTHERN STYLE

SERVES: 4 START TO FINISH: UNDER 30 MINUTES

1½ to 2 pounds strongly flavored greens, such as collards, kale, mustard, turnip greens, or a mixture (see Note)
5 chicken bouillon cubes
Black pepper to taste
¼ cup bacon bits, or ¼ cup Super Sofrito (page 388), for serving (optional)
4 teaspoons cider vinegar, for serving (optional)

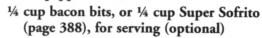

SUPER-CHEAP!

1. Cut away and discard any tough portion of the greens' stems. Fill a clean sink with water and submerge the greens in the water. Let the greens soak in the water, undisturbed, for at least 2 minutes. Lift the greens from the water. (If you have two sinks, you can go ahead and place them in clean water in the second sink.) Drain the water from the sink and wash out all of the grit that's on the bottom of the sink. Repeat this rinsing process until there is no grit left in the sink when the water is drained out.

2. Bring 1 quart water to a boil in a covered 4½-quart or larger pot. Add the bouillon cubes and stir until they dissolve in the water. Shake the excess water from the washed greens and add them to the pot. (If all the greens don't fit at once, add them gradually—they'll make room as they wilt.) Cover the pot and bring the water back to a boil. Then reduce the heat to low and cook at a slow boil, stirring occasionally, until the greens are just tender, 7 to 10 minutes.

3. Remove the pot from the heat and drain the greens in a colander. Pour the greens into a serving bowl. Using two sharp knives and a sawing motion, cut the greens into bite-size pieces. Drain all but a little of the collected juice from the bowl. Season with black pepper and serve right away. If desired, top each serving with a sprinkling of bacon bits and 1 teaspoon of vinegar.

NOTE: At certain times of the year, frozen greens may be cheaper than fresh. Test the frozen greens after 5 minutes of cooking and adjust the cooking time as necessary to produce tender greens.

SWEDISH PICKLED CUCUMBERS

SERVES: 4 PREP TIME: 10 MINUTES

1 pound seedless (hothouse) or Kirby cucumbers
¼ cup cider vinegar
4 teaspoons sugar
¼ teaspoon salt
⅛ teaspoon black pepper

1. Peel the cucumbers and cut them into thin rounds. Place the slices in a 1-quart serving bowl.

2. Combine the vinegar, sugar, salt, and black pepper in a 1-cup or larger glass measure. Whisk until the sugar is mostly dissolved. Pour the mixture over the cucumbers.

3. Cover the cucumbers and refrigerate for 30 minutes or up to 48 hours. If you are marinating them for less than an hour, stir the cucumbers occasionally. If marinating longer, stir once or twice before serving.

before, the idea of cooking 2 pounds for 4 people may seem absurd, but greens shrink as they cook—a lot. And in the unlikely event you happen to have left-overs, you'll be glad you do.

From Beverly:

These are not actually pickles—that's just the name for this way of preparing these marinated cucumbers. We like to serve them as a light summer side dish when neighborhood vegetable gardens (and supermarkets) are overflowing with free (or very reasonable) cukes.

There are lots of ways to make pickled cucumbers. The version my mother makes contains a bit of vegetable oil, but those that her mother (my grandmother) makes contain only vinegar—no oil or sugar. This version with vinegar and sugar—but no oil—is the result of a social studies project my son Sam did, researching the foods of his Swedish heritage. The big surprise for us was how long the cucumbers lasted. Even after two days, they were still incredibly crisp and tasty.

This salad, with its beautiful, bright green color, makes a festive side dish for either a celebration or a midweek family dinner. Beverly's teenage son Sam liked it so much that he ate three helpings. Even though there's no meat, it's hearty enough to serve four for lunch or as a light dinner entrée.

SPINACH PESTO PASTA SALAD

SERVES: 6 START TO FINISH: UNDER 25 MINUTES

Salt for cooking the pasta
8 ounces short pasta, such as penne
1 rib celery (for about ½ cup chopped)
1 cup grape or cherry tomatoes
½ cup frozen green peas
¼ cup Spinach Parsley Pesto (page 372)
¼ teaspoon garlic powder
½ teaspoon salt
⅛ teaspoon black pepper

1. Bring 2½ quarts lightly salted water to a boil in a covered 4½-quart pot. When the water reaches a rapid boil, add the pasta and cook, uncovered, just until firm-tender, following the package directions.

2. Drain the pasta in a colander and throw in 2 handfuls of ice cubes. Rinse the pasta under cold running water and toss with the ice cubes until it reaches cool room temperature. Set it aside to drain.

3. Meanwhile, dice the celery and place it in a 3-quart or larger serving bowl. Cut the tomatoes in half and add them to the bowl. Rinse the peas under warm water to defrost; drain the peas well and add them to the bowl.

4. Remove any unmelted ice cubes from the colander and shake it well to remove as much water as possible from the pasta. Add the pasta to the bowl. Stir the pesto to mix in any oil that may have separated and add it to the bowl. Sprinkle the garlic powder, salt, and black pepper evenly over the ingredients. Stir gently to mix well, coating the pasta and vegetables with the pesto. Serve at room temperature or refrigerate, covered, until ready to serve, up to 12 hours. Bring back to room temperature before serving.

OLD-FASHIONED TWICE-BAKED POTATOES

SERVES: 8 PREP TIME: 15 MINUTES

SUPER-CHEAP!

Cooking oil spray
4 already-baked Russet baking
  potatoes (see page 366)
3 tablespoons butter
⅓ cup regular or reduced-fat sour cream
Salt and black pepper, to taste
1 cup shredded Cheddar cheese

1. Preheat the oven to 350°F. Spray a baking sheet with cooking oil spray and set it aside.

2. Slice the potatoes in half and scoop the centers into a bowl, leaving a shell about ¼ inch thick. Set the potato shells aside.

3. Place the butter in a microwave-safe dish, cover it with a paper towel, and microwave on high power until it melts, about 30 seconds.

4. Add the melted butter, sour cream, and salt and pepper to the bowl of potato pulp. Using a potato masher or a large fork, mash the potatoes well, mixing in all the ingredients. Season with more salt and pepper, if necessary.

5. Place the potato shells on the prepared baking sheet and fill each shell with the potato mixture. Top each one with about 2 tablespoons of the cheese.

6. Bake until the potatoes are heated through and just beginning to bubble, about 30 minutes. Serve immediately.

From Alicia:

My mom and grandmother always used leftover baked potatoes to make twice-baked potatoes. We'd eat baked potatoes on Saturday night and then enjoy the leftovers the next day at lunch (it was called Sunday dinner when I was growing up).

It's easy to pull off this old-fashioned favorite if you bake extra potatoes and then wait to use your bounty. Feel free to dress these up any way you like. Bacon bits, chopped broccoli, ham, other varieties of cheese, and even corn have found their way into my twice-baked potatoes.

I grew up thinking my mom's mashed potatoes were standard fare. Boy, was I wrong. I never really appreciated them until mashed potatoes became the "new" gourmet side dish at restaurants around town. Every time I ordered a dish with mashed potatoes, I envisioned my mom's amazing creamy potatoes. But after one bite, I realized that not all mashed potatoes are created equal.

"Creamed" potatoes like my mom used to make aren't really the same as standard mashed potatoes. Creamed potatoes are both lighter and silky smooth, a texture achieved by using an electric mixer. By any name, these potatoes make a fabulous, inexpensive side dish for just about any kind of meat—pork, steak, meat loaf, chicken. If you have a crowd, double the recipe—any leftover potatoes will keep for 3 days in the refrigerator and are delicious reheated in the microwave oven. These potatoes also make a wonderful topping for our Texas Cowboy's Pie (page 63.)

GAYLE'S CREAMED POTATOES

SERVES: 4 START TO FINISH: UNDER 30 MINUTES

6 medium (1½ pounds) white potatoes
¼ cup regular or reduced-fat sour cream
2 tablespoons butter
2 tablespoons whole milk or half-and-half
Salt and black pepper to taste

1. Peel and cube the potatoes and place them in a Dutch oven or large soup pot. Cover the potatoes with water and bring to a boil over high heat. Then reduce the heat to medium-high and cook, uncovered, until the potatoes are tender, 15 minutes.

2. Drain the potatoes and place them in the large bowl of an electric mixer or use a hand mixer. Add the sour cream, butter, and milk. Mix on medium speed, scraping down the sides of the bowl frequently, until the potatoes are very smooth, about 3 minutes. Then turn mixer to high speed and mix for 1 more minute to whip air into them. Season with salt and black pepper and serve at once.

GARLICKY SMASHED POTATOES

SERVES: 4 START TO FINISH: UNDER 30 MINUTES

8 medium (about 2½ pounds)
    red potatoes
2 tablespoons butter
¼ cup whole, low-fat,
    or skim milk
1 clove fresh garlic, minced,
    or 1 teaspoon bottled minced garlic
Salt and black pepper to taste

SUPER-CHEAP!

1. Pour 4½ cups water into a 3-quart or larger saucepan. Cover the pan, place it over high heat, and bring to a boil. Meanwhile, scrub the potatoes to remove any dirt. Cut out any bruises or large eyes, then cut the potatoes into 2-inch pieces (quarters or eighths, depending on their size).

2. When the water is boiling, add the potatoes carefully to avoid any splash-ups. Bring the water back to a boil, then reduce the heat to medium-high to maintain a steady boil (but not so hot as to boil over). Cook until the potatoes are tender when pierced with a sharp knife, about 10 minutes.

3. Remove the pan from the heat and drain the potatoes in a colander. Set aside to drain.

4. Return the potatoes to the saucepan and add the butter, milk, and garlic. Using a potato masher, smash the potatoes until they reach the desired consistency. Season with salt and pepper, stir well, making sure the butter and garlic are well distributed, and serve at once.

The next time you need a simple, really cheap side dish, think smashed potatoes. The idea of smashing potatoes seems easier than mashing them, because the word implies that you'll want to leave a few lumps. Here are a few tricks for pulling off this satisfying, homey dish:

Invest in a potato masher if you don't already have one. An age-old tool consisting of a thick wavy wire or round cutout grid attached to a sturdy handle of plastic or wood, the potato masher is very effective. They're available in variety and kitchen stores starting at about $3.

We choose red potatoes because you don't have to peel them—and because the peel adds color and texture. Cutting the potatoes into smaller than normal pieces (about 2 inches) allows them to cook faster. Use only enough cooking water to cover the potatoes—4½ cups works for this recipe.

The next time you're tempted to serve mashed potatoes, go easy on yourself and smash them instead.

333

From Alicia:

My husband, Ron, is a meat-and-potatoes man—always has been and probably always will be. So when it's Father's Day or his birthday, it seems silly to serve him anything wimpy for dinner. Although Ron would be perfectly happy with a plain steak and baked potato, the kids and I thought that was a bit boring for his big day, so we came up with this recipe for Dad's Spicy Spuds—which is anything *but* boring. The bell peppers, chiles, onion, and spices would liven up any plain meat-and-potatoes meal. If the dad at your house can handle the heat, serve the potatoes with salsa instead of that red stuff best saved for fries.

DAD'S SPICY SPUDS

SERVES: 4 START TO FINISH: UNDER 25 MINUTES

2 tablespoons vegetable oil
4 cups diced already-baked Russet baking potatoes (see page 366), or 1 package (1 pound, 4 ounces) refrigerated diced potatoes with onion
1 large onion (for about 1 cup chopped)
½ large green bell pepper (for about ¾ cup chopped)
1 can (4 ounces) diced green chiles
2 cloves fresh garlic, minced, or 2 teaspoons bottled minced garlic
½ teaspoon chili powder
Salt and black pepper to taste
Salsa or ketchup, for serving (optional)

1. Heat the oil in an extra-deep 12-inch skillet over medium heat for 1 minute. Add the potatoes and cook, stirring occasionally. Meanwhile, peel and coarsely chop the onion, adding it to the skillet as you chop. Stem, seed, and coarsely chop the bell pepper, adding it to the skillet as you chop. Cover the skillet and cook, stirring every 2 minutes, until the potatoes begin to brown, 12 to 13 minutes.

2. Meanwhile, drain the chiles and set them aside.

3. When the potatoes are brown, uncover the pan and add the chiles and garlic. Add the chili powder and stir and toss until it is evenly distributed. Season with salt and black pepper. Remove the skillet from the heat and serve at once, with salsa if desired.

Mrs. McDaniel's Southern Potato Salad

MAKES: 1 QUART SERVES: 8 TO 10 PREP TIME: 25 MINUTES

Salt for cooking the potatoes
6 medium (1½ pounds) red-skinned potatoes
1 medium-size onion (see Notes)
½ cup mayonnaise
1½ teaspoons cider vinegar
1 teaspoon prepared mustard
½ teaspoon sugar
½ teaspoon salt, or to taste
½ teaspoon celery salt or celery seed
¼ teaspoon black pepper, or to taste
¼ cup sweet pickle relish, drained (see Notes)
1 hard-cooked egg
2 large ribs celery (for about 1 cup diced)

1. Bring 2 quarts lightly salted water to a boil in a covered 6-quart pot over high heat. While the water is heating, scrub the potatoes and cut them (unpeeled) into ½-inch pieces.

2. When the water comes to a boil, add the potatoes, cover the pot, and bring the water back to a boil. Then uncover the pot, reduce the heat to medium-high, and cook at a moderate boil until the potatoes are very tender, 13 to 15 minutes.

3. Meanwhile, peel the onion and grate it on the smallest holes of a box grater into a 2-quart or larger bowl until you have about 2 tablespoons grated onion and juice. (Reserve the remaining onion for another use.) Add the mayonnaise, vinegar, mustard, sugar, salt, celery salt, black pepper, and pickle relish. Whisk until well combined.

From Beverly:

After you taste this potato salad, you'll never even think of purchasing it at the deli again. When I tasted it for the first time nearly three decades ago, I thought it was perhaps the best on the planet. When my husband first took a bite, this is what he said: "Usually when you eat potato salad, well, you're just eating potato salad. This elevates potato salad to a whole new dimension."

The recipe comes from a seriously fine Southern cook, Janice McDaniel of North Carolina. One of the secrets to success here is to mix the dressing with the potatoes while they're still warm (but not hot); then wait until the salad cools to adjust the seasonings. (The dish mellows as it cools.) This salad just isn't the same without real mayonnaise—it's definitely worth the calories. The recipe can be doubled if you're serving a crowd.

Oven-Baked Sweet Potatoes

"Sweet potatoes frequently go cut-rate around Thanksgiving."

Sweet potatoes are a thrifty choice during most seasons of the year, but of course they're almost always cheaper in the fall and frequently go cut-rate around Thanksgiving. Stock up, because they can be stored at cool room temperature for a couple of weeks. You'll want to eat sweet potatoes often, as they are virtually fat-free and very high in vitamins A and E. Sweet potatoes have more fiber than oatmeal, yet a medium-size sweet potato has just 118 calories.

Baked sweet potatoes are wonderful topped with a pat of butter and eaten just like a baked white potato. Their special natural sweetness, however, is further enhanced by a drizzle of maple syrup and a sprinkling of cinnamon. If you want to get really fancy, dust the cooked potatoes lightly with both cinnamon and chili powder. The contrast in flavors is heavenly.

Sometimes there's a bit of confusion between sweet potatoes and yams. In the United States, the two terms usually refer to the same thing. A true yam is generally imported from the Caribbean, has white flesh instead of orange, and tastes starchy instead of sweet. In the United States, the Department of Agriculture requires that the label "yam" be accompanied by "sweet potato" if the flesh is orange and sweet.

Sweet potatoes are a cinch to bake, in an oven preheated to 375°F. First, wash and pat them dry with paper towels. Prick them in several places with a fork. Line a baking sheet with aluminum foil and place the potatoes on the foil. This will help avoid any of the potatoes' sticky sweet juice burning on the pan. Bake until they are tender, about 45 minutes. (Test for doneness by piercing them with a fork or a small paring knife. The potatoes are done when the center is tender.) Sometimes only very large sweet potatoes are available. In that case, 1 potato will serve two people and will take 1 to 1¼ hours to bake. Sweet potatoes can also be baked in the microwave. Just prick them and bake one at a time (to avoid spotty cooking) until tender. A medium-size sweet potato will take 5 to 8 minutes.

4. When the potatoes are tender, drain them well in a colander and let them cool until they are warm, not hot. (You can rinse them with cool water to speed this process.) Add the well-drained potatoes to the bowl and stir until they are coated with the mayonnaise mixture.

5. Peel and finely chop the egg and add it to the bowl. Dice the celery and add it to the bowl. Stir to mix well. Refrigerate, covered, until ready to serve, up to 12 hours.

6. Just before serving, taste the salad and add more salt and pepper, if desired.

NOTES: Using a slightly larger than necessary onion makes the grating process easier and helps avoid scraping your knuckles.
■ Sweet pickle relish is sometimes called "sweet salad cubes." If you can't find it, substitute any sweet pickles, drained and chopped.

Inventing Your Own Rice Pilaf Recipe

The best thing about rice pilafs is that they are so full of flavor, they don't need any gravy. That means you can serve rice pilaf as a side dish even when you aren't serving a turkey or a roast.

Rice pilaf recipes are plentiful (see pages 303, 339, and 340), but you don't have to have a set recipe. Experimenting with different combinations is easy and fun, and they are a great way to use up bits and pieces you find in the fridge.

The flavor possibilities are practically endless. Try cooking the rice in chicken stock or beef broth—or even tomato juice—instead of plain water. Then add some sautéed onions or garlic. Or get fancy one night and throw in some chunky fruit, such as pineapple or mango, just before serving. A few toasted nuts on top add the perfect crunch.

While you're getting the hang of creating your own pilaf recipes, it helps to think in terms of international cuisines. An Italian pilaf might have diced tomatoes, lots of garlic, a teaspoon of dried Italian seasoning or basil, and maybe even sliced olives. An Asian pilaf would be nice with a couple of tablespoons of soy sauce, a teaspoon of dark sesame oil, and some grated ginger (either bottled or fresh). If you have any leftover asparagus spears or a few mushrooms, by all means cut them up and throw them in, too.

The only thing you have to remember is to be sure that the combination of liquids you choose adds up to the amount of water recommended in the package directions for cooking the rice. (The rule of thumb for long-grain rice is twice as much liquid as rice.)

When you invent your own rice pilafs, they may never turn out exactly the same way twice. And since you'll never tire of them, that's a definite plus.

"The flavor possibilities are practically endless."

JAMAICAN RICE PILAF

SERVES: 4 GENEROUSLY START TO FINISH: UNDER 25 MINUTES

3 chicken bouillon cubes
1 tablespoon dehydrated
   minced onion
2 teaspoons Worcestershire sauce
¼ teaspoon ground allspice or
   ground cinnamon
1 cup long-grain rice
½ cup frozen green peas

This pilaf relies on a flavorful combination of chicken bouillon and allspice. Allspice is a typical Jamaican ingredient, but you could substitute ground cinnamon. Adding the peas at the last minute ensures that they remain a lovely brilliant green; the heat from the rice is sufficient to warm them through.

1. Pour 2 cups water into a 2-quart saucepan and place it over high heat. Add the bouillon cubes, dehydrated onion, Worcestershire sauce, and allspice. Bring the mixture to a boil. Add the rice, stir, cover the pan, and reduce the heat to low. Simmer until the rice is tender, about 20 minutes.

2. While the rice cooks, pour the frozen peas into a colander and rinse them with cool water to remove any ice crystals. Set the peas aside to drain.

3. Remove the pan from the heat and stir the rice well. Stir in the green peas. Re-cover the pan and let it stand until the peas have warmed through, 1 to 2 minutes. Serve at once.

When the summer bounty hits its peak, and both corn and tomatoes hit their lowest prices of the year, this is a perfect dish. The acid from the tomatoes plays off the sweet milky corn and results in a performance that ought to require admission tickets. Forget plain rice when you need a side dish for any kind of meat or seafood and serve our Summer Corn Pilaf instead.

SUMMER CORN PILAF

SERVES: 4 START TO FINISH: UNDER 25 MINUTES

1 can (14 ounces) fat-free chicken broth, or 2 cups homemade chicken stock (see page 10)
2 cloves fresh garlic, minced, or 2 teaspoons bottled minced garlic
1 cup long-grain rice
4 ears fresh corn (for about 2½ cups kernels)
1 large ripe tomato (for about 1 cup chopped)
3 scallions (for ¼ cup chopped)
Salt and black pepper to taste

SUPER-CHEAP!

1. Pour the broth and ½ cup water into a 2-quart or larger saucepan and place it over high heat. (If you are using 2 cups homemade chicken stock, omit the water.) Add the garlic to the broth. When the broth comes to a boil, add the rice, stir, cover the pot, and reduce the heat to low. Simmer until the rice is tender, about 20 minutes.

2. While the rice cooks, fill a 4½-quart or larger pot with about 1½ quarts water—enough to fill it about one third of the way. Place it over high heat, cover, and bring to a boil. While the water is heating, shuck the corn and remove the silks.

3. When the water comes to a boil, add the corn, cover the pot, and bring it back to a boil. Cook the corn at a rolling boil until the kernels are just tender, 4 to 5 minutes. Remove the corn from the pot and place it in a colander in the sink. Run cold water over the corn until it is cool enough to handle.

4. Carefully slice the kernels from the corncobs into a 2-quart or larger serving dish. Scrape the cobs with the back of the knife to remove any remaining kernels and milk; add them to the dish. Core the tomato and cut it into roughly ¼-inch dice. Add the tomato to the dish. Chop the scallions, including enough of the tender green tops to make ¼ cup. Add them to the dish. Toss to mix well, then pour the hot rice into the serving dish. Toss it with the corn mixture. Season with salt and black pepper and serve.

Saving to Share

We'd expect the reasons for saving money on food to be different for everyone. One of the many reasons we practice thrift at the supermarket and in the kitchen is that it leaves a little more money at the end of the month to help out somebody who otherwise wouldn't have anything to eat at all. We don't mean to get on a soapbox, but the fact is, it really bothers both of us to throw away food simply as a result of poor planning or carelessness. At a time when over 12 percent of Americans live in poverty (a figure that's been growing annually), wasting food simply isn't right.

Perhaps it's because our careers center on food that we are so acutely aware that not everyone has as much to eat as we do. When the refrigerator is stuffed beyond capacity because we're testing recipes, we feel a responsibility to be good stewards of this abundance. (We often take extra food to our churches to help with various programs that feed the hungry and homeless or to neighbors who have lost their jobs.)

We aren't the only food professionals who feel this way. That's how Share Our Strength's annual benefits for the hungry got started. Every spring, chefs, restaurateurs, and others in the culinary industry donate their products, time and talents at more than 100 Taste of the Nation fund-raising events throughout the United States and Canada. The events have raised over $54 million since 1988, supporting 450 groups working to end hunger and poverty. (Visit the website www.tasteofthenation.org for more information and a schedule of events.) We also have lots of "foodie" friends who've gotten involved in food banks, soup kitchens, and programs to feed orphans in Africa, Haiti, and Mexico. Their experiences, as well as our own, have made us even more determined to change our wasteful ways.

We're not kidding ourselves about our minimal efforts to conserve food and make what are, in the grand scheme, nominal contributions to fight hunger. But if a lot of people participate even minimally, the combined efforts *will* make a difference.

"When the refrigerator is stuffed, we feel a responsibility to be good stewards of this abundance."

If you're like us, there's often a half-empty jar of salsa in the refrigerator. Time to make a Mexican rice pilaf. If you also happen to have any Cheddar or Mexican-blend cheese in the fridge, a sprinkling on top is great.

RIO GRANDE RICE

SERVES: 4 START TO FINISH: UNDER 25 MINUTES

2 chicken bouillon cubes
1 tablespoon dehydrated minced onion
½ cup mild or hot salsa
½ cup frozen yellow corn kernels
1 can (2½ ounces) sliced black olives (optional)
1 clove fresh garlic, minced, or 1 teaspoon
 bottled minced garlic
1 cup long-grain rice

1. Pour 2 cups water into a 2-quart saucepan and place it over high heat. Add the bouillon cubes, dehydrated onion, salsa, corn, olives (if using), and garlic. Bring the mixture to a boil.

2. Add the rice, stir, cover the pan, and reduce the heat to low. Simmer until the rice is tender, about 20 minutes. Remove the pan from the heat and fluff the rice with a fork, stirring to mix the ingredients. Serve at once.

STEWED ZUCCHINI WITH TOMATOES AND PARMESAN

SERVES: 6 START TO FINISH: UNDER 25 MINUTES

2 teaspoons olive oil

1 medium-size onion (for about ¾ cup chopped)

3 cloves fresh garlic, minced, or 1 tablespoon bottled minced garlic

4 medium-size (about 1½ pounds) zucchini

1 can (14½ ounces) diced tomatoes

2 teaspoons dried Italian seasoning

Salt and black pepper to taste

¾ cup shredded regular or part-skim mozzarella cheese (see Note)

¼ cup shredded or grated Parmesan cheese (see Note)

1. Heat the oil in a 2-quart saucepan over medium heat. While the oil is heating, peel and coarsely chop the onion, adding it to the pan as you chop. Peel and mince the garlic, if using fresh, and add it to the pan. Cook, stirring occasionally, while you cut the zucchini into ½-inch-thick rounds, adding them to the pan as you cut. Add the tomatoes with their juice and stir in the Italian seasoning. Bring the mixture to a boil, then reduce the heat to medium-low and cover the pan. Cook, stirring occasionally, at a moderate boil until the zucchini is crisp-tender, 10 to 13 minutes.

2. Remove the pan from the heat and season with salt and black pepper. Sprinkle the cheeses evenly over the mixture, cover the pan, and let it stand until the cheese melts, about 2 minutes. To serve, spoon the vegetables with some of the juice into small bowls.

NOTE: You can use a combination of cheeses, such as Parmesan, Cheddar, and mozzarella, to make the full cup.

We love the jokes about zucchini crawling out of the garden under their own power and being left for dead on unsuspecting neighbors' doorsteps. If it's free food, we say bring it on! When you get tired of zucchini bread, zucchini casseroles, zucchini fritters, and zucchini plain, try this, our favorite zucchini side dish. We could eat it every day for a week straight—and have many times, as a matter of fact.

CHAPTER EIGHT

BUDGET-MINDED BATCH COOKING

When we eat in restaurants, it's often not because we've planned a special outing or celebration; we find ourselves sitting in a booth simply because our busy schedules have forced us to. We forgot to plan a menu; we didn't get around to shopping; we were just too tired to face the kitchen.

If we're going to avoid expensive restaurant meals and take-out, we need strategies for getting dinner on the table. Some people deal with the problem by spending their entire Saturday cooking for the week ahead. But even if we wanted to spend all those precious weekend hours in the kitchen, let's be honest: Between soccer schedules, laundry piles, overgrown lawns, and grocery shopping, it's never going to happen. Our solution is simple: Compromise and make choices.

The compromise part of our solution brings us to Budget-Minded Batch Cooking. The concept is simple: Instead of trying to cook entire meals ahead, you just double up on some basic building blocks that will speed you on your way in the future. For example, when you're going to the trouble of browning ground beef and onions to make spaghetti sauce, you simply brown several pounds at one time. (Browning a lot of beef at once takes about the same amount of time, and you only have to wash the skillet once!) Then, before adding any spices to the meat, you refrigerate or freeze the extra portions to use later. That extra already-cooked ground beef is like gold in the bank—which brings us to the choices part of our solution. With just a few additional ingredients, your already-cooked beef can become any one of a host of different meals, such as Chow-Down Chili, Beefed-up Chinese Burritos, and a Tex-Mex-inspired shepherd's pie. And any of these dinners can find their way to the table in a matter of minutes.

The same concept works with chicken, and with this versatile bird you have even more options. You can use our Perfect Poached Chicken as the basis for an array of speedy recipes, including Greek Chicken over Orzo, Fiery Chicken with Vegetables, and Quickie Cacciatore. But wait! You could also use either Poached Chicken Thighs or Chunky Seasoned Chicken. (Each recipe lists the specific how-tos.) And if you're lighting up the grill for chicken anyway, throw on a big batch and cook extras for later. Then, with a ready supply of Great Grilled Chicken Breasts on hand, you can turn out sophisticated meals like Fall Chicken Salad or Chicken and Onion Pizza on days when you're too rushed to grill.

Another bonus for batch cooking is this: Cooking a lot of meat at one time dovetails nicely with the bonanza of buying a large quantity of something when it's on sale. And because supermarkets are notorious for offering the best prices on meat in giant "family-size" packages, you might as well go ahead and cook those multiple pounds all at once. The only real tricks involved in batch cooking are to stock a good supply of freezer-weight plastic bags (or other storage containers) and to keep a list of what's in the refrigerator and freezer so you don't forget to use those building blocks.

As we started to get the hang of batch cooking, it didn't take long to figure out that meat isn't the only food that

"Meat in the freezer that's already cooked is like gold in the bank."

benefits from the concept. First we tried baking a batch of potatoes all at once, and the result was that after a dinner featuring Amazing Baked Potatoes or Super Stuffed Potatoes, we were ready for another potato dish a couple of days later—Loaded Baked Potato Soup, August Vichyssoise, Chili in Spud Bowls, and side dishes like Dad's Spicy Spuds and Old-Fashioned Twice-Baked Potatoes. Before long we branched out to sauces. Thai-Style Peanut Sauce and Spinach Parsley Pesto pack a flavor punch so powerful that entire meals can be transformed with a little sauce here and there. Winter Minestrone anyone? Feel like a little Thai Salad with Pork? All it takes is a blender and our amazing recipes.

All in all, batch cooking gives coping with dinnertime a new dimension. And if you're like us, you need all the strategies you can get.

BASIC BEEF

MAKES: ABOUT 6 CUPS **PREP TIME:** 15 MINUTES

2 pounds ground beef
2 large onions (for about 2 cups chopped)
3 cloves fresh garlic, minced, or 1 tablespoon
    bottled minced garlic
1 tablespoon Worcestershire sauce

1. Place the beef in an extra-deep 12-inch skillet over medium heat. Begin browning the beef, stirring often to break up the meat. Meanwhile, peel and coarsely chop the onions, adding them to the skillet as you chop. Cook, stirring often, until all the meat is crumbled and cooked through, 8 to 12 minutes. Drain any accumulated fat from the skillet.

2. Add the garlic and Worcestershire sauce to the skillet and stir until well blended, 30 seconds.

3. Remove the skillet from the heat and allow the beef to cool enough to be refrigerated or frozen for use in future recipes.

STORAGE NOTES:

Basic Beef can be refrigerated for up to 3 days or frozen for 2 to 3 months. Refrigerate or freeze the beef in 1-cup portions in microwave-safe containers. To defrost, remove the lid and microwave on the defrost setting according to the oven manufacturer's instructions. Or defrost in the refrigerator overnight.

USING BASIC BEEF:

You can use Basic Beef in most of the recipes in this book that call for ground beef. (Individual recipes give substitution notes.) Some of them are:

- Hearty Homemade Beef and Vegetable Soup (page 4)
- Chow-Down Chili (page 48)
- Lynne's Mom's Mince (page 119)
- Salsa-Cheese Beef and Rice (page 124)

Planning ahead is not a luxury for every cook or every situation. We don't always know where we'll be at 6 o'clock or how many family members will actually make it to the table. What we need is a secret weapon—something that's flexible yet also helps get dinner on the table in a flash. For us, one such secret weapon is a big batch of Basic Beef. It saves money and time.

We find that, in general, the "family-size" packages of ground beef command a better price per pound. And sometimes, maybe only once every couple of months, ground beef goes on sale and you can buy a lot to take advantage of the rock-bottom price. But what to do with so much beef when you get it home? Brown it up! (If you have more than 2 pounds of ground beef, cook it in batches to prevent overcrowding your pan.)

Stash the already-cooked beef in your freezer, and dinner is one step closer. You may never buy ground beef at full price again!

BIG BEEF ROAST

SLOW COOKER METHOD

MAKES: ABOUT 8 CUPS PREP TIME: 5 MINUTES

You'll love having cooked roast beef on hand to use on short notice. We like the slow-cooker method for its fuss-free convenience, but we have provided the oven-roasting instructions as well. Cooking the beef to 170°F ensures that the meat will shred easily. When cooked in the slow cooker, it tends to fall apart almost on its own.

The average yield of shredded beef for a 4½-pound roast is 8 cups, so there's plenty for several meals down the road.

1 beef chuck roast (4 to 5 pounds), defrosted if frozen
1 teaspoon onion powder
1 teaspoon garlic powder
½ teaspoon salt
¼ teaspoon black pepper
1 can (14 ounces) fat-free beef broth
1 large onion (for about 1 cup sliced)

1. Trim off and discard any excess fat from the roast and place it in a 5-quart or larger slow cooker. Sprinkle the onion powder, garlic powder, salt, and black pepper over the roast and press the seasonings into the roast with your fingers. Pour the broth *around* the roast, taking care not to pour it over the meat. Peel and thinly slice the onion. Separate the slices into rings and add them to the pot. Cover the slow cooker and cook on low until the beef is fork-tender, 8 to 10 hours.

2. Turn off the slow cooker but leave the beef in the pot. Using two forks, carefully tear the beef into the shreds. Stir the shredded beef well to mix it with the liquid in the pot. The cooled beef can be refrigerated or frozen for use in future recipes.

CONVENTIONAL OVEN METHOD

MAKES: ABOUT 8 CUPS   PREP TIME: 5 MINUTES

1. Preheat the oven to 350°F.

2. Trim any excess fat from the roast and place it in a large (15- x 13- x 4-inch) roasting pan. Sprinkle the onion powder, garlic powder, salt, and black pepper over the roast, pressing the seasonings into the roast with your fingers. Pour the broth *around* the roast, taking care not to pour it over the meat. Peel and thinly slice the onion. Separate the slices into rings and add them to the pan.

3. Cover the pan with aluminum foil and bake until an instant-read meat thermometer registers 170°F, 2½ to 3 hours. Baste the meat several times during the cooking time, if desired. Make sure to re-cover the pan with the foil after basting.

4. Transfer the beef to a plate or shallow bowl. Using two forks, carefully tear the beef into shreds. Return it to the pot and stir well to mix it with the liquid in the pot. The cooled beef can be refrigerated or frozen for use in future recipes.

STORAGE NOTES:

The shredded beef mixture can be refrigerated for up to 3 days or frozen for 2 to 3 months. Refrigerate or freeze the beef (and any cooking liquid) in 1-cup portions in microwave-safe containers. To defrost, remove the container lid and microwave on the defrost setting according to the oven manufacturer's instructions. Or defrost in the refrigerator overnight.

USING BIG BEEF ROAST:

Here are some recipes that use Big Beef Roast:

- My Beef and Barley Soup (page 7)
- Beef Stew à la Guatemala (page 45)
- Barbecue Beef on a Bun (page 239)

MoneySaver

Sometimes the expiration date on a package of meat can mean big savings. Often, a day before the date (and sometimes two days before), the supermarket will mark the meat "reduced for quick sale." (Some stores use dollar-off coupons on the package to accomplish the same purpose without the stigma.) Just because the meat is about to expire doesn't mean it's gone bad. As long as you cook or freeze the meat by the expiration date, it's perfectly good. And cheap.

Keeping Tabs on Your Grocery Inventory

From Beverly:

Before I became our family's grocery inventory manager, I used to wonder: If I got my act together and used up all the food in the pantry, freezer, and refrigerator, how long would it take before I was forced to go spend money at the supermarket? I discovered that, except for milk and lettuce, we didn't need to shop for several weeks!

When it comes to groceries, the typical home operates on some of the same principles as a business, and an inventory manager is definitely called for. The food stored on the shelves represents tangible assets. And if those assets stay on the shelf too long, that's money that could have been invested somewhere else.

But like many other aspects of budget cooking, the issue of grocery inventory requires trade-offs and compromise. If your pantry is stocked with every flavor of canned tomatoes and broth, your freezer crammed with meats and breads, your refrigerator resplendent with a myriad of vegetables and condiments, it means you can decide at the drop of a hat to make practically any recipe that piques your taste buds. A bigger stockpile means more choices.

On the other hand, that stockpile is expensive to maintain. Cans of tomatoes cost roughly a dollar each, and let's say you always keep a dozen cans on hand, replacing each and every can as you use it. Under this scenario, you'll never run out of tomatoes, and your pantry carries a liability of $11. (All but one can falls into the liability category.) It's as if that $11 is just sitting in your pantry for no reason. Multiply that times the cans of broth, beans, and so forth, and suddenly you're talking about a significant amount of money sitting on those shelves.

To my way of thinking, the biggest inventory decision for the budget-conscious cook is the question of time in storage. Any package or can of food that remains uneaten for longer than two months changes from an asset into a liability. The longer the food sits there, the less likely it is to be consumed—chances increase that you'll simply forget about an item or it will pass its expiration date. (Indeed, up to 12 percent of all food items purchased are never used, according to a recent survey by a University of Illinois researcher.) And the longer the food goes uneaten, the more alternatives you would have had for the money you spent on that abandoned food.

Here are some tips for becoming a more efficient inventory manager and thus saving money:

- Organize your pantry and freezer so like items are grouped together. That way you can see at a glance how many cans of tomatoes you have (and eliminate the can hiding in the back behind the taller can).

- Do a food purge. Go through the pantry and freezer and take note of all the food that's been sitting a long time. Make a point to consume it, donate it to a food pantry, or pitch it if it's past its use-by date. And while you're at it, don't forget the condiments in the refrigerator.

- Plan to do a major food purge again in three months, and every three months after that. Write it on your calendar.

- The contents of the freezer can be most difficult to keep track of, particularly if you have a large chest freezer. Two things help: Invest in a roll of freezer tape, and label and date each item that goes in. Keep a list taped to the freezer door, and attach a pen with a string. Write down each item as it goes in. (Group the list by shelf.) Cross off each item as it comes out. A quick glance at the list helps with menu planning and is better than shivering while you rifle through the contents.

- Speaking of menu planning, just do it. Following weekly menus means you buy only what you need. (For more details, see page 74.)

"A stockpile that's too big is expensive to maintain."

From Beverly:

My son Sam ran in from school several years ago shouting "Hooray" and waving a piece of paper. This recipe would end his troubles—he was sure of it. Sam was the only person he knew who didn't adore Mexican food. Now was the time to conquer his dislike of the taco.

"My Spanish teacher says she's given this recipe out in class for a hundred years, and no student has never *not* liked it," Sam said that fateful day. "Do you think I could try it tonight?"

A quick glance at the recipe, and no problem-o—we'd have a burrito-eating bandito by sundown. Not wanting to jinx the spell, I dared not change a single ingredient. (However, I did transform the recipe into a skillet-only affair.)

Sam is pleased to report that he finally likes Mexican food—"so long as it's the stuff from Spanish class." Fortunately, this filling is perfect for many Mexican meals, everything from a topping for pasta to soft tacos, nachos, and taco salad.

FLEXIBLE MEXICAN FILLING

MAKES: ABOUT 5 CUPS PREP TIME: 20 MINUTES

1 pound ground beef
1 large onion (for about 1 cup chopped)
½ package (2 tablespoons) taco seasoning
1 can (10¾ ounces) condensed tomato soup
2 cups shredded Cheddar or Mexican-blend cheese
1 cup (8 ounces) sour cream

1. Place the beef in an extra-deep 12-inch skillet over medium heat. Begin browning the beef, stirring often to break up the meat. Meanwhile, peel and coarsely chop the onion, adding it to the skillet as you chop. Cook, stirring often, until all the meat is crumbled and cooked thp7.5am. Serve at once or cool and store for future use.

STORAGE NOTES:

Flexible Mexican Filling can be refrigerated for up to 2 days or frozen for 2 to 3 months. Refrigerate or freeze the filling in 1-cup portions in microwave-safe containers. To defrost, remove the container lid and microwave on the defrost setting according to the oven manufacturer's instructions. Or defrost the filling in the refrigerator overnight.

USING FLEXIBLE MEXICAN FILLING:

Use Flexible Mexican Filling in these recipes:

- Enchanting Enchiladas (page 64)
- Taco Twists (page 210)
- Make-Your-Own Soft Tacos (page 268)
- Beef and Cheese Quesadillas (page 269)
- Fiesta Dinner Nachos (page 270)
- Easiest Taco Salad (page 285)

MARVELOUS MEATBALLS

MAKES: 48 MEATBALLS   PREP TIME: 15 MINUTES

Cooking oil spray
2 pounds ground beef
1 cup purchased or homemade dry
    bread crumbs (see page 235)
2 large eggs
⅓ cup whole, low-fat, or skim milk
1 teaspoon onion powder
1 teaspoon dried basil
1 teaspoon salt
½ teaspoon black pepper

1. Preheat the oven to 375°F. Line the bottom of a broiler pan with aluminum foil for easier cleanup and spray the broiler pan rack with cooking oil spray.

2. Place the beef in a 2-quart or larger bowl. Add the bread crumbs, eggs, milk, onion powder, basil, salt, and black pepper. Mix well with a spoon or with your hands.

3. Using a cookie dough scoop, form 48 meatballs, giving each one a quick roll with your hands to make it smooth and then placing it on the broiler pan rack. (Or use heaping tablespoons of the meat mixture to form the meatballs with your hands; see Note.)

4. Bake the meatballs until they are brown and cooked through, 35 to 40 minutes. Serve at once or cool and store for future use.

NOTE: The best way to mix the meat mixture quickly is to use your hands, and it's difficult to get a well-formed meatball without at least a quick roll with the hands. When you have finished handling the raw meat, wash your hands well and clean any affected kitchen surfaces.

There's nothing ordinary about homemade meatballs, and they're a great comfort food. Until we started experimenting a few years ago, we never realized how easy meatballs are to make, going together with just 15 minutes of prep. To make shaping them even easier, use a cookie-dough scoop (like an ice-cream scoop with a smaller bowl). This handy gadget is sold at department stores, cookware shops, and even in some supermarkets. Once you taste these mini-marvels, you'll never want to be without them. Keep a stash in the freezer and you can satisfy your family's cravings at the spur of the moment.

STORAGE NOTES:

The meatballs can be refrigerated for up to 2 days or frozen for 2 to 3 months. Refrigerate or freeze them (20 to 24 meatballs per portion) in microwave-safe containers. To defrost, remove the container lid and microwave on the defrost setting according to the oven manufacturer's instructions. Or defrost in the refrigerator overnight.

USING MARVELOUS MEATBALLS:

Use Marvelous Meatballs in these recipes:

- Mindless Meatball Minestrone (page 8)
- Speedy Meatball Stew (page 46)
- Hawaiian Meatballs (page 128)
- Sam's Swedish Meatballs (page 211)
- The Kids' Favorite Meatball Hoagies (page 241)

Penny Wise and Pound Foolish: Time vs. Cost Savings

There are only so many hours in a day, and the decision about how to spend them is a daily dilemma. If saving money and saving time are both priorities in your life, welcome to the world of trade-offs!

The amount of money we can save on food will likely vary according to where we live, the nature of our jobs, and our commitment to leisure activities.

The smartest way to strike the balance between saving money and spending time is this: Pick the money-saving effort that will yield the most savings in the least time. Or, put another way, use the money-saving tricks that give back the most actual dollars per hour spent.

For example, if your supermarket doubles coupons so that a 50-cent coupon is worth a dollar, the time you spend clipping and organizing coupons might be worth more than the same amount of time spent driving around to take advantage of sale prices.

The other crucial factor in deciding how much time to spend on cost-saving techniques is whether or not you are employed and, if you are, how flexible your earning power is. It's important to calculate how much your time is worth so you can decide whether the block of time you spent saving money on food could have been worth more in actual dollars if you'd spent the same number of hours in gainful employment. For example, if your job includes pay for overtime, one extra hour spent on the job could be worth more money than three hours spent clipping coupons.

And then there's leisure time. If you give up an hour of tennis or television and instead go to the pick-your-own farm, you can perhaps save $5 or so on fresh produce. But is the trade-off worth it? If you're the type of person who thinks bargain-hunting is a sport, it probably is. Only you can decide.

"Don't forget to calculate how much your time is worth."

When we think of pot roast, we don't typically think of pork. But the pot roast treatment turns an economical cut of pork into scrumptious fare that's sure to warm the tummy on a frosty night. Better yet, this recipe makes enough pork for a delicious second-time-around meal. The trick to keeping pork moist is to cook the roast slowly in a pleasing blend of juices, and a slow cooker is perfect for this job. (If you don't have a slow cooker, you can also make it on top of the stove.) The combination of orange juice, lime juice, and white wine flavors the pork way beyond the ordinary.

Choosing a lean boneless roast, such as pork loin roast, will mean less waste, so it's actually more economical although the per-pound price might be higher than for a fatty, bone-in roast. Most boneless pork roasts weigh between 3 and 3½ pounds. A 3-pound roast yields about 2 pounds of cooked meat. If you serve half of the roast for dinner the night it's cooked, you'll have enough leftovers to make 2½ cups of cubes,

SAVORY PORK POT ROAST

SLOW COOKER METHOD

MAKES: 2 POUNDS ROAST PORK (5 CUPS CHUNKS), PLUS 3 CUPS BROTH
PREP TIME: 15 MINUTES

1 boneless pork loin roast (3 to 3½ pounds)
4 medium-size potatoes (see Notes)
2 medium-size onions
2 medium-size ribs celery
3 medium-size carrots, or 1 cup (about 12) baby carrots
1 cup orange juice
½ cup dry white wine or apple juice
¼ cup ketchup
Juice of 1 lime (see Notes)
2 tablespoons Worcestershire sauce
3 cloves fresh garlic, minced, or 1 tablespoon bottled minced garlic
1 teaspoon salt

1. Trim off and discard any excess fat from the roast and place it in a 5-quart or larger slow cooker. Peel and quarter the potatoes and add them, making sure they are at the bottom of the pot. Peel the onions and cut them in half. Cut each half into crescent-shaped slices about ½ inch thick. Put the onions in the pot. Cut the celery and carrots into 1-inch-long pieces. (If using baby carrots, there's no need to cut.) Add them to the pot.

2. In a 1-quart container or glass measure, whisk together the orange juice, wine, ketchup, lime juice, Worcestershire sauce, garlic, and salt. Pour the mixture over the meat and vegetables. Cover the slow cooker and cook on low until the roast and vegetables are very tender, 8 to 10 hours.

3. Turn off the slow cooker and remove the roast. Cut the roast in half and slice one half for serving with the vegetables. Allow the remaining half to cool until you can handle it safely, then cut it into bite-size chunks for future use.

STOVETOP METHOD

MAKES: 2 POUNDS ROAST PORK (5 CUPS CHUNKS), PLUS 3 CUPS BROTH
PREP TIME: 20 MINUTES

1. Heat 1 tablespoon vegetable oil in a 4½-quart Dutch oven or heavy pot over medium heat. Add the roast and brown on both sides, about 3 minutes per side.

2. Meanwhile, whisk the orange juice, wine, ketchup, lime juice, Worcestershire sauce, garlic, and salt together in a medium-size bowl.

3. Pour the juice mixture over the browned roast. Slice and add the onions, pushing them toward the bottom of the pot, and bring the mixture to a boil. Then reduce the heat to low and simmer, covered, for 1½ hours.

4. Cut up and add the potatoes, carrots, and celery. Cover and simmer until an instant-read meat thermometer inserted in the roast registers 170°F and the roast is very tender, about 1 hour more.

5. Remove the roast from the pot and cut it in half. Slice one half for serving with the vegetables. Allow the remaining half to cool until you can handle it safely, then cut it into bite-size chunks for future use.

NOTES: To avoid the chore of peeling the potatoes, use thin-skinned red potatoes and leave the tasty skin intact.

■ When buying limes that you are going to use right away, choose firm, unblemished fruit that has turned slightly yellow. The yellow color indicates that the fruit is ripe and will yield more juice than a dark green lime.

enough for two future recipes. The slight variations in the amount of cooked meat you wind up with won't matter for using leftovers in future recipes, as they're very flexible. Be sure to save the delicious cooking broth to make Super-Saver Tortilla Soup (page 16).

STORAGE NOTES:

The pork chunks can be refrigerated for up to 2 days or frozen for 2 to 3 months. Refrigerate or freeze the chunks in 1¼-cup portions in microwave-safe containers. The broth can be refrigerated in a microwave-safe container for up to 3 days or frozen for up to 1 month. To defrost both the pork and broth, remove the container lid and microwave on the defrost setting according to the oven manufacturer's instructions. Or defrost the frozen pork and broth in the refrigerator overnight.

USING SAVORY PORK POT ROAST:

Here are some recipes for using Savory Pork Pot Roast:

- Super-Saver Tortilla Soup (page 16; the stovetop method will not yield the full 3 cups of broth, but the broth will be more concentrated, so just add enough water to equal 3 cups liquid before making the soup.)
- Calle Ocho Cuban Hash (page 132)
- Savory Pork with Mexican Flavors (page 133)
- "Twice-Cooked" Pork Stir-Fry (page 134)

CHUNKY SEASONED CHICKEN

MAKES: 5½ TO 6 CUPS CHUNKS PREP TIME: 20 MINUTES

4 teaspoons vegetable oil

2 large onions (for about 2 cups chopped)

2¼ to 2½ pounds skinless, boneless chicken breast halves

3 cloves fresh garlic, minced, or 1 tablespoon bottled minced garlic

1 tablespoon Worcestershire sauce

From Alicia:

When I pick up skinless, boneless chicken breasts on sale, I know I'll be cooking Chunky Seasoned Chicken in triple batches when I get home. Having my private stash of seasoned chicken waiting in the freezer means I'm minutes away from dinner on even the most hurried nights. Not only have I made use of the

1. Pour the oil into an extra-deep 12-inch skillet, and place it over medium heat. Peel and coarsely chop the onions, adding them to the skillet as you chop. Cook, stirring occasionally, while you cut the chicken into roughly ½-inch cubes.

2. When all of the chicken is cut, add it to the skillet and cook, stirring constantly, until the chicken is no longer pink in the center, 7 to 9 minutes.

3. Add the garlic and Worcestershire sauce to the skillet and stir until well blended, about 30 seconds. Remove the skillet from the heat and allow the chicken to cool enough to be refrigerated or frozen for future use.

STORAGE NOTES:

The chicken and onions can be refrigerated for up to 2 days or frozen for 2 to 3 months. Refrigerate or freeze the mixture in 1- or 2-cup portions in microwave-safe containers. To defrost, remove the container lid and microwave on the defrost setting according to the oven manufacturer's instructions. Or defrost in the refrigerator overnight.

USING CHUNKY SEASONED CHICKEN:

You can use Chunky Seasoned Chicken in most of the recipes in this book that call for chicken. (Individual recipes give substitution notes.) Some of them are:

- Simple Chicken Stew (page 49)
- "Barbecued" Chicken and Black Bean Burritos (page 98)
- Island Chicken (page 152)
- Chicken and Green Bean "Casserole" (page 156)
- Curried Chicken with Spinach and Tomatoes (page 160)
- Chicken and Broccoli Lo Mein (page 194)
- Corkscrews with Chicken and Zucchini (page 202)

big savings at the store, I also don't have to wait for chicken to cook when I'm throwing together a soup, stew, skillet, or pasta dish.

The following recipe is easily doubled or tripled for those times when you find a really great price on chicken breasts.

When you're heating up the grill, why not cook more than you need for just dinner tonight? That's what we often do with these basic chicken breasts, and we use the bounty later in everything from soups, stews, and salads to skillet meals and pizzas. You can easily double this recipe (if your grill has the capacity) when skinless, boneless chicken breasts go on sale.

GREAT GRILLED CHICKEN BREASTS

MAKES: 8 BREAST HALVES (12 CUPS CHUNKS)
PREP TIME: 5 MINUTES

8 skinless, boneless chicken breast halves
   (about 3½ pounds; see Note)
¼ cup vegetable oil
2 teaspoons garlic powder
2 teaspoons onion powder
1 teaspoon salt
½ teaspoon black pepper

1. Place the chicken breast halves in a 2-gallon zipper-top plastic bag.

2. Combine the remaining ingredients in a small mixing bowl and whisk to mix well. Pour the mixture into the plastic bag, seal it tightly, and shake to coat the chicken well. Refrigerate the bag, positioned so that the breasts are in a single layer, for 15 minutes or up to 8 hours.

3. When you are ready to cook the chicken breasts, turn a gas grill to medium-high.

4. Place the chicken breasts on the hot grill, close the lid, and grill until lightly browned, 6 to 7 minutes. Turn the chicken over, re-cover the grill, and grill until the breasts are cooked through, 5 to 7 minutes more. Serve at once or allow the chicken to cool until you can handle it safely, then cut it into bite-size chunks for future use.

NOTE: We tested this recipe with breast halves that weighed about 7 ounces each. Smaller pieces will cook faster, while larger ones will take longer.

FOR AN INDOOR GRILL:

We love our closed (Foreman-style) countertop grill for indoor grilling. Most appliances of this sort are not big enough to handle 8 chicken breast halves, though. If you are using an indoor grill, cook the chicken in batches. Preheat the grill according to the manufacturer's instructions. After preparing the chicken according to the recipe, place the breasts (with space between the pieces) on the hot grill. Close the grill and cook until the chicken is no longer pink in the center, 10 to 12 minutes. Serve at once or cool for future use.

STORAGE NOTES:

The chicken chunks can be refrigerated for up to 2 days or frozen for 2 to 3 months. Refrigerate or freeze the chicken in 1-cup portions in microwave-safe containers. To defrost, remove the container lid and microwave on the defrost setting according to the oven manufacturer's instructions. Or defrost frozen chicken chunks in the refrigerator overnight.

USING GREAT GRILLED CHICKEN BREASTS:

You can use Great Grilled Chicken Breasts in many of the recipes in this book that call for chicken. (Individual recipes give substitution notes.) Some of them are:

- Spinach Pesto Pasta with Chicken (page 183)
- Chicken and Onion Pizza (page 263)
- Sweet and Savory Chicken Salad (page 275)
- Fall Chicken Salad (page 276)

If you can boil water, you can poach chicken. The tricky part is to have a little faith in the method, because it does sound too easy to be true. Taking the pot off the heat is the secret to ending up with tender, moist meat. Although this method specifies 3 pounds of chicken, you can easily increase the amount. Just use a larger pot and double the quantity of vegetables.

Poaching chicken is one of our favorite tricks for producing moist meat that forms the basis for speedy dinners later on.

PERFECT POACHED CHICKEN

MAKES: 5½ TO 6 CUPS CHUNKS PREP TIME: 10 MINUTES

2½ to 3 pounds skinless, boneless chicken
    breast halves (5 to 8 ounces each; see Notes)
1 large onion
1 large rib celery
1 large carrot
¼ teaspoon black pepper
Salt to taste (optional)

1. Place the chicken breasts in a 4½-quart Dutch oven or soup pot. Peel the onion, cut it into 4 pieces, and add them to the pot. Cut the celery into 4 pieces and add them to the pot. Peel the carrot, cut it into roughly 1-inch pieces, and add them to the pot. Sprinkle the black pepper over the chicken and vegetables. Add just enough cold water to completely cover the chicken and vegetables, then sprinkle in the salt, if using.

2. Cover the pot and bring to a rolling boil over high heat. As soon as the water reaches a vigorous boil, remove the pot from the heat and let it stand, covered, until the chicken is no longer pink in the center, about 25 minutes for average-size pieces. (Test for doneness by cutting into a breast half.) Do not overcook.

3. When the chicken is done, remove it from the pot, using tongs or a slotted spoon. Allow the chicken to cool enough to cut into bite-size chunks for future use. Allow the poaching liquid to cool, transfer to a storage container, cover, and refrigerate for up to 3 days or freeze for up to 3 months (see Notes).

NOTES: The poaching liquid won't be as flavorful as chicken stock but can be used instead of water when making soup.

■ This method works for chicken breast halves that are of typical size, about 5 to 8 ounces each. However, every now and then you'll run across very thick chicken breast halves of up to 12 ounces each.

Our best advice is to avoid poaching pieces this large. However, if your chicken pieces are huge and you still want to poach them, you'll need to alter our method slightly. Here's how:

In Step 2, after the water comes to a boil, reduce the heat to low and cook the chicken at a very slow boil for 5 minutes. Then remove the pot from the heat and proceed with the recipe as written. The chicken should be done (no longer pink in the middle) after standing in the hot water for 35 minutes, but be sure to test it by cutting into a piece.

STORAGE NOTES:

The chicken chunks can be refrigerated for up to 2 days or frozen for 2 to 3 months. Refrigerate or freeze the chicken chunks in 1- or 2-cup portions in microwave-safe containers. To defrost, remove the container lid and microwave on the defrost setting according to the oven manufacturer's instructions. Or defrost in the refrigerator overnight.

USING PERFECT POACHED CHICKEN:

You can use Perfect Poached Chicken in any recipe calling for already-cooked chicken. (Individual recipes give substitution notes.) Some of the recipes in this book include:

- Old-Fashioned Chicken and Rice Casserole (page 92)
- Individual Chicken Cobblers (page 164)
- Magically Modern "Croquette" Sandwiches (page 250)
- Chicken and Onion Pizza (page 263)
- Fall Chicken Salad (page 276)
- Waldorf Pasta Salad (page 278)
- Chicken Caesar Salad (page 279)

I t's a simple matter to poach chicken thighs, after which the skin slips off easily and the tender meat practically falls off the bones. Once the skin and bones have been banished, the juicy chicken can be used in any recipe that calls for cooked chicken, such as casseroles and salads.

The process for poaching chicken thighs is similar to that for breasts, with a few modifications. You'll have to use a larger pot because chicken with bones takes up more room, and you need more poundage to yield the same amount of meat. In our poaching method for boneless breasts, the pot is removed from the heat as soon as it comes to a vigorous boil. However, thighs require a bit more heat, so you'll need to simmer them for a bit before they finish cooking off the heat.

Cooking thighs with the skin and bones gives you an added bonus for your efforts: an extremely flavorful cooking stock that can be used in place of canned chicken broth in all of our recipes. Just remove the vegetables from the broth

Poached Chicken Thighs

MAKES: 5½ TO 6 CUPS CHUNKS PREP TIME: 10 MINUTES

4½ to 5 pounds chicken thighs (see Notes)
1 large onion
1 rib celery
1 large carrot
1 teaspoon dried tarragon (see Note)
¼ teaspoon black pepper
Salt to taste (optional)

1. Place the chicken thighs in a 6-quart Dutch oven or soup pot. Peel the onion, cut it into 4 pieces, and add them to the pot. Cut the celery into 4 pieces and add them to the pot. Peel the carrot, cut it into roughly 1-inch pieces, and add them to the pot. Sprinkle the tarragon and black pepper over the chicken and vegetables. Add just enough cold water to cover the chicken and vegetables completely, then sprinkle in the salt, if using.

2. Cover the pot and bring to a rolling boil over high heat. As soon as the water reaches a vigorous boil, reduce the heat to low and cook the chicken, uncovered, at a very slow boil for 10 minutes. Then remove the pot from the heat and let it stand, covered, until the chicken is no longer pink in the center, 25 to 35 minutes. (Test for doneness by removing a thigh and cutting into it. The exact time will depend on the size of the thighs.)

3. When the chicken is done, remove it from the pot, using tongs or a slotted spoon. (Reserve the chicken stock in the pot for later use.) Allow the chicken to cool enough to remove the skin and any visible fat. Pull the meat from the bones. Cut the chicken into bite-size chunks for future use.

NOTES: If you don't have a 6-quart pot, use a 4½-quart pot and cook only 3 pounds of chicken thighs.

■ Other dried seasonings beside tarragon work well, too, such as basil, marjoram, herbes de Provence, thyme, or Italian seasoning blend.

■ Because chicken thighs are poached bone-in and with skin on, the poaching liquid should be flavorful enough to use as stock.

STORAGE NOTES:

Refrigerate or freeze the chicken chunks in 1-cup portions in microwave-safe containers. To defrost, remove the container lid and microwave on the defrost setting according to the oven manufacturer's instructions. Or defrost in the refrigerator overnight.

USING POACHED CHICKEN THIGHS:

You can use Poached Chicken Thighs in most of the recipes that call for already-cooked chicken. (Individual recipes give substitution notes.) Some of them are:

■ Simple Chicken Stew (page 49)

■ "Barbecued" Chicken and Black Bean Burritos (page 98)

■ Island Chicken (page 152)

■ Chicken and Green Bean "Casserole" (page 156)

■ Curried Chicken with Spinach and Tomatoes (page 160)

■ Chicken and Broccoli Lo Mein (page 194)

■ Corkscrews with Chicken and Zucchini (page 202)

and then strain it. (We like to use a strainer lined with a paper towel. Ladle the stock through the strainer, and replace the paper towel whenever the accumulating fat slows down the draining: You may have to do this three times. Discard the accumulated fat along with the paper towel.)

Refrigerate the stock until it is cold. Then skim the hardened fat off the surface and discard it. The remaining stock can be refrigerated for 3 days or frozen for up to 2 months. We like to freeze the stock in 1-cup portions for flexibility.

The baked potatoes I had always made at home were perfectly fine, but never truly amazing like those at my favorite steak house. (I used the "grease them and wrap in tinfoil" method.) Then I got into a conversation with my friend Ryon Wilder, who owns several restaurants, about how to bake a truly wonderful potato.

"If you want potatoes with crunchy skin and a moist, fluffy middle, you'll have to use the high-heat method," he said.

I would never have been brave enough to put unwrapped potatoes on a bare oven rack at 475°F and leave them there for an hour. But that's the secret to the best potatoes ever. And if I was going to the trouble, I realized I should do a big batch and save some for later in the week. It takes only a few extra minutes to scrub and prick 10 potatoes instead of 4. Because baked potatoes don't freeze well, only bake the number of potatoes you'll need to fit your menu. Plan to serve your potato dishes within three days of baking the potatoes.

AMAZING BAKED POTATOES

MAKES: 10 BAKED POTATOES **PREP TIME: 5 MINUTES**

10 large (8 to 12 ounces each) Russet baking potatoes (or more as desired)

1. Preheat the oven to 475°F.

2. Scrub the potato skins under cold running water and pat dry. Prick each potato twice with a fork. Bake, uncovered, directly on the oven rack (no baking pan needed) for 1 hour.

3. Using oven mitts or tongs, carefully remove the potatoes from the oven. Serve immediately or let the potatoes rest until cool. For later use, place the potatoes in a zipper-top bag or covered container and refrigerate for up to 3 days. (Do not freeze.)

USING BAKED POTATOES:

Once you have your stash of potatoes, you have a world of options:

- Enjoy them, fresh-baked or reheated, as Super Stuffed Potatoes (page 91).

- Scoop out the middle of the leftover potatoes, leaving a potato shell about ¼ inch thick to form a "cup" for Chili in Spud Bowls (page 68). Save the centers for use in August Vichyssoise (page 31) or Loaded Baked Potato Soup (page 30).

- Dice them or slice them for use in Homey Chicken Hash (page 162) or Dad's Spicy Spuds (page 334).

- Or enjoy Old-Fashioned Twice-Baked Potatoes (page 331).

Super Potato Toppers

When you have a stash of Amazing Baked Potatoes on hand, it's easy to slice them in half and pop them in the microwave for dinner. To keep baked potatoes lively and never boring, here are some suggestions for toppers:

- Lynne's Mom's Mince (page 119)

- Flexible Mexican Filling (page 352)

- Chunky Seasoned Chicken (page 358), Great Grilled Chicken Breasts (page 360), or Perfect Poached Chicken (page 362) and cheese of choice

- Spinach Parsley Pesto (page 372)

- Sheri's Romesco Sauce (page 378)

- Super Sofrito (page 388)

Cooking your own dried beans is absolutely the cheapest way to serve them. A 1-pound bag of beans generally costs less than $1. That one bag yields more than 6 cups of beans and broth. A can of beans, at the same price, yields only 1 cup. It doesn't take a genius to do the math.

Dried beans must be soaked before cooking, and we've given instructions for a quick 1-hour soak in addition to the traditional overnight method.

DRIED BEAN BONANZA

MAKES: 6 CUPS

1 pound dried beans, such as Great Northern red kidney
1 teaspoon salt
¼ cup ham pieces (½-inch pieces; optional)

1. Pour the beans into a colander and pick over them to remove any debris. While you rinse the beans under cool water, run your fingers through them to find and rinse away any clumps of dirt.

2. *For a quick soak:* Place the beans in a 4½-quart Dutch oven or soup pot and add water to cover. Place the pot over high heat, cover, and bring to a boil. Then remove the pot from the heat and let the beans soak for 1 hour.

For an overnight soak: Place the beans in 4½-quart Dutch oven or soup pot. Cover the beans with water and cover the pot. Let the beans soak for 12 hours.

3. Drain the beans, discarding the soaking water. Return the beans to the pot and add 6 cups water, the salt, and the ham (if using). Place the pot over high heat, cover, and bring to a boil. Uncover, reduce the heat to low, and simmer the beans until they reach the desired tenderness (see the chart on page 370), 1½ to 2½ hours. Add more water if necessary to keep the beans covered during the cooking time.

4. Remove the beans from the heat and set them aside to cool or to use in a recipe. Discard the ham pieces. The beans can be covered and refrigerated for up to 4 days or frozen in 1-cup batches for up to 1 month. (See page 370 for freezing tips.)

USING HOME-COOKED DRIED BEANS:
You can use home-cooked dried beans instead of canned in any of the recipes that call for beans in this book. Some of them are:

- South-of-the-Border Bean and Tortilla Soup (page 42)
- Mixed Bean Meatless Cassoulet (page 57)

- Cinco de Mayo Skillet (page 126)
- Old South Hoppin' John (page 170)
- Red Bean and Pasta Salad (page 293)
- Three-Bean Salad (page 294)

LOTS OF LENTILS

MAKES: 6 CUPS

1 pound brown lentils
1 teaspoon salt

1. Pour the lentils into a colander and pick over them to remove any debris. Rinse the lentils under cool water, running your fingers through them to find and rinse away any clumps of dirt.

2. Place the lentils, salt, and 5 cups water in 4½-quart Dutch oven or soup pot. Place the pot over high heat, cover, and bring to a boil. Then uncover, reduce the heat to low, and simmer the lentils until they reach the desired tenderness, 30 to 40 minutes. Add more water if necessary to keep the lentils covered during the cooking time. (The cooking time may vary depending upon the age of the lentils, but 30 minutes should produce still-firm lentils, while at 40 minutes they should be very tender. If not, continue to cook until the lentils are tender, adding more water if necessary.)

3. Remove the lentils from the heat and set them aside to cool or to use in a recipe. The lentils can be covered and refrigerated for up to 4 days, or frozen in 1-cup batches for up to 1 month. (See page 370 for freezing tips.)

USING LOTS OF LENTILS:
To speed your way, use already-cooked lentils:

- Lentil Chickpea Soup with Cilantro (page 23)
- Very Veggie Lentil Chili (page 58)
- Italian Lentils over Rice (page 174)

Though they may be small, humble lentils do have a lot going for them. They're fat-free, packed with protein, versatile, and full of fiber and flavor. Unlike dried beans, they don't need to soak before cooking. Because lentils cook so much faster than dried beans, we often cook them the night before, just letting the pot simmer while we're making something else or while we're cleaning up the night's dishes.

How to Cook and Store Dried Beans

From Alicia:

The only things necessary for successfully cooking dried beans are patience and water. You simply can't hurry the process, and if you try, it usually spells disaster. (Don't get me started talking about my bean disasters.)

The following chart should help you gauge if you have enough time to cook the beans. The quickest dried beans you can cook are lentils (legumes, really, but for our purposes let's call them beans)—less than an hour because you don't have to soak them first. For other beans, the minimum time is about 3 hours, using the quick-soak method and cooking the beans to a slightly firm texture.

If you're freezing the beans, you'll get a better result if you cook them to a fairly firm texture. For easy use in our recipes, we like to freeze our cooked beans in 1-cup batches in quart-size zipper-top plastic freezer bags. If you lay them flat to freeze, they'll defrost faster. Defrost frozen beans overnight in the refrigerator or in the microwave following the oven manufacturer's directions. Be sure to include some of the broth when you are packaging the beans for freezing. You can drain it off later if your recipe doesn't call for it, but it will help protect the beans while they're frozen. All the figures in the chart are based on 1 pound of beans.

COOKING BEANS

Bean Type	OK to Quick Soak?	Water*	Cooking time	Yield
Black beans	Yes	about 6 cups	1½ hours	6½ cups beans and broth
Black-eyed peas	Yes	about 6 cups	2 hours	7 cups beans and broth
Chickpeas	Yes	about 7 cups	2½ hours	7 to 8 cups beans and broth
Lentils	No soaking required	5 cups	30 to 40 minutes	6 cups beans and broth
Pinto beans	Yes	about 6 cups	2 hours	7 cups beans and broth
Red beans	Yes	about 6½ cups	2¼ hours	7 cups beans and broth

*This refers to the cooking water only, not the soaking water in Step 2 of the recipes on pages 368 and 369. The amount of water you use depends on how old your dried beans are. The older the bean, the more water it takes to tenderize it. The amount stated in the chart is an average. Check the beans frequently, and make sure they do not dry out during simmering. Add water as necessary to keep them covered during cooking.

Pesto almost always conjures thoughts of basil and pine nuts, and indeed these are the classic Italian ingredients. There's only one problem: In the winter, a generous supply of fresh basil can be hard to come by, not to mention quite expensive. Never fear. If you've run out of the pesto you prepared and froze in the summer, when basil is cheaper, here's a solution. In the centuries since the Italians started making it, pesto has evolved. If you just follow the basic method, you can make pesto out of a host of herbs—or even spinach, olives, or sun-dried tomatoes. In the winter, spinach and parsley make a luscious combination. Our inexpensive winter pesto provides an easy way to push some summer flavor into an ordinary weeknight meal.

SPINACH PARSLEY PESTO

MAKES: ABOUT 1²/₃ CUPS PREP TIME: 10 MINUTES

½ cup walnut pieces
2 cloves fresh garlic
½ bunch parsley, preferably flat-leaf
  (for about 1 cup packed leaves)
3 cups (5 ounces) packed fresh baby spinach leaves
½ cup extra-virgin olive oil
Juice of ½ lemon
½ cup shredded or grated Parmesan cheese
⅛ teaspoon salt

1. Place the walnuts on a microwave-safe plate and microwave, uncovered, on high power until fragrant and lightly toasted, 2 to 4 minutes, stopping halfway through to stir. Set aside to cool.

2. While the walnuts are toasting, peel the garlic. Turn on a food processor and drop the cloves through the feed tube; process until finely chopped.

3. Rinse the parsley leaves and pat dry. Remove the tough stems and discard them, but do not worry about the smaller, upper stems. With the motor running, drop the parsley into the processor and mince it finely. Stop the machine.

4. If the spinach is gritty, rinse it thoroughly and dry it in a lettuce spinner or with paper towels. (There shouldn't be any tough stems, but if there are, discard them. Do not worry about the tender stems.) Add half of the spinach to the processor bowl. With the motor running, drizzle a tablespoon or so of the oil through the feed tube; process until the spinach is finely minced, about 10 seconds. Scrape down the sides of the bowl. Repeat with the remaining spinach, drizzling in another tablespoon or so of the oil. (You do not need to remove the first batch of spinach from the processor bowl.) Add the walnuts and process until well chopped, 5 to 10 seconds. Scrape down the sides of the bowl and pulse the motor 3 times.

5. Add the lemon juice to the bowl, pouring it through a strainer to catch the seeds. Add the Parmesan cheese and salt. With the motor running, drizzle the remaining oil through the feed tube. As soon as the oil is incorporated, turn off the motor and scrape down the sides of the bowl. Pulse 2 more times. Serve at once or store for future use.

STORAGE NOTES:

The pesto can be refrigerated in an airtight container for up to 4 days. To freeze the pesto for up to 2 months, line the cups of a muffin tin with plastic wrap and scoop ¼ cup pesto into each cup. Twist the plastic wrap to close it around the pesto, secure the bundle with a twist-tie, and then freeze the bundles in the muffin tin for 48 hours. Once they are frozen, remove the pouches from the tin and drop them into a zipper-top plastic bag. (Or for tablespoon-size amounts, use an ice tray instead of a muffin tin and spray it with cooking oil spray instead of using plastic wrap. When frozen, the cubes can be snapped out of the tray, placed in a freezer bag, and stored in the freezer.) To defrost, let the pesto sit on the counter (still in the plastic wrap) at room temperature for 30 minutes. Or defrost the pesto in the refrigerator overnight. Before using defrosted pesto, stir it to mix in any oil that may have separated.

USING SPINACH PARSLEY PESTO:

Try Spinach Parsley Pesto in these recipes:

- Winter Minestrone with Pesto (page 24)
- Spinach Pesto Pasta with Chicken (page 183)
- Perfect Spinach Pesto Pizza (page 265)
- Spinach Pesto Pasta Salad (page 330)

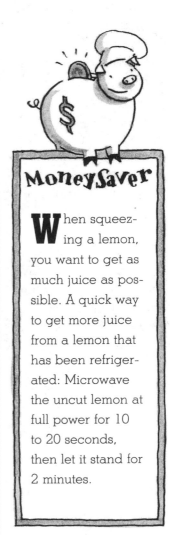

MoneySaver

When squeezing a lemon, you want to get as much juice as possible. A quick way to get more juice from a lemon that has been refrigerated: Microwave the uncut lemon at full power for 10 to 20 seconds, then let it stand for 2 minutes.

Those who know me well (and those who have read our Desperation Dinners cookbooks and newspaper column) know how much I adore peanut sauce. I first encountered this sweet and complex condiment when it was served with grilled chicken satay at my favorite Thai restaurant. Once I figured out how easy it is to make peanut sauce at home, I saw no reason to stop at satay. In my opinion, if a little peanut sauce is good, a lot is better. So I started experimenting, and suddenly peanut sauce became the basis for soup, stews, noodle dishes, and even salad dressing. Served cold, the sauce makes a great dip for raw vegetables such as cucumbers, carrots, and bell peppers. This recipe makes enough sauce to use in two recipes. Or you can just eat the peanut sauce straight up. But do use a spoon.

THAI-STYLE PEANUT SAUCE

MAKES: ABOUT 2 CUPS   PREP TIME: 10 MINUTES

4 cloves fresh garlic
Juice of ½ lime
½ cup creamy peanut butter
¼ cup ketchup
¼ cup regular or reduced-sodium soy sauce
¼ cup firmly packed light brown sugar
2 tablespoons vegetable oil
4 teaspoons finely minced fresh ginger or bottled minced ginger
1 tablespoon red wine vinegar or cider vinegar
1 tablespoon onion powder
1 tablespoon Asian (dark) sesame oil
½ teaspoon red pepper flakes (see Note)

1. Peel the garlic. With the blender on, drop the garlic cloves, one at a time, through the opening in the lid. Chop fine.

2. Pour the lime juice into the blender container. Stop the blender and add all the remaining ingredients, along with ½ cup water. Pulse on high speed until the ingredients are just combined, about 5 seconds. Scrape down the sides of the blender container and pulse 3 or 4 more times. The sauce is now ready to use in recipes or as a dipping sauce, or it can be refrigerated or frozen for future use.

NOTE: Omit the red pepper flakes if serving young children.

STORAGE NOTES:

The peanut sauce can be refrigerated in an airtight container for up to 1 week or frozen in an airtight container for up to 1 month. Defrost it in the refrigerator for 24 hours. Do not defrost in microwave oven.

USING THAI-STYLE PEANUT SAUCE:

Use Thai-Style Peanut Sauce in these recipes:

- Pumpkin Peanut Soup (page 32)
- Curried Groundnut Stew (page 50)
- Thai Spaghetti Toss (page 184)
- Noodles and Vegetables with Peanut Sauce (page 227)
- Thai Salad with Pork (page 286)

CHAPTER NINE

SASSY SAUCES AND TOPPERS

"For a minimal cost, you can transform plain into perfectly awesome."

There's nothing like a sassy sauce to brighten up a meal that seems a bit humble, like chickpea burgers, or a little too plain, like baked chicken breasts. For a minimal cost and a negligible investment of time, you can transform plain into perfectly awesome.

Suddenly your boring chicken breast tastes as if it hails from Madrid, Provence, or the Caribbean. If chicken's on sale and you've stocked up, you can put so many twists on the same old bird that your family may not even notice you're serving chicken yet again this week. And chicken is just for starters. Here's a whole chapter of salsas, relishes, and flavored mayonnaise combos that are also great for dressing up fish, pork chops, ham, turkey, hamburgers, baked potatoes, and sandwiches.

Our Super Sofrito takes garlic, onions, bell pepper, and cilantro and marries them into a versatile condiment that can be served alongside roasted meat, stirred into a soup or sauce, or used to top off beans. Lemon Aïoli is a French garlic mayonnaise that's perfect for anything you'd use plain mayo for, but oh-so-much better. Pineapple Salsa brings the bright taste of the tropics to an ordinary meal. Sheri's Romesco Sauce takes us to Spain with an aromatic blend of roasted red peppers, almonds, garlic, and herbs that can make you feel like a true gourmet.

We also couldn't resist sharing a couple of basics, partly because they're economical, but mostly because they're terrific. Sure, there are lots of commercial barbecue sauces around, but you'll pay dearly for a premium boutique brand. Ours is simply the best barbecue sauce we've ever tasted. We've been known to eat Fred's Red straight from the spoon. No-Waste Roasted Garlic is part condiment and part recipe building block; this easy technique will ensure that you'll never let fresh garlic wither in your pantry again.

All it takes is a spoonful here or a dollop there to get an intense flavor-booster. So get sassy with a homemade sauce or topper and never be plain again.

From Alicia:

Here's an easy twist on a classic Spanish sauce that transforms everything it touches. It comes from our friend Sheri Castle, who used to run a cooking school in Raleigh. Instead of the traditional combination of peppers and tomatoes, Sheri uses red peppers only, and because the already-roasted peppers in the jar work well, this fancy sauce becomes a quick possibility. With a recipe making 2 cups, you'll get a lot of bang for your batch. I've served Sheri's Romesco Sauce on steak, fish, chicken, pork tenderloin, and even hamburgers. When we serve baked potatoes, a little ends up over them too. Sautéed summer squash and onions? A drizzle here or there is delicious. Leftovers will keep for up to a week in a covered container in the refrigerator. Allow the sauce to come to room temperature before serving.

SHERI'S ROMESCO SAUCE

MAKES: 2 CUPS   START TO FINISH: UNDER 10 MINUTES

¼ cup almonds (see Note)
2 cloves fresh garlic
1 teaspoon dried rosemary, or 1 tablespoon fresh rosemary leaves
1 teaspoon dried oregano, or 1 tablespoon fresh oregano leaves
1 large jar (12 ounces) roasted red bell peppers, or 2 large home-roasted red bell peppers
2 tablespoons red wine vinegar
1 teaspoon sugar
1 teaspoon salt (see Note)
Pinch of cayenne pepper
½ cup extra-virgin olive oil

1. Place the almonds in a food processor and process on high speed until they are finely chopped. Peel the garlic and add it to the work bowl. Add the rosemary and oregano. Pulse the motor to finely chop the herbs and garlic.

2. Drain the peppers and add them to the processor. Add the vinegar, sugar, salt, and cayenne pepper. Pulse the motor to chop the peppers and mix the ingredients.

3. With the motor running, slowly drizzle the oil through the feed tube. Process just a few more seconds to blend thoroughly. Serve immediately or store in a covered container in the refrigerator for up to 1 week. Allow the sauce to come to room temperature before serving.

NOTE: Any type of almonds—raw, blanched, or roasted—will work. Unsalted almonds work best, but it is fine to use lightly salted. Don't add more salt without tasting first. Sliced, slivered, or whole almonds will work here.

MUSHROOM WINE SAUCE

MAKES: ABOUT 1⅔ CUPS START TO FINISH: UNDER 10 MINUTES

8 ounces fresh button mushrooms
1 tablespoon butter
¼ cup full-bodied red wine, such as Cabernet Sauvignon (see Note)
1 envelope (about 1 ounce) brown gravy mix

1. Rinse, pat dry, and coarsely chop the mushrooms, discarding any tough stems. Set aside.

2. Melt the butter in a 2-quart saucepan over medium heat. Add the mushrooms and raise the heat to medium-high. Cook, stirring frequently, until the mushrooms release their liquid, 2 to 3 minutes.

3. Add the wine to the pan and cook, stirring, for 1 minute. Then add the amount of water called for on the gravy mix package *minus ¼ cup* (the amount of water is decreased to account for the wine). Add the gravy mix. Using a whisk, stir constantly until the sauce comes to a boil, about 2 minutes. Remove the pan from the heat and serve.

NOTE: You can substitute a fortified wine, such as Marsala, Madeira, Port, or sherry, for the red wine.

If you want to dress up a simple London broil, roast chicken, or a pork chop, just whip up this quick sauce. It's so versatile, it goes with practically anything. Thanks to the splash of wine and fresh mushrooms, the gravy mix takes on a special flavor. One batch serves 6 to 8 people.

Here's a quick way to add some oomph to plain steamed vegetables or seafood. It's also a good way to use up dried or fresh herbs that are reaching the end of their freshness.

QUICK HERB BUTTER SAUCE

MAKES: ⅓ CUP **START TO FINISH:** 5 MINUTES

4 tablespoons (½ stick) butter
1 chicken bouillon cube
½ teaspoon dried herb, such as basil, thyme, dill, marjoram, herbes de Provence, or Italian seasoning (see Note)

SUPER-CHEAP!

1. Put the butter in a 1-cup or larger glass measure. Crush the bouillon cube and place it in the measure with the butter. Cover tightly with plastic wrap and microwave on full power until the butter is almost completely melted, about 45 seconds. Remove from the microwave and stir with a fork until the butter melts completely. Add the herb of choice and stir well.

2. Serve at once, drizzling the butter sauce over cooked vegetables or seafood. The sauce will keep, covered, in the refrigerator for up to a week. If you store it in a microwave-safe container, you can rewarm it by placing the open container in the microwave, covering it with a paper towel, and microwaving at full power for about 45 seconds, until butter has melted.

NOTE: You can also use 1½ teaspoons finely minced fresh herbs. Fresh cilantro and parsley make particularly nice butters.

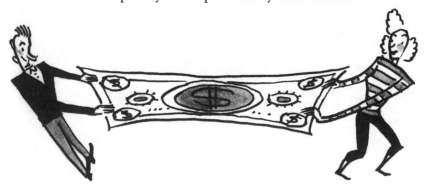

A Refrigerator Check-up Makes Good Cents

When a friend complained that her dairy products never stayed fresh as long as the expiration date on the package, we started wondering about the health and well-being of her refrigerator. If your refrigerator isn't cooling properly, your food simply won't stay fresh as long as it should. That leads to wasted food—and wasted money.

Unless your refrigerator is brand-new, it's a good idea to run a few quick checks once a year. First, check the door gasket to be sure it doesn't have any tears. If the gasket is dirty or sticky, give it a wash. Second, vacuum or wipe down the condenser coils. If there's an air filter, clean that, too.

If your dairy products aren't staying fresh or if you suspect a cooling problem, test the temperature with a refrigerator thermometer. (Hardware stores and some supermarkets sell inexpensive ones.) Put the thermometer in the middle of the refrigerator (not on the door and not way in the back). While you're at it, check the freezer, too. Generally, 37°F is ideal for the refrigerator compartment, and 0°F is best for the freezer.

If the temperatures don't measure up, first check to be sure the thermostat is at the right setting. Other culprits (besides dirty condenser coils or a damaged door gasket) could be a sagging door or frost accumulation. Also be sure the door isn't left open.

Be aware, too, that proper air circulation is key to proper refrigeration; a refrigerator should not be crammed so full that air can't circulate around the items.

Although the door shelves are a convenient place to stash food you use frequently, these shelves are the warmest area of the refrigerator; highly perishable foods like milk shouldn't be kept on the door. If none of these factors is the problem, it's time to call a repair person. Spending just a few minutes (or a few dollars) on refrigerator maintenance each year makes good sense when you consider the total value of the food you store there.

"Spending a few dollars on refrigerator maintenance each year makes good sense."

Mayonnaise Saves the Sandwich—and a Lot of Other Stuff

From Beverly:

I'll never forget the Labor Day when Alicia and I decided things would be different. Forget fancy picnics and complicated cook-outs. We longed to laze our way through summer's last hurrah just like everybody else. And that's how we came to the conclusion that the family could survive quite nicely on sandwiches. They would be served outdoors, after all—and they wouldn't have to break the family budget the way grilled steaks would. But alas, just as we gave a definitive handshake to seal our pact, motherly guilt reared her wicked head, screaming, "This is a *holiday!*"

Okay, so how about taking a plain-old sandwich and doing something different—something dressy, but something simple and not so expensive? And that's how we came up with seven mouth-watering mayos, including a Terrific Tartar Sauce (opposite) and an Almost Classic Rémoulade (page 386). All you have to do is scoop out a little store-bought mayonnaise (we like Hellmann's, and reduced-fat works well) and add some full-flavored stir-ins—like pesto, garlic, curry powder, lemon, sweet pickles, mustard, and fresh herbs. Don't hesitate to get creative and make up your own flavored mayonnaise: A tablespoon or so of chopped roasted red peppers, roasted garlic, chopped black or green olives, grated ginger, prepared horseradish, orange zest, or chutney—all are good choices.

While the only actual work is opening a few jars, the result is an array of gourmet spreads sure to elevate the humble sandwich to holiday heights. The mayos are equally wonderful in tuna salad, pasta salad, or on top of a simple fish fillet, bean burger, or beef burger. Meanwhile, you can relax—just like everybody else.

"Don't hesitate to get creative."

TERRIFIC TARTAR SAUCE

MAKES: ABOUT ⅔ CUP START TO FINISH: UNDER 5 MINUTES

½ cup regular or reduced-fat
  mayonnaise
2 tablespoons sweet pickle relish
  (see Note)
Slice of ½ lemon

Place the mayonnaise in a small mixing bowl. Drain the relish, discarding the juice, and add the relish to the bowl. Squeeze the lemon juice through a strainer directly into the bowl. Stir to mix well. Serve at once or refrigerate, covered, until ready to serve. The sauce will keep, covered and refrigerated, for up to 1 week.

NOTE: Sweet pickle relish is sometimes called "sweet salad cubes." If you can't find it, substitute sweet gherkins, drained and chopped. After it has been opened, a jar of relish will keep in the refrigerator for up to 6 months.

This 3-minute sauce is truly terrific with Shrimp Po' Boys (page 253), Salmon Cake Sandwiches (page 252), Golden Broiled Fillets (page 114), or any other seafood you're serving.

Prepared pesto is available in jars, found with the imported foods in larger supermarkets, and is also sold in plastic containers alongside the other refrigerated pasta sauces. Beverly's son Sam especially likes this on turkey and sandwiches.

PESTO MAYONNAISE

MAKES: ABOUT ¼ CUP PREP TIME: UNDER 5 MINUTES

¼ cup regular or low-fat
mayonnaise
2 teaspoons prepared basil pesto

Spoon the mayonnaise into a small bowl. Stir in the pesto. Serve at once or refrigerate, covered, for up to 1 week.

Fresh or roasted garlic fans will rave over this mayo. And while garlic lovers might swear it needs to be on everything, the rest of us will certainly appreciate a dab to liven up a ham sandwich or a BLT.

GARLIC MAYONNAISE

MAKES: ABOUT ¼ CUP PREP TIME: UNDER 5 MINUTES

¼ cup regular or low-fat
mayonnaise
2 cloves fresh or roasted garlic
(see page 69)

Spoon the mayonnaise into a small bowl. Peel the garlic and squeeze it through a garlic press directly into the bowl. (If using roasted garlic, peel and finely chop or mash it.) Stir well to blend. Serve at once or refrigerate, covered, for up to 2 days.

HERBED MAYONNAISE

MAKES: ABOUT ¼ CUP **PREP TIME:** UNDER 5 MINUTES

¼ cup regular or low-fat
   mayonnaise
2 tablespoons fresh herb leaves,
   such as parsley, cilantro,
   basil, thyme, or tarragon

Spoon the mayonnaise into a small bowl. Finely mince the
herb leaves and stir them into the mayonnaise. Serve at once
or refrigerate, covered, for up to 2 days.

Any sandwich benefits from mayo blended with a fresh herb. We particularly like it smeared on a hero piled high with whatever's in the fridge. Dagwoods, anyone?

CURRY MAYONNAISE

MAKES: ABOUT ¼ CUP **PREP TIME:** UNDER 5 MINUTES

¼ cup regular or low-fat
   mayonnaise
1 teaspoon curry powder

Spoon the mayonnaise into a small bowl.
Stir in the curry powder. Serve at once or refrigerate, covered,
for up to 1 week.

Curry is a strong blend of flavors, so you don't need a lot. If you can find it, use imported curry powder. If you have time, make this mayo a couple of hours or even a day in advance to give the flavors time to develop. And if you want a slightly different twist, try adding a tablespoon of mango chutney. Either way, this is great in chicken salad, tuna salad, or egg salad.

Our version of aïoli, a French mayonnaise with a generous amount of garlic, contains a touch of olive oil along with lemon juice and zest. (You could also use orange zest and juice to make Orange Aïoli.) We especially like it atop our Sassy Chickpea Burgers (page 256).

LEMON AÏOLI

MAKES: ABOUT ⅓ CUP   PREP TIME: UNDER 5 MINUTES

2 cloves fresh garlic
1 teaspoon grated lemon zest
1 tablespoon lemon juice
⅓ cup regular or low-fat mayonnaise
1 teaspoon extra-virgin olive oil

Peel and finely mince the garlic or use a garlic press. Place the garlic in a 2-cup or larger bowl. Add the lemon zest and lemon juice to the bowl. Add the mayonnaise and oil and stir well to blend. Serve at once or refrigerate, covered, for up to 2 days.

Rémoulade is a French mayonnaise sauce that's usually served as a condiment with cold meat and seafood. A traditional recipe would include capers and anchovies, but we don't think you'll miss them.

ALMOST RÉMOULADE

MAKES: ABOUT ½ CUP   PREP TIME: UNDER 5 MINUTES

2 scallions (for 2 tablespoons chopped)
1 clove fresh garlic
¼ cup regular or low-fat mayonnaise
1 tablespoon grainy or country Dijon mustard
1 tablespoon sweet pickle relish (see Note)
¼ teaspoon cayenne pepper

Chop the scallions, including enough of the tender green tops to make 2 tablespoons. Place them in a small serving bowl. Peel the garlic and finely mince it or use a garlic press. Add the garlic to the bowl. Stir in the mayonnaise, mustard, pickle relish, and cayenne pepper. Serve at once or refrigerate, covered, for up to 3 days.

NOTE: Sweet pickle relish is sold alongside the other pickles. It is sometimes called "sweet salad cubes." If you can't find it, substitute 2 sweet gherkins, finely chopped.

FRED'S RED BARBECUE SAUCE

MAKES: 1 QUART **START TO FINISH:** UNDER 25 MINUTES

1½ cups ketchup

1 small can (8 ounces) tomato sauce

½ cup lightly packed light brown sugar

½ cup red wine vinegar or cider vinegar

⅓ cup Worcestershire sauce

2 tablespoons regular or reduced-sodium soy sauce

Juice of 1 lemon

1 teaspoon finely minced fresh ginger or
  bottled minced ginger

½ teaspoon black pepper

½ teaspoon dry mustard or prepared Dijon mustard

½ teaspoon garlic powder

½ teaspoon onion powder

½ teaspoon dried oregano

½ teaspoon dried basil

½ teaspoon red pepper flakes, or more to taste (optional)

¼ teaspoon ground allspice (optional)

Place all the ingredients in a saucepan and stir to mix well. Bring to a boil over high heat, then reduce the heat to low and simmer, stirring occasionally, for 15 minutes to blend the flavors. Remove the sauce from the heat. The sauce will keep in an airtight container in the refrigerator for up to 1 month.

From Beverly:

One of my brother-in-law Fred Bisel's favorite sports is to see how much Tabasco sauce he can stand in a single sitting. So when he started bragging about his barbecue sauce, I retorted, "Yeah, yeah, it's going to turn my ears into smoke-stacks, and I won't be able to eat again for a week, right?"

This banter continued as he stoked up his grill. Later, as we sat down to a platter of barbecued chicken, I clutched a fork in one hand and a glass of ice water in the other. Boy, oh, boy! Truly it was the best barbecued chicken I'd ever eaten—slightly sweet, with an undercurrent of complex spices and the faintest bit of burn.

Fred's Red is equally good for grilling pork and ribs. The amount of red pepper flakes called for here gives the sauce just the slightest zing, but you can omit it or add more.

Here's a slightly adapted version of my now-favorite barbecue sauce, along with my apologies to Fred for the jokes, the barbs, the jabs, and the doubts.

This is the seasoning secret behind every-day cooking in many Latin cultures. Sofrito can be as varied as the individual cook. Some versions contain chile peppers and thyme, while others include annatto seeds, parsley, and bacon fat or lard. But the mainstays of sofrito—garlic, onions, bell pepper, and cilantro—are all that's really required to add tons of flavor to plain cooked beans, soups, or simple seared meats such as chicken and pork chops. We like to add tomatoes to our sofrito when we have them on hand, but they aren't mandatory. One of our Peruvian friends always puts ground cumin in hers, and if you have some, it is a lovely addition.

Using a food processor or blender makes quick work of the chopping required for the sofrito. You can cook the sofrito in advance and keep it in the refrigerator, and then just stir in a little to flavor basic beans. The entire bean pot can be flavored, or you can apply just the preferred amount to an individual serving. Ditto with meat and soups.

SUPER SOFRITO

MAKES: ⅔ CUP, 1 CUP WITH TOMATO
START TO FINISH: UNDER 20 MINUTES

2 small ripe plum tomatoes
(for about ½ cup chopped; optional)
4 teaspoons olive oil
1 small onion (for about ½ cup chopped)
1 medium-size green or red bell pepper
(for about ¾ cup chopped)
4 cloves fresh garlic
¼ teaspoon salt, or more to taste
½ teaspoon ground cumin (optional)
½ cup loosely packed fresh cilantro leaves

1. If you are using the tomatoes, core and cut them into roughly ½-inch dice (do not peel them). Set aside.

2. Heat the oil in a 10-inch or larger skillet over medium heat. While the oil is heating, peel the onion and cut it into quarters. Place the onion pieces in a food processor or blender and pulse until they are finely chopped but not mushy. Use a rubber spatula to scrape the onion into the skillet and cook, stirring frequently, until the onion is transparent, about 4 minutes.

3. Meanwhile, stem, seed, and cut the bell pepper into quarters, then cut the quarters in half again. Place the pieces in the food processor or blender and pulse until they are finely chopped but not mushy. (It is not necessary to wash the work bowl first.) Add the pepper pieces to the skillet, reduce the heat to low, and cook, stirring frequently.

4. While the onion and pepper are cooking, wipe out the processor bowl with a paper towel. Peel the garlic, turn on the processor, and drop the cloves through the feed tube; process until finely minced. As soon as the garlic is chopped, use a rubber spatula to scrape it into the skillet. Add the salt, chopped tomato (if using), and cumin (if using) to the skillet. Continue to cook, stirring frequently, until all the vegetables are soft, about 5 minutes.

5. With the processor running, drop the cilantro leaves through the feed tube and process until finely minced. (It is not necessary to wash the work bowl first.) Use a rubber spatula to scrape the cilantro into the skillet. Cook, stirring, for 1 minute.

6. Remove the sofrito from the heat and serve at once. Or cool and refrigerate in an airtight container for up to 1 week or freeze for up to 1 month. Thaw frozen sofrito in the refrigerator for 24 hours prior to serving. Reheat in a microwave-safe container, covered with a paper towel, by microwaving on full power for about 1 minute, stirring halfway through.

PINEAPPLE SALSA

MAKES: ABOUT 1²⁄₃ CUPS   PREP TIME: UNDER 10 MINUTES

1 small can (8 ounces) pineapple tidbits packed in juice
½ small sweet onion, such as Vidalia (for about ⅓ cup diced)
1 medium-size plum tomato (for about ½ cup diced)
1 large clove fresh garlic
3 tablespoons loosely packed chopped fresh cilantro or parsley leaves
1 tablespoon fresh or bottled lime juice
⅛ teaspoon salt
⅛ teaspoon red pepper flakes (optional)

1. Drain the juice from the pineapple and reserve it for another use (see Note). Place the pineapple in a medium-size mixing bowl. Peel and finely dice the onion half, adding it to the bowl.

2. Core the tomato and finely dice it, adding it to the bowl. Peel and finely mince the garlic and add it to the bowl. Add the cilantro, lime juice, salt, and red pepper flakes (if using). Stir to blend well. Serve at once or refrigerate, covered, until ready to serve, up to 2 hours.

NOTE: The pineapple juice can be used in Alicia's Fruit Smoothies (page 415) or in Bits-of-Fruit Salad with Strawberry Yogurt Dressing (page 321).

In the past few years, chefs have made an art form out of salsa combinations. We especially like this version (which originally appeared in our first cookbook, *Desperation Dinners*), because its main ingredient is something we always have on hand: a can of pineapple. With the fresh ingredients added, you'll never suspect such humble beginnings.

PINEAPPLE CRANBERRY RELISH

MAKES: 2½ CUPS START TO FINISH: UNDER 10 MINUTES

1 can (16 ounces) whole-berry cranberry
    sauce (see Note)
1 can (8¼ ounces) crushed pineapple
    packed in juice
¼ cup pecan pieces
¼ teaspoon apple pie spice

SUPER-CHEAP!

Pour the cranberry sauce into a 4-cup or larger glass or ceramic bowl. Drain the pineapple, reserving the juice for another use, and add the pineapple to the bowl. Finely chop the nuts and add them to the bowl. Add the apple pie spice and stir well to mix. Serve at once or refrigerate, covered, until ready to serve. The relish will keep in an airtight container in the refrigerator for up to 1 week.

NOTE: Be sure to buy cranberry sauce that specifies "whole berry," not the smooth "jellied" cranberry sauce.

No-Waste Roasted Garlic

PREP TIME: 5 MINUTES

Fresh garlic cloves
Olive oil

1. Preheat the oven to 375°F.

2. Do not peel the garlic. Cut about ¼ inch off the top of each clove. (If you are roasting a whole bulb, leave it intact and cut across the top portion of the entire bulb.) Place the garlic on a sheet of aluminum foil. Drizzle a small amount of oil over the garlic. (The exact amount doesn't matter—roughly ½ teaspoon for the first clove and ¼ teaspoon for each additional clove or 1 generous tablespoon for a whole bulb.) Wrap the foil around the cloves and seal it to make a package. Shake the package to distribute the oil.

3. Place the foil package, seam side up, in a baking dish and bake until the garlic cloves are soft, about 30 minutes. To test for doneness, unwrap the foil packet and test a clove or two with a toothpick. It should slide in easily with no resistance from the garlic. Remove the foil package from the oven and let it cool to room temperature before opening it.

4. To use the garlic, squeeze it from the skins. Store the cloves in a zipper-top plastic bag or other airtight container in the refrigerator for up to 10 days.

There's no need to ever waste fresh garlic by letting it sprout or wither when you can roast the cloves to make a wonderful condiment that boosts the flavor of practically anything. Roasted garlic turns slightly sweet and is sublime spread directly onto French bread, chopped and tossed into spaghetti or other Italian-style sauces, added to corn muffin mix (see page 310), tossed with steamed vegetables, added to mashed potatoes or beef stew . . . well, you get the idea. And once garlic is roasted, it will keep, covered and refrigerated, for up to 10 days. You can also whir the roasted cloves in a food processor to make a paste, which then becomes even easier to spread and add to sauces.

It doesn't matter how much garlic you roast at any one time. Just drizzle a fine stream of olive oil over it and roast away. The only type of garlic we don't like roasted is the very large elephant garlic—it does not develop the same sweet flavor. An average roasted whole bulb of garlic will yield about ¼ cup of chopped cloves.

391

CHAPTER TEN

SPECIAL BREAKFASTS AT HOME

Most days, breakfast at our house is a bowl of Cheerios. But here's a true confession: Both of us like nothing better than to settle into a restaurant booth on a Saturday morning and wolf down overstuffed omelets, dishes of cheese grits, a fancy breakfast casserole, or fruit-filled pancakes smothered in sweet syrup. And the bill for that guilty pleasure? Don't even ask.

Where we live, pancake houses and other breakfast restaurants are so crowded on the weekends that you have to wait well over an hour for a table. That fact alone—plus the motivation to save money—got us to thinking. We'd long experimented with quick-and-easy breakfast recipes for our Desperation Dinners books and newspaper columns, but we'd mostly advised our readers to serve "breakfast for dinner." And while we still think serving breakfast items at dinner-time is a great idea, we realized that many of our recipes would also make wonderful weekend breakfasts. Having a stash of stress-free recipes that could help keep us out of restaurants, without making us feel deprived, could only leave us smiling all the way to the bank. And with the recipes in this chapter, you'll be smiling—and saving—too.

When you need something hearty, try the Sausage-Pepper Strata, the Back-to-Barcelona Tortilla (think potato omelet), or either of our skillet frittatas. Omelet lovers will delight in our flexible omelet formula that lets you customize based on the ingredients you have on hand. And our doctored-up version of old-fashioned hash browns is wonderful as a side dish or as the morning main event. Myra's Monkey Bread, Apple Pie Quesadilla, Croissants with Chocolate Gravy, and Pumpkin Raisin Biscuits satisfy those cravings for sweet breakfast breads in fine style.

When you have overnight guests, you want to serve an especially great breakfast. It's all in the details—those little touches that, served alongside a platter of basic scrambled eggs and toast, turn a plain breakfast into an extraordinary one. Our homemade Easy-Strawberry Freezer Jam and Spiced Pear Butter push toast to new heights.

Go ahead, pour those Cheerios during the week. But on the weekend, try out these amazing breakfast recipes.

"Having a stash of stress-free recipes helps keep us out of restaurants."

There's nothing like a hearty stuffed omelet to turn breakfast into a celebration. This is a large omelet that serves two quite generously, and it's quick enough to make so that you can just keep repeating the process to serve however many people happen to be at the table. Just put the already-cooked portions on serving plates and stash them in a warm oven (on the lowest setting) until you've cooked all the omelets you need.

For this versatile omelet, use whatever combination of vegetables and cheeses you happen to like or find in the fridge. For meat lovers, replace half of the veggies with ham chunks or bacon bits.

A CELEBRATORY BREAKFAST OMELET

SERVES: 2 START TO FINISH: UNDER 20 MINUTES

4 teaspoons olive oil or vegetable oil
1 small onion (for about ½ cup chopped)
1 clove fresh garlic, or ½ teaspoon bottled minced garlic
½ cup chopped vegetables, such as mushrooms, green bell pepper, tomato, ripe olives, or a mixture (see Note)
3 large eggs
½ teaspoon dried Italian seasoning or dried basil (optional)
½ cup finely shredded or grated cheese, such as Cheddar, Parmesan, Swiss, or a mixture
Salt and black pepper to taste

1. Heat 2 teaspoons of the oil in an extra-deep 12-inch skillet over medium heat. Peel and coarsely chop the onion, adding it to the skillet as you chop. (If you are using mushrooms, add them now.) Cook the onion, stirring frequently, until it is soft, 2 minutes.

2. When the onion is soft, add the garlic and the other vegetables to the skillet and cook until they are tender, 2 to 3 minutes. (See Note.)

3. While the vegetables cook, break the eggs into a 1-quart or larger bowl, add 1 tablespoon water, and beat with a whisk or a fork until foamy. Set aside.

4. When the vegetables are tender, transfer them to a small bowl and set it aside. Discard any juices that may have accumulated in the skillet.

5. Add the remaining 2 teaspoons oil to the skillet and heat it over medium heat. Reduce the heat to medium-low. Pour the eggs into the skillet and cook without stirring until the edges are set and the middle is only slightly runny, 3 to 4 minutes. Turn the heat to low and sprinkle the Italian seasoning (if using) over one half of the omelet. Drain off any juices that may have accumulated around the cooked vegetables and sprinkle the vegetables evenly over half of the omelet. Sprinkle the cheese over the vegetables and season with salt and black pepper.

6. Using a wide metal spatula, fold the plain half of the omelet over the filled half. Then cover the skillet and cook until the cheese melts, 1 to 2 minutes. Cut the omelet in half and serve.

NOTE: Tomato and ripe olives don't need to be cooked, so add them after all the other vegetables are tender and just stir for about 30 seconds to warm them. Mushrooms will take longer to cook, so add them with the onion as indicated.

MUSHROOM-SWISS FRITTATA

SERVES: 4 START TO FINISH: UNDER 25 MINUTES

½ large green bell pepper (for about ¾ cup chopped)
8 ounces fresh button mushrooms
2 tablespoons olive oil or vegetable oil
1 medium-size onion (for about ¾ cup chopped)
2 cloves fresh garlic, minced, or 2 teaspoons bottled minced garlic
6 large eggs
¾ cup shredded Swiss cheese
¼ cup shredded or grated Parmesan cheese
2 tablespoons real (not imitation) bacon bits (see Note)
Salt and black pepper to taste

1. Turn on the broiler to high.

2. Stem, seed, and coarsely chop the bell pepper and set it aside. Rinse the mushrooms, pat them dry, and slice them, discarding any tough stems. Set them aside.

Every now and then we find ourselves with an abundance of eggs. To avoid letting good eggs go to waste, we make frittatas. A frittata is an Italian omelet, with the ingredients mixed throughout instead of folded in the middle. Frittatas also tend to be firmer—and round, because they're not folded over. A quick run under the broiler finishes the top.

Frittatas are also a nice way to use up bits and pieces of leftover meats, vegetables, and cheeses. This frittata is made with onions, mushrooms, and bell pepper, but you could also use sliced ripe olives

(continued)

(continued)

and about a cup of finely chopped ham. Crumbled bacon left over from a previous breakfast makes tasty bacon bits. No Swiss cheese? Cheddar and a blend of Colby and Monterey Jack are nice, too.

Of course, frittatas make wonderful breakfast or brunch fare, but we also find they work great at dinnertime. So don't let those eggs sit past their expiration date. Put them to work in a filling frittata.

3. Heat the oil in a 12-inch cast-iron or other ovenproof skillet over medium heat. Peel and coarsely chop the onion, adding it to the skillet as you chop. Add the mushrooms to the skillet and continue to cook, stirring occasionally, until the mushrooms begin to release their juices, about 2 minutes. Add the garlic, then the bell pepper, and continue to cook, stirring frequently, until all the vegetables are tender, about 2 minutes more.

4. While the vegetables cook, beat the eggs with a whisk in a 2-quart or larger bowl until foamy. Add the Swiss and Parmesan cheeses and stir to mix.

5. Shake the skillet to distribute the vegetables evenly, and pour in the egg mixture. Lightly shake the skillet to help distribute the egg mixture. If necessary, use the back of a spoon to spread the vegetables out. Sprinkle the bacon bits evenly over the top and season lightly with salt and black pepper.

6. Cook without stirring until the bottom is set but the surface is still runny, about 5 minutes, then immediately put the skillet under the broiler and cook until the surface is just set but not brown, 1½ to 2 minutes.

7. Run a knife around the edge of the frittata to loosen it. Cut the frittata into 4 wedges and serve. You may have to cut the first wedge in half to remove it from the pan.

NOTE: Turn any leftover cooked bacon into bacon bits by crumbling it with your fingers or chopping it with a chef's knife. Use the bacon bits as salad or soup toppers. They can be frozen for up to 2 months.

An Orange Juice Dilemma

From Alicia:

We've been in an orange juice quandary. For years my family has used premium "not from concentrate" orange juice for cooking and drinking. I decided we needed to save a bit on the grocery bill, and premium orange juice was an obvious target. So I started buying the frozen concentrated juice.

Gone was the convenience of opening the carton and immediately pouring out what I needed. What's more, we seemed to be drinking less of one of our favorite beverages. When I questioned my family, they said they simply didn't enjoy the "new" orange juice as much, so they stopped drinking such huge quantities. It was a sure way to save money, but when juice started to spoil in the fridge, any savings went down the drain. Besides, orange juice is so good for us: 100% pure, no sugar or other additives, and a terrific source of vitamin C.

So now we're back to premium. However, instead of sticking to the one expensive brand I used to buy, I have branched out to the other not-from-concentrate brands, including house brands. Practically every week, one of the premium brands is on sale, and now I simply buy whatever brand that happens to be. Although my kids profess that they can tell a difference in the individual brands, they are back to drinking the juice at the same rate as before. So we're saving a little, definitely not wasting money, and still drinking a healthy beverage.

"When the juice started to spoil, any savings went down the drain."

Here's a dish to add to the breakfast repertoire when the zucchini supply gets out of control. You could also use yellow summer squash, if that's more abundant. Beverly's mom, Dot Mills, points out that if you're a fan of spicy foods—as her husband, Jay, is—a few shakes of Tabasco sauce blended with the eggs in Step 4 makes a nice addition.

ZUCCHINI FRITTATA

SERVES: 4 START TO FINISH: UNDER 25 MINUTES

½ large green bell pepper (for about ¾ cup diced)
12 ounces (about 2 small) zucchini
2 tablespoons olive oil or vegetable oil
1 medium-size onion (for about ¾ cup chopped)
2 cloves fresh garlic, minced, or 2 teaspoons bottled minced garlic
6 large eggs
½ cup shredded or grated Parmesan cheese
½ cup shredded regular or part-skim mozzarella cheese
2 tablespoons real (not imitation) bacon bits (see Note, page 396)
Salt and black pepper to taste

1. Turn on the broiler to high.

2. Stem, seed, and coarsely chop the bell pepper and set it aside. Trim and discard the zucchini ends, cut the zucchini into 4 strips, and then cut the 4 strips into ¼-inch dice. Set the zucchini aside.

3. Heat the oil in a 12-inch cast-iron or other ovenproof skillet over medium heat. Peel and coarsely chop the onion, adding it to the skillet as you chop. Add the garlic, bell pepper, and zucchini, and cook, stirring frequently, until the zucchini is crisp-tender, 2 to 3 minutes.

4. While the vegetables cook, beat the eggs with a whisk in a 2-quart or larger bowl until foamy. Add the Parmesan and mozzarella cheese and stir to mix.

5. Shake the skillet to distribute the vegetables evenly, then pour the egg mixture into the skillet. Shake the skillet to help distribute the egg mixture. If necessary, use the back of a spoon to spread the vegetables out. Sprinkle the bacon bits evenly over the top and season lightly with salt and black pepper.

6. Cook without stirring until the bottom is set but the surface is still runny, about 5 minutes, then immediately put the skillet under the broiler and cook until the surface is just set but not brown, 1½ to 2 minutes.

7. Run a knife around the edge of the frittata to loosen it. Cut it into 4 wedges. (You may have to cut the first wedge in half to remove it from the pan.) Serve immediately.

BACK-TO-BARCELONA TORTILLA

SERVES: 4 TO 6   START TO FINISH: UNDER 25 MINUTES

6 large eggs
⅛ teaspoon black pepper
1 tablespoon olive oil
1 large onion (for about 1 cup chopped)
1 large green or red bell pepper
    (for about 1½ cups chopped)
1 clove fresh garlic, minced, or 1 teaspoon bottled
    minced garlic
2 cups already-cooked potato chunks (see Note),
    or 1 can (14½ ounces) sliced new potatoes
1 cup (about 6 ounces) coarsely chopped ham

1. Turn on the broiler to high.

2. Break the eggs into a 1-quart or larger bowl and whisk until foamy. Whisk in the black pepper. Set aside.

3. Heat the oil in a 12-inch cast-iron or other ovenproof skillet over medium heat. Peel and coarsely chop the onion, adding it to the skillet as you chop. Stem, seed, and cut the bell pepper into ¼-inch dice. Add the bell pepper and the garlic to the skillet. Raise the heat to medium-high and cook, stirring occasionally, until the vegetables are tender, 2 to 3 minutes.

From Beverly:

On a trip to Barcelona a few years back, I fell in love with the Spanish tortilla—sort of like an omelet with potatoes thrown in. It's often cut into small wedges and served as a snack or as part of a meal made up of appetizers, called tapas. A meal of tapas in Barcelona is heavenly, but I think the tortilla also makes a wonderful budget breakfast dish at home. The Spanish serve their tortillas at room temperature, but at breakfast I like to eat them hot. Part of the beauty of the dish is its simplicity—a true example of "less is more."

4. Drain the potatoes if you are using canned.

5. When the vegetables are tender, add the potatoes to the skillet, distributing them evenly. Sprinkle the chopped ham evenly over the mixture. Give the skillet a shake to distribute the ingredients evenly, then add the eggs and cook without stirring until the edges and bottom begin to set, 2½ to 3 minutes.

6. Place the skillet under the broiler and cook until the top of the tortilla is very lightly browned, 2½ to 3 minutes. Let the tortilla stand for a minute or so to cool, then run a knife around the edge to loosen it, cut it into wedges, and serve. The tortilla can also be served at room temperature.

NOTE: You can use 2 cups potato cubes from Amazing Baked Potatoes (page 366).

This is a versatile breakfast casserole that is a great way to use up bread that's in danger of going stale. The casserole can be assembled and refrigerated overnight before it is baked, which makes it particularly convenient for weekend breakfasts when you want something hearty and a little special. If you don't happen to have any Cheddar, use Parmesan, Swiss, Monterey Jack, or any other flavorful cheese.

SAUSAGE-PEPPER STRATA

SERVES: 6 GENEROUSLY PREP TIME: 20 MINUTES

1 package (12 ounces) spicy breakfast-style bulk sausage
  (see Notes)
1 large onion (for about 1 cup chopped)
1 medium-size green or red bell pepper
  (for about 1 cup chopped)
Cooking oil spray
4 cups white or whole wheat bread cubes (see Notes)
6 large eggs
1½ cups whole, low-fat, or skim milk
¼ teaspoon salt
¼ teaspoon black pepper
1 cup shredded Cheddar cheese

1. Crumble the sausage into a 12-inch skillet and cook over medium heat, stirring frequently to break it up. Meanwhile, peel and coarsely chop the onion, adding it to the skillet as you chop.

Continue to stir the sausage and onion frequently while you stem, seed, and coarsely chop the bell pepper. Add the pepper pieces to the skillet and continue to cook until the sausage is browned and fully cooked, about 10 minutes total. Pour the mixture into a colander and drain well. (If you use reduced-fat sausage, draining may not be necessary.)

2. Spray a 13- x 9-inch glass or ceramic baking dish with cooking oil spray. Spread the bread cubes out in the dish and sprinkle the sausage mixture evenly over the bread.

3. Whisk the eggs, milk, salt, and black pepper together in a 1-quart or larger bowl until well combined. Pour the egg mixture evenly over the sausage. Use a fork to press the sausage and bread into the milk mixture until all of the bread is moist. Cover with plastic wrap or aluminum foil and refrigerate for at least 1 hour or overnight.

4. When you are ready to cook the strata, preheat the oven to 375°F.

5. Bake, uncovered, until the strata is light brown and puffy and the eggs have cooked through, 50 to 55 minutes. If the top begins to brown too quickly, cover it with foil for the remainder of the cooking time.

6. Remove the dish from the oven, sprinkle the cheese on top, and return it to the oven. Bake just until the cheese melts, about 5 minutes. Remove the dish from the oven and let it stand for 10 minutes. Cut the strata into squares to serve.

NOTES: Breakfast-style sausage sold in a log without casings is sometimes called bulk sausage. If you cannot find bulk sausage, buy links and remove the casings. Spicy sausage is often referred to as "hot" on the package label. You can also use reduced-fat turkey-pork sausage blend.

■ If you don't have leftover bread cubes in your freezer, cut or tear 6 slices of loaf bread for 4 cups of cubes.

MoneySaver

Want to get your kids to eat the cheaper store-brand cereal? When the name-brand box is empty, don't throw it away. Save the box and fill it with a similar generic cereal. Then wait to see if your kids can tell the difference. If not, you'll save money by continuing to refill the box. (Just be sure to toss the no-brand box before anyone sees it!)

These hash browns are not just a side dish—they're the whole meal. This recipe is based on those delicious hash browns you usually find at joints that serve up short-order breakfasts 24 hours a day. But we've doctored them up a bit, adding sausage, lots of onions, and a sprinkling of cheese. So brew up the coffee, get out the ketchup, and enjoy.

DOCTORED-UP BREAKFAST HASH BROWNS

SERVES: 4 START TO FINISH: UNDER 25 MINUTES

1 package (12 ounces) breakfast-style bulk sausage (see Note)
2 large onions (for about 2 cups chopped)
4 already-baked Russet baking potatoes (see page 366), or 1 package (1 pound, 4 ounces) refrigerated hash-brown potatoes, such as Simply Potatoes
Salt and black pepper to taste
1 cup shredded Cheddar cheese
Ketchup, for serving (optional)

1. Crumble the sausage into an extra-deep 12-inch skillet (preferably nonstick) and cook over medium heat, stirring frequently, to break it up. Meanwhile, peel and coarsely chop the onions, adding them to the skillet as you chop. Cook the sausage until it is almost browned, 6 to 8 minutes.

2. Meanwhile, peel and coarsely chop the potatoes, if using baked. Add the potatoes (whichever you're using) to the skillet after the sausage is almost browned and stir well. Cook without stirring until the potatoes start to brown, about 3 minutes. Then stir and turn the mixture. Again, let the potatoes brown for about 2 minutes, then stir and turn. Continue until the potatoes are tender (if using the purchased potatoes), and until they are browned to the desired crispness. Season with salt and black pepper.

3. Reduce the heat to low and sprinkle the cheese evenly over the potatoes. Allow the cheese to melt, about 1 minute. Serve with ketchup on the side, if desired.

NOTE: There are all types of sausage available, from hot to mild to reduced-fat to maple syrup–flavored. Choose your favorite for this recipe. If you choose the reduced-fat type, add 1 tablespoon vegetable oil to the skillet when you add the potatoes. If your sausage is extremely fatty, you may want to drain off some of the rendered fat before adding the potatoes; leave about 2 teaspoons to aid in browning. If you can't locate bulk-style breakfast sausage, you can use links and remove the casings before browning the meat in Step 1.

CHILE CHEESE GRITS

SERVES: 4 START TO FINISH: UNDER 20 MINUTES

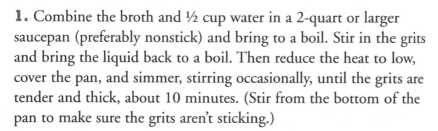

1 can (14 ounces) fat-free chicken broth, or 1¾ cups homemade chicken stock (see page 10)
½ cup quick-cooking (not instant) grits
¾ cup (4 ounces) shredded Cheddar cheese
1 can (4 ounces) diced green chiles

1. Combine the broth and ½ cup water in a 2-quart or larger saucepan (preferably nonstick) and bring to a boil. Stir in the grits and bring the liquid back to a boil. Then reduce the heat to low, cover the pan, and simmer, stirring occasionally, until the grits are tender and thick, about 10 minutes. (Stir from the bottom of the pan to make sure the grits aren't sticking.)

2. Remove the pan from the heat. Stir in the cheese and the green chiles with their juice. Serve at once.

There's nothing like a pot of good old grits. That's what we Southerners think, anyway, probably because we grew up eating lots of this good, inexpensive breakfast food. But if you're not from the South—and if you're looking for a wake-me-up dish to round out your breakfast—dressing up your pot of grits might be in order.

Green chiles add a Southwestern kick, but if you prefer, leave out the chiles and just serve wonderful cheese grits. The chicken broth adds lots of flavor, but you could make the grits with 2½ cups of water instead. (If you're using all water or unsalted stock, add ½ teaspoon salt when you add the grits in Step 1.)

Pancake Mix Fix-ups

From Alicia:

There's nothing easier (or much cheaper) for a quick breakfast—or even dinner—than pancakes. We love to have a pancake night every now and then, and they are a perennial favorite weekend breakfast. Finding an inexpensive pancake mix is as easy as going to the store. Granted, there are a lot of "gourmet" mixes out there, but after experimenting, we've found that we prefer the most inexpensive ones—usually the store brand at the local discount grocery.

When you're paying only a couple of pennies per ounce for the mix, you can afford to splurge on the fix-ups. We find that the best technique is to add the fix-ups just after pouring the batter onto the skillet. This also makes it easy to customize the pancakes to individual tastes. Just sprinkle your favorite add-in over a pancake, and then when you flip it over, you're cooking the extras right into it. Here are our favorite pancake mix fix-ups.

- Fresh blueberries, blackberries, or raspberries
- Chopped or sliced fresh strawberries
- Sliced bananas (the riper the better)
- Thinly sliced or finely chopped fresh pears or apples
- Pineapple tidbits, fresh or canned
- Granola
- Chopped nuts, such as pecans, walnuts, and/or toasted almonds
- Chocolate chips
- Butterscotch chips
- Shredded coconut

Get creative and add more than one ingredient. In our book, whipped cream and maple syrup are mandatory toppers for those really special occasions.

"Get creative and add more than one ingredient."

BEV'S ULTIMATE OATMEAL

SERVES: 1 **START TO FINISH:** UNDER 5 MINUTES

For the oatmeal
⅓ cup old-fashioned rolled oats
1 tablespoon lightly packed light brown sugar
(see Note)

Optional toppings
2 tablespoons raisins
2 tablespoons dried cranberries
2 tablespoons chopped toasted walnuts or pecans
¼ teaspoon ground cinnamon

1. Place the oats and ⅔ cup water in a microwave-safe cereal bowl that has a capacity of at least 2 cups. Microwave, uncovered, on high power for 2 to 2½ minutes. (The exact time depends on the power of your microwave. If the oatmeal still contains a lot of water after 2 minutes, microwave for 30 seconds more. My experiments showed that microwaving for longer than 2½ minutes causes the oatmeal to bubble over the sides of the bowl.) Remove the bowl from the microwave oven and stir the oatmeal well. Let the oatmeal stand for 1 minute so that all of the water is absorbed.

2. Sprinkle the brown sugar evenly over the oatmeal. Sprinkle with the additional toppings, as desired. Serve at once.

NOTE: Honey or maple syrup can be used instead of the brown sugar.

From Beverly:

When you start me talking about my favorite breakfast, it's hard to get me to hush up: This oatmeal tastes terrific, is unbelievably healthy, and is incredibly quick to microwave.

First, if you make it in an individual bowl you won't have to wash anything else. Because it takes just a couple of minutes, you can quickly microwave enough individual bowls for the whole family. The bowl should be microwavable and hold at least 2 cups with some room to spare. Since the oatmeal will bubble up as it cooks, it will spill over the sides, if your bowl isn't large enough.

Importantly, make the oatmeal only with the proportions listed in this recipe. I've tried microwaving more oatmeal and less oatmeal, and it simply doesn't work. However, ⅓ cup uncooked oatmeal is the perfect portion size for most people.

If you want the ultimate oatmeal, load it with all of the toppings listed, and when nobody is looking, drizzle on a little half-and-half or heavy cream. Amazing!

From Beverly:

I keep homemade granola on hand most of the time, but sometimes my best intentions go astray, particularly when I'm on a writing deadline.

"I know you've been busy trying to finish your new book and all," my husband ventured one day, "but now that it's almost done, do you think you might start making granola again?"

It's so easy to stir up a big batch—even deadline pressure is no excuse. This recipe can easily be cut in half if your family isn't as granola-crazy as mine is.

GREAT GRANOLA

MAKES: ABOUT 13 CUPS   START TO FINISH: UNDER 45 MINUTES

Cooking oil spray
½ cup vegetable oil
½ cup pure maple syrup or honey (see Notes)
1½ cups lightly packed light brown sugar
6 cups quick-cooking or old-fashioned rolled oats
(not instant oatmeal)
2 cups chopped walnuts, almonds, or pecans
1 cup wheat germ (optional; see Notes)
1 cup sweetened shredded coconut
1 cup raisins
1 cup sweetened dried cranberries or cherries
(optional; see Notes)

1. Place oven racks in the two center positions and preheat the oven to 350°F. Spray two 17- x 11-inch jelly-roll pans with cooking oil spray.

2. Combine the oil, maple syrup, and brown sugar in a 1-quart microwave-safe bowl. Microwave, uncovered, on high power until the sugar starts to melt, about 3 minutes. Remove the bowl from the microwave oven and whisk until any lumps dissolve.

3. Combine the oats, nuts, wheat germ (if using), and coconut in a 3-quart or larger bowl. Toss to mix well. Pour the syrup mixture over the oat mixture and stir until well mixed. Spread evenly onto the jelly-roll pans.

4. Place a pan on each oven rack and bake for 10 minutes. Taking note of which pan was on the top rack, remove the pans from the oven, stir the granola, and return it to the oven, rotating each pan to the opposite rack. (If your oven will accommodate the two pans side-by-side on the same rack, it is not necessary to rotate them.) Bake for 8 to 10 minutes, taking care not to let the granola get too brown.

5. Cool the granola in the pans until it reaches room temperature, about 1 hour. Sprinkle the raisins and dried cranberries (if using) over each pan, dividing them evenly. Stir to mix well. Store in air-tight containers, preferably glass jars or tins, for up to 2 weeks.

NOTES: Use only real maple syrup, not artificially flavored pancake syrup.

■ Look for wheat germ in the supermarket cereal aisle.

■ The dried cranberries or cherries make for a colorful granola, but you can increase the raisins to 2 cups instead.

About:
GRANOLA: THE ALL-PURPOSE TREAT

From Beverly:

It's true that you can buy granola at the supermarket, but compared to homemade, that supermarket stuff might as well be sawdust. And nothing makes my hubby happier in the morning than to sprinkle his cereal with toasted oats, nuts, and a dash of coconut, all glazed with pure maple syrup.

It is also a wonderful breakfast addition and all-purpose snack. My family loves granola sprinkled over fresh fruit, yogurt, oatmeal, and ice cream. And when you're off on a stroll, walk, hike, or run, instead of raisins and peanuts, pack a zipper-top bag to help keep your energy up. Going to the movies? Granola makes a nice break from that overpriced bag of popcorn.

MoneySaver

If you've become accustomed to breakfast cereals with sugary flakes, dried fruit, and nuts but don't like the expense, try this: Fill a bowl with the inexpensive plain cereal, then sprinkle just a little of our granola on top as a garnish. You'll probably like this mixture better anyway, because most of those embellished cereals are too sweet—and not healthful.

When we were growing up in the South, folks used to put thick slices of Cheddar cheese on top of leftover apple pie and eat it for breakfast—a flavor combination made in heaven. This recipe combines those flavors and then gives them a Mexican flair by putting them inside flour tortillas. We were surprised to find that, at our supermarket, the house brand of apple pie filling was the superior choice in taste and texture.

APPLE PIE QUESADILLA

SERVES: 4 START TO FINISH: UNDER 25 MINUTES

Cooking oil spray
1 tablespoon butter
2 large (10- to 12-inch) flour tortillas
1 can (21 ounces) apple pie filling
½ cup finely shredded Cheddar cheese
1 tablespoon sugar
½ teaspoon ground cinnamon

1. Preheat the oven to 375°F. Spray a large baking sheet with cooking oil spray.

2. Place the butter in a small microwave-safe dish, cover it with a paper towel, and microwave on high power until melted, about 15 seconds. Set aside.

3. Place 1 tortilla on the prepared baking sheet. Spoon the apple pie filling onto the tortilla and spread it out almost to the edge. Sprinkle the cheese evenly over the filling. Place the second tortilla over the apple mixture, forming a top crust.

4. Drizzle the melted butter evenly over the top crust of the quesadilla. Mix the sugar and cinnamon together in a small dish and sprinkle it evenly over the melted butter.

5. Bake until the quesadilla is crisp and the edges are just beginning to brown, 8 to 10 minutes. Remove it from the oven and, using a pizza cutter or a sharp knife, cut the quesadilla into 4 wedges, then serve.

CROISSANTS WITH CHOCOLATE GRAVY

SERVES: 8 START TO FINISH (SAUCE ONLY): UNDER 10 MINUTES

4 large croissants, biscuits, or
    crescent rolls (see Note)
¾ cup sugar
2 tablespoons all-purpose flour
¼ cup unsweetened cocoa powder
Pinch of salt
1½ cups whole or low-fat (not skim) milk
2 tablespoons butter
2 teaspoons vanilla extract
Fresh fruit, such as strawberries, raspberries,
    or pineapple chunks, for serving (optional)

SUPER-CHEAP!

1. Heat or bake the croissants, biscuits, or crescent rolls according to the package directions.

2. Meanwhile, stir the sugar, flour, cocoa powder, and salt together in a 2-quart or larger saucepan. Place the pan over medium heat and gradually add the milk, whisking constantly, until the mixture is well blended and smooth. Cook, stirring frequently, until the sauce has thickened slightly, 5 to 6 minutes. It should have the consistency of hot fudge sauce.

3. Reduce the heat to low. Add the butter and stir until it has melted and is well blended into the chocolate. Remove the pan from the heat and stir in the vanilla.

4. Cut the croissants, rolls, or biscuits in half and pour ¼ cup of the sauce over each half. Garnish each plate with fruit, if desired, and serve immediately.

NOTE: You can use croissants, biscuits, or crescent rolls from a bakery, heat up frozen ones, or bake your own biscuits or rolls using refrigerated dough or a mix.

When a reader of our Desperation Dinners newspaper column, Avis June Thompson, told us about the chocolate gravy that her mother used to serve as a special breakfast, we knew we'd love it. This is guaranteed to jolt you out of the breakfast doldrums. Instead of the homemade biscuits Avis June grew up with, we drizzle this sauce over warm croissants that we bake up flaky and delicious from our stash in the freezer. But lots of breads will work. Any leftover sauce can be refrigerated for up to a week and reheated in the microwave oven.

409

From Alicia:

From Alicia:

I first fell in love with this bread on the day my youngest child started kindergarten. There, at a "new parent" tea, I beheld the most sinful-looking, ooey-gooey bread sitting on a beautiful crystal cake plate. Later, after I had enjoyed several servings, I found out that my dear friend Myra Fisher had baked it.

I was in awe. How could a mother of four young children, and the president of the PTA, possibly have the time or brain space to bake something that obviously took so long to prepare? Then Myra told me how easy it was to make. A friend had given her the recipe years before, and it had become a family favorite for their Christmas-morning breakfast.

The flexibility of this sweet bread makes it perfect for overnight guests, PTA teas, special family breakfasts, or just as a surprise for your kids. Especially around the holidays, you can often find frozen yeast rolls at half price. Stock up: The dough will keep in your freezer for up to 6 months.

MYRA'S MONKEY BREAD

MAKES: ABOUT 12 SERVINGS   PREP TIME: 15 MINUTES

Cooking oil spray
1 package (1 pound) unbaked frozen yeast roll dough
½ cup granulated sugar
½ teaspoon ground cinnamon
½ cup chopped walnuts
½ cup firmly packed light brown sugar
10 tablespoons (1¼ sticks) butter

1. Lightly spray a Bundt or tube pan with cooking oil spray. Empty the entire package of rolls into the pan and distribute them top side up evenly in the pan.

2. Mix the sugar and cinnamon together in a small bowl and sprinkle it over the rolls. Scatter the nuts and the brown sugar over the rolls. Slice the butter into ½-tablespoon pieces and dot them over all. Cover the pan with plastic wrap, place it in a cold oven, and leave it for at least 8 hours or as long as overnight (see Note).

3. Remove the pan from the oven and preheat the oven to 350°F.

4. Uncover the pan, place it in the preheated oven, and bake until the bread is golden brown and slightly bubbly, about 30 minutes.

5. Remove the pan from the oven and let the bread rest for 10 minutes in the pan. Place a cake plate over the top of the pan and flip upside down so the bread falls onto the plate. If it doesn't fall out easily, give the pan a shake. Serve warm or at room temperature, pulling the individual rolls apart with your fingers. (Covered well with plastic wrap and then with aluminum foil, the bread will keep for 3 days at room temperature.)

NOTE: It's important to let the bread rise in a draft-free environment, and a cold oven is perfect for this.

Turn Everyday Coffee into a Gourmet Treat

If the idea of amaretto coffee or cinnamon coffee seems like heaven, there's no reason not to treat yourself. You don't have to buy expensive gourmet coffees or "international" coffee mixes at the supermarket. Just buy regular (inexpensive) coffee and spice it up yourself.

This is way too easy: Simply pour the ground coffee into the filter basket as usual, add just a few drops or a sprinkling of the flavoring or spice of choice, and then brew the coffee as usual.

You don't need specialty syrups. We just use the extracts that you find in the spice section of the supermarket—such as vanilla, almond, and orange. Ground cinnamon, ground allspice, ground cardamom, unsweetened cocoa powder, and ground nutmeg also make good coffee additions. Orange zest is wonderful. Mix and match flavors to your personal preference.

There's no exact science to how much flavoring to add to the coffee. The quantity depends on the amount of coffee you're making and on how strongly flavored you want it to be. In general, we add 3 drops of a flavored extract and/or ½ teaspoon of a ground spice to the grounds for making 6 cups of coffee.

An added benefit: The aroma of the brewing coffee is as wonderful as its flavor.

"Mix and match flavors to your personal preference."

Pumpkin turns these biscuits a lovely light orange, and the raisins and spices make them special. We love serving them to guests, especially in the fall. They're so pretty and unusual that we have bagged them up for gifts as well.

PUMPKIN RAISIN BISCUITS

MAKES: 9 BISCUITS START TO FINISH: UNDER 25 MINUTES

Cooking oil spray
2¼ cups buttermilk baking mix, such as Bisquick
3 tablespoons sugar
1 teaspoon ground cinnamon
1 cup canned 100% pure pumpkin (see Note)
½ cup whole, low-fat, or skim milk
¾ cup raisins

1. Preheat the oven to 450°F. Spray a 17- x 11-inch baking sheet with cooking oil spray.

2. Combine the baking mix, sugar, and cinnamon in a medium-size mixing bowl and stir until well combined. Add the pumpkin, milk, and raisins and stir until well blended.

3. Drop the batter, 2 heaping tablespoonfuls at a time, onto the prepared baking sheet, 1½ to 2 inches apart. Bake until the biscuits are just brown on the bottom, 11 to 13 minutes.

4. Remove the biscuits from the oven and allow them to cool for about 5 minutes on the baking sheet. Serve warm or at room temperature.

NOTE: Do not confuse canned pure pumpkin with canned pumpkin pie filling. Do not use pie filling for this recipe. It must be 100% pure pumpkin.

Easy Strawberry Freezer Jam

MAKES: ABOUT 5 CUPS PREP TIME: 20 MINUTES

About 1 quart whole fresh strawberries
4 cups sugar
1 package Sure-Jell fruit pectin (see Note)

1. Make sure the jam containers and lids are clean and thoroughly dry. (We used 1-cup plastic containers purchased at the supermarket.) Set them aside.

2. Rinse the strawberries and drain them in a colander. Hull the berries, place them in a food processor, and pulse until they are coarsely chopped. (Do not overprocess—you want some chunks.) Or use a potato masher. Measure out exactly 2 cups mashed berries.

3. Place the fruit in a large bowl. Stir in the sugar and let the mixture stand for 10 minutes, stirring it occasionally.

4. Pour ¾ cup water into a small saucepan and stir the pectin into the water. Bring the mixture to a boil over high heat and then boil for 1 minute, stirring constantly. Remove the pan from the heat. Pour the pectin mixture into the bowl containing the fruit and stir until the sugar has dissolved. (A few sugar crystals may remain.)

5. Pour the jam into the prepared containers, leaving about ½ inch at the top for expansion during freezing. Let the containers stand for 24 hours at room temperature, then immediately refrigerate or freeze the jam. (The jam can be refrigerated for up to 3 weeks or frozen for up to 1 year. Thaw frozen jam in the refrigerator.)

NOTE: We tested this recipe using Sure-Jell fruit pectin. Other pectin products are available but may require a different amount of water, fruit, and/or sugar. Follow the directions exactly.

From Alicia:

My friend Paula Henderson gave us a lovely jar of homemade strawberry jam, and the minute it was gone, my kids started asking if I could please make some more. Me, make jam? They had to be kidding. My crazy schedule doesn't include time for jam. Well, I was wrong.

Freezer jam simply involves fruit, sugar, pectin, and a bit of boiling water. That's it. (The reason it's called "freezer jam" is that it must be stored in the freezer because it does not go through the traditional canning process.) The only secret is that you must follow the directions *exactly.* (That means no substitutions, doubling, decreasing, or other variations if you want successful jam.)

I did some research. It turns out that the various manufacturers of pectin products have calculated the exact proportions needed for successful jam and have made it as simple as one, two, three. So anyone can make Easy Strawberry Freezer Jam in a snap.

From Alicia:

One of my fondest memories of fall in my childhood involves my grandmother's pear preserves and pear butter. We'd spend the cool afternoons gathering the pears in burlap sacks and then lugging them back to the kitchen for canning the next morning. Even peeling what seemed like a thousand pears was fun—and then we'd get to "cook down" the pears until they were ever-so-tender, spice them, and can them. Jar after jar would line the countertops with our day's labors. Hard work for sure, but, *ahhhh,* the results!

Gourmet fruit butters are everywhere now, but at hefty prices. I believe I'll pass. Or maybe not. This recipe for Spiced Pear Butter is so close to my grandmother's, she'd have a hard time telling the difference. While the flavor and texture are all there, the hours in the kitchen are not. No peeling required! Serve pear butter over any style of breakfast bread, from croissants to biscuits to buttered toast. Over ice cream, it makes a yummy dessert.

SPICED PEAR BUTTER

MAKES: 2 CUPS PREP TIME: 20 MINUTES

2 cans (about 15 ounces each) pears in light syrup
¼ cup dry white wine, such as Chardonnay
1 tablespoon fresh lemon juice
¾ cup sugar
1 teaspoon pure vanilla extract
½ teaspoon ground cinnamon
¼ teaspoon ground cloves

1. Make sure the jam containers and lids are clean and thoroughly dry. (We used 1-cup plastic containers purchased at the supermarket.) Set them aside.

2. Drain the pears, place them in a food processor, and pulse several times to finely chop. Be careful not to puree or liquefy the pears.

3. Place the pears, wine, lemon juice, sugar, vanilla, cinnamon, and cloves in a heavy 2-quart or larger saucepan. Place the pan over medium heat and bring to a slow boil, stirring frequently. Continue to boil, stirring frequently, until the mixture thickens slightly, about 15 minutes.

4. Remove the pan from the heat and spoon the pear butter into the prepared containers. Allow to cool, uncovered, for about 30 minutes, then cover and refrigerate for up to 2 weeks.

ALICIA'S FRUIT SMOOTHIES

MAKES: 2 SMOOTHIES START TO FINISH: UNDER 10 MINUTES

6 to 8 ounces fruit yogurt,
  any flavor (see Note)
1 cup fruit juice, such as
  orange juice or a blend
½ to 1 cup fresh fruit, such as
  sliced bananas or peaches,
  or whole or sliced berries
2 cups ice cubes

SUPER-CHEAP!

Combine the yogurt, juice, and fruit in a blender and process until smooth. Add the ice cubes, a few at a time, blending well after each addition. Process until the mixture reaches the desired consistency. Serve in glasses.

NOTE: Low-fat or fat-free yogurt will work just fine. We buy whatever is on sale.

From Alicia:

My kids adore fruit smoothies. Shops that offer this special treat seem to be located on every corner, but making a smoothie at home is easy and inexpensive.

Instead of relying on prepackaged frozen fruit, which can jack up the price, we use ice, fruit juice, yogurt, and seasonal fresh fruit. Everything from bananas to grapes to berries can be added to boost the flavor. These smoothies make a delicious addition to breakfast, and they're a great afternoon snack.

CHAPTER ELEVEN

DELECTABLE DESSERTS

When you get really serious about saving money on groceries, dessert becomes an obvious target. It's one "food group" you don't have to eat, after all. But what happens to the quality of life when there's never any dessert? There are occasions when life simply demands something sweet.

For us, homemade dessert comes in two basic categories: elegant desserts that you'd serve at a family celebration or to company, and homey desserts for regular nights. (Of course, these desserts are worthy company fare, too.)

For Southern women, desserts are a point of pride. We know women who stake their culinary reputations on their desserts alone. So being Southern ourselves, we cannot imagine printing a dessert recipe in one of our cookbooks unless we can truly say we'd be proud to serve it—whether at a party or at the kitchen table. If we're going to take the time and trouble to make dessert, it has to be worth the cost and the calories. No mediocre desserts allowed!

However, by its very nature dessert does not usually come cheap. The ingredients required for rich, satisfying homemade confections—butter, cream, chocolate, nuts, fruit—are costly. And let's face it: When a box of cake mix or brownie mix goes on sale, that's a tough bottom line to beat. If your family would just as soon have an Oreo or a dish of Jell-O to top off dinner, that's also a pretty inexpensive point of comparison. So when we started thinking about making special desserts on a budget, we realized we had our work cut out for us.

We eliminated a host of recipes on the cost factor alone. Making a dessert from scratch is not automatically cheaper than purchasing a comparable dessert at the supermarket or bakery, especially if the recipe would require you to buy a lot of ingredients that you wouldn't use up. We quickly realized that the cheapest homemade desserts were the simplest. And sometimes the simplest desserts are simply the best. So here we have over two dozen desserts that can be made for pennies (for example, our Chocolate Bread Pudding cost us 30 cents per serving, Grandma's Eclair Cake, 45 cents per serving, and our Old-Fashioned Gingerbread with Lemon Glaze weighed in at 20 cents per slice).

"The cheapest homemade desserts are the simplest."

Whether it's Individual Chocolate Shortcakes with Strawberries, Ron's Favorite Sweet Potato Pie, Banana-Pineapple Crumb Cobbler, or Caffe Latte Granita, we know you'll be proud to serve these desserts, too.

Strawberries are one of our favorite fruits. We love to make a summertime trip to "the patch" to pick them straight from the field—and get the best possible price. Of course we always pick too many, so it's strawberries at every meal for at least a few days. We crave traditional strawberry shortcake, but after a while, we welcome something a bit different. Here, powdered cocoa transforms ordinary baking mix into elegant chocolate biscuits, giving us that little something extra. Although they are yummy straight out of the oven, we sometimes like to slice the biscuits and let them cool while we eat our evening meal. The assembly takes only about 5 minutes.

INDIVIDUAL CHOCOLATE SHORTCAKES WITH STRAWBERRIES

SERVES: 6 START TO FINISH: UNDER 20 MINUTES

2 cups buttermilk biscuit mix, such as Bisquick
¼ cup unsweetened cocoa powder
3 tablespoons sugar
⅔ cup whole or low-fat milk
1½ pounds fresh strawberries (for 4 cups sliced), plus 6 small whole berries for garnish
¾ cup strawberry jam (see Notes)
Whipped cream, to taste (see Notes)

1. Position a rack in the center of the oven and preheat the oven to 450°F.

2. Pour the biscuit mix into a 2-quart or larger mixing bowl. Stir in the cocoa powder and sugar. Add the milk and stir to blend well. (The dough will be sticky.)

3. Drop the dough onto an ungreased baking sheet by heaping quarter-cups, making 6 drop biscuits. Bake until a toothpick inserted into the center comes out clean, 9 to 11 minutes.

4. While the biscuits bake, rinse and drain the strawberries. Reserve the 6 small whole berries for garnish. Hull and slice the remaining berries and set them aside.

5. When the biscuits are done, slice each one in half. (You can let the biscuits cool at this point or proceed with the recipe.)

6. Assemble the shortcakes: Place the bottom halves of the biscuits on individual dessert plates. Place the jam in a 1-cup or larger glass measure, cover it with microwave-safe plastic wrap, cut a vent in the plastic wrap, and microwave on high power just until the

jam is loose enough to drizzle, about 1 minute. Meanwhile, scatter the sliced berries over the bottom halves of the biscuits. (Berries will spill over the sides.)

7. Drizzle 2 tablespoons of the jam over each serving of berries, then top with whipped cream. Place the biscuit tops over the whipped cream. Spoon a small dollop of whipped cream over each biscuit top, and place a whole strawberry in the cream as a garnish. Serve at once.

NOTES: You can use our Easy Strawberry Freezer Jam (page 413) or any good-quality purchased strawberry jam.
■ The cheapest option is to whip your own cream, but whipped cream from an aerosol can is fine too.

MoneySaver

We always shop after-the-holidays sales. Once the celebrations are over, many grocery stores will pull those expensive holiday delicacies off the shelf, discount them drastically, and cram them into a cart or an aisle display in the hope of selling them quickly. Some of our favorite after-holiday deals include jars of chestnuts, eggnog, holiday-motif napkins and paper plates, and holiday cookies and candy. Who cares if the M&Ms are red and green in January? They're still chocolate.

Eating fresh-baked gingerbread is like gobbling up a warm hug. It's rare to find ginger-bread made from scratch anymore, and yet it is so easy and inexpensive to do.

Laurie Colwin said it best in her book *Home Cooking:* "Gingerbread made from scratch takes very little time and gives back tenfold what you put into it. Baking gingerbread perfumes the house as nothing else. It is good eaten warm or cool, iced or plain. It improves with age, should you be lucky or restrained enough to keep any around."

This recipe cuts down on the huge amounts of molasses called for in some recipes and is a great way to use up that extra cup of coffee that's lingering in the pot. (If you are not a coffee drinker, use instant coffee granules. Just follow the brewing instructions on the jar.)

We enjoy this delicious treat straight out of the oven with no topping, or cooled slightly and topped with a lemon glaze.

OLD-FASHIONED GINGERBREAD WITH LEMON GLAZE

SERVES: 8 PREP TIME: 15 MINUTES

Butter or cooking oil spray
    for preparing the pan
2¼ cups all-purpose flour, plus
    more for preparing the pan
¼ cup vegetable oil
¼ cup sugar
½ cup dark or light molasses (see Note)
1 cup brewed coffee, at room temperature
2 large eggs
1½ teaspoons baking soda
¼ teaspoon salt
¾ teaspoon ground cinnamon
¾ teaspoon ground cloves
1½ teaspoons ground ginger
Lemon Glaze (recipe follows; optional)

SUPER-CHEAP!

1. Preheat the oven to 300°F. Lightly butter (or spray with cooking oil spray) and flour an 8-inch square glass baking dish. Set it aside.

2. Cream together the oil, sugar, and molasses in the large bowl of an electric mixer or with a hand-held mixer. Add the coffee and eggs and mix until combined.

3. In a separate bowl, sift the 2¼ cups flour, baking soda, salt, cinnamon, cloves, and ginger together. Add the dry ingredients to the molasses mixture and blend until no lumps remain. The batter will be very thin and smooth.

4. Pour the batter into the prepared baking dish and bake until a toothpick inserted into the center comes out clean, 45 to 50 minutes.

5. Remove the gingerbread from the oven and allow it to cool for about 15 minutes in the dish. Then cut it into squares and serve with glaze, if desired.

NOTE: There are several different kinds of molasses—sulfured and unsulfured, mild and full-flavored. Any kind is fine for this dish. An equal amount of brown sugar can be substituted.

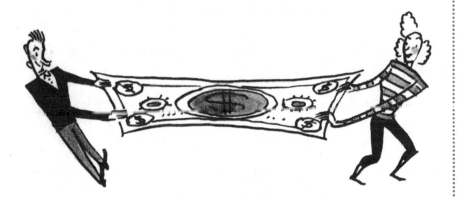

MoneySaver

Don't throw out brewed coffee. Freeze leftovers in ice cube trays for cooling iced coffee. Or use it to make Caffe Latte Granita (page 451) or Old-Fashioned Ginger-bread (opposite).

LEMON GLAZE

MAKES: ABOUT ⅔ CUP **PREP TIME:** 5 MINUTES

Perfectly sweet-tart, this easy glaze is a nice complement to the spicy gingerbread.

¼ **cup fresh lemon juice**
1 **cup confectioners' sugar**

Mix the lemon juice and confectioners' sugar in a small bowl until completely blended and smooth. Spoon over squares of gingerbread before serving.

NOTE: The glaze will keep, covered, in the refrigerator for 3 to 5 days. Bring back to room temperature before serving.

If you have some bananas that are ripening before you can get to them, don't throw them away. Just peel the bananas, toss them into a gallon-size zipper-top plastic bag, and freeze them. Keep adding to the bag until you have enough for this grand cobbler of sorts—it's a lot easier than baking banana bread or muffins. If the bananas are frozen, do not thaw them or they'll turn to mush. Just use a sharp knife to slice the frozen bananas carefully, and place them over the pineapple as described in the recipe.

The cobbler tastes great with only these five ingredients, but we find it's also a good way to use up the last bits of this and that we find in the refrigerator and pantry. You could add a little sweetened flaked coconut, a few chocolate chips, some frozen blueberries, or canned mandarin oranges. A third of a cup of quick-cooking oats, sprinkled in along with the cake mix, adds interest. Get creative—your family and friends will be glad you did!

BANANA-PINEAPPLE CRUMB COBBLER

SERVES: 12 PREP TIME: 20 MINUTES

12 tablespoons (1½ sticks) butter,
   plus more for preparing the pan
1 can (8 ounces) crushed pineapple packed in juice
8 very ripe medium-size bananas, fresh or frozen
1 box (18.25 ounces) white or yellow cake mix
½ to 1 cup pecan pieces (see Note; optional)

1. Preheat the oven to 350°F. Butter a 13- x 9-inch glass or metal baking dish and set it aside.

2. Cut the butter into 6 pieces, place them in a microwave-safe dish, and cover with a paper towel. Microwave on high power until the butter just melts, about 1 minute. Set aside.

3. Spread the pineapple (with its juice) evenly in the prepared baking dish. Cut the bananas into ¼-inch-thick slices and place them over the pineapple.

4. Sprinkle the cake mix evenly over the fruit, spreading it all the way to the edges of the pan. Drizzle the melted butter in a fine stream over the cake mix, covering the cake mix completely. If you are using the pecans, sprinkle them over the top.

5. Bake until the top is golden and the edges are bubbling, 45 to 55 minutes. To serve, spoon into individual dessert bowls. Serve warm or at room temperature. Leftovers can be covered and refrigerated for up to 2 days. Reheat, covered with foil, in a 325°F oven for 10 minutes, if desired.

NOTE: Walnuts, almonds, cashews, or macadamia pieces can also be used.

Cheap Desserts from the Store

Snagging an inexpensive prepared dessert from the supermarket—something that you're not embarrassed to serve—may seem impossible, but it's not. We've scouted out all kinds of ways to get dessert on the table quickly and not break the piggy bank in the shuffle. Here are some of our favorites:

- Supermarkets often sell fresh pound cakes (and flavored cakes with similar textures) in halves. This smaller cake is perfect for topping with fresh berries that you've mixed with a little sugar and a dollop of whipped cream. If you can't find a half cake, buy the whole thing and freeze half: Cut the cake, wrap the extra half well with plastic wrap, and place it in a freezer-weight plastic bag. The cake thaws at room temperature in about 2 hours. When the cakes are on sale, they usually cost less than the ingredients for a homemade pound cake.

- Frozen pound cake often goes on sale in the summertime, and our freezer pantries are never without one or two. For frugal fondue, cube the cake and dip it into melted chocolate frosting (zap the frosting in the microwave oven for a few seconds).

- Layer ice cream sandwiches in a rectangular glass dish, and top them with whipped cream (any type works, including frozen whipped topping that's been defrosted for spreading). Freeze for 1 hour, then slice and serve. Voilà! A layered ice cream dessert. With a spoonful of chocolate sauce, it's miraculous!

- Shortbread or pecan shortbread mini cookies are perfect for making miniature cookie sandwiches. Just spoon a bit of purchased frosting (any flavor) between these buttery beauties, and dessert is complete. Unopened frosting stores for 3 months, so buy a stash when it goes on special.

"When cakes are on sale, they usually cost less than homemade."

423

CAROLINA PUMPKIN COBBLER

SERVES: 12 PREP TIME: 15 MINUTES

For the crust
8 tablespoons (1 stick) butter
(not margarine)
1 cup all-purpose flour
1 cup granulated sugar
4 teaspoons baking powder
½ teaspoon salt
1 cup whole or low-fat milk
1 teaspoon vanilla extract

For the filling
2 large eggs
1 cup evaporated milk
2 cans (15 ounces each) 100% pure pumpkin
(also called solid-packed pumpkin),
or 3 cups cooked mashed pumpkin (see Note)
1 cup granulated sugar
½ cup lightly packed light brown sugar
1 tablespoon all-purpose flour
1 teaspoon ground cinnamon
¼ teaspoon ground ginger
¼ teaspoon ground nutmeg
½ teaspoon salt

For the topping (optional)
Vanilla ice cream or whipped cream

1. Prepare the crust: Turn the oven on to 350°F. Place the butter in a 13- x 9-inch baking dish and place it in the preheating oven. When the butter has melted, after about 3 minutes, remove the dish from the oven and set it aside. Allow the oven to continue to preheat.

2. Meanwhile, mix the remaining crust ingredients together in a medium-size bowl and pour the mixture evenly over the melted butter. Do not stir. Set aside.

3. Prepare the filling: Lightly beat the eggs in a large bowl. Add the evaporated milk and pumpkin and stir to blend. Stir in the remaining filling ingredients and mix well.

4. Spoon or slowly pour the filling evenly over the crust batter in the baking dish. (The crust ingredients will be almost completely covered.) Do not stir.

5. Bake the cobbler, uncovered, until the crust has risen over the sides of the filling and is golden brown and bubbling, 45 to 50 minutes. (The crust will not cover the cobbler completely.) Remove the dish from the oven and allow the cobbler to cool for 10 to 15 minutes. Serve warm, in shallow dessert bowls, topped with vanilla ice cream or whipped cream, if desired.

NOTE: Do not use pumpkin pie filling. We have found pure pumpkin in several different places in the supermarket. Check the canned vegetable aisle and the baking aisle.

MoneySaver

Stock up on cake mixes when they go on sale. A good time to check is around major holidays, when you can often find them for less than a dollar. Check the expiration date on the package; typically they last for at least a year.

The thing that makes an apple betty a "betty," as opposed to a crisp, is the bread crumbs. This makes it a good choice when we're trying to use up the last of a loaf of bread or when we need a quick dessert from ingredients we typically have on hand. Apple betty dates to Colonial days, and we suspect those Revolutionary cooks liked the dessert for the same reasons—plus the fact that it's delicious and comforting. What more could you ask for?

BUDGET BROWN BETTY

SERVES: 10 TO 12 PREP TIME: 20 MINUTES

8 tablespoons (1 stick) butter,
  plus more for preparing the pan
1 tablespoon lemon juice
2 pounds (about 4 medium) apples
  (any variety except Red Delicious)
⅓ cup granulated sugar
3 cups soft white bread crumbs (see page 235)
⅓ cup firmly packed light or dark brown sugar
2 teaspoons apple pie spice or ground cinnamon
Vanilla ice cream, for serving

1. Preheat the oven to 375°F. Butter a 13- x 9-inch glass or ceramic baking dish and set it aside.

2. Cut the butter into 4 pieces, place them in a microwave-safe measuring cup or small dish, and cover it with a paper towel. Microwave on high power until melted, 45 seconds to 1 minute. Set aside.

3. Pour the lemon juice into a medium-size mixing bowl. Peel and core the apples. Cut them into bite-size chunks, adding them to the bowl as you cut and tossing them in the lemon juice. Add the granulated sugar and stir well. Set aside.

4. Mix the bread crumbs, butter, brown sugar, and apple pie spice together in a medium-size mixing bowl. Stir well.

5. Spoon half the apples into the baking dish. Top with half the crumbs. Repeat with the remaining ingredients.

6. Bake, uncovered, until the apples are tender and the top is crisp and browned, 45 to 55 minutes. Remove the dish from the oven and allow the apple betty to cool for 15 minutes. Serve in small dessert bowls, topped with vanilla ice cream.

GRANDMA'S ECLAIR CAKE

SERVES: 8 PREP TIME: 15 MINUTES

- 1 cup whole, low-fat, or skim milk
- 1 small box (3.4 ounces) French vanilla–flavored instant pudding mix
- 1 carton (8 ounces) whipped topping, such as Cool Whip, defrosted if frozen
- ½ box (7.5 ounces) graham crackers
- 1 cup purchased milk chocolate frosting, at room temperature

1. Mix the milk and the pudding mix together in a medium-size bowl. Stir in the whipped topping and set the mixture aside.

2. Arrange a single layer of graham crackers in the bottom of an 8-inch square glass baking dish. Spread about 1 cup of the pudding mixture over the crackers. Top with another layer of crackers and another layer of pudding mixture. Continue layering until all of the pudding mixture is used. Top with a final layer of crackers.

3. Spread the chocolate frosting over the top layer of crackers, spreading it all the way to the edges. Cover with plastic wrap and refrigerate for at least 4 hours, or up to 24 hours, before serving.

NOTE: Leftover chocolate frosting can be covered and refrigerated for up to 2 weeks. Let it stand at room temperature for at least 20 minutes before spreading.

From Alicia:

My mother-in-law, Betty Ross, is a master at feeding a hungry crowd. Way back when, she had three sons, a daughter, and a husband to feed every day. I can hardly imagine the amount of food those boys consumed. Now she feeds an additional son-in-law, three daughters-in-law, and nine grandchildren when we all gather at her house. So when I need a great dish to serve to a crowd, I call Betty. She's got a recipe box full of ideas and is always willing to share them.

My kids love Grandma Ross's eclair cake, which shows up on the holiday menu at least once a year. Because I don't need to feed the hungry masses that Betty does, I've halved the original recipe. There's still plenty to serve eight.

From Beverly:

Somehow the joys of bread pudding escaped me for decades. My mom didn't make it, and the plain-sounding name never enticed me to experiment. Then my daughter Grey came home from summer camp and announced: "Mom, we have *got* to make bread pudding. It's my new favorite dessert."

And so the grand bread pudding experiment began. As Grey and I served our creations to friends and family, I noticed a pattern: People who like bread pudding don't simply like it—they're passionate about it. Bread pudding is indeed wonderful, something that still surprises me because it's so utterly simple: You just stir together some cream, milk, sugar, and eggs, dump the whole she-bang over bread cubes, and bake. The result? An elegant, easy, and economical dessert that'll elicit raves.

Bread pudding is traditionally served with whiskey sauce—but not to children, of course! They'll like it plain or with our Rich Caramel Sauce.

Grey's Favorite Bread Pudding

SERVES: 12 PREP TIME: 15 MINUTES

SUPER-CHEAP!

4 tablespoons (½ stick) butter, plus more for preparing the pan
6 cups loosely packed, bite-size white bread cubes (see Notes)
2 cups heavy or whipping cream
1 cup whole milk, low-fat milk, or half-and-half (not skim milk)
5 large egg yolks (see Notes)
⅔ cup sugar
1 teaspoon vanilla extract
Whiskey Sauce (recipe follows) or Rich Caramel Sauce (page 450), for serving (optional)

1. Lightly butter a 13- x 9-inch glass or ceramic baking dish.

2. Place the bread cubes in the prepared baking dish.

3. Place the 4 tablespoons butter in a microwave-safe measuring cup or bowl, cover it with a paper towel, and microwave on high power until melted, about 45 seconds. Drizzle the melted butter over the bread cubes, tossing the cubes to distribute the butter as evenly as possible. Set the dish aside.

4. Combine the cream and milk in a small saucepan and bring just to a boil over medium heat. While the mixture is heating, place the egg yolks in a small bowl and beat them lightly.

5. When the cream mixture comes to a boil, remove the pan from the heat. Whisk in the sugar and vanilla well, then whisk in the egg yolks. Pour the mixture over the bread cubes, making sure all the bread is covered. Use the back of a spoon to even out the mixture, if necessary. Cover the baking dish with aluminum foil and refrigerate for at least 1 hour and up to 4 hours.

6. When ready to bake the pudding, preheat the oven to 325°F.

7. Remove the baking dish from the refrigerator and cut six small vent holes in the foil. Bake, covered with the foil, until the pudding is just set, 50 minutes to 1 hour.

8. Remove the bread pudding from the oven, uncover it, and allow it to cool for 15 to 20 minutes. Spoon the warm pudding into dessert bowls and top with sauce, if desired.

NOTES: If the crust is hard, cut it off the bread.
■ You can use 3 of the egg whites to make our Chocolate Meringue Cookies (page 437).

WHISKEY SAUCE

MAKES: 1½ CUPS **START TO FINISH:** UNDER 10 MINUTES

    4 tablespoons (½ stick) butter
    ¾ cup milk
    ½ cup sugar
    1 tablespoon cornstarch
    2 tablespoons cold water
    5 tablespoons bourbon, brandy, Cognac,
       or Scotch whiskey
    1 teaspoon vanilla extract

1. Melt the butter in a heavy saucepan over low heat. Add the milk and sugar and cook, stirring often, until the sugar dissolves, 2 to 3 minutes.

2. Meanwhile, combine the cornstarch and water in a small jar that has a lid. Cover and shake until the lumps dissolve.

3. Add the cornstarch mixture, bourbon, and vanilla to the saucepan. Raise the heat to medium and bring to a boil, stirring constantly. Boil, still stirring constantly, until thickened, about 1 minute.

The kids may pass on this sophisticated sauce, but the adults will be thrilled. It is a Southern cousin to hard sauce, which has similar ingredients and is the traditional accompaniment to plum pudding. Hard sauce is typically chilled, while whiskey sauce is served warm. You can make the sauce up to a day ahead.

429

4. Remove the pan from the heat and let stand for 2 to 3 minutes to cool the sauce slightly before serving. Or allow to cool completely and then refrigerate, covered, for up to 1 day; reheat the sauce briefly in the microwave oven.

NOTE: The sauce can be prepared up to 1 day ahead and refrigerated in an airtight container. To reheat, place the sauce in a microwave-safe bowl, cover with a paper tower, and microwave on high until warm, about 1 minute. Stir the sauce before serving.

CHOCOLATE BREAD PUDDING

SERVES: 12 PREP TIME: 15 MINUTES

**4 tablespoons (½ stick) butter,
  plus more for preparing the pan
6 cups loosely packed, bite-size white bread cubes
  (see Note)
2 cups heavy or whipping cream
1 cup whole milk, low-fat milk, or half-and-half
  (not skim milk)
5 egg yolks
1 bag (12 ounces) semisweet chocolate chips
⅔ cup sugar
1 teaspoon vanilla extract
Rich Caramel Sauce (page 450), for serving (optional)**

1. Lightly butter a 13- x 9-inch glass baking dish.

2. Place the bread cubes in the prepared baking dish.

3. Place the 4 tablespoons butter in a microwave-safe measuring cup or bowl, cover it with a paper towel, and microwave on high power until melted, about 45 minutes. Drizzle the melted butter

"This is about as close to heaven as you can get while you're still alive." That's a direct quote from our friend Bill, who tasted this fudgy pudding when we served it at a casual dinner party. When somebody mused about the number of calories the pudding might contain, Bill didn't miss a beat. "That's like pondering the gas mileage of a Rolls-Royce," he replied.

We especially love it when a Rolls-Royce dessert can be made with a few simple ingredients (and even with slightly stale bread if need be).

over the bread cubes, tossing them to distribute the butter as evenly as possible. Set the dish aside.

4. Combine the cream and milk in a 2-quart or larger saucepan and bring just to a boil over medium heat. While the mixture is heating, place the egg yolks in a small bowl and beat them lightly.

5. When the cream mixture comes to a boil, remove the pan from the heat and add the chocolate chips, sugar, and vanilla. Stir with a whisk until the chocolate has melted and the mixture is smooth. Then add the egg yolks and whisk well.

6. Ladle the chocolate cream evenly over the bread cubes, making sure all the bread is covered. Use the back of a spoon to even out the cream mixture, if necessary. Cover the dish with aluminum foil and refrigerate for at least 1 hour and up to 4 hours.

7. When you are ready to bake the pudding, preheat the oven to 350°F.

8. Remove the baking dish from the refrigerator and cut six small vent holes in the foil. Bake, covered with the foil, until the pudding is just set, about 1 hour.

9. Remove the bread pudding from the oven, uncover it, and allow it to cool for 10 to 15 minutes. Spoon the warm pudding into dessert bowls and top with sauce, if desired.

NOTE: If the crust is hard, cut it off the bread.

From Alicia:

What better way to use that last cup of cooked rice than in a delicious, old-fashioned rice pudding? I've tasted all kinds of fancy rice puddings that make my head swim with all the additions, but I still keep coming back to this recipe—rice pudding in its simplest form. You can leave out the raisins if you don't have any or if your family prefers the pudding unadorned.

BAKED RICE PUDDING WITH CINNAMON

SERVES: 6 PREP TIME: 15 MINUTES

Butter or cooking oil spray
  for preparing the pan
1 cup already-cooked
  medium-grain or
  long-grain rice
½ cup raisins (optional)
3 large eggs
½ cup sugar
2 cups whole or 2-percent milk (see Note)
1 teaspoon vanilla extract
½ teaspoon ground cinnamon

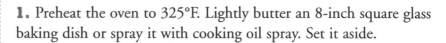

SUPER-CHEAP!

1. Preheat the oven to 325°F. Lightly butter an 8-inch square glass baking dish or spray it with cooking oil spray. Set it aside.

2. Combine the rice and raisins (if desired) in a 2-quart or larger saucepan, add 1 cup water, and heat over medium heat until the rice is rehydrated, about 10 minutes. Drain, if necessary, and set aside.

3. Meanwhile, whisk the eggs, sugar, milk, vanilla, and cinnamon together in a medium-size bowl. Add the drained plumped rice and raisins to the mixture. Stir well and pour into the prepared baking dish.

4. Bake the pudding, uncovered, until the center is almost set and a knife inserted within 1 inch of the side of the dish comes out clean, about 45 minutes. Serve warm, at room temperature, or chilled.

NOTE: We do not recommend using low-fat or skim milk in this recipe.

STRAWBERRY RICE DELIGHT

MAKES: 6 SERVINGS **START TO FINISH: UNDER 25 MINUTES**

1 cup already-cooked medium-
  grain or long-grain rice
1 cup heavy or whipping cream
¼ cup sugar
¼ cup strawberry jam or preserves
Fresh strawberries, for garnish (optional)

SUPER-CHEAP!

1. Place the rice in a 2-quart or larger saucepan, add 1 cup water, and heat over medium heat until the rice is rehydrated, about 10 minutes. Drain, if necessary, and set aside to cool completely.

2. In the small bowl of an electric mixer, whip the cream on high speed until soft peaks form. Gradually add the sugar, 1 tablespoon at a time, and continue to whip until stiff peaks form.

3. Stir in the rice and the jam, and spoon the mixture into individual serving dishes. Garnish with strawberries, if desired, and serve.

Children go mad for this unbelievably simple rice pudding. All it takes to whip it up is a mixer (hand-held is fine) to whip the cream; then you just stir in the other ingredients. It's a perfect spring and summer treat. Easy Strawberry Freezer Jam (page 413) works beautifully, or stir in any other strawberry jam you happen to have on hand.

Every year when the fresh apple crop floods our farmer's markets, we face the bounty with glee, splurging with apples at every meal. On those nights when we don't have time to transform them into a pie, we pull out this recipe. These microwave-"baked" apples combine the flavors we crave—succulent tender apples, brown sugar, and cinnamon—and you don't have to peel a thing.

AMAZING BAKED APPLES

SERVES: 4 START TO FINISH: UNDER 30 MINUTES

¼ cup walnut or pecan pieces
4 medium-size tart apples, such as Granny Smith or Braeburn
About 6 tablespoons lightly packed light brown sugar
½ teaspoon apple pie spice or ground cinnamon
4 teaspoons butter, cut into 4 pieces

SUPER-CHEAP!

1. Spread the nuts out on a microwave-safe plate and microwave, uncovered, on high power until fragrant and toasted, 1 to 3 minutes, stopping halfway to stir. Set aside.

2. While the nuts microwave, core the apples all the way through (do not peel them). Place the apples in a shallow microwave-safe dish, such as a glass pie plate. (If an apple doesn't sit upright in the dish, cut a little off the base to flatten it.)

3. Microwave the apples, uncovered, on high power for 6 minutes to partially cook them.

4. While the apples microwave, finely chop the nuts and set them aside. Place the brown sugar in a small dish, add the apple pie spice, and stir well; set aside.

5. Using oven mitts, carefully remove the plate of apples from the microwave oven. Spoon 1 tablespoon of the chopped nuts and 1 tablespoon of the brown sugar mixture into the cavity of each apple. Using your fingers or the spoon handle, pack the sugar mixture into the cavity. (Depending on the size of the cavity, you may want to use a little more sugar or a little less.) Place a piece of butter on top of the sugar in each apple. (It's okay if the butter just sits on top.)

6. Return the plate to the microwave oven and microwave, uncovered, on high power until the apples are tender when pierced with the tip of a sharp knife, 6 to 8 minutes (see Note).

7. Using oven mitts again, carefully remove the plate from the microwave. Use a large serving spoon to place each apple in a shallow dessert bowl. Spoon the sugar syrup and any nuts that have accumulated in the baking dish evenly over the apples. Allow the apples to cool for 10 to 20 minutes before serving. Serve warm.

NOTE: We tested this recipe using apples that weighed about 7 ounces each. Microwave times may vary, depending on the power of your microwave oven and on the size of the apples. If the apples are large, you will need to increase the cooking time: Just microwave until the apples are tender when pierced with a sharp knife. They will continue to soften a bit during the cooling time.

MoneySaver

Buy nuts in bulk when they're on special (especially around the holidays) and bag them in ¼-cup portions (zipper-top sandwich-size bags are great for this). Then gather all the bags and pop them into a large freezer-weight zipper-top bag and freeze them for up to 6 months.

From Beverly:

If you need a quick-and-easy confection to contribute to the bake sale, or if there's a horde of hungry kids descending on your house, this is the cookie for you. It was my favorite when I was a child, and after we printed the recipe in our Desperation Dinners newspaper column several years ago, readers from all around the country wrote to say that it was their childhood favorite as well. Be sure to use quick oats (not old-fashioned oats and not instant oatmeal). P.S. There's no baking involved!

Our Favorite Peanut Butter– Chocolate Cookies

MAKES: ABOUT 30 COOKIES   PREP TIME: 20 MINUTES

8 tablespoons (1 stick) butter (not margarine)
2 cups sugar
½ cup unsweetened cocoa powder
½ cup whole or low-fat milk
Pinch of salt
¾ cup smooth peanut butter
1 teaspoon vanilla extract
2⅔ cups quick oats

SUPER-CHEAP!

1. Cut the butter into 4 pieces and place them in a 2½-quart or larger pot. Melt the butter over medium-low heat, then stir in the sugar, cocoa powder, milk, and salt. Stir until few lumps of cocoa remain. Raise the heat to medium and cook, stirring frequently, until the mixture just comes to a boil, 2 to 4 minutes.

2. Cook at a boil, stirring constantly, for exactly 2 minutes. (Start timing when it is bubbling around the edges. Boiling too long will cause the mixture to become grainy and harden too fast. If not boiled long enough, the cookies won't harden at all.) Immediately remove the pot from the heat and stir in the peanut butter and vanilla until well blended. Add the oats and stir until they are completely mixed in and covered with chocolate.

3. Place two 18-inch-long sheets of waxed paper on a work surface. Using a cookie dough scoop or a tablespoon measure, drop heaping tablespoons of the cookie mixture onto the waxed paper. Let the cookies stand until they are at room temperature and firm, 30 minutes to 1 hour. Store the cookies in an airtight container at room temperature for up to 3 days.

CHOCOLATE MERINGUE COOKIES

MAKES: 60 TO 70 COOKIES   PREP TIME: 10 MINUTES

½ cup semisweet or milk
    chocolate chips
3 large egg whites, at room temperature
⅓ cup sugar
1 teaspoon vanilla extract

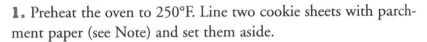

1. Preheat the oven to 250°F. Line two cookie sheets with parchment paper (see Note) and set them aside.

2. Place the chocolate chips in a microwave-safe dish and microwave, uncovered, on high power for 1 minute. Remove the chips from the microwave oven and stir until they are completely melted. Set aside.

3. Using an electric mixer, beat the egg whites on medium speed until soft peaks form, about 1 minute. With the mixer running, slowly add the sugar. Increase the mixer speed to high and beat until the egg whites are stiff but not dry, about 1 minute. Using a spoon or a spatula, gently fold the chocolate and the vanilla into the egg whites.

4. Spoon the mixture into a pint-size zipper-top plastic bag and seal the bag. Use scissors to cut a small opening in one corner of the bag. Squirt the meringue onto the parchment paper in bite-size dollops. Bake for 1 hour.

5. Remove the cookies from the oven and allow them to cool completely on the cookie sheets, about 30 minutes. Then peel them off the parchment and serve at once or store the cookies in an airtight container at room temperature for up to 2 weeks.

NOTE: These cookies are too fragile to remove from a cookie sheet that has not been lined with parchment paper. It's available in some supermarkets and at kitchenware shops.

From Beverly:

There were four teenagers on hand for my son's birthday on the afternoon I was testing this recipe. Everyone liked the birthday cake, but what really drew the raves were these chocolate cookies! They're crisp outside and slightly chewy inside, incredibly light, and definitely addictive. You'd have to use formidable willpower to stop at just one.

I whip up these incredibly easy cookies—just four simple ingredients—whenever I've used egg yolks in a recipe—they are a great way to use the leftover whites.

One bit of advice: There's a good reason why the cookies need to be bite-size. The outsides are so crisp that you'll end up with crumbs all over yourself if you try to bite into one. So just pop the whole thing into your mouth and enjoy.

We almost always have some flour tortillas handy, and if you combine them with some simple ingredients, you can whip up a quick and delicious dessert or snack that will taste as if it cost a fortune. If you want to double the recipe, you can: Just use two baking sheets and rotate them halfway through baking for even browning.

MoneySaver

Don't give up on that crystallized honey left in the bottom of the jar. Place the jar in the microwave oven (as long as there is no metal on it) and microwave for 30 seconds. The hardened honey will turn back to liquid.

SWEET CINNAMON CHIPS

MAKES: 16 CHIPS **START TO FINISH:** UNDER 20 MINUTES

SUPER-CHEAP!

2 large (10- to 12-inch)
  flour tortillas
3 tablespoons butter
2 tablespoons sugar
1 teaspoon ground cinnamon
¼ cup honey, chocolate syrup,
  or Rich Caramel Sauce (page 450),
  or more to taste

1. Preheat the oven to 375°F.

2. Stack the tortillas on top of each other and cut them into 8 equal triangles, using a pizza cutter or a sharp knife.

3. Place the butter in a shallow microwave-safe dish and microwave, uncovered, on high power until melted, about 25 seconds. Meanwhile, combine the sugar and cinnamon in a small bowl and set it aside.

4. Drag one side of each tortilla triangle through the melted butter, then over the side of the dish to remove the excess. Place the triangles, butter side up, on an ungreased 15- x 10-inch baking sheet. Sprinkle evenly with the cinnamon sugar.

5. Bake until the tortillas barely begin to crisp, about 8 minutes. Transfer the crisps to a serving plate and let them rest for 2 minutes to cool and crisp.

6. Meanwhile, place the honey in a microwave-safe dish and heat on high power for 30 seconds to 1 minute. Drizzle the warm honey over the crisps and serve.

SUGARY PASTRY CRISPS

MAKES: 12 COOKIES START TO FINISH: UNDER 20 MINUTES

Two 9-inch unbaked pie crusts, purchased
 or homemade (see page 446)
3 tablespoons firmly packed light or
 dark brown sugar
1 teaspoon ground cinnamon
¼ cup pecans or walnuts (pieces are fine)
¼ cup honey, or to taste

SUPER-CHEAP!

1. Preheat the oven to 450°F.

2. If you are using homemade pie crusts that are not already rolled
out, roll them out to form a 9- to 10-inch round. If you are using
purchased pie crusts, follow the directions on the package for
bringing the crusts to room temperature in the microwave oven.

3. Place 1 pie crust on an ungreased cookie sheet or pizza pan.
Repair any cracks or tears with wet fingers, pinching the dough
back together. Crumble the brown sugar evenly over the entire
crust. Sprinkle the cinnamon evenly over the sugar. Finely chop
the nuts and sprinkle them evenly over the cinnamon.

4. Place the second pie crust over the top and press it down firmly
with a flat hand. Press the edges of the two crusts together with
your fingertips.

5. Bake the cookie until it is light brown, about 11 minutes.

6. Using a pizza cutter or a knife, slice the cookie into 12 wedges.
Place the wedges on a serving plate, drizzle the honey evenly over
them, and serve.

From Alicia:

When I was growing
up, it was always
a treat to take the
scraps of Mom's pie pastry,
sprinkle them with sugar
and nuts, and bake them
on a piece of foil. Drizzled
with honey, they were a
special treat for kids who
couldn't wait for the pie
to finish baking. (And not
a crumb of that precious
pie pastry went to waste.)
If you don't have time to
make your own pastry,
you can still indulge in
this simple dessert. Using
two refrigerated pie crusts,
you can have steaming,
sugary homemade cookies
that will delight kids and
grownups alike. They're
best hot out of the oven,
but if you have any left-
overs, wrap them tightly in
aluminum foil and serve
them later. They will keep
for 2 to 3 days.

439

There are a few certainties in life, but one of them is that fresh cranberries will go on sale a week or so before Thanksgiving, and probably again at Christmas. When cranberries are so cheap, it's a shame not to make this simple yet beautiful pie. This is one of those less-is-more recipes, and if you like cranberries, you'll love it. Our thanks go to our friend Ada Winters, who adapted the pie from a recipe she found in a Shaker cookbook published in the 1950s that belonged to her aunt Ada.

AUNT ADA'S CRANBERRY PIE

SERVES: 8 PREP TIME: 10 MINUTES

Two 9-inch unbaked pie crusts,
   purchased or homemade
   (see page 446)
1 cup sugar
1 tablespoon all-purpose flour
2 teaspoons vanilla extract
2½ cups fresh cranberries
Vanilla ice cream, for serving (optional)

1. Position a rack in the center of the oven and preheat the oven to 350°F.

2. Place 1 pie crust in a 9-inch pie plate.

3. Mix the sugar and flour together in a small bowl. Add the vanilla and stir until it is evenly distributed.

4. Pour the cranberries into the pie crust and sprinkle the sugar mixture evenly over them. Place the second pie crust over the fruit, folding the edges over the edge of the bottom crust. Crimp the edges together with your fingers or with a fork.

5. Bake the pie until the top crust is light golden brown, 35 to 40 minutes.

6. Let the pie cool. Serve it slightly warm or at room temperature, topped with vanilla ice cream, if desired. Store leftover pie, covered, at room temperature, for up to 3 days.

REX'S OATMEAL PIE

SERVES: 8 PREP TIME: 10 MINUTES

4 tablespoons (½ stick) butter,
   at room temperature
¾ cup sugar
3 large eggs
1 cup light corn syrup
1 teaspoon vanilla extract
½ teaspoon salt
1 cup quick oats (not instant oatmeal)
½ cup raisins (optional)
One 9-inch unbaked pie crust, homemade or purchased
   (page 446)

SUPER-CHEAP!

1. Preheat the oven to 325°F.

2. Using an electric mixer, cream the butter and sugar well in a large mixing bowl. Add the eggs, one at a time, mixing gently after each addition. Add the corn syrup, vanilla, and salt. Beat until smooth. Stir in the oats and raisins (if using).

3. Place the pie crust in a 9-inch pie plate and pour the mixture into it. Place the pie plate on a cookie sheet.

4. Bake until the top is golden brown and firm to the touch, 55 minutes to 1 hour. Let the pie cool for at least 1 hour before serving. Store leftover pie, covered, in the refrigerator, for up to 3 days.

From Alicia:

To my mind, hospital food ranks right up there with the mystery morsels served on airplanes. So imagine my surprise when, as a recipe columnist for my local newspaper, I kept receiving requests for the oatmeal pie served at Rex Hospital in Raleigh.

The hospital's executive chef at the time, Paul Johnson, was happy to share the recipe with our readers, and over the years I've made slight changes as I've adapted the recipe to my family's preferences.

Be sure to use quick-cooking oats, not instant oatmeal. Quick-cooking oat flakes are smaller than old-fashioned oats and will form a nutlike crust on the top of the pie. The raisins are optional, but my husband can't imagine this pie without them.

No Need to Be a Gadget Junkie

"We do recommend spending a little extra money on knives."

You simply don't need a lot of gee-whiz gadgets to be a good cook, and stocking your kitchen with every tool on the market would cost a pretty penny indeed.

We've learned this lesson the hard way. The pasta maker we used once and finally sold at a yard sale comes to mind. Then there was the tiny electric chopper that took more time to clean than it saved doing the chopping. The rice cooker went in the trash soon after it spewed starchy water all over our kitchen cabinets. And the deep-fat fryer, used once, was donated to Goodwill.

You will, of course, need some basic kitchen equipment. Chief on the list are sharp knives, a large skillet that has a lid, measuring cups and spoons, a wire whisk, a cutting board, wooden spoons, spatulas (rubber for scraping bowls and a stiff one for removing food from a skillet), mixing bowls, a medium-size saucepan, baking pans, and cookie sheets.

One area where we do recommend spending a little extra money is knives. Properly cared for, good-quality knives will last practically forever. (Show us someone who hates to cook, and we'll show you the owner of a dull knife!) You can get by with three basic knives: a paring knife, a chef's knife, and a slicing knife.

Some of our recipes do call for an electric mixer, but this appliance need not be industrial-strength or expensive. In fact, our mixers are the cheapest models we could find, and they work well unless you're kneading a stiff yeast dough. Some of our recipes (mostly sauces and salad dressings) also call for a food processor or blender. Again, the cheapest models work fine, and as you'll see in the recipes, if you don't have a processor you can often use a blender—and vice versa.

If you think there's a kitchen gadget you might like to own, first try borrowing one from a friend and take it for a test drive. You'll save yourself a lot of money and storage space!

SOUTHERN BUTTERMILK PIE

SERVES: 8 PREP TIME: 10 MINUTES

One 9-inch unbaked pie crust,
   purchased or homemade (page 446)
2 large eggs
1½ cups sugar
3 tablespoons all-purpose flour
8 tablespoons (1 stick) butter
1 cup regular or low-fat buttermilk
1 tablespoon lemon juice
2 teaspoons vanilla extract
Seasonal berries, for serving (optional)

1. Position a rack in the center of the oven and preheat the oven to 350°F. Line a pie plate with the unbaked crust and set aside.

2. Using an electric mixer, beat the eggs until well mixed, about 1 minute. Add the sugar and flour and beat at medium speed until very well combined, 2 minutes.

3. Cut the butter into 4 pieces, place them in a microwave-safe dish, and cover with a paper towel. Microwave on high power just until melted, 45 seconds to 1 minute.

4. Add the butter and buttermilk to the sugar mixture and mix on high speed for 2 minutes. Add the lemon juice and vanilla and beat until mixed in. Pour the mixture into the pie crust.

5. Bake until the top is golden brown and a toothpick inserted in the center comes out clean, 55 minutes to 1 hour. Remove the pie from the oven and allow it to cool until it is just slightly warm, about 30 minutes. (The pie can also be served at room temperature.) Serve each slice of pie with berries on the side, if desired. Store leftover pie, covered, in the refrigertor, for up to 3 days.

A pie made out of *what*? you ask. To be precise, this is a chess pie, one of those heavenly concoctions that requires you to ignore the ingredients list and put your faith in generations of Southern cooks who wouldn't dream of serving a dessert that doesn't make you quiver in your hoop skirt. Chess pie is, by definition, simple. It's comfort food—smooth as velvet and slightly tart from the buttermilk and the shot of lemon juice. If you can't imagine using the rest of a quart of buttermilk, look for 1-cup cartons, which are available in some stores and are perfect for this recipe. (Do *not* use reconstituted powdered buttermilk.) If strawberries, blueberries, or raspberries are in season, a few served on the side make for an even more special dessert.

RON'S FAVORITE SWEET POTATO PIE

SERVES: 8   PREP TIME: ABOUT 1 HOUR

3 medium sweet potatoes
(about 1½ pounds, for 2½ cups
cooked and mashed)
One 9-inch unbaked deep-dish pie crust,
purchased or homemade (page 446)
1 cup firmly packed light brown sugar
8 tablespoons (1 stick) butter, at room temperature
1 teaspoon ground cinnamon
¾ teaspoon ground ginger
½ teaspoon ground nutmeg
2 large eggs, at room temperature
½ cup evaporated milk
¼ cup granulated sugar
Whipped cream, for serving (optional)

1. Place the sweet potatoes in a 4½-quart or larger pot, add water to cover, and bring to a boil. Cook at a moderate boil (lower the heat if necessary to prevent splatters) until the potatoes are very tender when pierced with a small sharp knife, 35 to 45 minutes.

2. Using tongs, remove the potatoes from the water. Set them aside to cool or refrigerate until ready to use. (See Note if you refrigerate the potatoes.)

3. Preheat the oven to 400°F. Line a deep-dish pie plate with the crust and set it aside.

4. Peel the potatoes (the skin usually just slips right off) and lightly mash the flesh. Measure out 2½ cups of mashed sweet potato. (Reserve any extra for another use.) Combine the mashed sweet potato, brown sugar, butter, cinnamon, ginger, and nutmeg in a mixing bowl and mix on medium speed until light and fluffy, about 2 minutes.

5. Separate the eggs, placing the whites in a small mixing bowl and set it aside.

6. Add the yolks to the sweet potato mixture and mix well. Add the evaporated milk and mix just until well blended.

7. Beat the egg whites, adding the granulated sugar, 1 tablespoon at a time, until stiff peaks form, about 3 minutes. Gently fold the egg whites into the sweet potato mixture.

8. Spoon the mixture into the prepared pie shell. (There will be a significant amount of filling. Mound it in the middle, taking care not to let any spill over the edge of the crust.) Bake for 10 minutes, then reduce the oven temperature to 350°F and continue to bake until the top is just starting to brown lightly, 45 to 50 minutes. When the pie is done, the center will be just set—it will still jiggle slightly.

9. Remove the pie from the oven and let it rest for 20 to 30 minutes. Serve with whipped cream, if desired. Store leftover pie, covered, in the refrigerator, for up to 3 days.

NOTE: If you precook and refrigerate the sweet potatoes, warm them slightly in the microwave oven before blending them with the butter and seasonings—you'll get a smoother finished pie.

Chew on This

As some fruits ripen, they emit a gas called ethylene that can cause apples to become soft, mealy, or spotted. For the longest apple life, don't store these gas-producing fruits in the same bowl with apples: apricots, bananas, cantaloupes, honeydews, kiwis, mangoes, nectarines, papayas, peaches, pears, and plums.

FLAKY HOMEMADE PIE CRUST

MAKES: TWO 9-INCH UNBAKED PIE CRUSTS
START TO FINISH: UNDER 25 MINUTES

1 cup cold water (see Notes)
4 to 5 ice cubes
2 cups all-purpose flour
1 teaspoon salt
¾ cup solid vegetable shortening,
    chilled (see Notes)

1. Measure the water in a 2-cup glass measure, add the ice cubes, and stir. Set aside.

2. Stir the flour and salt together in a large mixing bowl. Cut the shortening into pieces and add them to the bowl. Using a pastry blender or two knives, blend the shortening into the flour until most of the mixture is coarse, with some pea-size pieces. (Some of the mixture will be as fine as cornmeal.) Add the very cold water (water only, no ice chunks), 1 tablespoon at a time, to the flour mixture, tossing the mixture with a fork after each addition. When the dough forms loose balls that hold together when pressed with your fingers, you have added enough water. It should take between 5 and 8 tablespoons. Work quickly, trying to avoid overworking the dough. Divide the dough in half.

3. With your hands, press each dough portion out to form a disk that is 5 to 6 inches in diameter. Lightly flour both sides of the disks, wrap them in plastic wrap, and refrigerate for at least 15 minutes (this keeps the crust from shrinking when baking) or up to 2 days. (Or wrap the dough well, place it in a freezer-weight zipper-top plastic bag, and freeze for up to 6 months. Defrost it completely in the refrigerator when ready to use.)

From Alicia:

Ready-made pie crusts have improved a good deal in recent years, but it is still much cheaper to make your own.

All that's required for a successful crust is cold vegetable shortening, flour, and very cold water. My grandmother taught me to make homemade pie crust when I was very young, and I still enjoy the activity. As she always said, just remember, the less you handle the dough, the more tender and flaky the crust will be.

The theory behind any pastry is to break up the flour. Water dough with tiny pieces of fat—in this case, vegetable shortening—to prevent the development of the gluten, which would make the pastry tough. When the water is added, the fat forms gaps in the flour, preventing the gluten from forming. Then when the pastry is baked, the fat melts, creating steam that expands and leaves the layers of a wonderful flaky crust. Most of the time, novice pastry makers add too much water, which produces a crust that is either hard or

4. To shape the dough into a pie crust, remove the plastic wrap and lightly flour the dough again. Carefully center 1 disk between two 12- to 13-inch squares of waxed paper. Lightly dampen your work surface and place the "sandwich" on the work surface. Using a rolling pin, roll from the center in all directions, forming a round that's 11 to 12 inches in diameter. Remove the top layer of waxed paper. Flip the dough round, using the bottom waxed paper as a handle, into a 9-inch glass or metal pie plate. Peel off the remaining waxed paper. Press the dough into the pie plate. The edge of the crust should hang over the plate by about ½ inch or so. Fold this overhang under along the edge, making a small double layer of crust. To form a decorative edge, hold the tips of your thumb and index finger in a V, and place the V on the outside edge of the crust, lifting the crust slightly off the pie plate. With the other index fingertip, push the dough on the inside edge of the crust into the V shape. This will indent the crust and make it stand upright. Repeat this shaping all the way around the crust. Fill or bake the crust as directed in the recipe.

NOTES: Each time you make a pie crust, the dough might require a different amount of water depending on the age of your flour, the air temperature in your kitchen, and the humidity. You want to add just enough water to have the pieces of dough hold together in a loose ball but not be sticky. Adding water 1 tablespoon at a time, as described in Step 2, is the way to get just the right consistency. Toss and stir the mixture after each addition, and you shouldn't go wrong.

■ Vegetable shortening is now available in sticks, which are easy to keep in the refrigerator and make it simple to cut off what you need. The manufacturers have even printed the tablespoon amounts on the package, just like butter wrappers. If your vegetable shortening is in a can, measure out the amount you need and refrigerate it for at least 30 minutes before starting the pie crust recipe.

chewy and breadlike. (See the Notes about adding water.)

Using a pastry blender is definitely the easiest way to blend homemade pastry dough, but two knives will also work. Simply hold one knife in each hand and pull the knives through the mixture in opposite directions in quick, short strokes to "cut" the shortening into the flour mixture. Keep moving the flour toward the center of the bowl to make sure you have incorporated all of the shortening.

One final tip for foolproof pastry: Keep the dough cold. Work away from the hot oven or stovetop, and, if the dough becomes too soft and squishy, refrigerate it for 15 to 30 minutes. Then proceed with the recipe.

Given these ingredients, you can afford to practice a few times as you gain confidence. If you don't want to use your practice crusts for a pie, try the quick-and-easy recipe for Sugary Pastry Crisps (page 439).

When you need to produce a stand-out dessert and you don't have a lot of time or money, go to the supermarket freezer case and buy the least expensive carton of vanilla ice cream you can find. Then whip up this fabulous sauce of canned pineapple, brandy, brown sugar, and a bit of butter. The sauce turns any ice cream it touches into pure gold.

PINEAPPLE UPSIDE-DOWN SUNDAES

SERVES: 6   START TO FINISH: UNDER 15 MINUTES

1 can (15¼ ounces) pineapple
    tidbits packed in juice
1 tablespoon butter
½ cup firmly packed light brown sugar
¼ cup brandy (see Notes)
2 tablespoons orange juice
6 scoops vanilla ice cream

SUPER-CHEAP!

1. Drain the pineapple, reserving the juice for another use. Set the fruit aside.

2. Melt the butter in a small saucepan over medium-low heat. Add the brown sugar, brandy, and orange juice. Stir constantly until the brown sugar melts, about 2 minutes. Add the pineapple. Raise the heat to medium-high and bring the sauce to a boil. Boil, stirring occasionally, until the sauce is slightly thickened, about 2 minutes. Remove it from the heat and set aside, covered, to keep warm.

3. Place a scoop of ice cream in each of the six dessert dishes and spoon the sauce evenly on top. Serve at once.

NOTES: For an alcohol-free sauce, substitute ¼ cup of the drained pineapple juice for the brandy.
■ The sauce can be prepared ahead of time and refrigerated in an airtight container for up to 3 days. To reheat, place the sauce in a microwave-safe bowl, cover with a paper towel, and microwave on high power until warm, about 1 minute. Stir the sauce before serving.

BANANAS FOSTER

SERVES: 4 START TO FINISH: UNDER 15 MINUTES

2 ripe bananas (see Notes)

2 tablespoons butter

⅓ cup lightly packed light brown sugar

¼ cup rum, brandy, or Cognac (see Notes)

⅛ teaspoon ground cinnamon

4 scoops vanilla ice cream

1. Peel the bananas and cut them in half crosswise. Slice each half lengthwise, and then cut those pieces in half lengthwise again. You will have 16 pieces. Set them aside.

2. Melt the butter in a 10-inch or larger skillet over medium-high heat. Add the brown sugar, rum, and cinnamon. Stir to mix well. Cook until the mixture comes to a boil, 2 to 3 minutes. Then reduce the heat to medium and cook, stirring constantly, until the sauce begins to thicken, about 2 minutes. Add the bananas and cook, stirring constantly but gently so as not to break them up, until the bananas are heated through, 1½ to 2 minutes.

3. Remove the skillet from the heat. Serve the warm bananas and sauce over scoops of ice cream.

NOTES: Bananas that are ripe but still white (not bruised) and firm are best for this dish.

■ For a nonalcoholic sauce, substitute orange juice for the rum.

Here's something terrific to do with bananas before they get too ripe. Bananas Foster was created in the 1950s at the famous Brennan's Restaurant in New Orleans. It was named for Richard Foster, a regular customer. All of these ingredients are easy to keep on hand for a quick, festive dessert that won't cost a mint. Speaking of mint, a garnish of a few fresh mint leaves would turn this into company fare.

MoneySaver

Some grocery stores sell produce that's past its peak at a substantial discount. Think before passing it by since, for example, very ripe bananas make the best bread and smoothies!

It may have only five ingredients, but this simple caramel sauce tastes anything but simple. And it's so easy to make, you'll find yourself relying on it to turn a bowl of plain ice cream into a gourmet delight. In fact, just about anything you pour caramel sauce over is vastly better for it. Take that bargain apple pie you picked up at the supermarket: With a drizzle of caramel sauce, it's suddenly elevated to star status. The same goes for brownies from a box or a cake from a mix. Even simple apple slices can be dipped into caramel sauce for a tasty treat kids love.

RICH CARAMEL SAUCE

MAKES: ABOUT 1⅔ CUPS   START TO FINISH: UNDER 10 MINUTES

8 tablespoons (1 stick) butter
1 cup lightly packed light brown sugar
½ cup heavy or whipping cream
2 tablespoons light corn syrup
1 teaspoon vanilla extract

SUPER-CHEAP!

1. Cut the butter into 4 pieces and place them in a 4-cup glass measure. Add the brown sugar, cream, and corn syrup. Stir to mix. Cover with microwave-safe plastic wrap and cut a small hole in the plastic to vent. Microwave on high power until the mixture boils, 3 to 4 minutes. Remove the measure from the microwave oven, uncover, and stir well. Stir in the vanilla.

2. Let the mixture cool; serve the sauce warm or at room temperature.

NOTE: The sauce can be prepared up to 1 week ahead and refrigerated in an airtight container. To reheat, place the sauce in a microwave-safe bowl, cover with a paper towel, and microwave on high power until warm, about 1 minute. Stir the sauce before serving.

Caffe Latte Granita

MAKES: ABOUT 1 QUART   PREP TIME: 5 MINUTES

3 to 4 cups brewed coffee,
 well chilled
⅓ cup half-and-half or milk,
 or to taste
¼ cup sugar, or to taste
Whipped cream, for serving (optional)

1. Combine the coffee, half-and-half, and sugar in a mixing bowl and stir until the sugar dissolves. (If you've stored the coffee in a jar and there's room, add the sugar and milk and shake the jar instead.)

2. Pour the mixture into a 6-cup or larger rectangular glass or metal baking pan. (You'll need enough room to stir the ingredients.) Place the pan, uncovered, in the freezer and freeze until ice crystals begin to form around the edges, 30 to 45 minutes.

3. Remove the pan from the freezer and, using a fork, stir to break any chunks into small ice crystals. Return the pan to the freezer for 30 minutes.

4. Remove the pan and stir again, poking any chunks with the fork to break them up completely. Continue freezing, stirring with the fork every 15 minutes, until the granita is completely frozen, 45 minutes to 1 hour longer. The granita should have the texture of shards of glass throughout. (At this point the granita can be transferred to an airtight container and frozen for up to 2 days. If it freezes solid, thaw the granita slightly in the refrigerator and break it up with a fork before serving.)

5. To serve, spoon the granita into ice cream dishes or glasses, such as wine or parfait glasses, topping each serving with whipped cream, if desired.

If you're like us, you've gotten spoiled by drinking really good coffee from the shop on the corner. You're probably also brewing better coffee at home than you once did. Some mornings we don't finish off a pot, so save the extra for this yummy icy dessert. If you like coffee ice cream, you'll love coffee granita.

Since you'll need at least three cups of coffee and it may take several days of leftovers to accumulate that much, just pour each day's coffee into a quart jar and keep it, covered, in the refrigerator for up to a week. (If your storage jar is glass, be sure to let the coffee cool almost to room temperature before adding it to the cold jar to avoid any chance of the jar shattering.) When the jar is almost full, you'll know it's time to freeze the brew and recycle it as dessert. If you find you're making coffee granita often, you can vary the flavors by adding a little ground cinnamon or flavored extracts such as almond, vanilla, orange, or cherry.

We both bought electric ice cream freezers in order to re-create a scoop of our own childhood for our kids: homemade ice cream on the Fourth of July. What we didn't expect was that this handy appliance would become the source of amazing fat-free desserts for the whole family all year long.

Sorbet is frequently served in upscale restaurants. Flavors run the gamut from passion fruit to lavender, but our favorites are the clean, bright tastes of citrus. This recipe can be used with lemons, limes, oranges, or a combination of all of them. Serve with a simple cookie, such as a sugar cookie.

Citrus sorbet is so economical and elegant that it has become our dessert of choice for summer entertaining. Making your own sorbet is easier than you think. Ice cream freezers used to mean messy ice and rock salt, but most modern freezers require neither. Just stash the fluid-filled freezing compartment in your own freezer a day ahead; then plug it in and you're good to go. Non-electric ice

ANY-FLAVOR CITRUS SORBET

MAKES: ABOUT 1 QUART PREP TIME: 20 MINUTES

1 cup sugar
4 lemons, limes, or oranges
   (or a combination)
1 teaspoon finely grated lemon,
   lime, or orange zest
   (the colored part of the skin only,
   not the bitter white part underneath)
Mint leaves, for garnish (optional)

SUPER-CHEAP!

1. Combine the sugar and 1 cup water in a small saucepan and place it over high heat. Cook, stirring constantly, until the sugar dissolves, about 1 minute. Then bring the syrup to a boil and let it boil, without stirring, for 1 minute. Remove the pan from the heat and set the sugar syrup aside.

2. Squeeze the juice from the lemons, limes, or oranges (including the one with the zest removed) into a 4-cup glass measure. (Use a strainer to catch any seeds.) Stir in the sugar syrup and the zest. Add enough water to make 3½ cups, stirring well. (You will use less water for orange sorbet, but that's fine, because the flavor of orange juice is less intense than that of lemons or limes. Just make sure you have 3½ cups total liquid.) Refrigerate the mixture until is it is well chilled, about 1 hour.

3. Transfer the sorbet mixture to an ice cream maker and freeze according to the manufacturer's instructions, typically 20 to 30 minutes. (If you don't have an ice cream maker, see the alternative instructions in the Note.)

4. Transfer the sorbet from the ice cream maker to a covered container and leave it in the freezer until the desired consistency is reached, about 1 hour. Serve at once or keep in the freezer until ready to serve. Garnish with mint leaves, if desired.

NOTE: If you don't have an ice cream maker, it's still easy to make sorbet. Just pour the chilled liquid into a metal baking pan and freeze it until ice forms at the edges of the pan, about 1 hour. Then, using a fork, break up the ice and distribute the frozen parts evenly. Continue freezing, stirring every 30 minutes, until the desired consistency is reached, 2 to 3 hours.

cream makers are also affordable, with a wide range of models that make about a quart. And the really good news is, if you don't have an ice cream maker, you can still make our sorbet. You just have to a do a little more stirring instead of letting the machine do it for you.

Homemade sorbet differs from the supermarket variety in that the taste is more vibrant and the texture is softer. (Commercial sorbets contain additives to control their texture.) In order to get homemade sorbet firm enough to hold a ball shape when scooped, you'll have to let it sit in the freezer to "ripen" for about an hour after it is churned. However, if you store homemade sorbet in the freezer for 4 hours or longer, it may freeze solid and then you'll need to defrost it slightly before scooping.

After you experience the refreshing taste of homemade sorbet, you may never scream for ice cream again.

CONVERSION TABLES

APPROXIMATE EQUIVALENTS

1 stick butter = 8 tbs = 4 oz = ½ cup

1 cup all-purpose presifted flour or
     dried bread crumbs = 5 oz

1 cup granulated sugar = 8 oz

1 cup (packed) brown sugar = 6 oz

1 cup confectioners' sugar = 4½ oz

1 cup honey or syrup = 12 oz

1 cup grated cheese = 4 oz

1 cup dried beans = 6 oz

1 large egg = about 2 oz = about 3 tbs

1 large egg yolk = about 1 tbs

1 large egg white = about 2 tbs

Please note that all conversions are approximate but close enough to be useful when converting from one system to another.

LIQUID CONVERSIONS

U.S.	IMPERIAL	METRIC
2 tbs	1 fl oz	30 ml
3 tbs	1½ fl oz	45 ml
¼ cup	2 fl oz	60 ml
⅓ cup	2½ fl oz	75 ml
⅓ cup + 1 tbs	3 fl oz	90 ml
⅓ cup + 2 tbs	3½ fl oz	100 ml
½ cup	4 fl oz	125 ml
⅔ cup	5 fl oz	150 ml
¾ cup	6 fl oz	175 ml
¾ cup + 2 tbs	7 fl oz	200 ml
1 cup	8 fl oz	250 ml
1 cup + 2 tbs	9 fl oz	275 ml
1¼ cups	10 fl oz	300 ml
1⅓ cups	11 fl oz	325 ml
1½ cups	12 fl oz	350 ml
1⅔ cups	13 fl oz	375 ml
1¾ cups	14 fl oz	400 ml
1¾ cups + 2 tbs	15 fl oz	450 ml
2 cups (1 pint)	16 fl oz	500 ml
2½ cups	20 fl oz (1 pint)	600 ml
3¾ cups	1½ pints	900 ml
4 cups	1¾ pints	1 liter

WEIGHT CONVERSIONS

US	METRIC	US	METRIC
½ oz	15 g	7 oz	200 g
1 oz	30 g	8 oz	250 g
1½ oz	45 g	9 oz	275 g
2 oz	60 g	10 oz	300 g
2½ oz	75 g	11 oz	325 g
3 oz	90 g	12 oz	350 g
3½ oz	100 g	13 oz	375 g
4 oz	125 g	14 oz	400 g
5 oz	150 g	15 oz	450 g
6 oz	175 g	1 lb	500 g

OVEN TEMPERATURES

°F	GAS MARK	°C	°F	GAS MARK	°C
250	½	120	400	6	200
275	1	140	425	7	220
300	2	150	450	8	230
325	3	160	475	9	240
350	4	180	500	10	260
375	5	190			

Note: Reduce the temperature by 20°C (68°F) for fan-assisted ovens.

APPENDIX

Eating on $100 a Week— Our Experimental Cheap Extravaganza

So, how low can you go? What's the absolute bottom line for what you have to spend on food and still get a nutritionally balanced diet?

According to the 2003 figures from U.S. Department of Agriculture, that bottom line was $107.70 a week for a family of four. This is what the government called a "thrifty" meal plan. Wow! Exactly what would it be like to *really* eat on the cheap? We decided to conduct the Grand Cheap Experiment—keeping track of every penny we each spent for a week to see what we'd be cooking if we toed what was the government's thrifty line at the time.

As you might imagine, we have good news and bad news to report.

The good news is that dinner wasn't nearly as expensive as we expected, but more on that later. The news on just about everything else is mixed.

First of all, figuring out how to follow the government's thrifty meal plan wasn't quite as simple as buying bargains. We actually spent quite a bit of time thinking about this before we started. First we needed to figure out how much we had to spend per meal. We decided to subtract $7.70 from the food total, figuring that's about what you'd have to pay for taxes (give or take $1 to $2 depending on where you live). That left us with $100 a week to spend on food, which divides out to exactly $14.285714 per day. (To avoid brain cramps we rounded up part of a penny to $14.29 a day.)

That's not a lot of money for 12 individual healthful meals per day (about $1.19 each) for a family of four, and we figured we had to start with some general (and we hope smart) assumptions and guidelines. Here are the assumptions and guidelines we used:

- We thought dinner would be the hardest and most expensive part, so we decided to stick to very cheap breakfasts and lunches. (It turned out we were wrong in our assumptions, but for purposes of the experiment, we stuck to our plan.)

- We decided to allow 60 cents per person per day for a microwave breakfast of Bev's Ultimate Oatmeal (page 405) and an eight-ounce glass of milk.

- For lunch, we allotted $1 per person per day, which frankly doesn't leave a lot of options unless you have leftovers. (You can't always count on leftovers, so we didn't work them into the plan.) We decided everybody would have to eat a low-priced sandwich—we offered a choice of egg salad on wheat bread (27 cents per sandwich; see page 258), or peanut butter (29 cents per sandwich), an apple (in season we found that at 27 cents each; out of season, double that amount) or banana (13 cents), some chips (19 cents per serving), and a couple of cookies (25 cents).

- This left $1.97 per person per day for dinner. In almost all of our menus that amount turned out to be too generous (yes, really!), which was very good news indeed. That meant we ended up having more money to expand our breakfast and lunch options. (See the actual dinner menus, costs, and notes.)

- Because of the strict budgetary restraints of the thrifty menu plan, we did not include dessert as a general rule. (There were a couple of exceptions; see the menus on pages 461 and 463.)

- Except for the glass of milk at breakfast, we also did not include beverages. Our thinking was that beverage choices are incredibly personal, and we figured that, if necessary, a brewed cup of coffee wouldn't upset the apple cart. (After the experiment, Alicia decided to allot some of her leftover money for milk at dinner; see the notes below.)

In the end, we learned a lot from this experiment. The most important lesson was that, with a little careful menu planning, eating sensibly and interestingly on $100 a week is definitely workable.

"Dinner wasn't nearly as expensive as we expected."

Tips for Eating on $100 a Week

- It's easier for you to take the broad view. Your food dollar will likely go further if you consider your total budget as $400 over a month, or even $800 over two months, rather than thinking of it as only a strict $100 a week. This will allow you to vary what you spend in any given week to buy larger sizes and stock up when you find special sale prices. (With a little discipline, the total comes out the same in the end!)

- To come up with the cost per serving for the recipes in this experiment, we counted only the food actually used in making the recipe. For example, if the recipe called for a tablespoon of ketchup and we happened to be out of it, we didn't count the cost of buying the whole bottle, only the tablespoon. (For more information on how we arrived at specific cost figures for ingredients, see page 465.) That leads us to the next point . . .

- In order for any $100 weekly budget to work, the cost of staples like ketchup, flour, sugar, spices, and such have to be averaged out over their entire span of use. If you have to replace more than one of these staples in a single week, the food tally might be a bit higher, which brings us back to the point of taking the broad view. (Speaking of flour, if you seldom bake, buy the smallest package you can find. Twenty-five pounds of flour sitting around will get bug infested and wind up no bargain.) For more information on stocking staples and other food inventory issues, see Keeping Tabs on Your Grocery Inventory, page 350.

- Consider ingredients and staples you have on hand when choosing recipes. If you have to buy a $4 condiment only to use a tablespoon with the rest going to waste, that's not smart. In general, recipes using common, everyday ingredients will be cheaper.

- Another consideration crucial to making the budget work is to eat all of the food you prepare. A recipe that serves six might have a low cost-per-serving figure, but it typically will

"Eat all the food you prepare."

cost more to make than a recipe that just serves four because of the extra amount of food required. Therefore, the overall impact to the weekly budget will depend on using the leftovers at another meal in the same week, or freezing them for use later on.

- Before we started the experiment, we thought it would be easier emotionally to stick to the budget if we used a "scrimp/splurge" approach. That meant if we scrimped by eating a meatless meal on, say, Tuesday night, we'd have extra money to splurge on a special meal (with dessert!) on another night. But what we actually found after calculating the meal costs was that many of our soups and skillet meals with meat were just as cheap as the meatless dinner. (Of course that wouldn't be true if you served he-man–size steaks or pork chops instead!)

- Soups, skillet meals, and pasta dishes that include meat, a vegetable, and starch all in the same recipe tend to be cheaper than serving a just-meat entrée accompanied by separate side dishes. (Our fish entrée and meat loaf are exceptions to this.) That's often because the noodles or rice make a little meat go a long way. Beware when it comes to stand-alone meats and sides—the more you serve, the more it costs. In the old days Mom might have served three veggies every night, but she grew her own in the vegetable garden out back. Unless you do too, those multiple dishes can quickly add up.

- For the purposes of this experiment, we often served a basic salad as our side dish. A basic salad, per person, consisted of 1 cup of torn iceberg lettuce, ½ carrot, ½ celery stalk, ¼ cup Crisp Homemade Croutons (page 281), and 2 tablespoons of Dot's Salad Dressing (page 295). It's nutritious and tasty, and at 25 cents per serving, rock bottom cheap. Seasonal fresh vegetables or frozen vegetables in big bags would probably also come in on budget.

- For the purposes of this experiment, we served half a loaf of French bread per meal at $1.28 per loaf (64 cents per meal); or half a package of purchased "brown and serve" rolls at 99

"Rice and noodles make a little meat go a long way."

cents a package (50 cents per meal); or saltine crackers at 16 cents per meal.

■ There's more expense required to run a kitchen than just food. The cost of dish detergent, paper towels, and plastic wrap can really add up. In our experiment, we did not include these in our figures. Take advantage of sales on these items, and seek out stores with the best prices (even if it means an extra shopping trip to the "discount" store to stock up every so often). And considering the "hidden" costs of soap, water, and electricity to run the dishwasher, we like to make sure we've got a full load before starting the machine.

"Consider ingredients and staples you have on hand when choosing recipes."

Our Eating on $100 a Week Experiment, By the Numbers

For purposes of the following examples, a month has 30 days, and a year has 365 days. To make the numbers less cumbersome, the costs for individual meals have been rounded up to the nearest dollar. That rounding makes our total meals $15.85 higher for the year (or about 30 cents higher per week) than eating on a straight $100 per week.

Breakfast: $2.40 per day (60 cents per person) for a family of 4; $16.80 per week; $72 per month; $876 per year

Lunch: $4 per day ($1 per person) for a family of 4; $28 per week; $120 per month; $1,460 per year

Dinner: $7.89 per day ($1.97 per person) for a family of 4; $55.23 per week; $236.70 per month; $2,879.85 per year

Total food cost budgeted for the year: $5,215.85 for a family of 4

ALICIA'S DINNER MENUS AND COSTS FOR THE WEEK

Monday: Chicken and Onion Pizza, page 263 ($1.70 per serving); basic salad (25 cents per serving). *Meal total for 4:* $7.80 (see menu notes below)

Tuesday: Liz's Tuna Toss, page 220 (47 cents per serving, serves 6); basic salad (25 cents per serving); brown and serve dinner rolls (13 cents per serving). *Meal total for 4:* $4.34 (includes all six servings of entrée; see menu notes below)

Wednesday: Cure-All Chicken Soup, page 12 (88 cents per serving); Simply Southern Coleslaw, page 318 (22 cents per serving); saltine crackers (4 cents per serving). *Meal total for 4:* $4.56

Thursday: Good Ol' Beans and Rice, page 173 (83 cents per serving); basic salad (25 cents per serving); brown and serve rolls (13 cents per serving); bonus dessert: Rex's Oatmeal Pie, page 441 (44 cents per serving, serves 6). *Meal total for 4:* $7.48 (includes whole pie; see menu notes)

Friday: Lynne's Mom's Mince over rice, page 119 (72 cents per serving); Simply Southern Coleslaw, page 318 (22 cents per serving); French bread (16 cents per serving). *Meal total for 4:* $4.40

Saturday: Mexi-Chicken Skillet, page 154 ($2.31 per serving, serves 4 generously); basic salad (25 cents per serving); chips (99 cents for the bag). *Meal total for 5:* $11.48 (one dinner guest; see menu notes)

Sunday: Golden Broiled Fillets, page 114 (31 cents per serving); Terrific Tartar Sauce, page 383 (12 cents per serving); Pasta with Bread Crumbs, page 234 (20 cents per serving); Simply Southern Coleslaw, page 313 (22 cents per serving); Old-Fashioned Gingerbread, page 420 (20 cents per serving). *Meal total for 4:* $4.20 (see menu notes)

Total actual dinner cost for the week: $44.26
Total budgeted: $55.23
Amount left over: $10.97

How Alicia allocated her extra money: My kids drink milk at dinner (they really like it!), so I used $2.52 of my "extra money" for milk. (That's 14 servings, 8 ounces each, at 18 cents per serving.) Lunch is the hardest place to stay "on budget." We had one "free" lunch entrée with leftovers from Tuesday, but generally if we "go over" on budget it's because of lunch. I was thrilled that we could loosen the strict lunch budget with the money we saved on dinner. We were able to add nearly $9 to the lunch budget.

Alicia's additional menu notes:
Monday: Pizza is a must around my house at least once a week, so even though the total meal cost pushes the daily average, I made it up with more "budgetary" meals later in the week.

Tuesday: The bonus here is that I get two more servings and still land solidly under the target dinner budget. My husband and I take these servings to lunch on Wednesday or Thursday. It's our "free" lunch entrée.

Thursday: Beans and rice are so basic, I try to make these nights special with dessert. There are two servings of dessert left over (but within our dinner budget) that will be a special "I made it to the end of the week after-school snack" for the kids on Friday.

Saturday: There's hardly a Saturday night that we don't find ourselves with an "extra" child at dinner. So we allowed an extra person (since the skillet meal feeds 4 generously—read 5 normal appetites). We counted the whole bag of chips, too, so there'd be snacks during the movie watching later.

Sunday: Half of the gingerbread is not included in this meal total. It can be used for breakfast or a dinner dessert during the next week. (The per-serving cost for gingerbread is 20 cents.)

BEVERLY'S DINNER MENUS AND COSTS FOR THE WEEK

Monday: Winter Minestrone with Pesto, page 24 ($1.01 per serving); basic salad (25 cents per serving); French bread (16 cents per serving). *Meal total for 4:* $5.68

Tuesday: Confetti Fried Rice, page 175 ($1.04 per serving); Bits-of-Fruit Salad with Strawberry Yogurt Dressing, page 321 (42 cents per serving); French bread (16 cents per serving). *Meal total for 4:* $6.48

Wednesday: Perfect Spinach Pesto Pizza, page 265 ($1.18 per serving); canned pineapple slices (18 cents per serving). *Meal total for 4:* $5.44

Thursday: Ham and Broccoli Pasta Toss, page 213 (65 cents per serving, serves 6), basic salad (25 cents per serving), French bread (16 cents per serving). *Meal total for 4:* $5.54 (includes all six servings of entrée; see menu notes below)

Friday: Spinach Pesto Pasta Salad, page 330 ($1.57 per serving); basic salad (25 cents per serving); French bread (16 cents per serving). *Meal total for 4:* $7.92

Saturday: My S-t-r-e-t-c-h-e-d Meat Loaf, page 71 (44 cents per serving); Gayle's Creamed Potatoes, page 332 (27 cents per serving); frozen yellow corn kernels (12 cents per serving); French bread (16 cents per serving); Chocolate Bread Pudding, page 430 (30 cents per serving). *Meal total for 4:* $5.16

Sunday: Shipwreck Skillet Dinner, page 129 (88 cents per serving); Simply Southern Coleslaw, page 318 (22 cents per serving); French bread (16 cents per serving); Chocolate Bread Pudding (left over from Saturday; 30 cents per serving). *Meal total for 4:* $6.24

"Generally, if we go over budget it's because of lunch."

Bonus Meal (Saturday-morning breakfast for 6): Sausage Pepper Strata, page 400 (74 cents per serving); Bits-of-Fruit Salad with Strawberry Yogurt Dressing, page 321 (42 cents per serving); orange juice (31 cents per serving); coffee (28 cents per serving for 4 adults only). *Meal total for 6:* $9.94

Total actual dinner cost for the week: $41.16
Total budgeted: $55.23
Amount left over: $12.77

How Beverly allocated her extra money: I decided to splurge on a special Saturday morning breakfast with friends, see "bonus meal" menu above, which ended up costing $9.94. However, I subtracted the $2.40 I would have spent on a basic oatmeal breakfast for four. Taking this into account, I still had $5.23 extra to spend to beef up the week's lunches (plus I had two "free" lunch entrees leftover from Thursday's dinner). I agree with Alicia's opinions on lunch! See her notes above.

Beverly's additional menu notes:
Three meals during the week took advantage of a big batch of Spinach Parsley Pesto (page 372), and after making the three entrées, there was still enough pesto left for another use.

Thursday: The pasta recipe makes six servings, so the extra two servings were used as a "free" entrée for Friday's lunch.

Saturday: The meat loaf makes eight servings, so we ate meat loaf sandwiches for Sunday lunch on slices of French bread (76 cents per sandwich). The sausage strata for Saturday's special breakfast serves six, so we were able to invite two friends over to join us. The bread pudding makes 12 servings, so we finished it up on Monday of the next week.

"Consider the hidden costs of soap, water, and electricity to run the dishwasher."

About Our
Cost-Per-Serving Analysis

Here's how we determined our prices per serving:

- Alicia checked ingredient prices in Raleigh, North Carolina. Beverly checked prices in Minneapolis, Minnesota. We used the average price between these two.

- All prices were reduced to either a price per pound or per ounce so the only amount used for the analysis is the exact amount required for the recipe.

- The prices on meat were the average "on sale" prices (or the lowest price we could find), since that's the only way we recommend buying meat if you're on a budget. Some of the meat prices required buying several pounds at once. For example, our price for skinless, boneless chicken breasts was $1.94 per pound. Ground beef was $1.59 per pound.

- Produce prices were in-season prices when those differed greatly from nonseasonal prices. For example, in-season asparagus is $1.99 per pound. Out-of-season asparagus costs up to $5.99 a pound.

- Prices on staple ingredients (broth, flour, sugar, salt, and so on) were for store-brand items when store brands were available.

- Prices for bottles, packages, cans, and cartons are for the middle-range size—not the largest and not the smallest. We tried to pick sizes we thought average consumers would use. For example, we used the price for apple juice in a 64-ounce bottle, which came out to 2 cents an ounce.

- Ingredients listed as "optional" in recipes were not included.

- The actual costs-per-serving were analyzed by Chris Lowden of Reston, Virginia, a registered dietitian who uses the Genesis R&D computer program.

Our Best Coupon Advice

If you've never clipped grocery coupons before, the process seems fairly simple. Just cut 'em out and cash 'em in, right? Well, yes—more or less. After several months of serious clipping, we've come up with some observations and advice you may find helpful. We quickly figured out that the biggest drawback is the time required—not only to clip the coupons but also to file and locate them again when you're ready to shop. Therefore, a lot of our tips involve time management.

Here goes:

- Think of couponing as a game, hobby, or sport. If you can't find a way to enjoy the process, this isn't for you.

- Be selective. Coupons quickly multiply, and if you clip them all—including coupons for items you're unlikely to buy—keeping track of them becomes difficult indeed. The time required to find the specific coupon you want corresponds directly to the number of coupons you keep on file.

- Develop a system. Beverly files her coupons in three categories: First is coupons for items she always buys (so these are the coupons she knows she'll use soon). The second category is food items she might buy if the price is right, and the third is anything that's not edible. She keeps the "always-buy" coupons together in an envelope. Might-buy foods go in one card file box, and the not-edible items go in another file box. She files these coupons alphabetically according to type (pasta sauces under "P," toothpaste under "T," ice cream under "I," and so on). Alicia prefers to file all of her coupons together in the same mini-accordion file under these categories: produce, canned goods, breakfast, beverages, snacks, other general food, soaps/detergents, toiletries, paper goods, frozen foods, and dairy. This is also the general floor plan for the supermarkets where she shops.

- Invest in a coupon carrying case. This can be anything from a small accordion-type file from an office supply store to business-size envelopes to a special "coupon wallet." If you're redeeming a lot of coupons, you'll need a way to keep them organized between home and the cash register.

- Weed out expired coupons. It's a good idea to purge your files once a month. The fewer coupons you have, the easier it is to locate the one you can use.

- Coordinate with your shopping list. When making out your grocery list, write a "C" by any item you're buying with a coupon and specify the item by brand name. This cuts down on shopping time and cuts back on flipping through a stack of coupons in the grocery aisles. Alicia likes to paper clip the coupons she knows she'll be using to the side of her grocery list.

- Coordinate with the advertised grocery specials. We've already mentioned how supermarkets often coordinate with manufacturers to put an item on sale the same week a coupon is offered. The added savings can be significant.

- Depending on how many you have, you might want to carry all of your coupons to the store in case there are unadvertised specials.

- Shop smart. Some items aren't cheaper than a competing brand even if you do have a coupon, so comparison shop. Likewise, if your family isn't likely to use the item, it's not a good deal no matter how cheap it is.

- Be flexible. Some items seem to always have coupons on one brand or another. (Cereal, toothpaste, and laundry detergent are prime examples.) If you're willing to switch brands to buy with a coupon, you'll save more.

- Some coupons are seasonal. During one June and July, Beverly clipped 31 different coupons for ice cream. Although many of them did not expire until the end of

"A lot of our tips involve time management."

September, the coupons represented way more ice cream than the family needed to buy. But since ice cream stays frozen for months, it's wise to stock up during the "coupon season," provided you have the freezer space.

- Carry a small calculator in your wallet for last-minute calculations. Often the best coupon deal means buying the smallest size of the product. (This runs contrary to the common wisdom of buying the largest size for biggest savings.) You'll need to calculate the cost per ounce (or pound or unit) to figure out what size is the best deal with your coupon. Be sure to check the coupon for any size restrictions.

- Watch for restrictions on doubling. Some manufacturers print "no doubling" directly on the coupon beside the expiration date. When you *can* double, savings really add up.

- Look for coupons not only in your Sunday newspaper, but also in your favorite magazines. There are sometimes cents-off coupons in the advertisements, especially for new products.

- Some products also contain coupons printed directly on the packaging or attached with a sticker to the outside of the package.

- Look for coupon dispensers on the aisle shelf in the grocery store. "Point-of-purchase" coupons, as they are called, have become very popular. Just be sure to calculate the savings. You may have a better coupon in your collection.

- Be extra nice. A lot of coupons can add up to extra time for the checkout attendant and the person behind you in line, and you may as well be pleasant about it.

- Tally your winnings. This is a sport (remember?), so you'll need to keep track of the score. Many supermarkets print a coupon savings total at the bottom of the receipt. We also like to figure out what percentage of the total bill we've saved.

- Finally, realize that coupons save money if they reduce the overall amount of your grocery bill. This tends to happen if the items you buy with coupons replace other items rather than simply adding extra items to your weekly menus. For example, if you buy canned corn with a coupon and serve it for dinner tonight rather than fresh corn (purchased without a coupon), then you've probably saved money. If, however, you serve the canned corn as an extra vegetable (and it therefore doesn't replace anything), then you probably won't save.

Alicia's Coupon Experience

When my kids were in diapers, I was the Coupon Queen. Back then, those one- and two-dollar-off coupons for disposable diapers seemed like gold. So while I was paging through newspapers scouting out the diaper coupons, I eagerly clipped other coupons as well. But back then I had a lot more time. Because of the ages of the kids, naps and strict schedules were the rule. Now those babies are teenagers, and my family of four seems to be going in ten different directions at once. So, how does coupon clipping fit into the chaos? Honestly, not very well.

On the other hand, Beverly was playing the game to the hilt. Every week she'd tell me about the huge savings she was racking up. It felt like I was sitting on the sidelines.

One of my problems was simply timing. In my hometown, the grocery coupons appear in the Sunday newspaper, while the grocery store ads for sales come out on Wednesday. Within the first week, I noticed my biggest savings would come when I could buy something on sale and use a coupon, too. But with the delay of three days between the coupons and store ads, fitting clipping and shopping according to the ads into my busy week just wasn't happening. I was in the habit of shopping at the beginning of the week—not in the middle or at the end, when I would be able to cash in on all of those compounded savings of coupons plus store sales. When I missed the sale and waited for the next time my item was discounted, my coupon would have already expired. (That's

"Often the best deal means buying the smallest size of the product."

another big difference from 15 years ago: The coupon expiration dates are often not more than a month out. I used to have at least six months to cash in.)

Because I wasn't having much luck with traditional coupons, I turned to other ways to save on groceries. For example, most of the sale prices at my grocery stores are only available if you have a special store-issued, free, "preferred customer saver card." I am now the proud owner of five saver cards, because there are five major grocery chains in my town. If you don't have a card, you pay the full price, while the saver card entitles you to save, say, between 10 cents and a dollar on the week's featured items.

In addition to the weekly specials, several area supermarkets run long-term promotions that stretch for 16 weeks. If you spend roughly $40 at the store for 13 out of the 16 weeks, you're given a bonus at the end. At Thanksgiving you might get a free turkey, at Easter a free ham, in the spring a free grill, or at the December holidays, free shrimp or free knives. Getting the freebies requires spending the minimum amount (not usually a problem) for the 13 weeks of the promotion and keeping up with the special coupons proving you did shop for all of those weeks.

Well, for me, that wasn't happening, either. Keep a specially printed coupon for 16 weeks? Really, what are these people thinking? But then I'd hear my friends rave about the cool free grill, the new set of steak knives or the free turkey, while my coupons were spread from the car to my purse to the box at home—all unredeemed.

It became obvious that if I was going to save with any of these methods, I needed to get organized. I knew what I needed to do. The challenge was motivating myself to do it.

First, I stopped complaining about the three-day lag in coupons versus the store sale ads, and went ahead and clipped and filed my coupons on Sunday. This only takes me about 10 minutes. (It takes zero when I can bribe the kids to do it for me.) I no longer highlight the expiration date unless it is hidden in the small print. That one annoying step is often not necessary because many coupons already have the date printed in yellow. I've whittled down the kinds of coupons I clip, since so many of them would expire before I could redeem them. Or the food would go bad before I could use it (a big waste of money).

"If you don't have a saver card, you pay the full price."

Next, I lowered my expectations a bit. I talked to my sister-in-law, Lynn, about couponing. Her philosophy is that if she redeems enough coupons to pay for the newspaper the coupons came in, then she's already ahead of the game. I liked those perimeters. I could live with feeling good about a $2 savings a week . . . after all, it paid for the Sunday paper! Facing the pressure of needing to save $15 to $20 a week (like Beverly reported) had made me feel like a major failure.

One thing that does take longer with coupons is making out my grocery list on Wednesday. Because I get the biggest savings when I buy what is on sale *and* with a coupon, I have to menu-plan according to the sales and coupons. This takes me about 30 minutes. Then I have to work in my running list of necessities, which takes another 10 minutes. I paperclip the coupons I know I'm going to redeem directly to the list so they don't get misplaced. But I still take along my other coupons just in case I see something in the store that is a good price.

Switching my shopping day to Wednesday has been the hardest adjustment, but now I'm fairly used to it. In fact my whole shopping experience has changed. It's more deliberate and efficient. I don't go to the store without a list, and I know what we're having for dinner practically for a whole week. Now if I plan to shop at more than two stores because of the good deals, I spread that over a couple of days. I know my limits in driving around to stores around town. (See The When, Where, and How of Shopping, page 54.)

Most grocery stores in my area total my savings at the bottom of the receipt, which means I know exactly how much I saved for instant gratification. This includes the coupons redeemed as well as the sale price (with the store's saver card). My savings (including coupons redeemed and sale items) range from a few dollars to more than $20 each week, depending on how much my total bill is. I can live with that kind of savings, for sure, and it's paying for more than the newspaper, too!

I still haven't been able to keep up with the

"extra" store coupons to cash in on the free goodies after 13 weeks, but that's my next goal. Then I'll really be winning the couponing game. No more sitting on the sidelines for me!

Beverly's Coupon Experience

I have a love/hate relationship with my grocery coupons. Some days they seem like unexpected treasure stashed in my purse, and I can't wait to cash in. Yet there are also times when my unwieldy coupon file feels more like a nagging boss who wouldn't recognize quitting time if it blasted a foghorn.

Sure, I save money every time I shop with coupons—between 14 and 16 percent of my total bill on a good day. But no matter how organized I try to be, shopping with coupons just seems to take way longer than it should. Enter Beverly's Coupon Rationalizations—on both sides of the issue.

Rationalization, Side 1: I spent an extra 90 minutes to use coupons today, and I saved $24.80, or 14 percent of my bill. That's not bad "wages" for my "work." The pay-out is even higher considering this is tax-free "income," averaging out to nearly $21.50 an hour at my tax bracket. That's more than I make per hour at my real job.

Rationalization, Flip Side: With real job deadlines looming and Grandma coming for a visit, I'll be lucky to get to the supermarket at all today. Think I'm gonna flip through two dozen little pieces of paper to find the one that'll save 25 cents on a can of pineapple? Do I have the patience to inch my way down the grocery aisles comparing jar ounce sizes to the sizes printed on a coupon? Not a chance!

For me, the bottom line is that sometimes coupons make sense, but at other times using them would drive me senseless. The following is a list of my personal observations that you may find helpful if you're just starting out on the coupon-cashing quest. Here goes:

- I spend between 20 and 30 minutes per week clipping and filing coupons from two (and sometimes three) Sunday newspapers. (Buying an extra paper more than pays for itself in coupon savings.)

- It takes me about 20 minutes longer than it ordinarily would to make out my grocery list when I match coupons to my list and cross-reference the store advertisements. Most of this time is spent searching for the coupons in my file and writing the specific coupon item info on my list.

- It takes me an average of 30 to 45 minutes longer to shop for groceries using coupons. The extra time is spent tracking down the specific coupon item on the store shelf, and then double-checking the item against my coupon to make sure I've got the right size. I find I need to double check even though I've written specifics on my grocery list.

- Because I know coupons can save so much money, I feel something akin to guilt and a sense of failure when I don't use them. (This occurs regularly.) Even though I know this isn't rational, I haven't been able to shake these nagging feelings. They tend to strike when I buy an item and know for sure there's a coupon wasting away at home.

- On the staying organized front, after experimenting with various filing systems, one approach has been key for me: If I find a coupon on a brand item that I always buy, I file those coupons in a special envelope I call "current to use." These are the coupons I'm most likely to use—and sooner rather than later.

- The conventional advice from the real coupon experts is to clip every coupon. But for me, clipping them all isn't a worthwhile time investment. After experimenting with different philosophies on which coupons to clip and which to bypass, here are my rules: I clip (almost) all coupons valued at $1 or more. (If the item is offered on store special *and* I have a dollar-off coupon, it's often a very attractive bargain.) However, I don't clip coupons (even $1 ones) for items that I have never used, knowing that life will continue in fine fashion without this item, no matter how cheap it is.

"I don't clip coupons for items I have never used."

(Scented room deodorizers are one example.) I do clip all coupons on brands of items I always buy, even if the coupon is only for 20 cents. (If I always buy the item anyway, even 20 cents is a bonanza!) If the coupon is for a food I know my family will not eat, I just don't clip it. (Wasted food is never a bargain.) However, I do sometimes clip coupons for food I know my family should not eat. (A very cheap cookie every so often never hurt anyone!)

- For me, resisting the temptation to buy something I'm not likely to use just because I have a great coupon (and the item is on sale and therefore very cheap) requires an ongoing discipline. I guess couponing brings out the competitive and thrill-seeking aspects of my personality. I truly *love* a bargain! But think about it: Money saved on coupons is only a true savings if using them lowers your overall grocery bill.

- It took some time for couponing to become part of my weekly habit. Even now I often need to remind myself to clip and file coupons, and to grab my "current to use" coupon envelope when making an unplanned dash to the store.

- One benefit of couponing for my family is that we often get to eat and use better quality items because—taking the coupon savings into consideration—the "premium brand" item costs the same as (or less than) the cheaper (and in many cases inferior) off brand or store brand.

- An unexpected benefit to coupon shopping has been an overall reduction in the number of times per month I need to do a "major" grocery shop for nonperishable items. The reason is that many coupons require buying two, three, or even four of the same item. If the item happens to be on sale—and I have two of the coupons (from my two newspapers)—I'll stock up. I recently purchased four cans of my family's favorite baked beans for half the regular price using this system, so I won't need baked beans again for weeks. Ditto with toilet paper, toothpaste, and laundry detergent.

"Money saved on coupons is only a true savings if using them lowers your overall grocery bill."

All in all, I do think using coupons is worthwhile, even though I'm not sure I'll ever love the extra time and energy it requires me to spend on grocery shopping, which, in truth, isn't my favorite way to spend time. But whenever I'm tempted to forget the whole coupon thing, I just use this trick:

As soon as I get home from the store, I look at the grocery receipt and see how much I saved using coupons. I then "pay" myself by putting the actual cash into an envelope. At the end of the month, I can see the rewards that have added up in plain green. That's usually all the green light I need to keep me going.

INDEX